Bilingual Press/Editorial Bilingüe

Studies in the Literary Analysis of Hispanic Texts

Address:

Editorial
Bilingual Press
Department of Foreign Languages
York College, CUNY
Jamaica, New York 11451
212-969-4047/4035

Business
Bilingual Press
552 Riverside Drive Suite 1-B
New York, New York 10027
212-866-4595

The Significance and Impact of GREGORIO MARAÑÓN

Literary Criticism, Biographies and Historiography

Gary D. Keller

ISBN: 0-91650-04-2

Library of Congress Catalog Card Number: 76-45295

Printed in the United States of America

Acknowledgments

I wish to express my appreciation to Gonzalo Sobejano, Antonio Regalado, Ciriaco Morón-Arroyo, Karen S. Van Hooft and Jerome S. Bernstein for their valuable assistance in the preparation of this study. Also, my gratitude goes to Robert Gorham Davis who suggested to me many useful resources on psychological literary criticism. Finally, I wish to give thanks to Michael Walsh for his efforts in obtaining important materials from the Library of Congress and to my parents, Jack and Estelle, and my wife, Mary, for their help in the completion of this manuscript.

For
Gonzalo Sobejano,
with gratitude and deep affection

Table of Contents

INTRODUCTION

Gregorio Marañón was the most prominent and prolific member of a group of scientists and physicians who shortly after the First World War began to apply their scientific expertise to Spanish art, biography, history, and literary criticism. This group, including figures such as Ricardo Jorge, José Goyanes Capdevila, Gonzalo Lafora, José M. Sacristán and others, was formed under the sponsorship of teachers such as Ramón y Cajal and Letamendi and inspired by the impact Darwinism and Naturalism had on the novel and biography in the late nineteenth century, as well as by the clamorous effect psychoanalysis had on European arts and letters beginning shortly before the First World War. In addition, their orientation was supported by a number of philosophic outgrowths of Darwin's theory of evolution (e.g. Bergson, Driesh, Hertwig) which were in vogue in Europe during the period and which were commented upon in Spain by Ortega y Gasset, among others.

Marañón was primarily a medical researcher and clinician who explored aspects of human sexuality, emotion, and temperament. As a scientist, Marañón has been internationally recognized. Moreover, some of the humanistic implications of his scientific discoveries, together with his concern for the future of Spain and his boundless curiosity concerning cultural and literary phenomena led him to also write literary criticism, biography and history. Marañón's writings represent an effort to exemplify the useful contribution that biology and psychology are able to make within these humanistic disciplines. Our critic's characteristic procedure was to extend biopsychological constructs of his own creation for clinical use to literary or historical phenomena as well. On other occasions, he borrowed constructs such as the Oedipus complex, ambivalence, or the inferiority complex from the Freudians or Adlerians in order to explain the motivation of a writer, historical personage, or even a character in a fictional work. In my initial chapter, I shall outline the main influences on Marañón's theoretical approach, and shall briefly situate him within the movement of psychological or clinical literary criticism in Spain and elsewhere. This chapter also includes a general critical evaluation of his theories.

Marañón is generally interested in the human element in literature. Literary movements, esthetic manifestos, stylistic peculiarities are approached, not in themselves, but rather with regard to their social or psychological significance. For example, Marañón analyzes some of Baroja's favorite expressions in terms of what they may reveal about the author's psychology:

> . . .Baroja. . . .is not pleased or displeased [*gustar, disgustar*] by things, rather, they either enthuse him or they don't [*entusiasmar*]. This word, "enthusiasm," along with "farce and farceur" and the expression "somewhat" that he placed in front of almost all of his adjectives, always fearing to commit himself—"somewhat ridiculous, somewhat exact," etcetera—will be conspicuous among the vocabulary that future critics will encounter and comment on; and in this lexicon is summarized, . . .that which pertains most authentically to the psychological character of the author.[1]

Marañón's speciality in history is clinical biography, and, thus, when dealing with literature, he tends to devote himself either to biographies exploring the relationship between the author's personality and his themes, or to a biopsychological analysis of fictional characterization such as Don Juan, Pedro Crespo, the mayor of Zalamea, or Don Quijote. Marañón's methods are substantially the same whether he is discussing an author or a fictional character, a dramatist or several *dramatis personae*.

I have found it useful to divide Marañón's contributions to biography, history, and literary criticism into four chapters: *Biological and Psychological Criteria Applied to Fiction; Marañón's Contribution to Spanish Historiography and the Theory and Practice of Biography; Biographies of Artists and Writers;* and *Biographical History of the Experimental, Inductive Consciousness in Spain.*

Chapter II, *Biological and Psychological Criteria Applied to Fiction*, examines the application of Marañón's theories about body and personality types to a profoundly mythological protagonist: Don Juan. To a much lesser degree, these theories are reflected in the critic's brief comments on Don Quijote and the honor-bound characters in Calderón's plays. Don Juan was the subject of intense concern for the critic from as early as 1924, the date of his first contribution to the field of literary criticism. In addition to his interest in psychologically interpreting Don Juan, he was motivated by an educational purpose as well: to undermine the force of a myth that he judged modern endocrinology and psychology had shown to be detrimental to the mental health of many Spaniards.

The Don Juan writings have had a curious fate. They have been intensely and widely, but seldom closely and carefully, read; they have been translated into several languages and hotly debated. No one, to my knowledge, has ever accepted Marañón's position. Thus the Don Juan critiques have been influential in a paradoxical way. Critics comment on Marañón's position but only to define and distinguish their own in opposition. The Don Juan writings have served as a catalyst, as a sort of "inspiration" for critics determined to oppose Marañón's debunking of the Burlador. A literary phenomenon as unique as this one deserves careful scrutiny. I have attempted two things: first, a detailed, developmental analysis of Marañón's Don Juan criticism throughout his professional career, paying close attention to the emendations, revisions or amplifications in his theory over the years; second, I have sought to place Marañón in perspective, intellectually, by systematically contrasting his critical stance with that of his most significant contemporaries in Spain and elsewhere who were concerned with Don Juan, including, among others, Francisco Agustín, Corpus Barga, Albert Camus, Joaquín Casalduero, Arturo Farinelli, Otto Fenichel, Sigmund Freud, Georges Gendarme de Bévotte, Jacinto Grau, Gonzalo R. Lafora, Salvador de Madariaga, Ramiro de Maeztu, Ramón Menéndez Pidal, F. Oliver Brachfeld, José Ortega y Gasset, Ramón Pérez de Ayala, Otto Rank, Juan Rof Carballo, Víctor Said Armesto, and Miguel de Unamuno. In this fashion, I believe that not only are Marañón's theories elucidated but the contemporary cycle of Don Juan criticism serves paradigmatically to introduce a vast intellectual involvement with psicoliterary criticism in the early and mid-twentieth century.

Chapter III, *Marañón's Contribution to Spanish Historiography and the Theory and Practice of Biography,* treats within their intellectual context both the explicit and implicit assumptions that guided our critic's biographies and histories. As in chapter II, I have attempted to place Marañón in perspective by comparing his work in this area with that of other significant biographers such as Agustín González de Amezúa, Benjamín Jarnés, Emil Ludwig, Antonio Marichalar, André Maurois, Giovanni Papini, Lytton Strachey and Stefan Zweig, as well as historians who were his contemporaries or who followed him, including Manuel Fernández Alvarez, Angel González Palencia, J. Ernesto Martínez Ferrando, Francisco Tomás Valiente and Jaime Vicens Vives. For this reason I believe that the aforementioned chapter is useful not only for its analysis of Marañón's place in Western biography and Spanish historiography, but also as an introductory and rudimentary outline of Spanish historiography, taking up where Sánchez Alonso's *Historia de la historiografía española* (1947-50), leaves off. Contemporary Spanish historiography is a most neglected area and the interested reader should find the bibliography that I have compiled of value, although it does not presume to exhaustiveness.

The theoretical questions of greatest concern in Spain immediately prior to and during Marañón's career as an historian were the renewed debate over the perennial polemic of whether or not history is a science or an art. A similar polemic was the question of history as a system and the possibility of deriving historical laws. Rather curiously for a scientist, and in contrast to Ortega y Gasset, Marañón did not particularly concern himself with the philosophy of history. Nevertheless his utilization of biopsychological constructs as well as techniques intended to dramatize the past constitute an implicit, consistent (if dubious) historiography. Moreover, Marañón did speculate at length about the theory and craft of biography. He accepted the early twentieth-century assumption that the novel was a dying genre and went so far as to pronounce the historical novel an already extinct species. He conceived of the biography as a proper humanistic substitute for the moribund novel. He attempted in his own writing to plot a course between "biografía novelada" (fictionalized biography) of little historical account because of its slick catering to public fancy, and on the other, serious, fully-researched and documented scientific efforts, which, nevertheless, provided no amenities nor sense of pleasure for the reader. Marañón's ideas in this regard are not unique, nor are his biographies from the point of view of their guiding formula. His biographies share certain essential characteristics with those of Stefan Zweig, Emil Ludwig, André Maurois, Lewis Mumford, and others. All of these "intuitive" biographers have in common the idea that every personality is ultimately to be understood once the "key to character" can be detected. In contrast, say, to Ludwig who saw things in terms of conflicts (Goethe: genius vs. daemon; Bismarck: pride vs. ambition), or to Maurois who found motifs (Shelly: water; Disraeli: flowers), Marañón's deciphering instrument is the biopsychological construct: "resentment," "passion to rule," "will to overcome," and so on. Thus, in a certain sense Marañón's biographies are clinical histories, case histories,

4

but written in an often melodramatic, popular fashion so as to engage the general public and not lacking in the scholarly documentation that we normally associate with the work of the professional academic historian.

Chapter IV, *Biographies of Artists and Writers*, once again, applies biopsychological constructs to authors and artists, either to clarify or explain their motivations and the curious or significant incidents that affected them in the course of their lives, or to interpret their literary or artistic productions. Thus, El Greco is evaluated in terms of his Oriental temperament, Amiel in terms of his sexual timidity, Garcilaso in terms of his ambivalence, and so on.

Included as well within this heading are a number of circumstantial or commemorative writings in which Marañón does not significantly involve himself in literary criticism, but rather evokes his reminiscences or impressions of several prominent authors of his personal acquaintance. The recent publication of the (not entirely complete) *Obras completas* of Marañón gives me the opportunity and responsibility to briefly survey this body of circumstantial literature, almost all of which has been virtually unknown since its original appearance in various newspapers or periodicals in Spain, Mexico and Argentina. The writings of Galdós, Azorín, Emilio Castelar and others, including a number of prominent French authors, Valéry, Gide and Cocteau, will be considered within this special category of evocative biographical literature.

Chapter V, *Biographical History of the Experimental, Inductive Consciousness in Spain*, distinguishes and evaluates a group of biographical essays on thinkers and scientific essayists that reflect Marañón's interpretation of the evolution of a scientific consciousness in Spain. In these essays, Marañón not only applies, say, the construct of ambivalence to Servet or the notion of projection to certain incidents in Feijoo's life. He develops a broad intellectual, scientific and literary history. Basically, Marañón seeks to identify, seek out the origins of and trace the history of the objective, experimental attitude in Spain. Both the historical figures and their writings are considered, since the development of the experimental attitude brought with it, as well, the gradual development of a new genre, the objective, theoretical essay with its own peculiar style and language.

Marañón does not devote himself to tracing the experimental approach in Spain in a systematic way, in one coherent work. Rather, his contributions on the topic are written in separate works spanning his whole professional career. Nevertheless, his efforts have been substantial and the pattern is clear. The sequence finds its beginnings in the Golden Age, with essays on figures such as Luis Vives, Huarte de San Juan and Miguel Servet, and proliferates in the eighteenth century with works on Feijoo, Casal, Sarmiento, and Pablo de Olavide. In the nineteenth and twentieth centuries, we have essays on Menéndez Pelayo and Santiago Ramón y Cajal.

Naturally, in his effort to trace the development of the experimental attitude in Spain, Marañón is at the same time tracing his own cultural antecedents and identifying his own cultural progenitors. For Marañón himself has been considered one of the foremost theoreticians and cultivators of the theoretical essay of his time. This points to an important difference between the biographies in chapter IV and chapter V. For example, in the biography of Feijoo, Marañón identifies rather closely with his protagonist and displays a profound emotional attachment to him.

In sum, Marañón's literary criticism and biographies usually involve the application of theoretical constructs developed in scientific research either to fictional (e.g., Don Juan) or biographical topics. Marañón selected these topics because he felt that they readily exemplified the theoretical power and validity of his theoretical constructs. On the other hand, Marañón's biographical history of Spanish experimentalism, in a general way, in terms of the development of the Spanish scientific consciousness, and in a specific way, in terms of the development of new theories and scientific discoveries, presents a history of the methodological tools and theoretical constructs themselves.

I should note some particulars concerning the *Obras completas* of Gregorio Marañón as well as the footnoting and indexing procedure in this book. The *Obras completas,* begun in 1966 and finished in 1972, represent a prodigious accomplishment of anthologization. However, they do not encompass the complete works of Marañón. (There are nine volumes in the *Obras completas* themselves. The editor, Alfredo Juderías, had noted an additional book, *El Greco y Toledo,* should be considered in addition to the *Obras completas,* however, it *was* reissued in volume VII of the collection.) First of all, they basically represent the humanistic contribution of Marañón, and what scientific writings that are anthologized are included because of their overriding, general, intellectual or cultural importance. A complete bibliography of Gregorio Marañón's works that would include all of his scientific writings as well has yet to be done, although the bibliography in Almodóvar and Warleta's biographical *homenaje*[2] is almost complete through the year 1950. Finding the scientific writings from 1951 through 1960, the year of Marañón's death, is much more problematical, although the physician was not publishing much science during his last decade. Moroever, there are articles (particularly among the Don Juan writings) and prologues that are missing from the *Obras completas*.

This book, while it does not presume to exhaustiveness in the scientific domain, is as complete as I have been able to achieve in the areas of literary criticism, biography and history. For the sake of consistency I have referred to works published in the *Obras completas* wherever possible. If a title is not cited in that collection it is because it has been omitted from the complete works.

Because the "complete works" of Marañón include several, often scores, or in the case of the prologues, hundreds of titles in one volume, I have thought it more practical to note separately each of my citations of Marañón rather than include them in the main body of the text. These notes are categorized by chapter and appear after the text of the book. Investigators who may be interested in specialized areas of research that are significant to the concerns of this critical study are advised to consult the notes. Since this book of criticism has sought to place Marañón in historical, cultural and intellectual perspective, I have had occasion to compile specific sub-bibliographies of certain scientific, historical or psychological topics. The notes to chapter I contain a brief bibliography of psychological art and literary criticism prior to the Second World War, while the notes to chapter II contain references to contemporary psychological literary analyses of the text rather than of the character or author. In chapter II appears an extensive bibliography of Marañón's Don Juan writings as well as those of his contemporaries and the more recent critics. As I have noted earlier, the notes for chapter III contain a rudimentary bibliographic outline of contemporary Spanish historiography. The notes for chapter IV contain sub-bibliographies on El Greco art criticism, on the influence of Oriental art in Spanish Renaissance and Baroque painting and sculpture (particularly in terms of the sociocultural theories of Américo Castro), and on the personality and diary of Henri Frédéric Amiel. In the notes for chapter V there are sub-bibliographies on the "problem" of Spanish science according to the generations of 1898 and 1914, and on Fray Benito Jerónimo Feijoo.

7

Gary D. Keller

In addition, in order to avoid complicating critical discussions that often become quite involved, I have frequently used the notes as a medium for somewhat extended discussions of discursive matters that bear indirectly on the analyses at hand. The subject and author index incorporates both the text and the notes, but names in the notes only appear in the index if they are related to one of the discussions therein.

Finally, I need mention that this book was originally contracted with the series, *Studies in the Romance Languages and Literatures* of the University of North Carolina Press in 1971. It had been expected that the book would appear in 1973 but—alas!—the financial difficulties and ultimate suspension of operations at North Carolina have delayed the publication of my study until now. I have earnestly endeavored to keep the book up to date, both textually and bibliographically, and in a certain sense the book is perhaps a better, more complete one for the delay. On the other hand, I have also been engaged in other scholarly pursuits and have not been able to attend to this book with the single-minded devotion that characterized its genesis in years past. Thus, if for some reason I may have omitted a recent bibliographic entry, particularly in the ever-expanding areas of Don Juan writings and criticism and of Spanish historiography, I ask the sympathetic understanding of the reader to put my work into historical perspective just as I have attempted to do with the work of Gregorio Marañón.

I

ORIGINS AND DEVELOPMENT OF MARAÑON'S BIOGRAPHICAL AND LITERARY THEORIES

Science applied to humanities: general developments

Gregorio Marañón began his professional career as a medical researcher during a period when biologists, psychologists and other scientists had begun to apply clinical and physiological discoveries, as well as scientific methodologies, to all sorts of phenomena in the fields of ethics, literature, history, myth and art. Between the years 1915-1930, he was able to make at least one contribution in each of these fields. Moreover, he continued to contribute to the humanities and social sciences from a biopsychological viewpoint until his death in 1960, with notable success in terms of readership and influence.

Marañón was not a pioneer in the application of scientific constructs to the humanities or social sciences. As we shall see in our survey of his contributions on Don Juan, El Greco and Amiel, while our critic's efforts were peculiarly his own, they chronologically followed a substantial number of previous pathological studies.

In the latter half of the nineteenth century, the connection between science and art was fostered by Naturalism and Darwinism. Emile Zola's debt to Claude Bernard is well known. The novel was to become an experimental, in some instances almost a medical document. The influence of Naturalism was also pronounced in the field of biography. For example, in France, Charles Binet-Sanglé, a psychology professor, after writing books entitled *L'epilepsie chez Gustave Flaubert* and *La maladie de Blaise Pascal,* set out, in an exhaustive four-volume work, to prove that Jesus Christ himself was mad![1] Roberto Novoa Santos, a contemporary of Marañón, was astounded, repelled and attracted by the work.[2] Novoa Santos himself attempted to trace mysticism to its erotic, biological roots and in his *Patografía de Santa Teresa* (1932) treated the Spanish saint as a pathological case. Earlier, in 1892, Max Nordau had been discussing the pathology of mysticism in his book *Degeneration*.[3] Pompeyo Genér popularized Nordau's work in his own *Literaturas malsanas*.[4] The disenchantment with mysticism is echoed in the rationalism of Eugenio d'Ors and Ortega y Gasset. For d'Ors, mystic understanding entails the inability to judge the true weight of things. Ortega focuses on the hermeticism and incommunicability of mystic knowledge. Marañón himself, in his "Misterios de San Plácido," explores the relationship between mysticism and erotic delirium.

Similarly, Darwin's *The Origin of Species* had a profound influence on biography, supplying fuel for both the advocates of the role of heredity and those who pointed to the environment in the determination of human nature. Francis Galton, in his *Heredity and Genius* (1869), leaned toward the defenders of heredity. John Fiske defended the environmentalists. By 1896, Havelock Ellis was to claim that biography was really a branch of applied psychology. Ellis expressed his shock that few biographers knew anything of the theories of psychologists like Wilhelm Wundt, G. Stanley Hall and Joseph Jastrow, who "have taught us how to obtain by exact methods a true insight into the processes of the average human mind."[5]

Around the turn of the century, biography, literature, art, ethics, and myth were influenced by another current, Freudianism. In 1910, Freud attempted to demonstrate the applicability of psychoanalysis by choosing a subject for whom a conventional approach was severely handicapped by the shortage of evidence: Leonardo da Vinci. As John A. Garraty puts it: "Only the bare outline of Leonardo's career was known; of his personality scarcely a vestige remained. Yet Freud's study, published in 1910, attempted to penetrate the deepest recess of the artist's soul."[6]

A host of other works by Freud and his followers were soon published, including: *Totem and Taboo, Wit and its Relation to the Unconscious*, and *Moses and Monotheism* by Freud; *Art and Artist* by Otto Rank; and *Hamlet and Oedipus* by Ernest Jones.[7]

In Spain and Argentina, two figures who preceded Marañón and his generation were Santiago Ramón y Cajal and José Ingenieros. Cajal utilized a scientific approach to the problem of Spain's backwardness which was extremely influential, and, in addition, in 1905 published *Psicología de Don Quijote y el quijotismo*. José Ingenieros, in his *La psicopatología en el arte*, among other topics, discusses

the insanity of Don Quijote and the psychology of writers and theorizes, independently of Freud, on the psychopathology of dreams.[8]
Yet, it is with Marañón's generation, the Generation of 1914, that
biology and psychology truly make themselves felt over a wide cultural spectrum, particularly in the fields of biography, ethics, literature and myth. Biography, as in Europe and the United States, pro-
liferated in the 1920's and 1930's. Beside Marañón, Ortega y Gasset,
Manuel Azaña, Eugenio d'Ors, Salvador de Madariaga, Pío Baroja,
Benjamín Jarnés, Antonio Marichalar, Agustín González de Amezúa, Ramón Gómez de la Serna and many others tried their hands at
this literary form. Ortega y Gasset writes a biography of Goethe from
the "inside."[9] Salvador de Madariaga takes a clear psychological
approach to biography. Others, such as Gómez de la Serna, approach
biography from an esthetic, rather than psychological, orientation.

In an article entitled "Ni vitalismo ni racionalismo," Ortega proclaims his adherence to *biologismo* as a philosophic goal.[10] Of course,
Ortega's orientation toward biology is quite different from Marañón's, as their differing conclusions on the nature of Don Juan clearly
show.

Others of this generation who were making literary contributions
from a biological or psychological orientation were José Goyanes
Capdevila, José M. Sacristán, Gonzalo Lafora, Francisco Agustín
and Roberto Novoa Santos. We shall have occasion to compare all
of these figures with Marañón in specific instances.

Marañón's own application of biological and psychological constructs to literary and art criticism is a very eclectic one. The succession of hypothetical and methodological tools that the critic applies
to fiction, drama and biography reflects the professional development of Marañón as a scientist. The three basic sources upon which
he drew in his literary criticism were, successively, endocrinology,
morphology and Freudian psychology. Because his approach is so
eclectic, I have described the constructs and evaluated the theoretical
significance of each major study singly. For example, the reader will
find, in my evaluation of the *Don Juan*, a description of "primary
and secondary sexual energy"; in the El Greco writings, an outline
of pertinent morphological theories; in the study of Garcilaso and
Servet, respectively, an analysis of the application of the concepts
of ambivalence and the inferiority complex. Here I shall confine myself to indicating in a general fashion the theoretical sources which
Marañón applied to literary criticism and biography.

The Endocrinological Approach

The endocrinological approach

Marañón has been internationally recognized as one of the founders of modern endocrinology and as the leading researcher in that field in Spain during the first quarter of the twentieth century. Some of his most well-known experiments describe the effects of adrenalin (the hormone secreted from the adrenal glands) on human emotional states. The experiments were cited by W. B. Cannon in support of his general theory of emotion.[11] By 1915, the year that Marañón wrote a treatise on internal secretions, endocrinology had grown into a field of medical significance. Physiological experiments in the field had already been done by Claude Bernard, Brown-Sequard and others. Starling had created the concept and term "hormone" in 1905, and with a new generation of researchers, such as Marañón, Biedl and Pende, endocrinology emerged as a clinical discipline. Marañón's research in clinical endocrinology led him to conclude that the the glandular secretions are important determinants of human behavior. The normal personality is one whose glands work in harmony. No disproportionate function on the part of any one gland can be detected: in biology as in fashion, "perfect elegance must be free from notice."[12] Between normality and an overt pathological condition lies an intermediate zone. In this state one or more glandular secretions leaves traces of influences although these are to a large extent held in check by the remaining normal components of the system. The organism, therefore, appears quite normal, although it is inclined to pathological difficulties.[13] These pathological inclinations are more or less stable states.

> These states can be called *temperaments*, and truly many of the temperaments that commonfolk are diagnosing all the time are, in fact, *endocrine temperaments*. The person that displays one of these overt temperaments, as common people well know, borders on ill-health because of the ease with which his constitution, already inclined toward a given direction, can go beyond the point of normality.[14]

As early as 1915, Marañón displays his interest in these stable, abnormal dispositions somewhere between normality and a pathological temperament, thus foreshadowing his studies of figures such as Enrique IV or Tiberius:

> ...temperaments, in their infinte varieties, are more interesting than pathological states. In them the power of the abnormality is unable to overcome the natural energy of life which reveals itself to us without the sad one-sidedness of infirmity, but with a volatility and with inclinations not found in the perfect course of the normal, healthy constitution.[15]

Among the various temperaments that Marañón describes are those influenced by the hyperfunction or hypofunction of the thyroid, pituitary and superadrenal glands. For example, a constitution characterized by hypofunction of the thyroid tends to be short and overweight, with small, chubby hands. An example is the *Gioconda*, with her cold, white skin and her unarousable temperament.[16] Marañón claims that the type is particularly common among women. Let us note in this description, written in 1915, Marañón's reference to the *Gioconda*. As we shall see, in 1927 the critic initiates his studies on El Greco by hypothesizing that the artist modeled many of his figures on an antithetical type, the hyperfunctional type with respect to the thyroid, a temperament which he claims abounded among the Jewish population in Toledo during the painter's time. Moreover, as Pedro Laín Entralgo has pointed out,[17] as early as 1919, the date of the publication of *La edad crítica*, Marañón had begun to make consistent use of literary material. Passages from Pérez de Ayala, Ortega y Gasset, Eugenio d'Ors, Nietzsche, Michaelis and others are utilized to exemplify Marañón's theories of bisexuality and intersexuality.[18] One of the basic tenets of the doctor's theory of sexual evolution is that each individual's development, whether male or female, proceeds through various "critical" stages, each marked by a sexual crisis. For the male, adolescence is the most critical period. This is the period during which the characteristics of the undifferentiated child are overtaken by the forces of a newly emerging masculinity. On the other hand, for the female the climacteric or menopause "marks the passage from her stage of arrested development (which although the most specifically feminine is also considered a partial prolongation of childhood) into a terminal state, in some respects approaching masculinity."[19] Marañón finds that these sexual crises are marked by the tendency of the dominant sex to assume some determinants of its opposite: ". . .in the evolution of man during puberty there erupts an outbreak of femininity, while woman experiences an outbreak of virility during the climacteric period."[20]

Marañón's use of literary citations to support his theory of critical stages in the sexual evolution of man and woman is defended in the following way:

> Perhaps we could be reproached for our excessive use of literary examples. We offer them because we judge them to be just as instructive as clinical descriptions. The artist gathers his impressions directly from reality without the scientific prejudices that sap the human value from medical observations. . . . For this reason we need to turn to the great artists, who are also supreme psychologists. . . .[21]

13

The Endocrinological Approach

Naturally, in *La edad crítica*, the literary material is utilized to exemplify a biopsychological theory of sexuality. Nevertheless, the abundant use of such material, together with Marañón's admiration for the psychological verisimilitude of great art, foreshadows his first literary effort, the 1924 essay on Don Juan. Here the converse of *La edad crítica* takes place: biopsychological constructs are utilized by the author in an effort to clarify the nature of the Don Juan myth both in its literary and sociocultural aspects. The step from utilizing material to exemplify scientific theory to the converse, the use of theory to clarify literature, was made easy and natural by the precedents of others during the late nineteenth and early twentieth centuries. As we shall see, examples abound, in the fields to which Marañón initially contributed, of scientists and physicians whose scientific-humanistic approaches had gained a measure of recognition among scholars and among the general, educated public.

The morphological approach

Marañón's endocrinological research (1910-1915) almost exclusively concerned itself with the effects of glandular secretions on human sexuality, emotion and the susceptibility to illness. However, he soon became aware of the relationship between his own endocrinological research and the morphological analysis of personality types by Ernst Kretschmer. This awareness bore fruit in a number of studies culminating in the book *Gordos y flacos* (1926). In this work, Marañón notes that Kretschmer's pyknic and asthenic types, with their corresponding psychology, can be reconciled with the theory of endocrine temperaments.[22] Society is generally aware of the differences in character between two basic human types, the obese man and the thin man. In contrast to the social stereotypes concerning the obese and thin individuals, Kretschmer has provided "a rigorously scientific conception and terminology."[23] The *gordo* designated as the "pyknic type," is associated with a "cyclothymic character, that is, one given to frequent rapid alternations of exhilaration and depression, pessimism and optimism. Such types tend to manic-depressive psychoses."[24] The *flaco*, designated "asthenic," is associated with "schizothymic character, marked by restlessness, intenseness, and idealism. Asthenic types tend to schizophrenic psychoses."[25]

As Hoddie points out, Marañón concludes that

in accordance with this classification, it seems that certain types are better suited than others for specific activities: the pyknic type for the natural sciences, the asthenic for philosophy, literary activity, mathematics and political leadership. Although Marañón's notions closely parallel most of Kretschmer's, the former objects to the weakness of the theory in dealing with intermediate types whose morphology and psychic configuration do not correspond to any specific category. In his own analysis of the personalities of historical and literary figures, Marañón applies ideas based both on his research in endocrinology and on his interpretation of Kretschmer's concepts, in so far as they are not mutually exclusive.[26]

A combined endocrinological and morphological approach can be seen as early as 1927, the date of Marañón's first article on El Greco. It also supplies the basic theoretical orientation toward the biography of Enrique IV of Castile.

We should also mention that Kretschmer himself applied his physiognomic approach to the field of biography. One of the most enduring conventions of the nineteenth and twentieth centuries has been the attribution of abnormality to the creative artist. The creator, the "genius," allegedly gains his insights at the expense of his emotional stability. Kretschmer's *Geniale Menschen* (1929) reflects this notion and attempts to validate it on scientific grounds. The German psychiatrist's book was well known in Spain. It influenced Gonzalo Lafora's conception of "genius" as applied to Ramón y Cajal, and it may also have influenced J. M. Sacristán. The latter wrote a number of articles in the Spanish newspaper, *ABC*, on figures such as Amiel, Nietzsche, Kant, etc. that were later anthologized in a book entitled *Genialidad y psicopatología*.[27] Marañón also subscribed to this concept of genius that entails mental imbalance.[28]

The relationship between Marañón and Freudian psychology

In addition to the biopsychological constructs drawn from endocrinological and morphological research, Marañón, from the beginning of his career as literary critic and biographer, added to his methodology a substantial number of concepts from Freudian psychology as well as one or two from Adler. From an early date, he was fairly well acquainted not only with the work of Freud, but also with the contributions of Wilhelm Stekel and Otto Rank. Freudianism is given substantial attention in *Tres ensayos sobre la vida sexual* (1926).

The relationship between Freud and Marañón has been the subject of some debate. The controversies are understandable because they reflect the ambivalence of Marañón himself, who on certain

15

occasions praises and on others damns Freud. The doctor's *Los estados intersexuales en la especie humana* is a typical example of this phenomenon. On the one hand, he asserts:

> Freud's work, viewed dispassionately, has a contradictory effect on the Latin reader [*lector meridional*]. On the one hand we sense that surely the author has touched the nexus of many recondite tragedies of the human soul. Part of his studies on the child, on puberty, on the influence of sexuality on pathological life, on the ontological evolution of the instincts (and even several of his interpretations on everyday psychology, far from the tumultuous energies of the instincts) are so exact, so saturated with authentic, anguished humanity, that one has the impression upon reading them that we are confronted with facts of a definitive worth in the understanding of human souls. One would have to be blind not to see that never before has human psychology received through the influence of one man, a transformation so profound as that brought about by the work of Freud. The human spirit, before and after Plato, before and after Aristotle, Descartes, Kant, was not seen with insights so radically different than those which expand our knowledge after the advent of psychoanalysis. Even those who combat Freudianism are, without knowing it, trapped in its nets, and the truth is that in our time there are no physicians, no philosophers, no naturalists, no historians, no priests who are not more or less imbued with the spirit of Freud....[29]

On the other hand, Marañón points out the errors of Freud: "In my judgment, Freud's error lies in the following three circumstances: in the excessive generalization toward normality of phenomena that are merely pathological; in the universalizing of psychological data that are probably peculiar to his race [Jews] and perhaps, even within this confine, limited to the environment in which he has been working; and finally, in his lack of experimental understanding of animal sexuality."[30] Marañón goes on to claim that the infantile sexuality described by Freud is more Central European than Spanish! ". . .the outline of infantile sexuality that Freud describes for us in his works . . .we can affirm does not correspond to the nature of the children of our race. It is certain that our children are not like that."[31]

James Hoddie, Jr., supported by statements reflecting the doctor's antagonism toward Freud, concludes that Marañón's biographical approach is essentially nonpsychoanalytic.[32]

Perhaps at the other extreme, F. Oliver Brachfeld, an Adlerian extremely hostile to Marañón,[33] judges that the physician "contrabanded" Freudian psychoanalysis:

> . . .the overall view that Marañón presents is more than debatable. In order to confect it he has made use of various elements that were very fashionable during the time that he elaborated his doctrines. One of these is called psychoanalysis, on which Marañón performs an extra-

ordinary job of contraband. He prohibits it to enter the main door in order to open up a small lateral door for it. . .he has the plan of contrabanding psychoanalysis; when discussing the importance of the mother, etc., he is a psychoanalyst who is unaware of himself, a clear psychoanalyst but one who practices only unconsciously and in secret. If he had lived in Germany he would have declared himself a psychoanalyst. . .in a country like Spain, he seems to be a fallen psychoanalyst who still remembers the heavens.[34]

Despite the hostile phrasing, Oliver Brachfeld points to an important circumstance: Marañón's relationship to psychoanalysis was colored by the general disapproval of that theory in Spain. Moreover, Marañón hedged on psychoanalysis only partly because he feared the professional consequences that would fall upon him from his colleagues if he openly embraced that theoretical orientation. As Oliver Brachfeld's diatribe clearly shows, he *was* to some degree associated professionally with the psychoanalytic school. Marañón himself comments on the fact that he was accused of Freudianism: "I have been attacked because of the nefarious sin of an alleged Freudianism. Nevertheless. . .I have never crossed with the attitude of a believer but rather as a dispassionate observer, the threshold of that precinct filled with revelations and shadows that are the works of Freud."[35] In addition to the harm that might befall his professional credentials, the doctor was genuinely repulsed by some of the philosophic outcomes of Freudian psychology, particularly the religious outcome, inasmuch as Freud reduced the divine to a "paternal figure," a crutch upon whom immature personalities rely for authority and guidance. In addition, Marañón found that the ultimate psychoanalytic vision of man was in "bad taste:" ". . .Freud suffers from a defect which in human psychology is fundamental: the sin of bad taste. I believe that no reader, at least in our latitudes, has not felt at some moment, with Freud's books before us, an intimate sense of ill-being; something akin to a sense of outrage. . .on behalf of our allegiance to our species. . . ."[36]

Given Marañón's education as a classical biologist, his religious orthodoxy and his awareness of the professional dangers in advocating psychoanalysis, one could argue that Marañón's many statements of praise for Freudianism as early as 1919 represent an heroic stance. Precisely this has been done by Pedro Laín Entralgo.

F. Oliver Brachfeld, an Hungarian professor residing in Barcelona, was appalled by the inconsistency in Marañón's theories, for in truth, Marañón takes from psychoanalysis only what is convenient for him without giving up any of his endocrinological or morpho-

logical notions, without penetrating into the theoretical consequences of his assimilaion. For example, he utilizes the notion of the
Oedipus complex without ever discussing the Freudian concept of repression upon which much of the notion rests! Oliver Brachfeld terms
Marañón's theories a *fameuse salade.*

On the other hand, Pedro Laín Entralgo, a leading Catholic intellectual, medical historian and literary critic, is able to sympathize
deeply with Marañón:

> I want to emphasize the open intellectual attitude of our clinician already
> in 1919, when confronted with the findings of psychoanalysis which were
> still so recent. Marañón objects and with good reason to Freud's lack
> of attention to constitutional aspects and the actual states of his patients'
> organisms, in which, for example, somatic intersexuality and psycho-
> logical homosexuality are not really as independent as the first psycho-
> analyst claimed; yet, at the same time, he knows how to discover and
> accept the important role of the Oedipus complex in the psychological
> and somatic evolution of sexual life. How many internists, either Euro-
> pean or American, were capable of such "audacity" forty years ago?[37]

Perhaps the key to Marañón's attraction to Freudian psychology
lies in the fact, as J. Rof Carballo has pointed out, that both the Spanish doctor and the Viennese psychoanalyst discovered around the
same time, independently of each other, "the bisexual reality of
man."[38] Marañón and Freud arrived at comparable conclusions on
infantile sexuality.[39] As a result, Marañón consistently praised
Freud's research and theories in this area, while pointing to some
discrepancies with the psychoanalyst on important details such as the
origin of *libidinal* energy. Marañón never really made up his mind
with respect to the origin of the energy available to the *libido*. On the
one hand, he goes so far as to claim that the drive for glory and money
have a displaced sexual origin, causing him to be accused by Oliver
Brachfeld as an extreme pansexualist in the tradition of Freud and
Wilhelm Stekel. On the other hand, Marañón, as was extremely
common in the first quarter of the twentieth century, tended to explain behavior through recourse to innate instincts such as the "instinct to overcome," or the "wandering instinct." In reality, Marañón
never had an interest in formulating fundamental theories; he was an
inventor of explanatory constructs on an ad hoc basis. He gradually
incorporated several concepts from Freudian psychology, adapting
them to his own, practical, biographical needs. He assimilated and
adapted Freudian material as a result of his need to explain complex
psychological phenomena which the endocrinological and morphological approach was unable to encompass. L.S. Granjel has pointed

out a change of position by Marañón with respect to the scope and relevance of endocrinology in the explanation of human behavior. As late as 1930, Marañón claimed, ". . .even when our most rigorous critics have attempted to limit the flights of fancy of those who in the pre-war years took their cues from the fertile endocrinological perspective in order to interpret so many obscure phenomena in human biology, the process of adjustment to reality has not really been unnecessarily violent."[40] Yet, by 1935, Marañón was to change his position substantially:

> My current conception of endocrinological theory is rather direct, hypercritical, even harsh. Hormones are not mischievous elves nor magical fairies, but rather, strictly workers with clearly delimited functions; their activities are fixed and untransferable. . . .I don't deny nor have I ever denied that the fact that biological truth will be revealed not only by the constant hammering of the experimenter, but also by the sudden, inspired vision of the philosopher and even the artist. Moreover, as the years have gone by, I feel more committed to moderate, step by step advances. . .to responsibility and to critical postures rather than bold hypothetical flights.[41]

As Granjel points out, a comparison of the two passages, within the context that they were written, reveals a different scientific posture on the part of Marañón, one characterized by caution and a realization of a human reality that is not only biological but psychological and spiritual as well. Marañón still believes in the influence of hormones in human behavior, but "he no longer sustains that such an influence is unique or decisive."[42] Granjel cites Marañón's conclusion on the relative weight of internal glandular secretions in determining behavior: ". . .the theory of internal secretions has revealed to us one factor of human personality, yet it is but one factor. Certainly its importance is great, but rarely decisive."[43]

At the same time that Marañón's reliance on endocrinology was decreasing, his interest in Freudian constructs took an upsurge. His 1924 distinction between primary and secondary sexual energy has a certain connection with Freud's theory of the vicissitudes or transformations of the instincts, and specifically, the notion of sublimation.[44] But it is not until 1932 that Marañón actually uses an unmistakenly Freudian concept: the Oedipus complex. In 1939, he conceives of mysticism as a sublimation of sexual instincts; in 1940, he redefines the concept of ambivalence and then applies it to Garcilaso de la Vega. In addition, he assimilates at least two concepts from Adler, the inferiority complex and the will to power (the biography of the Conde-Duque de Olivares is subtitled *La pasión de mandar*.)

Marañón and Freudian Psychology

Marañón's utilization of Freudian material will be evaluated in various sections of this book. At this point, I will confine myself to noting that Marañón does not assimilate Freudian concepts in their original form. The basic terms are retained but the concepts themselves, to a greater or lesser degree, are reformulated in order to conform to Marañón's own opinions. Thus, when our critic discusses the Oedipus complex in Amiel, rather than emphasizing the desire to commit incest with the mother and to do away with the father, the Oedipus complex is merely asserted to be a symptom of an over-idealization of the mother's love. Similarly, ambivalence is not seen as a dynamic concept covering a situation in which any person may be pulled toward and repelled by the same object of his love-hate (as for example, the protagonist Acacia in Jacinto Benavente's *La malquerida*, a drama constructed along psychoanalytic lines), but rather, is associated by Marañón with a given personality type. For Freud (or Kurt Lewin), ambivalence is a phenomenon experienced by every human being; for Marañón it becomes a behavioral response typical of a certain type of personality.

Critics and successors of Gregorio Marañón

In conclusion, let us turn briefly to the criticisms directed toward Marañón's theories, both explicit and implicit, by some of his successors in the field of psychological literary criticism. Marañón is vulnerable to criticism on two basic grounds: his penchant for classification and labeling rather than explanation, and his tendency to explain human behavior with a deterministic model. Both of these criticisms also apply to almost all of the psychological literary criticism of the first half of the twentieth century.

Oliver Brachfeld notes Marañón's tendency to adjust data to an abstract, classificatory system, a procedure typical in classical biology:

> The classical biologist "Marañón style," appears to depart from concrete, individual empirical data; in fact, he departs only from a systematic viewpoint and when he approaches a concrete case he is already dominated by his schemes and by his preconceived system. These systems are abstractions and nobody will deny that in the sciences we are considering, that which is abstract...is simply false; abstract theories are automatically turned into *myths*.[45]

Indeed, Marañón, like so many other psychologists during this time, was content to explain phenomena through mere recourse to a name, a label. Often a certain distinguishable variety of behavior would be labeled as an instinct. As Robert C. Bolles has put it, "These constructs were the curse of the 1920's, the period of 'The Great Instinct Controversy.' "[46] Several individuals spent their professional careers compiling long lists of all the instincts allegedly residing in man. Bolles observes:

> For any activity it was possible to introduce an instinct of which the activity in question was the manifestation. No criteria were employed to determine if the alleged instinctive behavior was unlearned, or universal, or done without foresight or if it was purposive. Instincts were invoked ad hoc and ad lib. If the connotation had been purely descriptive, little harm would have been done; however, the attitude common in these accounts was that nothing more needed to be said of any behavior to explain it once an instinct had been invoked.[47]

Marañón uses such phrases as "undifferentiated instinct," "wandering instinct," "reproductive instinct," "instinct to overcome," and "the law of the instincts," among others. Don Juan, Othello and Amiel are classified according to this instinctual scheme. Oliver Brachfeld asks:

> What does this classification mean? Does it correspond to anything in reality? No. It would have a correspondence only if we could grasp the instinct and measure it with precise instruments. But that is impossible. Othello, Desdemona, or Don Juan are not physical nor physiological types. They are only characters, and in that sense fixed—since the notion of character implies something set—but fixed only from a psychological point of view. A fat Othello or a skinny Othello are able to represent their role in the same fashion and they will be credible, even though the actor may be the purest Don Juan type according to Marañón.[48]

Other examples of mere labeling without delving into the theoretical consequences abound. Personalities are described as governed by univalence, ambivalence or doubt. Revolutions are caused by "resentment," "envy" and "masochistic ferocity." Moreover Amiel, a "super-differentiated" psychobiological type, is systematically contrasted with Don Juan who is an example of an "undifferentiated instinct." The neat symmetry caused by the opposing of Amiel to Don Juan clearly reflects a theoretical scheme which Oliver Brachfeld has properly judged to be abstract and mythic rather than concrete and realistic.

Most of social science during the 1920's and 1930's has been classified as "metaphysical." Social scientists have adapted Comte's terminology, with respect to the general development of human society, to their own research methods, so that research done without rigorous experimental controls, the prior defining of theorems, the prior prediction of outcomes and the use of statistical or mathematical models in order to quantify results is properly termed "metaphysical." Marañón's psychological speculations must also be classified within this category. The influence of metaphysical research on current social science (or current literary criticism) is, on the whole, an historical question. This is not to say that a good portion of the pioneering speculations of the first thirty years of the twentieth century do not still have contemporary relevance. For example, the notion of the "pugnacious instinct," although now termed "aggression," defined and, above all, measured in a totally different manner from the 1920's, is still strongly debated. Nevertheless, the method itself of identifying and labeling psychological syndromes in fictional protagonists or their authors has been totally superseded by current psychologically oriented literary critics.[49]

Marañón has also been criticized for his neglect of human freedom and free will in his literary criticism and biography in favor of theories which explain man in a mechanistic, predetermined fashion. Pedro Laín Entralgo, without mentioning Marañón by name, protests the biographical approach of psychologists closely associated with our critic:

> Must the individuality of every person be no more than a determined "point" in the mixture of typically definable human qualities, as Hippocrates and Galen conceived of temperaments? Must each man be distinguished according to a somatic and psychobiological *crisis*?

> Contemporary characterology (Klages, Jaensch, Kretschmer, etc.) incurs in a myopic limitation by giving too affirmative an answer to this last question. Decidedly it is no easy task to understand *truly* what is a *person*.[50]

Oliver Brachfeld judges that Marañón's "biological prejudice" serves only to "strip responsibility from the individual, and consequently having him appear as an object without will, as one no longer the 'master of his own destiny'. . . ."[51] Such criticisms do not pertain merely to Marañón, but to virtually the whole body of psychological and particularly psychoanalytic literary criticism of the first half of the twentieth century (with the exception, perhaps, of Jungian mythography).

Yet these criticisms—labeling rather than explaining, and a reliance on a biological or psychological determinism—have been confronted and transcended by a recent group of neo-Freudian and neo-Jungian critics, such as Ernst Kris, Norman N. Holland, Northrup

Frye and R. Chasse. Spain as well has produced several excellent psychological literary critics and biographers who have practiced their art with infintely more subtlety and sophistication than the old guard of the 1920's and 1930's. We have, for example, Pedro Laín Entralgo, J. Rof Carballo, Juan José López Ibor and Domingo García Sabell. Yet, to a greater or lesser degree, all of these Spanish critics have admitted their debt to Marañón. Undoubtedly, however, Marañón's biographical formula and his approach to literary criticism are no longer viable. His methodology *in toto* is now a subject of historical study. Nevertheless, Marañón's writings *themselves* have continued to enjoy wide readership throughout the Spanish-speaking world and elsewhere as well. Although his method, strictly speaking, has failed to find continuance through a school of followers, his example and the critical and imaginative success of his writings have inspired others to follow in his general direction. Shortly after our critic's death in 1960, Rof Carballo, in a striking essay, attempted to explain what Marañón represented to him and others of his generation. He describes Marañón as a completely individuated man in the peculiarly Jungian sense.[52] Such a man, by definition, is deeply in touch with his personal and collective roots, and his ability to stand whole despite his inner contradictions permits him to serve as a model for youth:

> The 'Great Individual' is one who is not only a great man in the sense of being a significant figure; what really characterizes him is that which teems in his unconsciousness (and not only in his own, but also in the collective unconsciousness). . . .And it is here where the old—and very noble—sense of a stoic Spain which is *still* represented in Marañón, that Spain that adopts a dignified stance in order to conceal its emotions, the one that doesn't want to reveal and examine them, joins with the spirit of a new Spain, *that he also represented*: a Spain that examines and analyzes, without fear, without stupid apprehensions that the light will blind or confound us.[53]

II

BIOLOGICAL AND PSYCHOLOGICAL CRITERIA APPLIED TO FICTION

Marañón's first Don Juan theory: 1924

The most widely circulated theories of Marañón in the field of literary criticism have been contained in his essays on the mythical figure of Don Juan, whose popularity, according to Marañón, has led to a widespread social misconception about the nature of masculinity and virility. Marañón has produced a substantial number of lectures, articles, essays and prologues on the subject. Also, books devoted to other interests such as *La edad crítica, Tres ensayos sobre la vida sexual,* or *Amiel* have portions referring to Don Juan and Don Juanism.[1]

Marañón's writings on the subject as a literary critic embrace a period from 1924 through 1959. Although Marañón's theories on Don Juan are fundamentally stable, he put his thoughts to the test of continual revisions and expansions. We must remember that Marañón writes in a period extremely rich, not only in essayistic criticism, but also in literary interpretations of the Don Juan motif. During the periods before and contemporaneous to Marañón's first essay on Don Juan in 1924, among the many significant critical works which appeared, the following have a direct relevance to Marañón's work: Arturo Farinelli, "Cuatro palabras sobre Don Juan y la literatura donjuanesca del porvenir," 1899; Georges Gendarme de Bévotte, *La légende de Don Juan, son évolution dans la littérature des origines au romantisme,* 1906; Victor Said Armesto, *La leyenda de Don Juan,* 1908; Ramón Pérez de Ayala, *Las Máscaras,* 1919; Ramón Menéndez Pidal, *Estudios Literarios,* 1920; Otto Rank, *Die Don Juan Gestalt,* 1924; Ramiro de Maeztu, *Don Quijote, Don Juan y La Celestina,* 1926; Gonzalo R. Lafora, *Don Juan, Los Milagros y otros ensayos*, 1927; Francisco Agustín, *Don Juan en el teatro, en la novela y en la vida*, 1928.[2] In turn, Marañón's writings had a direct influence on several of the above works. Marañón formed his theories while immersed in the dense milieu created by the above works as well as by various other impressions, evocations, articles, essays, novels, plays, poems, polemics, etc. written throughout Europe both in the distant and immediate past.[3]

Furthermore, of particular importance for Marañón was the fact that a precedent for the use of medical, biological and psychological terminology had already been established with reference to Don Juan. Already in 1884 Armand Hayam, with whom Marañón was acquainted through Gendarme de Bévotte's book, used the phrase *donjuanisme* to depict a common attitude throughout the world toward love composed of the elements of inconstance, infinite curiosity, seductiveness, and the desire to triumph over women. Moreover, there is a physiological diagnosis of the Don Juan type: ". . .a Don Juan is neither a nervous type nor a bilious one; he is instead a sanguine individual, a perfect model of vigor and beauty. Grace, intrepidness, eloquence, cunning, and a rare gift of adaptability combine to make him the irresistible seducer."[4] Of more immediate significance were the ruminations of Ramón Pérez de Ayala who associated Don Juan (in his characteristic, sardonic, half-serious way) with the mathematico-sexual theories of Otto Weininger.[5] As we shall see, several of Pérez de Ayala's biopsychological speculations had much impact on Marañón.

Marañón's first known entry into the field of literary criticism occurred in 1923 at Santander, where he gave a lecture on "Biología de Don Juan," followed by his 1924 lecture at the Real Academia de Medicina de Madrid, entitled "Psicopatología del donjuanismo." The same work was published that same year in the *Revista de Occidente* with the title, "Notas para la biología de Don Juan."[6] It is not surprising that Marañón picked the Don Juan motif inasmuch as this topic had been the subject of the widest possible variance of comment in society. The Don Juan motif had the further allurement and security of having been primed with a medical perspective and terminology by critics such as Armand Hayam and Pérez de Ayala. In a sense, Marañón made the transition to literary criticism with great facility, judging that he was not substantially stepping into an alien arena, but bringing his knowledge as a specialist to a constituency of critics who were ready to embrace his orientation. The same kinds of factors are present in motivating Marañón's first substantial effort

The 1924 Don Juan Theory

in biography: El Greco. Here again, by the time the doctor was ready to make his contribution, pathological and physiological viewpoints had gained currency and were the subject of intense debate.

In 1924, Marañón enters the field of literary criticism out of a desire to puncture a pervading literary and cultural myth extolling Don Juan as a model of masculinity and virility. This misconception, Marañón claims, is harmful to society in general and particularly to the adolescent male. His 1924 essay may be understood as a therapeutic intervention into a literary and cultural milieu dangerous because it encourages a false and unhealthy model of sexual fulfillment. The 1924 essay is not only a literary critique but also a document of sexual re-education. The myth of Don Juanism, typically termed "the myth of quantitative virility"[7] or "the myth of pseudovirility,"[8] has "soured the youth of many men, and has caused them to lead incomplete lives, when it has not trapped them in the labyrinth of psychopathy."[9]

Marañón takes a clinical approach, attempting to isolate the critical biological factors of real men around whom, he claims, the Don Juan myth was formed in the past and is perpetuated in the present:

> Don Juan is not an ideal creature, as we all know, but rather a person of flesh and blood, possessing a characteristic anatomy and physiology, and, we might add, a characteristic clinical history. The legendary type was formed from this living matter. And it frequently happens that literary commentators start from this legendary stage and, as a result, lose contact with the living reality, with the authentic and eternal Don Juan. The latter, it is true, has not escaped either from the influence of his own myth, but in what is essential, his biological component, he continues to be the same as in his pre-Don Juanesque period.[10]

Thus, to a large extent Marañón's findings are not based upon the various Don Juan literary works, but rather upon living individuals whom the doctor claims to be the human stratum upon which the literary Don Juans are modeled. The "eternal and authentic" Don Juan is a biological type whose profile is established not by theory, but rather, by clinical observation.[11] As we shall see, once the biological Don Juan type is outlined, the findings are then extrapolated and applied to the literary Don Juans. Naturally, a basic assumption that must be made is that the literary models do, indeed, reflect the biological Don Juan with greater or lesser accuracy.

Marañón isolates two essential attributes of the Don Juan type: ". . .the authentic Don Juan lives exclusively for women's love.

And he situates himself, except in a few cases, in a passive position in relation to them: he is the center of gravitation."[12] He examines the biological significance of both characteristics.

The fact of Don Juan's devotion to women to the exclusion of all else is analyzed in terms of primary and secondary forms of sexual activity in man. Psychodynamically, a mechanism similar to the Freudian concept of sublimation is involved here. The theory, however, follows Otto Weininger.[13] Primary sexual activity is to be understood as "the fulfillment of the procreative act, common to both sexes, and of the functions of maternity inherent to woman."[14] Marañón judges that for women

> ... the fulfillment of that primary sexual function is all-absorbing, while secondary sexual functions occupy a limited place in her existence. In other words, woman—the ordinary woman, not the exceptional one—is made for love and maternity, but not for participation, unless by accident, in social struggles, nor for changing the course of events with the creations of her brain.[15]

On the other hand, secondary sexual activity seems to involve the diversion of energy from primary sexual activity to masculine social activities such as those necessary to support a home and children, or if the level of civilization permits, to support the ambition of doing some social good in order to secure personal renown.[16] The pursuit of science or war are examples of secondary sexual activity. In the following examples, Marañón attempts to demonstrate the displaced primary sexual content in scientific or warlike endeavor:

> For example, see the letters that Pasteur sent to his wife from Germany, shortly after his marriage, during a trip in search of racemic acid. The passionate ardor with which he speaks about his investigations to his mate has a clear sexual equivalence. And when he finally manages to obtain the coveted substance artificially, the discovery is as much a sexual brainchild as flesh and blood children are sexual products of a mother's womb. Another similar example, . . .is found in the letters that Napoleon writes to Jospehine during the Italian campaign. He is madly in love with his wife, but, being a formidable man of action, he finds no other means of expressing his passion, between one expedition and another, than a few laconic accounts which resemble battle orders, in which he speaks of his victories and his plans. But betwen the brief and apparently cold lines there is a strong sexual undercurrent a thousand times more intense than in all of the expressions of love in her letters.[17]

According to Marañón, a man is capable of functioning on a totally primary or totally secondary level. The ascetic for example, by an act of will, is able to divert all primary sexual activity. The Don

Juan type, however, is abnormal in the sense that, like women, he is unable to function on a secondary level. ". . .the type deviates toward femininity. . .where all sexual energy is converted into amorous activity, at the expense of a precarious social activity, just as we have seen occurs in women. This is the case of Don Juan."[18] For Marañón, the masculine man is not the Don Juan type but rather "the hard-working and active man, who is frequently monogamous, not rarely timid, and even at times secluded in a state of voluntary chastity. . . . The most virile man is the one who works the most, the one who succeeds the best in outdoing other men, and not the Don Juan who deceives poor women who are naturally disposed beforehand toward letting themselves be fooled."[19]

Marañón seems to be on safe ground when he claims the Don Juan type is an unordinary or even pathological man. However, when he attempts to associate the Don Juan type with femininity, his arguments become tortured. In order to assert that the Don Juan type deviates toward femininity he has to claim that, like women, this type only functions on a level of primary sexual activity. Yet, even if this were so, there is still no rationale for claiming that primary sexual activity *itself* is more feminine and secondary sexual activity is more masculine. Furthermore, there seems to be no strong reason why women are not equally capable of secondary activity in the way Marañón has described it. Marañón claims that this is "something impossible for woman, whom nature reminds in a periodic and spectacular way that she is subjected to her slavery during the best years of her life."[20] Presumably, nature would likewise remind even the most rigorous male ascetic of his sexual makeup through erections, phantasies, dreams, etc. Cloistered life styles and philosophies emphasizing chastity such as the medieval ideals of virginity have been very widespread in Spain.

As we recall, the second attribute that Marañón points to is that Don Juan, rather than the woman, is the center of sexual gravitation. Ramón Pérez de Ayala had already noted and commented in some detail on this phenomenon in his collection of essays on the theater, *Las Máscaras*. For example, the latter finds it a "curious paradox that the most masculine beau, one who has innumerable belles, might likewise say that he himself is the indifferent belle pursued by innumerable lovers [*galanas*], since women are the ones who seek, pursue and fall in love with him, and not he with them."[21] Apart from the above word play which suggests a certain consonance with Marañón's position, Pérez de Ayala explains the phenomenon by the assertion that "a diabolical agent, a magic spell of love, is confined inside Don Juan."[22] For Pérez de Ayala, Don Juan's bewitching powers are an indication of his Satanism as well as his absolute masculinity.

> . . .how can we accept, and accepting him, how can we interpret a man, Don Juan, who corresponds to all of the imaginable dimensions of femininity and who attracts and enamours all women? Undoubtedly this man is absolute masculinity, and just as pure alcohol possesses the qualities and different gradations of all alcoholic drinks, Don Juan sums up all those dimensions of masculinity that produces the affinity with and attraction to as many other dimensions of femininity. . . .[23]

For Marañón, however, this bewitching power is a psychological inversion. Throughout the animal world it is the male segment of the species that takes the initiative and is ready to fight and kill for the female while she contemplates the battle and awaits the victor. The passivity of Don Juan is but another attribute which is normally found in the woman. Other, lesser elements that Marañón enumerates to support his thesis of Don Juan's pseudovirility are: Don Juan's wandering tendency, his tactics of publicizing his adventures, his devotion to games of chance, his narcissism and his facility for lying. With respect to morphology, Marañón claims:

> The morphology that corresponds to men endowed with an extraordinary capacity for love is, generally, somewhat antiesthetic: reduced stature, short legs, extremely accused physiognomical traits, rough skin, and abundant beard and body hair. This, therefore, does not at all resemble the thin, elegant Don Juan whom we see in drawing rooms and on stages, with his fine skin, wavy hair, and either a beardless face or slight, pointed beard. His meticulous care in dressing, and the occasionally showy exaggeration of his dress, accentuate even more the blurring of the virile component of Don Juan's morphology.[24]

Having traced Marañón's fundamental arguments against the supposed virility of the Don Juan type, I will turn to some important critical appraisals, both implicit and explicit, of the literary Don Juan.

First of all, Marañón hypothesizes a set of Don Juan types which have been preeminent in literature at least from Greek mythology. For Marañón, Don Juan represents a biological reality, "a well-defined and classifiable variety of the fauna of love."[25] and as such has had an ancient literary history. Don Juan's history can be divided into two periods: "the pre-Don Juanesque and the Don

The 1924 Don Juan Theory

Juanesque proper."[26] Marañón makes reference to Gendarme de Bévotte who identifies a pre-Don Juanesque philosophy in Epicureanism and a pre-Don Juanesque profile in Zeus and Theseus.[27] Eventually, with Tirso de Molina, Don Juan surfaces and is named. He is "cast into a definitive literary mold."[28] Yet, while we may know and identify him by his traditional name, in order to understand his totality it is necessary to dissect his biological roots. This leads us to another characteristic peculiar to Marañón's analysis. For literary historians such as Victor Said Armesto and Menéndez Pidal, the original myth is founded on the *convidado de piedra* (inviting of the statue to supper) episode to which Tirso de Molina genially introduced the "deceiver of women" motif. Marañón considers the myth to be essentially one of *hombría* (manliness). "New myths are added to the original one of manliness—false manliness—which excuses everything. First he [Don Juan] is the rebel who breaks with the laws of a petty society and morality. Later he is the sinner whom God forgives regardless of his offense, as He forgives Mary Magdalene, for having loved a great deal."[29] Marañón, by emphasizing the slight antecedents studied by Gendarme de Bévotte as well as others that he proposes (Ovid, Sodom and Gomorrah), makes it very difficult to envision how the *Burlador de Sevilla* was created by Tirso. It becomes necessary to hypothesize an inverse order of formation from the generally supposed one. Yet, it seems eccentric to think that for Tirso the core of the drama revolved around the character of a woman deceiver and that to this personage was added the traditional *convidado de piedra* material.

Be this as it may, in his claiming of the virility notion as the common denominator of the various Don Juan representations, Marañón severely underestimates the importance of Don Juan as a rebel. This is a topic that we shall develop later, yet let us mention that Gendarme de Bévotte himself claims that Zeus is a Don Juan only in a sense. This is so because:

> . . .it is important to distinguish two elements in Don Juanism. Don Juan is not only, as the layman believes, a devotee of love; he is also the defender of natural laws and individual prerogatives against social and religious law. The debauchee who spontaneously obeys his instincts, and who is commonly called, with a vulgar but significant name, 'a lady's man,' is not a complete Don Juan; he is only a sensualist.[30]

Zeus is not a Don Juan type to the extent that his behavior is accepted by society.

Biology, Psychology and Fiction

As a consequence of the focus on Don Juan as a representation of pseudovirility, Marañón is led to judge the excellence of Zorilla's *Don Juan Tenorio* over other dramas. "...if it were necessary to choose the Don Juan who is most replete with Don Juanesque substance, I am sure that a flagrant injustice would be committed if the chosen one were not Zorilla's Don Juan."[31] The reason for this is that Zorilla's drama portrays the biology and psychology of the Don Juan phenomenon with "absolute biological exactitude." For example, Doña Inés declaims her attraction in the following way: "I am drawn to you as a river is drawn to the sea," evidence for Marañón of the play's capturing of the magnetic passivity of the biological Don Juan. Marañón considers the last scene in the cemetary to contain a deep psychological truth about the aging Don Juan. He even suggests that a "greying toupee" should be used by the actor to represent these "psychological moments in which the expiatory importance of [Don Juan's] decline is seen. . . ."[32] In a prologue written in 1928 entitled "La vejez de don Juan," the doctor charts out the typical outcomes in old-age of the Don Juan type:

> In practice, the old Don Juan can follow one of these three paths: either he gets married; or he continues to be a Don Juan, substituting his ability at flattery for his organic decline; or he devotes himself wholly to religion. This, then, is his end: husband, old rake, or monk.[33]

Zorilla's *Don Juan Tenorio* is significant in that it encompasses at least two (one could argue for all three) of the typical outcomes. Marañón agrees with Pérez de Ayala that Zorilla's Don Juan is quite willing to marry Doña Inés and that if it weren't for the intemperance of the Comendador, "he would end up by entering the peaceful brotherhood of husbands!"[34] After marriage is frustrated, Don Juan returns to his women-chasing ways, and finally, of course, with the intercession of Doña Inés, he makes his peace with God.

Marañón credits the *Don Juan Tenorio* with psychological accuracy in the famous braggadocio scene where Tenorio and Mejías recount to each other their social and sexual affronts. For the critic, this scene is another evocation of one of Don Juan's traits:

> ...the scandalous and deliberate ostentation of his amorous successes, the exaggeration and even invention of them, just as adolescents do.... Don Juan recounts his conquests in public to whomever wishes to listen to him; in part because his worldly instinct enjoys the satisfaction of revealing his triumphs to the world, both the doubtful and

the real ones; and also because scandal is the most effective weapon for his new adventures.[35]

It is instructive to compare this aspect of Marañón's interpretation with Unamuno's observations on Don Juan in the prologue to his play, *El hermano Juan*. According to Unamuno, notoriety is the basic goal of Don Juan.

> The legitimate, genuine, and pure Don Juan seems to devote himself to chasing females for the sole purpose of telling all and boasting about it. Remember the list of victims and conquests that is presented by the Don Juan of Zorrilla's drama. And remember his challenges. Were they because of jealousy? No, the *Burlador* does not experience this emotion, as perhaps he does not feel ardor. What plagues him is the desire to astonish, to make a name for himself and assure his reputation.[36]

This, for Unamuno, is Don Juan's goal—to make a name for himself. While Unamuno is no great admirer of Don Juan,[37] he presents in his introduction to *El hermano Juan* a philosophic interpretation of the legendary figure that is consonant with his typically agonic understanding of the struggle for selfhood. (In the play itself, however, Don Juan does not fare nobly. He emerges as a grotesque narcissist.) Don Juan is the eminently theatrical protagonist. "If Don Quijote tells us 'I know who I am!,' Don Juan tells us the same thing, but in another way: 'I know what part I'm playing! I know I'm playing a role!' "[38] And Don Juan's "act," his routine of possessing women and spreading his fame, is seen in terms of an existential quest, a quest for selfhood, a name. It is notable how the same starting point, the braggadocio of Don Juan, is guided to such disparate conclusions, depending on the personality of the interpreter! For Marañón, fearful of the virulence of the Don Juan myth, the Tenorio's self-proclaiming powers are the redress of a weak, adolescent, inferior masculinity. For Unamuno, the same syndrome is indicative in Don Juan of the sort of quest for immortality and selfhood that he perceived in Don Quijote or in Augusto Pérez, the protester in *Niebla*. Don Juan is an actor in a world that in itself is merely a theater. Hence, the subtitle of the play, *el mundo es teatro*. Such a role in such an environment is the quintessence of an authentic, "real" existence.

Unamuno, curiously enough, pities Don Juan because of reasons similar to Marañón's 1939 essay *Gloria y miseria del conde de Villa-mediana*: his essential childhood. Don Juan is successful because he inspires charity and maternal compassion. Intensely grotesque and ironic is the vision that Unamuno gives us of Don Juan as a

smothered success because he is the unconscious surrogate of woman's frustrated desire for a child.

> Why do Don Juan's victims fall in love with him? It is because they
> pity him. Above all, they are grateful to him for noticing them, for
> acknowledging their personality, even if only in its physical, corporeal
> aspect. And for desiring—even without exactly wishing it—to make
> them mothers. There is vanity in this, delight in being honored as his
> favorite and in being distinguished in this way. But, in addition, and
> perhaps above all, there is maternal compassion. 'May the poor thing
> not suffer on my account!' Perhaps the victim takes Don Juan, draws
> him to her breast, mothers him, and maybe even offers him a breast
> to suckle. Poor Don Juan![39]

Unamuno's profile has notable thematic analogues to Marañón's
lecture "Los misterios de San Plácido," where the doctor chronicles
a series of Don Juanesque incidents at the convent of San Plácido.
Marañón concludes that mysticism is a sublimation of more organic
drives—one of these, naturally, the maternity drive. There is always
the danger that the sublimation will deteriorate. Indeed, in *El Greco
y Toledo*, Marañón quotes Lhermitte to the effect that "the mystical
access entails a serious trial for delicate temperaments; and so we end
up asking ourselves up to what point phenomena of a pathological
nature might interfere with the purest spiritual drive!"[40]

Perhaps the most provocative reason that Marañón puts forth
for extolling *Don Juan Tenorio* as the version which has best expressed the *hombría* notion and general biological reality of the Don
Juan type is the popularity of the play itself. Presumably, Zorilla's
Don Juan Tenorio is popular because it is a highly faithful, naturalistic representation of the Don Juan type. The public, of course, reacts to the exactitude of the representation with a mistaken attitude.
The public accepts all of Don Juan's "symptoms" as if they were attributes of virility. What is needed is the proper medical, biological
and pyschological interpretation of these symptoms to convince the
public that they are witnessing a faithful representation of a pathological type rather than a hero. Marañón thinks it hopeless for critics
to protest the yearly resurrection of the *Tenorio*. The substitution
of the Don Juan of Tirso or Molière for the *Tenorio* will not be successful because "no other except the *Tenorio* would have the attraction for the unique and varied multitude which is the annual
clientele of the play which flocks to the theater because of the biological reasons which have been given."[41] Even Ramiro de Maeztu,
who conceives of Don Juan as a revolutionary and renewing force,
seems to concede the popularity of Zorilla's play on Marañón's

grounds. Commenting on Zorilla's second thoughts about having written the play, he wonders if Zorilla's "conscience bothered him on noticing the enthusiasm with which the public applauded the worst sentiments, because, as a rule, the audience becomes enthusiastic when Don Juan says: 'I held nothing sacred; / I slipped in through palace windows / scaled the walls of cloisters / leaving a trail of ruin, grief, and tears.' "[42] There is an interesting literary consequence in Marañón's explaining the popularity of the *Tenorio* in terms of the *hombría* notion. Traditionally, the Don Juan of Tirso (or Molière) is distinguished from Zorilla's Don Juan by identifying the former works as "classic" and the latter as "romantic." The popularity of the *Tenorio* has been explained by the intensity with which the play caters to romantic sensibilities. Particularly we have the ingenuous Doña Inés who acts as Don Juan's "guardian angel" and intercedes on his behalf, as well as other romantic elements such as the supernatural and Gothic air, the titanism of the *burlador*, the sword play on the stage, the use of choreography and lighting to create mood, etc. Marañón does not think that the romantic flavor explains the *Tenorio's* popularity. "Neither magic nor the presence of corpses and spirits can explain, as some would wish, the popularity of the *Tenorio*, which shows no signs of dying out. The reason for its success is simply its magnificent realistic exactitude."[43]

We must concede that Marañón, writing in 1924, the properly romantic period having been terminated for nearly seventy-five years, would have to provide an explanation of the *Tenorio's* continued popularity, perhaps greater than any other Spanish play, either romantic or classical, on arguments transcending the mere intensity of the romantic resources in the work. However, perhaps in Marañón's explanation there is a tendency to underestimate a change in the basis of the play's popularity. Does not the *Tenorio* gain its success in the twentieth century primarily because it is no longer represented "straight," but rather as a parody of swashbuckling masculinity and rebelliousness? The *Tenorio* appears to be the first, and certainly the most notable example of "camp" in Spanish Literature. One should suspect that the spectator, even in Marañón's time, would no longer have been aroused to admire Don Juan's personality and deeds, but rather would have taken delight in the fantastic exaggerations. One also expects that the production of the play, even in 1924, would have begun to take on the burlesque and farcical coloring that it clearly contains in current productions. That some of the sentiments were not taken seriously in 1924 is conceded even by Marañón who quotes J.M. Salaverría to the effect that "now not even swooning sentimentalists are moved on hearing the reading of the letter and the so-called 'sofa' *décimas* [ten-line stanzas]."[44] Yet, Marañón thinks that, while "the verses must be stale as a result of being common knowledge, and they will, perhaps, seem ridiculous if they are heard outside of an atmosphere of sexual excitement,"[45] in the theater itself, in the proper atmosphere, the verses "spoken as Don Juan speaks them, within earshot of Doña Inés as well as the spectators, continue to move all women from the lowly hag to the haughty princess."[46] In 1924, Marañón had a vested interest in asserting the virulence of the Don Juan myth. For him to concede the ridiculousness of some of the sentiments in the eyes of the public would be to weaken his basically medical and therapeutic rationale for speculating on Don Juan in the first place!

Yet, even Marañón himself, although he seems to be unaware of the implications of his distinction, claims that certain verses, hackneyed as they may be on the street, in the *theater*, with its own peculiar "unreal" ambience, reacquire their moving effect. The problem is that Marañón, in his zeal to define the character, Don Juan, with naturalistic accuracy, substantially disregards the "accuracy" of the *Don Juan Tenorio*, the total play itself, as a period piece. Marañón disregards the important unnaturalistic elements—play, staging, verse, rhythm, etc.—that are part of even the most socially conscious plays, not to mention a work such as *Don Juan Tenorio*! After all, the *Tenorio* is a poetic construct as well as a biological or a psychological construct, and the play beautifully exposes the theatrical techniques of romanticism.

Marañón, after citing the famous moment where Don Juan enumerates the five days he needs to pursue, seduce and abandon a damsel, goes to the length of claiming, first, that this is "a completely clinical explanation," and finally claims that Don Juan is a systematic liar. ". . .another of the Don Juan's characteristics is the ease with which he tells lies; the truth of all that he says must be questioned. . . ."[47] Here we have clearly reached a point where a biopsychological perspective has become counterproductive in its disregard for the spectacular function for which such lines were intended. Marañón forgets that the play was written to satisfy a specific type of audience during a specific historical period. Furthermore, the doctor sins in forgetting that any biological reality he may garner from the Don Juan motif must be garnered from a metaphor, a theatrical symbol. It is one thing to enumerate the symptoms of a distressed

35

patient, but it is a far different task to abstract what biopsychological reality a character on stage may represent. In doing the latter task, it is essential to remember that the stage character is not the real person. C.S. Lewis has some very pertinent observations on the subject:

> When I tried to read Shakespeare in my teens the character criticism of the nineteenth century stood between me and my enjoyment. There were all sorts of things in the play which I could have enjoyed; but I had got it into my head that the only proper and grown-up way of appreciating Shakespeare was to be very interested in the truth and subtlety of his character drawing. A play opened with thunder and lightning and witches on a heath. This was very much in my line: but oh, the disenchantment when I was told—or thought I was told—that what really ought to concern me was the effect of these witches on Macbeth's character!.... I do not say that the characters ... count for nothing. But the first thing is to surrender oneself to the poetry and the situation. It is only through them that you can reach the characters, and it is for their sake that the characters exist. All conceptions of the characters arrived at, so to speak, in cold blood, by working out what sort of man it would have to be who in real life would act or speak as they do, are in my opinion chimerical.[48]

The same sort of problem occurs in the controversy over what painting ought to represent. When a woman remarked to Matisse that the arm of a woman was too long, Matisse answered: "First of all, I am not creating a woman, I am creating a painting."[49] While on occasion Marañón terms Don Juan a "symbol" or a "myth," he often lapses in his critiques and classificatory schemes and handles Don Juan as if he were an actual human being. This distortion is not exclusive to Marañón but has been a drawback of most literary criticism except for the rigorous stylistic analyses (which usually avoid characterization altogether), and has particularly handicapped psychological, sociological and psychoanalytic literary criticism of the first half of the twentieth century.[50] Let us glance at one more example, which has its curious counterpart in English literary criticism.[51] Pérez de Ayala and Marañón pointed out that Don Juan never seems to father children. As Pérez de Ayala put it, "rarely did he leave flesh and blood children as tangible signs of his power."[52] This is viewed with suspicion and seen as a clue of sterility. Gonzalo Lafora, who opposes Marañón's theory of sexual indeterminacy with his own diagnosis of Don Juan as a hysterical sadist, comes to the seducer's defense in this instance. First of all, the critic claims that in real life Don Juan does have children and he has them with various lovers. Second: "In Tirso's play there is no time to ascertain the results of Don Juan's love affairs, and the same thing happens in the others."[53] What either argument, pro or con, fails to see is that the lack of children in the Don Juan literature has an internal consistency of its own—vis-à-vis Don Juan as myth and metaphor—and therefore cannot be explained in naturalistic, biological terms. Francisco Agustín readily recognized this: "Why not suspect a tacit, intuitive and artistic agreement?. . .A Don Juan who is as potent as the literary one cannot have children. . . . How could he be Don Juan if he had them? The index of Don Juan's potency and harmfulness is not expressed numerically in the foundling asylum, but rather in the exceptional and endless list of his love affairs."[54]

This lack of a clear distinction (in order to make a clear correlation) between Don Juan as literary myth and the Don Juanesque man in society, coupled with a disregard of formal elements which was very characteristic of psychological literary criticism during the period, was immediately pounced upon by other critics. In 1926, Ramiro de Maeztu wrote, "Don Juan is a myth; he has never existed, nor does he exist, nor will he exist except as a myth,"[55] and Corpus Barga, also in the same year, wrote: "Don Juan has never been a real man; he has been, in the strict sense of the word, a literary bias. . . ."[56] Much later Jacinto Grau protests Marañón's analyses of Don Juan as well as other psychiatric critiques on the same topic:

> By means of different nuances and conclusions, the ostentatious and self-assured *burlador* becomes a prosaic clinical subject, set apart from the dramatic and poetic atmosphere that normally surrounds him. It is only in the atmosphere in which he was born that he can be studied, because apart from it he is only a literary character transformed into a myth by successive legends and critical judgments.[57]

Jacinto Grau's comments, incisive as they are with respect to Marañón's pioneering yet faulted critical methodology, seem too fatalistic in that they leave little hope for psychology ever being able to make a useful contribution to literary criticism. Grau's attitudes, in reaction to the excess of Marañón, Francisco Agustín, Gonzalo Lafora or others who made a neurotic out of Don Juan, or Salvador de Madariaga who portrayed Hamlet as an egocentric, insensitive psychotic,[58] are a sophisticated articulation of a well-entrenched, yet not necessarily just or valid, antipathy toward psychological literary criticism in many literary quarters.[59]

At any rate, it is an important consequence of Marañón's methodology that the traditional classical-romantic categories are collapsed in favor of a criterion focusing on the comparative biological accuracy in representing a character type. This consequence is patently clear in the following assertion:

> ...it is useless to try to inquire, as some would do, into which ... is the real Don Juan. All or almost all of them are; some are more noble, others more affected, a few are more romantic, and others are even endowed with a certain greatness. But they are always the same in their psychopathological outline.[60]

Nowhere in his essay does Marañón make a conscious effort to distinguish the essence of the classical Don Juan from the romantic Don Juan. On the contrary, the essence is the same—quantitative virility—irrespective of the period. Likewise, the fact that one Don Juan is condemned while the other is pardoned is irrelevant either to the character himself or to the popularity of the play.

Another facet of Marañón's approach, the consequence of not distinguishing between fictional protagonists and real persons, is the classification of both into groupings based on biological and psychological considerations. Marañón hypothesizes three strata of lovers: the intellectual lover (examples, Don Quijote and Faust), the emotive lover (Werther) and the instinctual lover (Don Juan, Casanova, Othello). On the instinctual level, Othello is considered diametrically opposed to Don Juan, by virtue of the former's active masculinity. In 1939, Marañón, as we shall see, contrasts Calderón's *Médico de su honra* to Don Juan. Don Juan and Casanova are grouped together by virtue of their wandering tendency, passivity and general incapacity to function except on a primary sexual level. Like Casanova, Don Juan displays the "wandering instinct," hence in the *Burlador* the adventures, reflecting this biological fact, are set in varied sites such as Naples, Tarragona, Seville, and Lebriga. Similarly the horse is emphasized in Tirso's *Burlador* as an indispensable instrument for Don Juan. On one occasion, Don Juan says to his servant, "Ready the two mares, for I only entrust my deceptions to their winged hooves."[61]

Already in 1924, in Marañón's opposing Othello and other literary protagonists to Don Juan, we have a forewarning of the doctor's 1939 efforts toward disproving the Spanishness of Don Juan and extolling the Calderonian protagonists of the honor plays as reflecting the attitude of the typical Spaniard toward women. Much light can be shed on this later effort by clarifying the moral antagonism that Marañón evinces against Don Juan. We have already commented on the primary factor: the myth is in no way endemic to Spain, nor does it fatally reflect the Spanish way of relating to the opposite sex. On the contrary, Marañón feels that his efforts may have some impact in combating the pathologies that result from the assimilation of such an ideal. He speaks of "the enormous importance of education and environment in Don Juanism."[62] In a more general way, Marañón is antagonistic to Don Juanistic attitudes because:

'Don Juanism' is, therefore, the natural enemy of work. And towns where Don Juans abound are towns that inevitably have short attention spans and lack the ability to introspect; they tend to be easily diverted and to engage in the cult of the external qualities of things. In sum, they are incapable of scientific work.[63]

The above sentiments, expressed in a lecture on Pasteur in 1922, seem to be partially in reaction to attempts to represent Don Juan as a metaphor of potential progressivism in Spain. Ramiro de Maeztu is a preeminent example of that tendency. Maeztu, in direct opposition to Marañón, thinks of Don Juan as "the myth of inexhaustible energy. . . ."[64] Furthermore, according to Maeztu, Don Juan, historically has been a resource and ideal in times of crisis, and never so much as during the twentieth century.

Don Juan has appeared again among us because these years mark another crisis of ideals. It is already known what 1898 and the years following represented: confusion and polemics, in which we realized, after passionate words and premature judgments, that we were weak and poor, which is the same as saying that the ideal of power appeared among us.[65]

Finally, in commenting on the positive side of Don Juan, Maeztu asserts: "Because of the immensity of his energy, Don Juan is the ideal, the dream, the myth. And because he invests it in pleasure, and we do not know, in a time of crisis of ideals, how to live our lives better, he is our temptation."[66] For Maeztu, the positive energy of Don Juan, coupled with and tempered by the wisdom and love traditionally incarnated in la Celestina and Don Quijote respectively, can furnish the prototype for the future Spaniard. The sarcasm in the following lines by Marañón seems directly applicable as a critique of Maeztu: ". . .in these times when the salvation of the soul seems to concern people less, this lucky man [Don Juan] finds favorable critics who lend him a hand so that he does not condemn himself again, and they present him transformed into a prototype of anatomical and mental selection, a point of departure for future humanity."[67] Marañón's views could not be more removed from Maeztu's in this respect. He attacks the Don Juan type as a passive center of attraction, basically lacking energy, at least in terms of social interaction. He seeks to undermine Don Juan as an archetype of potency and virility. He claims that along with the "intellectual incomprehension of many women" a mortal enemy of science in Spain is "the 'Don Juanism' of many men."[68] Against the potentiality of the Don Juan type, Marañón pits "the authentic working man" who is almost always monogamous and adjusted to "a placid emotional life, which tones his sexual instinct and subsequently flowers splendidly in the form of activities and discoveries."[69]

In a more general way, Marañón is compelled to defend his notion of work and productiveness in terms of a bourgeois morality. Here the scientist finds himself in confrontation with the humanists and thinkers of both the Generation of 1898 and the Generation of 1914. This is a fact that goes a long way in explaining Marañón's peculiar political role, both before and after the Spanish Civil War. Opposed to the anarchistic-aristocratic stance of the most prominent members of the Generation of 1898, with their projections of revolutionary, prototypical Spaniards, likewise opposed to the primarily aristocratic notion of most of the protagonists of the Generation of 1914,[70] with their fear of an esthetic dictated by the masses, Marañón exalts the "great number of men and women who fulfill their duties as human beings, in their homes or in their shops. . . ."[71] Marañón is pained by the "intellectualistic arrogance" that has not understood that the "petite bourgeoisie . . . represents the true gravitational center of collective life."[72] Marañón conveniently uses *El alcalde de Zalamea* to oppose Don Juan from the criterion of productiveness. In 1939, he will oppose *El médico de su honra* to Don Juan with respect to sexuality and honor. Marañón terms Pedro Crespo, the mayor:

> . . .a bourgeois who is hated by the resentful and despised by the aristocrat and the intellectual. The bourgeois, the man from the small town where society was born and continues to have its roots . . . [is] the creator of a solid and stable prosperity and the depository of genuine honor. It is not, certainly, the honor that is visible in the everyday bustle, but rather the one that gives vitality and splendor each day and night to life, the family and the surroundings, thanks to the essentially virile virtue of sobriety.[73]

Thus, we may conclude that part of Marañón's motivation in the 1924 entry into the Don Juan controversy stems from a concern that a myth of pseudo-virility may be exalted into a blueprint for the future model Spaniard. Supported by clinical and medical observations, he discourages any attempt to portray Don Juan as a model of the "instinct to overcome." On the contrary, Don Juan is seen as a pathological type and literary excellence is evaluated in terms of works which represent this pathology, in Marañón's opinion, with a maximum of biological and psychological fidelity. As we shall see, Marañón's 1924 effort to undermine exemplary mythical or psychological interpretations of Don Juan is closely linked with his 1939 effort to negate the historical Spanishness of the myth or the speculation that Don Juan represents in any way, positive or negative, an innate or "intrahistoric" manifestation of the Spanish temperament.

Marañón's second Don Juan critique: 1939

Marañón's second main incursion into the Don Juan cycle took place in Buenos Aires in November 1939, where he gave a lecture entitled "Gloria y miseria del conde de Villamediana." This lecture, along with two other writings indirectly related to it, "Los misterios de San Plácido" and "La novia de Villamediana", was published in 1940 in a book entitled *Don Juan. Ensayos sobre el origen de la leyenda.* Part of Marañón's new effort is devoted to recapitulating, emending and justifying his 1924 essay. He complains that, although in 1924 he had some hard things to say about Don Juan, "more, however, were things that people put into my mouth, without my having said them. . . ."[74] Marañón is particularly chagrined that the public has concluded from his analysis that the Don Juan type is an effeminate man, usually a homosexual.[75] A prominent example of this sort of conclusion occurs in Unamuno's prologue to *El hermano Juan.* That Marañón is among the targets of Unamuno's sarcasms (although not personally mentioned) is apparent:

> Biologists, physiologists and doctors, and particularly psychiatrists, have taken possession of the historical figure of Don Juan and have even presumed to reduce him to an onanist, a eunuch, a sterile individual—when not impotent—a homosexual, a schizophrenic—and, what is this?—perhaps a frustrated suicide, an ex-future suicidal.[76]

We should recall that while Marañón indeed does indicate that the Don Juan type deviates toward femininity and that he also *may* be actively homosexual, the doctor's total theoretical position toward the development and evolution of sexuality, as we have surveyed in the first chapter of this book, is too complicated to permit a simple one-to-one attribution of homosexuality to Don Juan.

The 1939 Don Juan Critique

In his 1939 essay, Marañón emphasizes a different metaphor in his critique of Don Juan. He now asserts that Don Juan "possesses an immature, adolescent instinct, which is arrested in the generic stage of attraction to women in general, and not in the strictly individual stage, which is the ideal. He loves women, but is incapable of loving a woman."[77] Here, by commenting on Don Juan's immaturity, Marañón may be borrowing and converting to his own purpose, the epithet of Gonzalo Lafora. Lafora's 1927 essay, taking a psychological perspective similar to Marañón's, arrives at different conclusions. Lafora is struck by Don Juan's heroic plunging into the sea to save his servant, Catalinón. He remarks on the fact that Don Juan possesses admirable qualities, "traits of gallantry, nobility and humility,"[78] which to some degree compensate for his vices. Thus Lafora is led to reject Marañón's conclusion that Don Juan acts merely on a basic instinctual level. He formulates a Don Juan who is suffering from a "complex" tinged with sadistic and hysterical colorings. The "tan largo me lo fiáis" rejoinder is termed a "rationalization" that the hysterical Don Juan invokes in order to get his way without feeling the burden of a sinful consciousness. Furthermore, the hysterical symptoms are associated with childhood: ". . .the child experiences transitory hysteria; that is to say, he is egotistical, violent, capricious, emotional, stubborn, and a story-teller; his desires constantly change, and he throws a tantrum when he does not get what he wants."[79] Lafora concludes that Don Juan has remained in a state "that Freud has called psychic and emotive *archaism*. . . ," a state peculiar to those of a "psychopathic constitution."[80] Marañón incorporates the hypothesis of Don Juan as immature or underdeveloped, without, however, altering his theory. A characteristic of the Don Juans that remains throughout their lives is that they preserve the markings of "juvenile indetermination." Precisely, this is one of the secrets of the Don Juans' seductive powers.

Marañón provides evidence that Don Juan is represented as sexually undifferentiated in the classical *Burlador de Sevilla*, through his interpretation of the dialogue involving the seduction of the duchess Isabela.

> When the king, attracted by the cries of the deceived duchess, asks what is happening, Don Juan, with profound biological exactitude, answers: 'Who could it be? A man and a woman"; that is to say, not two individuals, Don Juan and Isabel, but two sexes face to face. Don Juan replies to Isabel herself, when she senses his approach in the darkness and asks him who it is: 'Who am I? A man without a name.'

Here is the definition of Don Juan, definitively expressed in his first literary version: *a man without a name*; that is, a sex and not an individual.[81]

A true man would, above all, demand to see his beloved and to be seen by her. Don Juan, on the contrary, is incapable of loving women except generically.

Marañón's explanation of this segment of the play is startling and provocative, but it is not totally convincing, primarily because the critic clearly extrapolates the dialogue from the total context in order to justify his pre-established position. There is neither an allowance for or even mention of the function of the lines within the tense, uncertain situation that has been evoked on stage, nor a recognition of the inherent rebelliousness in the lines toward the king and the values the king represents. While in 1924 Marañón tended to undercut Don Juan as a deviant toward femininity, and in 1939 he likened Don Juan to an eternal adolescent, there is no real contradiction or shift in his views. Among Marañón's writings on the development of intersexual states, there is much material indicating that male adolescence (in general) is a period of sexual indeterminacy in which various physical and psychological characteristics of femininity appear. Among the psychological characteristics is the appearance of "sexual overesteem"[82] (a variation of Adler's concept of "self-esteem"), which is the progenitor of Don Juanism. Thus, while for tactical reasons Marañón substitutes "undifferentiated instinct" in his 1939 essay instead of the 1924 "deviation toward femininity," there is no substantive change since within Marañón's theoretical framework adolescence in the male reflects a period during which feminine characteristics are strongest (although in the normal male adolescent they will *never* be as strong as the masculine traits). Thus, to say that the Don Juan type is perpetually an adolescent is to acknowledge implicitly that the Don Juan type tends abnormally toward the feminine.

Nowhere does Marañón equate, *a priori*, Don Juanism with homosexuality, although he asserts the possibility of homosexuality as a path resulting from a basic lack of sexual differentiation, usually during puberty. Likewise, he gives examples of Don Juans who were also homosexuals, particularly the count of Villamediana, who Marañón thinks may have provided some inspiration for Tirso's *Burlador*. Yet this in no way excludes the fact that many Don Juans lead a totally heterosexual life. There is an important theoretical point embodied here. For Marañón, the appearance of feminine characteristics (both physiological and psychological) in the male need not be associated with homosexuality. Marañón rejects Freud's insistence on universal infantile homosexuality. "Freud has expressed this great inaccuracy: 'I have never carried out the complete psychoanalysis of a woman or a man without finding an element, perhaps an important one, of homosexuality.' Actually, what occurs in childhood, from the time the libido is awakened until puberty, is an indetermination of the object of the libido rather than homosexuality; it is an 'undifferentiated sexual inclination.' "[83] The years of puberty are critical for men because of this sexual undifferentiation and because of the male's vulnerability during this period, but Marañón thinks homosexuality is typically the result of "an abnormal influence during childhood or puberty."[84] Such considerations lead Marañón to specific recommendations in the area of sexual education, one of which, naturally, is to combat the Don Juan myth through proper sexual education.

The basic intent of the 1939 essay, however, is not to justify and expand the biological thesis of 1924. In 1939, Marañón observes a social change that he was not about to admit in 1924, namely the lack of virulence in Don Juanism as a pathological phenomenon. "Speaking about Don Juan has lost its interest for critics and naturalists and is beginning to pass to the dominion of archeologists. . . . I myself realize that Don Juanism, which twenty years ago was a deep problem for the men and women of that time, today has almost stopped being one."[85] This is not to say that Marañón is satisfied with the outcome or that he claims any success for his therapeutic intervention of 1924. Far from it, he claims that rapid technological developments (the automobile and telephone) have led to substantial changes in courtship and the understanding of love. Marañón does not think that Don Juanism is definitely obsolete but rather that, inasmuch as the attitudes toward love are limited, in future cultural circumstances, Don Juan will be resurrected. ". . .either love is earned and enhanced, or love is given away and profaned. We are now in the stage of easy love. Don Juan hardly has a *raison d'être*. But no one can be sure that someday he will not have his day again."[86]

With the problem of Don Juanism as a noxious social phenomenon resolved in its own peculiar fashion, Marañón directs his attention to commenting on the origin of the Don Juan legend in Spain in terms of Spanish character traits, to exposing some of the social circumstances of the period which influenced the formation of Tirso's *Burlador* and to describing a hypothetical individual, the count of

Villamediana, who plausibly might have served as the model for the *Burlador*. Curiously, Marañón arrives at a conclusion totally opposed to the characteristic line of Spanish criticism with respect to the nationality of Don Juan. "I wish . . . to demonstrate that Don Juan, although born into the world of legend in Spain, is hardly Spanish at all."[87] In order to comprehend the advocacy of this startling position, we must keep in mind Marañón's hostility and combativeness toward Don Juan as a personality type in his 1924 essay.

Joaquín Casalduero, in his masterful study of the Don Juan theme, has some biting observations on the whole polemic concerning the nationality or paternity of the Don Juan legend. The following is taken from the section entitled, "Tendencias de la crítica que deben evitarse."

> Some nationalistic arguments are really amusing as far as Don Juan's character is concerned. An example: (naturally, it is a question of demonstrating that the Don Juan is not a Spanish creation), the critic and professor of nationality X is convinced that Don Juan could not have been conceived of anywhere in his country, and he shows it. As is natural, he does not offer proof of any kind, but he does present an argument that will make Spaniards think twice before rejecting it: Spain being the country of nobility, of honor, of loyalty to the King and respect for ladies, how could it have created a type like Don Juan? Don Juan could not have been created anywhere except in his country, in X.

> It was certainly to be expected that Spaniards would be perplexed before answering and that they would limit themselves, nobly, honorably, loyally and respectfully to affirming that the first work dealing with this theme, *El Burlador*, was written in Spanish and not in another language. But it does not happen like this; Spanish nationalistic critics assure us that Spain has at least as many charlatans as any other country or perhaps more, and that no one outdoes them at buffoonery.[88]

We are in agreement with Casalduero that nationalist perspectives are "perfectly useless" for a comprehension of the sort of work that Casalduero is engaged in: the depiction of the evolution of the Don Juan theme based primarily on a rigorous and methodical analysis and comparison of literary texts. Nevertheless, the polemics concerning the nationality of literary heroes and the desirability of extolling their character traits have a major claim to cultural significance even though they may be extra-literary in the formal respect inasmuch as references to literary texts are highly unsystematic, selective and invariably adjusted to exterior concerns such as instilling a social consciousness or a desirable moral outcome.

Certainly strands of nationalism are intertwined in the philology of the nineteenth century; for example, in the controversies over possible French or Germanic models for the Spanish epic form. Yet in the nineteenth century the passions were more insulated from the public domain and the polemics more confined to the specialist's journals and reviews. However, with the appearance of the writers of the Generation of 1898, an added dimension is superimposed on the philological disquisitions concerning the origin and nationality of certain literary productions. Essayists such as Ramiro de Maeztu (rather than the philologists such as Said Armesto or Menéndez Pidal) were not objectively concerned with the illumination of the classics for the edification of the literary specialist. They had, rather, a political-cultural priority to which they affixed their commentary of the classics. The essayists of 1898 were concerned, at first, with political reform, and shortly after, with mass and systematic cultural renewal. Often they referred to classical literary productions and fictional heroes as typically embodying a given Spanish virtue or vice. A political dramatization is apparent in Costa's famous remark about sealing the Cid's tomb, as well as in the pilgrimage of Azorín and others to the grave of Larra. Similarly, Ganivet attempted to describe and defend the peculiarities and extremities of Spanish justice as indicative of the national temperament, through recourse to the *Quijote*. The *Idearium español* and *El porvenir de España* are studded with references to literary works as examples of various political, social and cultural phenomena. Unamuno presents Don Quijote as a holy crusader engaged in serving his country by reviving his comrades from lethargy. Maeztu presents Don Juan, Don Quijote and Celestina as the three extremes which define the parameters of the Spanish character.

The same involvement in describing Spanish fictional protagonists as symbols of the national identity is detected in the essayists of the Generation of 1914. Likewise, we again see a group of essayists writing for a large public forum rather than a specialized group of critics, and with cultural goals transcendent of rigorous textual analysis.[89] Ortega y Gasset, for example, in his own peculiar variation, presents Don Quijote as a Nordic temperament struggling in a Latin environment. Both the 1924 and the 1939 Don Juan efforts by Marañón must be understood as entries into a milieu, the unique and defining characteristic of which is the effort to establish a Spanish national identity through recourse to classical Spanish literature. Hence, we can better understand Marañón's apprehension in 1924 that the Don Juan behavior traits might be accepted as a behavioral model of the typical Spaniard, and that the Don Juan character type might be extolled as somehow embodying the national temperament. Similarly, in 1939 Marañón attempts to discredit the alleged unique Spanishness of Don Juan, on the one hand, by asserting the universality of Don Juanesque literary creations, and, on the other hand, by implying a substantial Italian contribution to the specific origin of the classical *Burlador de Sevilla.* In so doing, Marañón returns to a basically philological controversy over the national origin of Don Juan between Victor Said Armesto and the Italian hispanist, Arturo Farinelli, which reached its emotional peak in 1908 with the publication of Said Armesto's *La leyenda de don Juan: orígenes poéticos del Burlador de Sevilla y Convidado de piedra.* The Said Armesto-Farinelli controversy was conducted within the specialist's confines. Both critics made use of scholarly erudition and copious references. The controversy did not notably overreach itself into a public forum nor did it concern itself with any contemporary social consequences of Don Juanism. The satire of Joaquín Casalduero which we have earlier quoted refers, at least partially, to the Farinelli-Said Armesto controversy. Although there is some exaggeration involved in the lampoon, Professor X could well be represented by Arturo Farinelli.

In order to support his thesis Marañón drew on material stemming from the Farinelli-Said Armesto controversy. However, Marañón was clearly addressing himself, not to a group of literary scholars, but rather to the general educated layman. The 1939 essay had its first exposure as a lecture at the Asociación Amigos del Arte in Buenos Aires, a clear indication of the sort of public for whom it was intended. More important, as we shall see, Marañón's concern with taking a "firm" stand against the notion of Don Juanism as peculiarly Spanish explains—although it does not justify—the informality, selectiveness and lack of objectivity in Marañón's use of philological research to support his thesis.

Let us now turn to Marañón's thesis itself. As I have cited earlier, Marañón attempts to disavow the Don Juan legend as typical of the Spanish national character. In so doing, he divides the legend into three basic components: 1) The fascinating man who attracts, seduces and abandons in a never-ending series. 2) A religious (or sacrilegious) theme that is intermixed with the carnal passion: the cynicism of the protagonist and his perpetual defiance of society,

Church and God. 3) The moral outcome and lesson. Sometimes, the libertine is punished, as in the *Burlador*. On other occasions, he is pardoned, as in Zorilla's *Don Juan Tenorio.*

Once having separated the components of the legend, Marañón makes the same assertion seen earlier in 1924. He judges that the only element that is essential to the psychology of the protagonist is the fascinating, seductive man. The defiance element "whatever its picturesque and legendary effect, adds nothing to the substance of the Don Juanesque personality."[90] He goes on to claim that the defiance element, "even if it were, at first, the most attention-getting element of the legend itself, the agent of its success and diffusion, did not take long to disappear."[91] As we shall see, very few critics would accept the defiance motif as having substantially disappeared.

If it is accepted that the only element that is really fundamental to Don Juan is the *hombría* notion (for Marañón, of course, a false *hombría* notion), then it follows that the Don Juan type is not particularly Spanish. Rather he is to be considered "a universal variety of human love, and, within his universality, as having fewer roots in Spain than in any other country on earth."[92] Marañón claims:

> It is easy to find perfect Don Juans in Greece and in pre-Christian Rome. In the latter, the first, most cynical and most complete manual of Don Juanesque love, Ovid's *Ars amandi*, was published. Ovid himself was a Don Juan, with all his triumphs, all his failures and all his blunders.[93]

The virulence of Marañón's antipathy toward the Don Juan character type is at its most evident in the following *coup de grâce!* "He is a product of decadent societies; and, therefore, he had already exhibited his cynicism in the decline of various civilizations, when Spain was still the embryo of a nation, without a national structure."[94]

Opposed to the modality of love which Don Juan represents is "the distinctly Spanish modality of Spanish love," which is well-represented by the main protagonist of *El médico de su honra.*

> The indigenous Castilian male is represented not by the Don Juan but rather by *el médico de su honra* [the healer of his own honor]; that is to say, by the husband, lover, father or brother who entrusts both conjugal and family honor to the woman's virtue. They never fail to defend or avenge it, not only when it is in fact offended, but even when it is suspected that it may be offended.[95]

In order to reflect the vengeful, honor-ridden type, Spanish dramatists such as Lope de Vega and Calderón de la Barca created "a literary modality that is unique in the world,"[96] namely, the honor dramas. Marañón considers that "this 'honor' literature is the strictly national one, more so even than mysticism; it is the only one that could not be anything but Spanish."[97]

He goes on to hypothesize a stupor that the Spanish audience, mostly austere and honor-conscious individuals, must have felt upon being besieged by such pre-Don Juans as Leucinio (Juan de la Cueva's *El infamador)* and Leonidio (Lope de Vega's *La fianza satisfecha)*[98] as well as Don Juan himself, inasmuch as these characters are profoundly anti-Spanish in the sense that they have no fear or hesitation to "affront what is as sacred as God for a pure-blooded Iberian: the honor of the lineage."[99] Clearly, behind this comparison of the *Burlador,* the *Infamador,* etc., versus *El médico de su honra* there is an intent that is extra-literary, namely to utilize Spanish literature in order to convince the public that the typical Spanish sense of love "was, above all at that time, that of the Castilian home: monogamous, austere as the surroundings of a mystic; a home with numerous offspring, conceived almost without sin, in which the bedroom has the rigorous dignity of a cell."[100]

Yet in his extra-literary zeal, through misadjusting his literary comments to propositions of moral concern, Marañón produces a muddled literary critique filled with misstatements and contradictions. For example, it is excessive to think that an exaggerated sense of honor (and its consequent manifestations in literature) is typical only of Spain.[101] More fitting within Marañón's general framework would have been an assertion to the effect that the motif of a jealous guardian of honor is just as universal a psychological modality as that of the attractive seducer. Nor is Marañón's vision of a Spanish audience stupified by the barbarity and excess of Don Juanesque types on stage at all convincing. Marañón's hypothesis is dissonant with what we know of the Spanish stage. Hugo Albert Rennert, in *The Spanish Stage in the Time of Lope de Vega,* provides a compendium of irregularities for which the Spanish stage in the seventeenth century was noted. Rennert lists such occurrences as men sneaking into the *cazuela* (the gallery where only women were permitted) in order to affront and scandalize them, crowds destroying a theater where an announced play had been cancelled by the Inquisition, duels resulting from an over-involvement in the action on stage, the suspension of plays because the disapproving groundlings pelted the actors with fruit and cucumbers and drowned out the action with rattles, whistles and keys, knifings and brawling at the theater entrance, and so on.[102]

The 1939 Don Juan Critique

We grant that a Spanish audience may have been silenced for a moment by the likes of a Leonidio, who Marañón judges "makes love to his own sister . . . not because he is trapped by a love that would justify him, no matter how monstrous; but instead [he does it] coldly to give 'his blood this affront' and in addition 'to challenge the world and God.' "[103] Yet, certainly a Spanish audience would not be "stupefied" by such an outcome since it was generally the insistence of the groundlings which led to such increasingly sensational plots. It is unjust to claim that the action of *La fianza satisfecha* was perpetrated on the Spanish public by a maniacal Lope de Vega! The real state of affairs was clearly that the Spanish public expected, vociferously demanded, and perhaps needed, psychologically, such theatrical extremes. Lope bowed, not unwillingly, to the pressure of the *vulgo*. In short we conclude that the common public demanded and obtained both plays portraying audacious efforts to preserve one's own honor and to disparage the honor of others. Moreover, the stage protagonists who defied society and God, on the one hand, were to be admired for their disdain and magnificent indifference to punishment, but were also expected to receive the punishment due to them.

Just as Marañón twists logic by attempting to trade off one behavioral and theatrical modality for another in his pursuit of a national temperament, his excessive zeal in explaining away the Spanish origin of the Don Juan legend in Spain leads him to distort the research before him. Let us examine his position. If it is true, as Marañón alleges, that Don Juan is representative of a behavioral modality that has little to do with the Spanish character, then why and how was the legend born in Spain?

In attempting to answer the above question in a way consistent with his general framework, the doctor alludes to earlier arguments by Farinelli to the effect that an embryonic Don Juan is to be found on the Italian stage before Tirso's *Burlador de Sevilla* had been produced. Marañón asserts, first that "Don Juanesque love . . . is nothing but the application of Machiavellianism to human love. Machiavellian morality, which permits the Duke of Valentinois to get rid of his enemies without a trace of scruples, is exactly the same morality that Don Juan employs in his relationships with women, whom he conquers and abandons, just as a mercenary soldier conquers strongholds without any other aim than to possess his booty and set out on a new conquest."[104] Having linked, *a priori*, and without further evidence,[105] Don Juanism to Machiavellian ethics, as a sort of

practical application of the latter to the area of amorous relationships, Marañón mentions the fact that allegedly in 1615, several years
before the production of Tirso's *Burlador*,[106] a Jesuit play was produced in Ingolstadt, the title of which the doctor translates from
German: *Historia del conde Leoncio, que, corrompido por Maquia-
velo, tuvo un desdichado fin.* Marañón believes that the critics'
search for a medieval historical antecedent in Seville or Galicia is
futile because Don Juanism does not "invade" Spain and the rest of
Europe until the Renaissance.

> Don Juanism invaded Europe just as Renaissance architecture in-
> vaded the continent. It came to Spain as to other countries and it took
> root, above all in Madrid, because the Spanish court was then in the
> capital of the greatest European state and the vital influences of the
> whole continent converged there. Madrid, in effect, became populat-
> ed with Don Juans, and the chronicles and news accounts of these
> centuries overflow with the adventures of those hotheaded and im-
> moral nobles, nearly all of whom were educated in Italy, that great
> university of life without scruples. Any one of them could have served
> as a living model for Tirso de Molina.[107]

Marañón does not think that Tirso created his *Burlador* by an
able addition of a seducer protagonist to an ancient myth of disrespect, blasphemy and retribution. Rather, he thinks that Tirso began
with a direct model, a contemporary figure or a number of such
figures, since there were many Don Juan types in Spain during the
time, and from this concrete, living model, Tirso was inspired to
create his Don Juan Tenorio. "We must look for the origins of the
Don Juan legend in this directly human apprenticeship of Tirso de
Molina, and not in the old chronicles, nor in the genealogies of the
Tenorio surname, as the scholars of the nineteenth century attempted
to do."[108] According to Marañón, the figure of the Don Juan type,
so common in the society of the period, was already beginning to
crystallize on stage. Both Juan de la Cueva and Lope de Vega, particularly Lope, "had some insight into the Don Juan character, without managing to really understand it."[109] Marañón has an ingenious
and provocative argument which fits perfectly into his thesis to explain why it was not until Tirso that the figure reached his plenitude
and was converted into a "human archetype." It is well accepted
that Tirso, inferior to Lope and Calderón in other respects, was the
greatest creator of female characters!

> His work is full of admirable women characters. The figure of Don
> Juan fits perfectly into the series, in part because of his ambiguous
> sexuality, and above all because his image is like a photographic

negative of the one his lovers project around him. Without them Don Juan would disappear. This is why only a great expert on the female soul would have been able to create that of Don Juan.[110]

It certainly appears plausible that Tirso would have been strongly influenced by the nature of the society he was immersed in, even to the point of modeling his don Juan Tenorio on one or a group of the extravagant "beaus" and "libertines" that were then in such abundance. What is extremely difficult to assert is the Italian nature of the Don Juanism in Madrid. Let us examine this problem. First of all, we wonder what relationship the Ingolstadt play had to the *Burlador* in Marañón's eyes. In no place, of course, does Marañón indicate that the Ingolstadt play may have directly (or indirectly, through some Italian play) influenced Tirso. Far from it, Marañón judges Tirso's play to be modeled on some nefarious Spanish Don Juan filled with Italian Machiavellianism. The Ingolstadt play itself has been bandied about by the critics. Marañón most probably came upon it in Farinelli[111] who, although with many vacillations, recorded its existence in order to imply, as Victor Said Armesto has pointed out, that "The sources of the Don Juan must be sought in the extremely fertile atmosphere of Renaissance Italy."[112]

Presumably, Marañón does not go to the lengths of Farinelli who claimed that the Ingolstadt play with its Italian flavoring provides evidence for the Italian origin of the *Burlador* in a *textual* sense. Inasmuch as Marañón considers the *Burlador* to be substantially modeled on persons living in the Spain of Tirso, his arguments do not imply a textual origin, but rather a psychological and ethical origin in Italy. As Marañón puts it, "Don Juan has never forgotten the corrupting example of Machiavelli." And in another place, " . . . I assert that Don Juanesque love is an exotic importation into Spain, without national roots or tradition."[113]

It is remarkable, however, even in so informal and layman-oriented an essay as "Gloria y miseria del conde de Villamediana," that Marañón neglects even to cite in the text or bibliography Said Armesto's *La leyenda de Don Juan*. This latter work contains many penetrating (and emotional) rebukes to Farinelli's efforts. Its tracing of the totally different sources of the Ingolstadt play (*Larva Mundi*, etc.) as compared to the sources of the *Burlador de Sevilla*, as well as its clear differentiation of the essential conflict in both plays is devastating both to Farinelli's arguments of a textual origin in Italy and to Marañón's arguments for a psychological-ethical origin in Italy. It is unthinkable that Marañón was not acquainted with such a well-known book, yet he prefers to ignore Said Armesto in order to pursue his thesis in a public forum. As remarkable as is his neglect of Said Armesto, his treatment of Menéndez Pidal's "Sobre los orígenes de *El convidado de piedra*" in *Estudios literarios* is even more incredible. Marañón does cite Menéndez Pidal in his bibliography yet makes no mention of the latter's corroboration of Said Armesto's analysis of the great differences between Leoncio and Don Juan. Menéndez Pidal also produces further evidence in some versions of popular *romances* for a medieval, autochtonous Spanish "deceiver of women." The critical point for us here is the psychological-thematic relationship between Leoncio and Don Juan. Menéndez Pidal (paraphrasing the German philologist J. Bolte) observes the following about the relationship between Leoncio and Don Juan. First, that which is comparable:

> The dead person who takes revenge on those who disturb his repose was, according to both poets, an instrument of God, who drags the sinner to hell when the latter has reached the allowable limit of transgressions. Both amply developed the corrupt life of the hero and placed the avenging dead man in intimate contact with him: Leoncio invites his own grandfather or uncle to dinner, although without knowing it, and Don Juan invites the statue of the *Comendador*, whom he himself killed.[114]

Finally, that which is different:

> The former [Leoncio], misguided by the teachings of Machiavelli, becomes an atheist and shows a systematic contempt for all moral laws; the latter [Don Juan] shows disdain for the afterlife only because he believes death to be far off. Don Juan is moved by an unquenchable thirst for sensual pleasure, and he savagely abuses anyone who opposes him.[115]

Menéndez Pidal goes on to demonstrate that the similarities between Leoncio and Don Juan can be accounted for by a "tradition in Spain . . .one which is deeply rooted, of inviting the corpse to supper. Not only are there Portuguese stories, but also Galician and Castilian tales, and not only are there stories, as in other countries, but also *romances*."[116]

What is most dramatically at variance with Marañón's hypothesis that Don Juanism is the application of Machiavellian ethics to human love is the complete lack of such elements in Leoncio's character. While Leoncio is represented as corrupted by Machiavelli, he in no way displays this corruption in the area of heterosexual love.[117] It is therefore superfluous to imply that the Ingolstadt play or the character of Leoncio provides a link between Machiavellianism in Italy and Don Juanism in Spain.

Don Juan, the "rebel:" the critics in perspective

Up to this point I have been tracing the omission of earlier critiques that Marañón committed in order to negate any Spanish responsibility for the birth of Don Juan. Yet, in my opinion, a more central contradiction appears in Marañón's attempt to explain why Don Juan was "born" in Spain rather than in France or Italy. In order to explain this circumstance Marañón claims that:

> Inasmuch as Don Juan is a rebel against the social and religious orthodoxy of his milieu, it is evident that his rebelliousness was more heroic and more attention-getting in Spain than anywhere else. This is because among us the powers which he rebelled against—God and the State—were also stronger than anywhere else.

> In no other European country could Don Juan's rebelliousness have the dramatic emotion that it had in a State with external and internal norms as rigorous as ours. In sum, nowhere else could Don Juan be the hero that he is in Spain.[118]

This argument closely follows Gendarme de Bévotte's 1908 observations, only a portion of which we shall reproduce here: "It was in Spain that, for the first time, a monk represented the claim of the flesh to overcome the spirit, a daring affirmation of the right of Nature to nullify the religious law of chastity."[119]

We are in complete accord with Marañón's statements in this instance. Within the social circumstances of Spain at the time, Don Juan functions perfectly as a rebellious mirror of the social norms. Yet, it must be realized that to assert the birth of Don Juan in Spain on such grounds as Marañón does is also to contradict the foundations of some of the earlier arguments. First of all, if Don Juan was born in Spain out of an overbearing presence of God and State, what relationship does this defiant, cynical, anarchic figure have to Machiavellian ethics as described by Marañón? On the one hand, Machiavelli's eminently practical philosophy was proposed not to overthrow or defy the state, but rather, to preserve it. At this point we should recall the speculations that King Ferdinand may have provided a partial model for *The Prince*. On the other hand, the question of whether or not Machiavellian ethics can be applied to human love seems irrelevant when we claim that Don Juan achieves his heroism from a dramatic rebellion against the rigorous norms of Spain.

Furthermore, how can one reconcile the explanation of the birth of a legend on the basis of its vigor of defiance with the claim that the only essential component of the legend is the fascinating-seductive component to the exclusion of the rebelliousness component? Marañón insists on both claiming the birth of Don Juan in terms of his rebelliousness and on asserting the superfluous nature of that component. "This sacrilegious impulse, in spite of being basically an accessory, is what gave heroic stature to the *Burlador* from the time of his birth on, and it was what spread his legend."[120] I fail to find any validity in this argument or in the assertion that I have cited earlier that, although the rebelliousness was the most beckoning component of Don Juan at first, it did not take a long time before it disappeared.

What is more, the great majority of critics and writers, while not neglecting the seducer in Don Juan, have given equal attention to the significance of his rebelliousness.[121] A sampling of other sources makes this apparent. The philologists, as we have already seen, invariably point to the connection between the Don Juan legend and the earlier, widespread double *convite* [invitation of the corpse] legend, which reflects the rebelliousness component. Gendarme de Bévotte, leaning heavily on the Catholic nature of the Don Juan conflict in Spain, claims that the motif poses "a theological problem of sufficient interest to keenly affect any population of believers."[122] Curiously, Gendarme de Bévotte thinks that Spain has emphasized the seductive element to a lesser degree than France or Italy.

> In the Don Juan legend, contrary to what happened in Italy and in France, it is not the gallant adventures of the hero nor his mores that have interested his compatriots: it is only the religious meaning of the myth, the theological lesson that it contains. Whereas in the other countries the legend, stripped more and more of its supernatural elements, no longer served to express the multiple conceptions of the seducer, in Spain, all of the authors who have taken up the subject since Tirso have subordinated the human drama to the divine mystery which dominates it. Their works have not ceased to be a type of *auto sacramental*, in which, punished or pardoned, Don Juan is the instrument of Providence's designs, a living example destined to edify and convert the public . . . Spaniards not only have never stripped the legend of its old religious and moral meaning, but they have had trouble understanding and allowing the multiple transformations that foreign authors have caused it to undergo.[123]

Let us sample some of the critics and essayists. We cannot provide an exhaustive study here; rather, our criterion has been to sample those whose viewpoints appear to have some direct relationship to Marañón's.

Pérez de Ayala, while considering that Tirso created the *Burlador* from a protagonist who was "merely an impious man, ostentatious of his impiety,"[124] goes so far as to equate this new amalgam of impiousness and seductiveness with the Devil himself.[125] As Pérez de Ayala puts it:

> Don Juan has an element of absolute evil, with all the irresistible and pleasurable allurements of absolute evil, which, for the same reason that it is absolute, is so close to resembling absolute good, that we consider it as such. There is nothing that so resembles God as the Devil himself. The saints, who are the ones who know most about these things, affirm this. . . .[126]

Américo Castro invokes a similar position, conceiving of Don Juan as "a rebellious angel, . . . an authentic Lucifer, who behind the mask of his arrogance permits us to detect the vestiges of a glorious being."[127] He claims that those who "confuse him [Don Juan] with the gross type of more or less bold and cynical courter of women"[128] are wasting their time. Further on, he explicitly criticizes Marañón.

> Don Juan is noble, attractive and heroic. Storybook princesses have never fallen in love with anything else. Far from being a passive and almost effeminate man, as my great friend, the distinguished Dr. Marañón would have him, Don Juan has here displayed the maximum degree of virility.[129]

The position of Ramiro de Maeztu is well known. Don Juan is the man who liberates us from the three yokes that oppress us. "We are oppressed by natural law, social law, and reason: Moira, Dike, and Logos. Don Juan overcomes the three. He has shaken off the three yokes."[130] One could argue that Ramiro de Maeztu's position is diametrically opposed to Marañón's. While Marañón focuses on the seduction component and concludes that Don Juan represents a pathology, Maeztu focuses on the rebellion component, concluding that Don Juan may be the prototype of a new, utopian Spaniard. Ortega y Gasset, in his *El tema de nuestro tiempo*, takes a position quite similar to Maeztu and represents Don Juan as a symbol of defiance against an oppressive morality, a figure to be emulated in his clinging to biological vitality.

> Don Juan rebels against morality because morality had previously rebelled against life. Only when an ethic exists that depends primarily on biological plenitude as its most important norm, will Don Juan

be able to submit to it. But that means a new culture: a biological culture. *Pure reason must yield its dominion to biologically vital truth* [la razón vital].[131]

Jacinto Grau despairs of "Marañón's disdain . . . his analysis has left this figure in a pitiful state . . . as just one more biological phenomenon."[132] Grau thinks Don Juan, that "indefatigable human stud," is not only a conquerer of women. The same image appears that we have noted in Pérez de Ayala and Américo Castro. "Don Juan's Catholicism . . . permits us to see him in a tragic light, in which he equals Lucifer in pride."[133]

Salvador de Madariaga's position shows a marked change from his earliest formulation. In 1923, Madariaga, using Valle-Inclán's Marqués de Bradomín as a critical point of departure, accepted the judgment that Don Juan is "an essentially feminine being" since he displays "the central tendency of the feminine being, for whom love is not a mere episode in life, as it is for man, but rather the very core of existence."[134] Madariaga's 1923 position is perfectly reconcilable with Marañón's concept of Don Juan as a being who functions only on the level of primary sexual activity. The rebelliousness dimension is collapsed and we have a vision of Don Juan as a man "who lives obsessed by women."[135] By 1951, Madariaga had changed his position. He now considered Don Juan as the "prototype or symbol of masculinity in its pristine and incipient state."[136] Madariaga ultimately feels that Marañón has validly traced the Don Juanesque type of man who "flits from one woman to another" and is "usually not a man of firm character."

> More oriented toward what is generally called love, than toward what is generally called action, Don Juanesque men reveal in this the femininity which the physio-psychologists assign to them; because it appears in fact that women prefer love to action, and men action to love.[137]

Madariaga quotes Byron in support of Marañón:

> Man's love is of man's life a thing apart,
> 'Tis woman's whole existence.[138]

Don Juan himself, on the other hand, is entirely different. Don Juan is the male; he is masculinity incarnate.

> For Don Juan there cannot exist either religious, or moral, or social law; but not because he examines them and then rejects them, but because these laws spring up into the human conscience at a later stage of its development than the one which he embodies; and, once sprung up, what is purely masculine, like brute force, dies, since with

laws of a religious-moral-social nature it becomes embellished, conditioned, qualified, and consequently it ceases to be spontaneous.[139]

However, Madariaga qualifies Don Juan's rebellious relationship to the law. Don Juan, strictly speaking, violates the law because it is in conflict with his instincts, not out of any revolutionary stance.

... whoever imagined that Don Juan, being a violater of the religious, moral and social laws, was a revolutionary denier of religion, of faith and of morality, did not observe that, if he pursued this line of reasoning he was obliged to postulate that Don Juan is a denier of women, since he also violates them.[140]

Emile Capouya takes a different tack, criticizing Marañón's deprecation of Don Juan as rebel as a moralistic stance. The doctor is seen as the voice of a society terrified of protest and unorthodoxy.

The question of whether or not promiscuity is connected with homosexuality and/or impotence is a technical one. . . . But I think that our imaginative strategy blunders badly when we apply the notion, whether clinical principle or popular cliché, to a legendary figure, to Don Juan.

Applying such human measure to the Don Juan of literature has the effect of devaluing what else is useful in the legend. It has the effect of denigrating and neutralizing the qualities that Shaw perceived in the character, and that led him to incarnate them in the revolutionist, John Tanner, in *Man and Superman*. Marañón is out to geld Don Juan, and that his attempt should find favor in our eyes is a commentary on our times . . . our era has suffered so much from the actions of outsize personalities that it is ready to condemn out of hand any unorthodoxy, any originality, any exuberance, any protest. . . . We like to be told that men are being molded to an innocuous, uncombative, asexual pattern. . . . It is easy to see why the notion that Don Juan is merely sick, sick, sick is congenial to a society that is made up of gelded men and altered women.[141]

The psychoanalytic perspective toward Don Juan has been formulated mainly by Otto Rank and Otto Fenichel. The psychoanalytic critics invariably judge the seduction component as a screen for and symptom of an underlying conflict. For Otto Rank (as well as for Otto Fenichel)[142] the Don Juan situation is analyzable in terms of the Oedipus conflict: desire for the mother and antagonism toward the father.

The past record clearly shows that the main motif in the Don Juan matter does not lie in the description of his unbounded sex urges . . . the literary development of the Don Juan theme does not expand the seduction motif, so attractive to popular consciousness, but rather—

as if pushed by a mysterious force—expands the ancient but painfully tragic motif of guilt and punishment. . . . From our knowledge of psychoanalysis we are prepared to derive this overpowering guilt and punishment—coupled with sexual fantasies—from the Oedipus complex. . . . The many women whom Don Juan has to replace again and again represent to him the irreplaceable mother, while his adversaries, deceived, fought and eventually even killed, represent the unconquerable mortal enemy, the father.[143]

Other critics who have written on Don Juan with a medical or psychological orientation have been Gonzalo Lafora, F. Oliver Brachfeld, Francisco Agustín and Juan Rof Carballo. Gonzalo Lafora, as on several other issues, tries to reconcile the conflict between those who emphasize the rebelliousness component and Marañón who proclaims the seducer element. The reason for Don Juan's popularity in the seventeenth century is attributed to his "spirit of rebelliousness"[144] which the Spanish people secretly admired "because in those times religion was the weapon that oppressed the people. . . ."[145] As we have seen before, Don Juan is termed a "new Lucifer who rebels against the power of God and of men. . . ."[146] However, following Gendarme de Bévotte, Lafora claims that the demoniacal character of Don Juan as well as the theological aspect of the motif were lost when Don Juan surpassed the boundaries of Spain. For Byron, Molière and Lenau, Don Juan is simply a soul tormented by an "impossible love." Lafora concludes:

> It is necessary, then, to agree that the human problem concerning Don Juan that has most interested everyone has been the *psychological enigma* of this man of abundant sexual apetites, who is never satisfied by one woman. He continually has to change lovers in order see if at last he may find in another what he is looking for so assiduously.[147]

As we have seen, Lafora goes on to treat Don Juan as a neurotic having a great deal more psychological "complexity" than Marañón recognizes.

Oliver Brachfeld, the implacable antagonist of Marañón, treats Don Juan often in connection with his criticism of Marañón's study of Amiel. Oliver Brachfeld characteristically speaks of Don Juan as not only a "seducer" but also a "chastizer, as the result of feelings of inferiority."[148] Even a critic such as Francisco Agustín, who follows Marañón closely with respect to the biological analysis of Don Juan, agrees with Maeztu to the effect that the Don Juan of Spain is a "deceiver" while the Nordic Don Juan is merely a "lover."[149]

59

The Critics in Perspective

Juan Rof Carballo, writing at a much later date than Marañón (1957), has produced a very sophisticated analysis of Don Juan based on neo-Freudian and Jungian depth psychology. A detailed critique of this engaging work is beyond my scope here but I shall mention two points, both of which negate any understanding of Don Juan as a figure bereft of theological significance or lacking in supernatural transcendence. For Rof, the *burlador* "has arisen from a mystery of the collective soul, for which reason the collectivity joyfully recognizes him and lends him its support when dramatists, poets, musicians, and philosophers, one after the other, present him again under various disguises."[150] Among the "disguises" that Don Juan can assume is that of the "trivial beau" who with technical ability conquers women. Likewise, Don Juan may be projected as "a transcendental myth: for example, that of the man who struggles with God, who resists Him and tries to vanquish Him. That is to say, a Promethean myth."[151] (Clearly, Rof Carballo is expressing Don Juan here as a manifestation of what Jung would term the "archetype of the shadow.") The above dichotomy helps us to glimpse that Don Juan's varied existence (and the varied interpretations of him) point to "the law of the subconscious, the possible coexistence in a single mental situation of states which to us, consciously, would seem incompatible. . . ."[152] For Rof Carballo, Don Juan "pursues an unattainable and paradisiacal ideal in each female that he humiliates and seduces: that of returning to his primary affective base, his infantile tie to his mother. Behind the young rogue in Don Juan there is something obscure that redeems him: a quixotic nostalgia."[153]

Albert Camus' brilliant existentialist evocation of Don Juan begins with a starting point precisely the same as Marañón's! We recall that Marañón claimed Don Juan symbolized a myth of "quantitative virility." Camus places attention on that same guiding principle. "What Don Juan realizes in action is an ethic of quantity, whereas the saint, on the contrary, tends toward quality."[154] Camus arrives at an existential glorification of Don Juan however. Don Juan is the man who realizes his own absurdity, his own limitations. "Not to believe in the profound meaning of things belongs to the absurd man."[155] Don Juan's adjustment to absurd reality is glorious, perfect. On the other hand, the stone Comendador "symbolizes the forces that Don Juan negated forever . . . all the powers of eternal Reason, of order, of universal morality, all the foreign grandeur of a God open to wrath. . . ."[156]

The list of critics, essayists and thinkers that have written about Don Juan is interminable and we have been content here merely to give a brief and selective sampling of attitudes toward the rebelliousness dimension. However, our sampling does give an inkling of the depth and breadth of perspectives which militate against Marañón's efforts to disavow the rebel component.

Marañón's arguments must bear the isolation in which they find themselves, for little reconciliation, if any, is possible with the mainstream of viewpoints which proclaim, to a lesser or greater degree, Don Juan as a significant rebel or iconoclast. The thesis of an Italian origin, in an ethical and psychological sense, is superfluous to Marañón's fundamental arguments, and could be discarded without weakening the coherence of his views. Indeed, upon further reflection, if Don Juan represents a universal modality of behavior then there is no need to point exclusively to Don Juanism as the application of Machiavellian ethics. However, we must bear in mind that Marañón's thesis that Don Juan is not an active engager in affairs (and hence, not a rebel) cannot be tampered with without distorting his viewpoint beyond recognition. For, if Marañón should accept the rebellion component as essential to the Don Juan syndrome, he would not be able to argue convincingly for Don Juan's deviance toward passivity and femininity. Accepting Don Juan as a defier of secular and religious law would grant secondary sexual activity to him and thus Marañón would be at a loss to effectively thwart Don Juan as a myth of superb masculinity.

Don Juan and mysticism in seventeenth century Spain

Whether we may be convinced by or reject Marañón's arguments against Don Juan as a model of virility or as a representative of Spanish characterology, nevertheless, there is much in the critic's "Gloria y miseria del conde de Villamediana" along with the two contiguous essays, "Los misterios de San Plácido" and "La novia de Don Juan" which make up the Colección Austral book, *Don Juan*, that is of objective value as an historical disquisition into the social climate of the period. These brief essays are supported by penetrating and well-documented research into the religious, social and sexual customs, the mores, superstitions and taboos, the political, religious and economic ideologies and heresies of the period that we find in the full-length biographies, *El Conde-Duque de Olivares (La pasión de mandar)* and *Antonio Pérez (El hombre, el drama, la época.)*

Don Juan and Mysticism

In the prologue to the *Don Juan* book, Marañón describes his essays as an "allusion" to the process of interaction between the budding Don Juan myth and an environment marked by violent crosscurrents of orthodoxy and heresy, traditionalism and exotic importations. In "Los misterios de San Plácido," an essay growing out of Marañón's biography of the Conde-Duque de Olivares (first published in 1936), Marañón presents some erotic, legendary aspects of the convent of San Plácido as well as some widespread scandalous tales involving the amorous adventures of Felipe IV which he associates thematically (but not chronologically) with the Don Juan legend. Marañón attempts to separate fact from fancy, noting that the Don Juan legend "was born, no doubt, in Madrid, from the same mixture of falsehoods and truths, both religious and salacious"[157] that gave birth to the alleged love affair between Felipe IV and a beautiful and virginal nun. The most interesting aspect of Marañón's speculations is his association of the *alumbrado* heresy with Don Juanism. In order to do this, he is first obliged to hypothesize that mystic consciousness is built upon a substratum of biological sexuality. Marañón takes a position similar to Novoa Santos' essay "Biopatología de la estigmatización." In turn, Novoa Santos' position appears clearly related to the Freudian hypothesis of the sexual origin of libido. Novoa Santos and Marañón take a biological and structural approach, however, while Freud explains libido and sublimation in psychodynamic terms. Marañón asserts:

> The physical upheaval that the great mystics experienced on entering into their relationship with God, and which Santa Teresa describes to us with sublime and chaste objectivity, is initially the same vegetative phenomenon experienced, for example, by the poor *alumbradas* of Llerena on taking part in raptures of shameful passion. According to their spitirual classification, emotions are either good or bad, but their organic nature is always the same.[158]

Novoa Santos, in 1933, wrote, "mystical stigmata, . . . in the final analysis. . . , are no more than variants, although certainly very unique ones, of what we doctors have been studying as *vegetative stigmata*."[159] Novoa's conclusion, in accord with his rejection of religion, would never be accepted by Marañón: "At the end of this frivolous study lies the conclusion that the causal factors behind so many events considered to be 'miraculous' are reducible to natural, physical, or physiological forces."[160] Indeed the doctor finds it distasteful that although "any religious attitude is ultimately based on love. In mysticism this love is sublimated, and in its delirium it acquires erotic tones, in the noble sense of this word."[161] This fact has been interpreted "with nearsightedness and stupidity by the anti-clerical commentators of the past century and by some pedantic psychiatrists of the present one."[162] There is probably in the above a rejection of Novoa Santos' treatment of Sta. Teresa as a madwoman.[163] Nevertheless, the relationship between the *alumbrados* and authentic mysticism is clear to Marañón. The *alumbrado* movement is to be understood as a degeneration of perfectly sublimated or spiritual mysticism. The connection, for Marañón, between the *alumbrado* movement and Don Juanism lies in both seeking a love which is fruitful only when mixed with sin. Whereas the Don Juan type is stimulated sexually by religious outrages (Marañón chronicles several notable incidents and legends of seduction of nuns, etc.), the *alumbrado* is active sexually under a religious guise. For example, Marañón chronicles an *Aviso* of Fray Antonio de Pastrana recommending "copulation with holy women in order to beget prophets."[164] Whereas the Don Juan type (here Marañón explicitly accepts the rebellion component) achieves sexual satisfaction partially through a confrontation with religious authority, the *alumbrado* makes religion an active ingredient of his sexuality. Marañón connects both sexual aberrations to the social conditions of the time. "I insist on the relationship between the social climate in which the *alumbrado* sect took root and grew and the appearance of Don Juan on the Spanish scene."[165] The rigid norms and preoccupations with orthodoxy favored two separate, yet contiguous, outcomes for those who could not achieve orthodoxy (an effective sublimation): the rebel and the dissimulator or hypocrite.

The portion of "Gloria y miseria del conde de Villamediana" that I have yet to discuss proposes the aforementioned Count as an archetypal Don Juan figure of the period and perhaps even the model for Tirso's Don Juan. As James Hoddie, Jr. puts it: "Marañón does not choose to state whether or not knowledge about Villamediana's life, personality, and the events surrounding his death inspired Tirso in his characterization of Don Juan. Rather, this is one among many possibilities offered to the reader."[166] Marañón bases his conjecture on several factors. The Conde de Villamediana, who died only eight years before the appearance of the *Burlador* in 1630 (we must recall that Said Armesto judged the play could have been written at least fifteen years earlier), was widely known for his gallant adventures. It was even suspected that he was carrying on an illicit love affair with doña Isabela de Borbón, the wife of Felipe IV and queen of

Don Juan and Mysticism

Spain. While Marañón concludes that this rumor was false, nevertheless, Gabriel Téllez could not have avoided being aware of such rumors, nor of the Count's violent death. Marañón also notes the resemblance between Don Juan Tenorio's and Villamediana's name, Juan de Tassis (or Tarsis). Marañón thinks that "Tirso de Molina was not thinking, when he wrote his play, about any Don Juan that he knew. Tirso de Molina without a doubt invented this name by chance. But, like all inspired ideas, it has such a deep significance that by itself it has contributed to the legendary status of the hero."[167] Marañón associates *tenorio* with *tener* [to have] and *poseer* [to possess] as well as "tenor," a man with an "equivocal voice, whose notes fly like poisoned arrows in the nocturnal serenade."[168] What Marañón implies is that, rather than having modeled his hero on an actual surname, *Tenorio*, by a process of free association, Tirso might have arrived at a name which embodied certain character traits such as possessiveness and sexual indeterminacy as well as echoing an historical model: Juan de Tassis.[169] Finally, irrespective of whether Villamediana's personality influenced Tirso or not, Marañón claims that the discovery that the renowned Don Juanesque Villamediana was actually a homosexual[170] lends support to his contention that the Don Juan type is not sexually differentiated. The third essay in the book *Don Juan*, "La novia de Don Juan," originally given as a lecture in Buenos Aires in 1939, as the other two, focuses on the relationship between the Conde de Villamediana and doña Isabela de Borbón. Marañón concludes—in contrast to Cotarelo y Mori—that their "affair" was merely a flirtation. Marañón also evokes the maturity, strength and good judgment of the queen in moments of crisis. One of the most interesting aspects of the essay is the doctor's ingenious explication of the function of courtly frivolity, which runs counter to the layman's view.

> ...it is a known fact that, for many women, the superficial, courtesan life not only is not a first step toward sin, but rather an activity that saves them from it, causing the urgent, imperative tendencies of passion to explode in colorful and innocent fireworks.[171]

He judges that the queen's frivolity and "game playing" was a creative resolution of her biological needs.

Other Don Juan Writings

We have already alluded to the prologue "La vejez de Don Juan" which was published in Francisco Agustín's *Don Juan* in 1928. A variant of the above prologue is also included in Marañón's complete works,[172] as we have cited earlier. (See page 31.) In this short essay, Marañón enumerates the possible psychological outcomes of Don Juanism, "husband, old rake, or monk," and associates these outcomes with various different artistic versions.

Casanova's memoirs portray the Don Juan who continues his activities through old age. Casanova is a man who, once having accepted his old age, lives it out, "an old age still graced with small victories in love, with low-key adventures, that are in accord with the calendar and, above all, with the world of his memories."[173] Lope de Vega is another who falls under the "old rake" category. Marañón cites the poet's affair with Marta de Nevares, coupled with several verses where Lope makes fun of the husband after having cuckolded him.

Marañón judges (as did Pérez de Ayala) that Zorilla's Don Juan was headed for the marriage altar had it not been for the intemperance of the *Comendador*.

The religious outcome is represented in history by such figures as Miguel de Mañara, a certain Lauzun, well-known in the court of Louis XIV, and in literature by Zorilla's Don Juan as well as the versions of Azorín and Unamuno.

In a 1933 prologue to a play written by Manuel Villaverde entitled *Carmen y Don Juan*, Marañón theorizes on the female counterpart to Don Juan. Represented in literature by Carmen, such a woman would be "passionate and insatiable, a devourer of men, just as Don Juan consumes in his fugitive embrace the women who, one after the other, share his nights of love."[174] Carmen would deviate toward masculinity and domination to the same degree that Don Juan deviates toward femininity and passivity. Marañón concludes that Don Juan and Carmen never go together in real life because if Don Juan were to be conquered by an aggressive Carmen type he would lose his "stature as an adventurer; it would make his seductive glibness useless, in addition to his ruses, his faithlessness, his gold, and his go-between: everything, in short, which endows him with the apearance of a bold conqueror."[175] Similarly, Carmen disdains the *burlador* "for the same reasons . . . she needs tragically virile men, men of such virility that it incapacitates them, and they are defenseless. Such is the case of Don José, the gruff soldier who let himself be dragged like a child into the whirlwind of his passion."[176] Hence, Marañón thinks it only just that, in Villaverde's play, Don Juan,

65

"whose hands were never meant to touch a woman except to caress her," is compelled to kill the flamboyant Carmen.

In 1927 the "Historia clínica del caballero Casanova" was published in *Sagitario*, Buenos Aires.[177] In this article, over the objections of Iwan Bloch, Ricardo Baeza, Corpus Barga, Gonzalo Lafora, (and later, Jacinto Grau), Marañón classifies Casanova as a Don Juan type. The essay is basically a classificatory exercise, with some additional comment on the lack of religious feeling in Casanova in comparison to the peculiar "faith" of Don Juan. The same morphological and psychological criteria we have enumerated earlier are applied to Casanova.

Don Juan versus Don Quijote

In a lecture, undated in the *Obras completas* but given in 1953 in Brazil,[178] entitled "Don Quijote, Don Juan y Fausto," Marañón contrasts the above three protagonists as archetypes of the three fundamental varieties of love. Don Quijote represents idealistic love, Don Juan, carnal love and Faust, metaphysical love. For Faust, love is a metaphysical being, just another pulsation in the thinker's anguished search for knowledge. Marañón's most earnest efforts in this essay are devoted to contrasting Don Quijote with Don Juan. Whereas Marañón condemns Don Juan as a dangerous psychopath, he protects Don Quijote from any medical diagnosis and proclaims him a hero.

> If we consider Don Quijote to be insane, we will not be able to understand him. Doctors, with naive erudition, have tried to label Don Quijote's madness using any of the known diagnoses: delirium, mania, paranoia. The attempt is futile. Don Quijote was not a man, but rather a hero. And the passions that paralyze heroes have nothing to do with the illnesses that are described in books.[179]

It is curious that Marañón rarely discussed Don Quijote systematically or in detail. He comments on Cervantes a good deal more, usually to contrast him with Lope de Vega. When he does treat the *Quijote*, as in this essay, it is to defend the wandering knight's integrity and exemplariness and, as in "Gloria y miseria del conde de Villamediana," to console Spain for his repudiation of Don Juan by implying that the *Quijote* is the true expression of the Spanish temperament. However, in 1932, José Goyanes Capdevila published a book, *Tipología del Quijote*, which shows the clear influence of Marañón's earlier morphopsychological techniques, and, like Marañón, applies classificatory concepts from Kretschmer to the study of characterization in literature. For example, Goyanes classifies Alonso Quijano (rather than Don Quijote) as ("a schizothymic temperament, following Kretschmer; and in Jung's classification he would be an introvert, an individual turned in on himself, guided by his subjectivity, whose fantasy world dominates reality."[180]

Marañón, in the prologue he wrote for Goyanes, defended the book for its "exceptional importance in Cervantine production, since for the first time rigorously scientific and modern methods of psychological and psychosomatic investigation are applied to the problem of understanding Quixotic heroes."[181] Because of Marañón's willingness to write prologues for the widest imaginable variety of books, some of which he was at odds with, it is unwarranted for us to assume that Marañón was totally convinced by Goyanes' study. The tone of the prologue seems to indicate that Marañón was willing to defend a biological and psychological approach toward Don Quijote just as toward Don Juan, although he was not necessarily approving of the work that had so far been done—e.g., the studies of Royo Villanova, Federico Oloriz and even Goyanes Capdevila.

III

MARAÑON'S CONTRIBUTION TO SPANISH HISTORIOGRAPHY AND THE THEORY AND PRACTICE OF BIOGRAPHY

Prevalent theories of biography and history: 1900-1930

Gregorio Marañón's major, book-length historical biographies are five: *Ensayo biológico sobre Enrique IV de Castilla y su tiempo*, 1930; *El Conde-Duque de Olivares. La pasión de mandar*, 1936; *Tiberio. Historia de un resentimiento*, 1938; *Antonio Pérez. El hombre, el drama, la época*, 1947; *Los tres Vélez*, 1960, published posthumously. In addition, Marañón has written a number of historical essays. The most significant or well-known include, "La medicina en las galeras en tiempos de Felipe II," "La visión de Cristóbal Colón," "Dos mujeres decisivas en la anexión e independencia de Portugal," "San Martín, el bueno, y San Martín, el malo," and "Notas sobre la vida y la muerte de San Ignacio de Loyola." Finally we have Marañón's *El "Empecinado" visto por un inglés*, a translation of Frederic Hardman's *Peninsular Scenes and Sketches*, as well as his edition of *Los procesos de Castilla contra Antonio Pérez*.

The three decades prior to the first of Marañón's historical works in 1930 were marked by increasing debate, speculation and theorizing concerning the notion of historiography, particularly as applied to the investigation of Spanish history. This Spanish concern with historical theory partially reflected the general interest throughout the West in the philosophy and methodology of history as well as the development of modern sociology (e.g., Comte, Marx, Spencer, Croce, Spengler, Weber, etc.) and was also the natural outgrowth of the intellectual crisis of 1898.[1] The sequence begins with the work of Menéndez Pidal, Gómez Moreno and especially Rafael Altamira, whose historical production was overtly stimulated by the devastation of 1898. In the succeeding generations Spain produced, among others, Ortega y Gasset, Sánchez-Alonso, Américo Castro, Sánchez Albornoz, and, subsequently, Vicens Vives and the Catalán school. In addition Latin American thinkers such as Edmundo O'Gorman and José Luis Romero participated in the speculations concerning historiography.

Among the topics of intense theoretical interest in Spain prior to and during Marañón's career as a historian was the renewed debate over the perennial question of whether or not history was a science (or art). Allied to this mainstay was the question of history as a system as well as the possibility of deriving historical laws. Other topics involved the problem of the validity of generic statements, the discontent with the unfolding of history according to the narrative method and the question of the proper relationship of fictionalized biography, "biografía novelada," to the writing and interpretation of history.[2]

Similarly, the years following World War I witnessed a great deal of theorizing on the nature of biography and the art of dramatizing a notable life. For example, José Luis Romero, the Argentine philosopher, published a brilliant monograph attempting to explain the great popularity of biography and its "warm reception by the cultured but not specialized reader."[3] Romero's thesis is based on a general exaltation of individualism after World War I, leading to a transformation from "archetypal" (e.g. Plutarch) biographies which reflect collective ideals and the conscience of society at large, to "individualistic" biographies seeking out that which is unique in every existence.

Some of the speculation in the area of biography paralleled and overlapped with the concern over adequate historiographical guidelines, as for example the debate over whether or not personality could be scientifically analyzed—in other words, whether or not biography was a science or an art. During the 1920's Freudian and other psychologies attained a marked influence on the craft of biography.[4] André Maurois clearly typifies this art/science tension. In his *Aspects of Biography*, first published in 1929, he devotes his second chapter to "Biography as a Work of Art" and his third to "Biography Considered as a Science." (Maurois concludes that biography, and history, for that matter, are essentially art.)

Prevalent Theories: 1900-1930

Nevertheless the problems and potentials of biography differed substantially from those of history. Of particular importance is the fact of readership. As Garraty notes, during the twenties and the thirties biography had become extremely popular all over the Western world. During the twenties, ". . .led by Papini's *Life of Christ*, Strachey's *Queen Victoria*, André Maurois's lives of Shelley and Disraeli, and Emil Ludwig's *Napoleon*, biographies crowded the best-seller ratings, and many lives sold upwards of 50,000 copies."[5]

Biography was (and continues to be) oriented toward the general public, the educated layman, thereby relying on certain dramatic and rhetorical formulas and flourishes, generalizations and insinuations, value judgments and poetic flights not typically found in the more serious histories.

Marañón's historical biographies should be seen from three different perspectives. First and foremost they represent the application of Marañón's clinical, biopsychological constructs to specific historical personalities in order to exemplify and concretize these very constructs. In a certain sense Marañón's biographies are clinical histories, case histories. They typify and validate the peculiarly Marañónian morphological, endocrinological and psychological methods that we have studied earlier. However, they are not merely clinical histories. Marañón's theories themselves, in their application, come to attain an implicit philosophy of history which must be evaluated and compared with the general body of historiographical theory. Moreover, there is a clear sequence of expansion in Marañón's work, his biographies become more and more ambitious in their documentation and scope. This sequence culminates in *Antonio Pérez*, subtitled, significantly, *El hombre, el drama, la época*. Finally, Marañón was clearly motivated to write not only in order to exemplify his biopsychological theories but to compose popular, readable, artistically wrought, successful biographies that would interest the educated lay public in Spain, just as Maurois, Strachey, Ludwig, Zweig, Papini and Bradford were accomplishing elsewhere and Jarnés, Amezúa, Marichalar, etc. were doing at home.

Biographies in Spain both before and after the Civil War

As we have noted earlier, between the Wars biography became very popular throughout the West. Garraty observes that, in America alone, in 1929, over six hundred biographies were published and in 1932 the figure reached six hundred and ninety-nine. The situation, albeit on a lesser scale, was similar in Spain. Between the years 1929 and 1936 a fraction of the biographies published in Spain included *Sor Patrocinio, la Monja de las Llagas*, by Benjamín Jarnés, *Luis Candelas, el bandido de Madrid*, by Antonio Espina, *Riesgo y ventura del Duque de Osuna*, by Antonio Marichalar, *Sagasta, o el político*, by the Conde de Romanones, *Bolívar, el Libertador*, by José María Salaverría, *Mina el Mozo, héroe de Navarra*, by Martín Luis Guzmán, *La santa furia del Padre Castañeda*, by Arturo Capdevila, *Juan Van Halen, el oficial aventurero*, by Pío Baroja, *Martí, el apóstol*, by Jorge Mañach as well as such obscure works as *Vida y empresas de un gran español: Maura*, by César Silió, *López de Ayala, o el figurón político-literario*, by Luis de Oteyza and *Fernán Caballero, la novelista novelable*, by Angélica Palma. By 1935, in one collection alone, Espasa-Calpe's "Vidas Españolas e Hispanoamericanas del Siglo XIX," forty-five biographies had been published. Marañón himself contributed *Ensayo biológico sobre Enrique IV de Castilla y su tiempo* and *El Conde-Duque de Olivares* during these years.

The output in biography can reasonably be divided into two categories. Marañón himself makes a distinction between serious, scientific biographies which make use of advances in biological and psychological theories and facile, shallow, often apocryphal confections. Marañón severely criticizes the latter type of biography as a "degeneration of what we may call a new literary genre." These biographies display an "apparent facility with words but are constructed with very little research." Their appearance on the publishing scene reflects the combination of "good publishing rewards and the taste of today's readers." Unfortunately these biographies have "capitulated to the monster of public caprice so that the writer may sustain himself."[6] Marañón notes that a similar situation occurred with respect to the historical novel of the 19th century which in its most worthy models appears, "rather than having imaginatively deformed history, to have added a new facet to known truths: a popular and legendary interpretation of the eternal, simple facts."[7] However, the ease with which the historical novels were constructed "quickly caused the rapid prostitution of the genre, and after a time, its disappearance."[8]

The vast majority of biographies written both before and soon after the Spanish Civil War were totally romantic and picturesque, usually very brief and subjective, barely, if at all, documented, tapping only the most easily available sources, having no pretensions of adding to historical understanding. These works were intended for the general public as would be a best-selling novel and they were quite inexpensive, purchasable for five pesetas or less. Many of these biographies were wont to leap beyond their sources, inventing dialogue, describing events that might have occurred, in order to introduce melodramatic tensions. They also presumed to expose not only the deeds and words of their heroes and villains, but their thoughts as well. A prime example of this type of popular biography is Marichalar's *Riesgo y ventura del Duque de Osuna*, generally credited as a masterpiece of its kind.[9] With its rhyming title it is a generally witty, fanciful, poetic, gossamer sort of book. The chapters are headed with such specimens as "A Title with Fripperies," "In the Lair of the Dandies," and "Splendor on the Steppes." There is no genuine bibliography or footnotes (author cites names but no books) but on the other hand there are numerous moral lessons to be garnered from a romantic life as Marichalar's conclusion amply shows:

> God save the Duke of Osuna, the imperiled Duke, the intrepid Duke, the refined Duke who consumed himself in his own brilliance. He gave to the wind the thrust of his own name; he was a being who sacrificed himself in a holocaust of his own design. And in the midst of his own combustion the sinner recognizes that it is the falling off of the sorrowful dross which finally realizes him. From the specters of embers arises the solid structure of a new-born soul. May his ruin and fate edify us all. . .[10]

In the second category we are able to place such biographies as *Gonzalo Pérez* by Angel González Palencia, *Jaime II* by J. Ernesto Martínez Ferrando and *Política del Rey Católico en Cataluña* by Jaime Vicens Vives. In contrast to most biographies of the time, these were major historical efforts, fully researched and documented, dense, involved, and above all, serious. A biography such as *Gonzalo Pérez* contains nothing at all to catch the fancy of the general reader, no sweeping historical or philosophical generalizations, no intimate details concerning the family life or boudoir of the subject, no dramatizations of trials, persecutions, executions, love affairs or other personal agonies. Indeed, González Palencia's biography reads almost like a carefully arranged anthology of documents and citations contemporaneous to the subject's life. However, works such as Marañón's *Conde-Duque de Olivares, Antonio Pérez*, and *Los tres Vélez* or Amezúa's *Isabel de Valois* clearly partake of the elements of both categories. They share with the scholarly works ambitious bibliographies, appendixes and documentation; they aspire to permanent historical validity. Yet they share along with the more humble or fanciful biographies the goal of entertaining and stimulating the imagination of the reader. As Amezúa puts it:[11]

> . . .without defaulting on the obligation of historical severity, I will also endeavor to provide amenity because amenity is the most discreet companion that the curious reader may find upon taking up the lesson of a book, inasmuch as books should be published not in order to fatuously display one's knowledge or ability, but rather to provide pleasant entertainment, honest and serene recreation.[11]

Marañón himself judged biography to be "almost a new literary genre" which "today has achieved prominence to the point of almost killing off imaginative literature, the novel. . ."[12] Marañón considered biography as an apt humanistic substitute for the novel which was in the midst of extinguishing itself because of its tendency toward "dehumanization" (in the Orteguian sense).

Marañón and the "intuitive" school of biography

Being a proper substitute for the novel, biography was considered by Marañón to some degree as an art form. In turn Marañón was attracted to biography (as well as literary criticism and essay) because of "the infinte glory of creating. . ."[13] Marañón confides that the scientist needs to "attach himself to the creative permanence of the work of art which is like a life-preserver for his name amidst the shipwreck of oblivion, from which he must escape at all cost."[14] A scientist's ideas eventually are separated from the scientist's name and become diffused into a culture. On the other hand, "the work of art floats in time perpetually united to the name of its author."[15]

Marañón's biographies, with their built-in tensions between aspirations of historiographical validity and the goal to supplant the novel as an art form, are masterful Spanish counterparts of the "intuitive biographies" that were being written during the same years in other Western languages. The biographies of Marañón share certain essential characteristics with those of Zweig, Ludwig, Maurois,[16] Lewis Mumford, etc. All of these writers tended to produce biographies, perhaps of literary worth, but with severe limitations on their historical usefulness, despite the historical pretensions of the biographers themselves.

While Garraty terms the approach of Maurois, Zweig, Ludwig, Mumford and others as "intuitive," Vicens Vives judges Spanish biography of the 1930's and 1940's to have been written under notions of a "romantic historiography."[17] Garraty observes that "the basic idea behind the intuitive school was that every personality is essentially simple once the 'key to character' can be located."[18] For example, Emil Ludwig's procedure was to begin with portraits and photographs of his subject in order to arrive at the coveted intuition. Ludwig judged that, "The biographer begins with a concept of character and searches in the archives for what is at bottom corroboration of an intuition."[19]

Garraty notes that "Ludwig always had a simple theme to unify his immensely popular lives. In *Goethe* it was the struggle between the poet's genius and his 'daemon,' in *Bismarck*, the conflict between pride and ambition. Kaiser William could be explained by his withered arm, which gave him a feeling of inferiority that he disguised behind a facade of vanity and bluster."[20] The search for an underlying motif was also characteristic of the biographies of Zweig as well as the early work of Maurois. Zweig comments: "When research firmly bound to visual experience ends, the free and winged art of psychological vision begins. . . . Intuition knows more of a man than all the documents in the world."[21] Similarly, Maurois claims: "Critical reasoning alone will not make a man understand. We get our understanding by a coup d'état."[22] Maurois emphasized the water motif in Shelley's life, and in Disraeli's, the flower motif.[23] It is these motifs which endow biography with a poetic value.[24] Maurois felt that biography as an art form even had an advantage over the novel inasmuch as we know in advance "what changes of fortune and what *dénouement* to expect."[25] In a way similar to a great tragedy, "when we read a life with the events and the end of which we are already familiar, we seem to be walking in a stretch of country which we know already, and to be reviving and completing our recollections of it. The peace of mind with which we accomplish this familiar walk is favorable to the proper esthetic attitude."[26]

The intuitive school was primarily concerned with the interpretative analysis of character.

> The biographical writing of the whole Western world felt the force of this trend. The Frenchman André Maurois, the German Emil Ludwig, the Austrian Stefan Zweig, the Italian Giovanni Papini, together with Americans like Gamaliel Bradford and Francis Hackett, and Englishmen like Hesketh Pearson and Philip Guedalla were all primarily concerned with portraying personality.[27]

Garraty criticizes this school of biographers as having forgotten "that biographies were supposed to describe what a man *did* as well as what he was like pesonally, and that, essentially, biography was a form of non-fiction, subject to the restraints imposed by fact and reliable records."[28] He concludes that with a few exceptions, intuitive biography contributed little to historical knowledge.

Certain aspects of Marañón's biography closely parallel the techniques of the intuitive school, which Marañón greatly admired. Marañón associated the intuitive biographers with the moderate, subjective utilization of new psychological techniques:

> The universal success of the famous life of Disraeli, by Maurois, and of some of Zweig's biographies, masterpieces of the genre, undoubtedly may be attributed to the new penetration of psychology, which in its ability to cast a beam on the protagonist, converts a heretofore rigid, starchy subject, almost a marionette, into a live man with blood that circulates and a soul gripped by dissolute or sublimated passion. Probably the success of the biographic result is a function of the living, psychological reconstitution of the figures portrayed. This has not been accomplished by a technician, a professional psychologist, much less a psychiatrist who, with nails of pedantry and scientism, would have crucified his subject to the truth, but rather *by a simple writer filled with intuitive penetration.* On occasion it is in this scientific spume which surpasses the bound of strictly technical minds and passes into the common domain, where all that is eternally valuable in scientific thought resides.[29] (Italics mine)

Marañón's use of unifying thematic epithets to characterize his subjects, "resentment," "passion to rule," etc., are very much in line with the procedures of other intuitives.

Similarly illustrative is Marañón's classification of biographies. There are three types of biographies (apart from the so-called "degenerate," popular biographies that we have noted earlier): 1) Those based on legends. These are antihistorical and unworthy of consideration. 2) Erudite biographies, carefully documented, yet not always useful because they lack ample interpretation on the part of the biographer and they bore the reader. 3) The biography which bases itself on documents for fundamentals, but without excessive details. This biography is written with "ample interpretations of the living truth."[30] Naturally, Marañón prefers this last category because "the biographer is able to apply common sense and his personal understanding of history to his subject."[31]

With respect to the problem of maintaining veracity, Marañón has a conclusion remarkably similar to Lewis Mumford's. Marañón claims that a biography is a scientific book, but one "from which all dogmatism has been purged, a book saturated with humanity, free of facts that do not have an immediate interpretative rationale stemming from the soul of the subject in question,—even when such interpretations are false, for the truth is also made up of lies. The lie is always the reverse of the truth, and the reverse, provided it is genuine, often permits us to identify the true mint better than blurred and confused truths."[32] Garraty characterizes Lewis Mumford's position in the following manner:

> . . .the biographer should not confine himself to those historical "facts" which a capricious fate has preserved. Instead, being essentially an "anatomist of character," he should fill in the gaps out of his imagination. "He must be able to restore the missing nose in plaster, even if he does not find the original marble." Every biographer *selects* certain facts from among the total available, Mumford reasoned; why not, therefore, go a step farther and make up evidence if doing so helps to provide a more convincing interpretation?"[33]

Of course there are aspects which distinguish Marañón's work from others of the intuitive school, such as his peculiarly original morphological and endocrinological hypotheses, and at least in *Conde-Duque* and *Antonio Pérez*, his detailed bibliographies and appendixes containing reprints of relevant documents. Also there is Marañón's attitude toward myth and legend. This concern runs very deep in Spanish historiography and, clearly, the obligation on the part of the Spanish historian to deal with the phenomenon of the "black legend" is a substantive factor. Rafael Altamira's *Psicología del pueblo español*, 1902, written as a direct outgrowth of the defeat of 1898, devoted significant attention to the analysis of Hispano-phobe writings of the past. Altamira was "astonished at the strength of the legends that blackened the Spanish name with acts of cruelty and bigotry. More than ever he was convinced that both native and foreign historians had perpetuated fables that imbued in Spaniards grotesque notions of the factors in the past which had brought them to their present state."[34] Similarly, the work of Salvador de Madariaga and others who dedicated much effort and scholarship to refute the legends that smeared Spain is well-known. While Marañón himself was not substantively involved in the refutation of the "black legend,"[35] his analyses of myths and legends in general is quite broad in scope. First of all there was the question, for Marañón, of certain literary or cultural myths such as Don Juan, who represents a certain type of pseudo-heroism. (See Chapter II). Then there is the question of all sorts of popular superstitions, beliefs, customs, taboos, subtly authoritarian or irrational patterns of thinking which must be overcome in order to achieve a truly inductive, experimental consciousness and methodology. (See Chapter V). Marañón deals with these types of irrational impediments to experimental procedures particularly in *Las ideas biológicas del Padre Feijoo*. Finally, with respect to the biographies of historical figures that we are concerned with here, Marañón was involved with separating the true, essential personality of his subject from the mythical, popular representation or projection. This project was standard during the period in Spain. For example, Jarnés proclaims:

> A folk biography is something inconceivable because the populace nourishes itself on irradiations, that is, on fables, on facts without contour. . . .The contemporary biographer does not consider the reconstitution of a personality according to some opinion mummified by group repetition. The contemporary biographer ought not heed any voice at all, but rather he should serenely contemplate the substance of possible documents and embark upon the same path with his resurrected subject that the subject himself once took.[36]

Similarly, Amezúa claims that his *Isabel de Valois* was penned in order to clarify the black legend revolving around Phillip II, particularly those aspects of the legend having to do with his private, intimate life with his wives and his behavior toward France.[37]

The peculiar and original aspect of Marañón's approach toward myths and calumnies is the way that he attempts to psychologically validate them by mining the hidden kernel of truth subsisting within the distortions. Marañón insists that the myth is born out of the same historical reality from which spring the hard facts. Since this is so, legends and myths "represent the reaction of the cultural milieu when confronted with the personality of a grand protagonist or when confronted with a transcendental event. Therefore myths and legends show much of what that milieu was like as well as of the personality of the hero, and thus, part of the strict truth of the event."[38] Myths are typically the fabrications of the masses who permit themselves to be led by their emotions in order to satisfy their unconscious needs. In the case of Tiberius, for example, "on the subconscious level the oppressed masses attributed to another man the virtues which were not to be found in the tyrant."[39] Thus history must be reconstituted both with precise facts and legends and popular myths, all interpreted according to a scientific spirit.

Marañón's biographies in critical perspective

Unfortunately, despite the newly awakened scientific, psychological approach toward biography, despite a conscientious search for documents on the part of some biographers, practitioners such as

Marañón in Critical Perspective

Marañón, Amezúa, Jarnés, fell far short of their goals of recording an historical moment with objectivity and veracity. Nor were they able to depict an historical personage liberated from clinging distortions. Marañón has been criticized directly by such historians as Tomás Valiente and Charles H. Carter. Moreover, the criticisms of this particular period of Spanish historiography made by Vicens Vives are also quite relevant to the work of Marañón. Tomás Valiente notes that Marañón's *Antonio Pérez* and González Palencia's *Gonzalo Pérez* have in common the characteristic that "they do not examine with much detail the administrative activities of both secretaries."[40] Valiente goes on to say that this is natural "due to the biographic character of these studies,"[41] an observation which reveals the rather low level of expectations associated with biographies. Valiente simply assumes that a biographer wouldn't normally examine such dry activities as how a Secretary of State actually administered his position! Carter, dealing with the same problem, is much harsher with Marañón. He laments the fact that "Gregorio Marañón made a lifetime career of telling and retelling the story of Olivares' 'passion to rule,' yet managed throughout to skirt the real questions of the effectiveness and wisdom of that rule."[42] He goes on to detail his objections:

> In the "definitive, corrected and completed" edition, for example (Gregorio Marañón, *El Conde Duque de Olivares. La pasión de mandar*, Madrid, 1945), Marañón devotes pp. 9-299 to Olivares' personal life and characteristics; only a brief chapter (pp. 303-325) to "La Obra" (and that concerned mostly with irrelevancies); and a generous 76 pages (pp. 329-405) to the fairly brief affair of his fall from power. . . .Elsewhere, too, he glosses over the question, even when ostensibly examining it; see, e.g., "La obra política del Conde-Duque de Olivares," *Revista de Occidente* (Madrid), LI (1936), 283-321.[43]

Similarly, Jaime Vicens Vives, in a considered monograph on the structure of the state in the 16th and 17th centuries, notes that one of the main factors that has impeded the examination of the "effective power structure" during those two centuries has been a general identification of power with the monarchy on the part of historians. Vicens concludes:

> Therefore it would be convenient, in order to clarify the exact relationship between Power and Rule (Power as theory; Rule as governmental administration), to promote a series of investigations concerning the stratification and regionalization of the mechanisms available to the absolute Monarchy in different European environments. In this way we may obtain a true idea of the internal structures

of the various states during those centuries.[44]

From the historian's point of view there are several basic criticisms to be made in connection with Marañón's biographies. Marañón clearly does not give an adequate account or evaluation of the policies of his protagonists, nor of their relationships to the ongoing political, economic and cultural institutions of their time. For example, even though Marañón became a sort of specialist in the biography of *validos* (favorites), he does not discuss the political relationship and tensions between the *validos* and the various Councils of the king such as the Council of State, the Council of Portugal, the Council of Flanders, and the Council of the Inquisition. Nor does he devote any attention to the structure of the role of *valido* as well as its evolution in history: its origin as the post of Secretary of State or Secretary to the King and its final development into Prime Minister of the King. For this sort of structural-developmental understanding, as well as an examination of the *valido* with respect to the Spanish bureaucracy, we must consult Tomás Valiente. From a contemporary historiographical perspective, Marañón's work is characterized by many such lacunae.

Marañón, despite his insistence on "the passion to rule" and the "instinct to overcome," does not examine the actual patterning and placement of power. Indeed, in his *Conde-Duque*, Marañón does not give this important question even the benefit of his benign neglect. Perhaps obliged by the weight of his own theoretical formulations, he merely assumes that Olivares, because he craved power, was eminently successful in his power quest. Marañón goes so far as to term Olivares (along with Richelieu) a dictator. The choice of the term dictator to describe Olivares or Richelieu was perhaps useful in 1936 to stimulate the Spanish public to relate seventeenth-century European history with contemporary events. The use of the term is an understandable artifact. Yet from the historical point of view, the term is completely inappropriate. In no way could Olivares be described with historical accuracy as a dictator. Similarly, in *Antonio Pérez*, Marañón identifies Phillip II as an absolute leader and a dictator. "While typically the psychological value of a human act depends principally on the conflict between the will to realize it and the inhibitions which impede it. . .such a conflict did not exist in Phillip II. He died a total, absolute king: the absolute monarch of the vastest empire on Earth. . . .There was no limit to his power. . . ."[45] Clearly, although Marañón was fixated on those historical personalities who

79

were noted wielders of power, he was unequipped methodologically and philosophically to even attempt an appraisal of how power was actually administered. If he had been able to make such an examination, no doubt his a priori assumption of absolute power, even in the hands of Phillip II, would necessarily have undergone significant revision. These are merely two examples of many which impose significant limitations on the historical usefulness of Marañón's biographies.

It is not until we examine the work of such historians as Vicens Vives, Tomás Valiente, Maravall and others that we depart significantly from the old molds. Vicens Vives has been an insistent critic of what he terms "romantic historiography." In the introduction to his *Historia crítica de la vida y reinado de Fernando II de Aragón*, (written in 1951, published in 1962), a veritable watershed for the biographical genre in Spain, Vicens devastates the earlier biographers of Fernando II. His criticisms are pertinent to Spanish biography in general. Vicens notes that he uses the term "critical" in his title to highlight "the absolute intranscendence of his personal attitude toward Fernando II."[46] and to frustrate "by means of a magnifying glass, the opinionated knitting and unknitting of apologies and affronts."[47] Vicens is amazed that at mid-twentieth century it is still possible to consider Fernando "as the illuminated apostle of the purest Hispanic mission. . .or as the crafty and tortuous politician of authoritarian, renaissance monism."[48] Unfortunately it has still not been possible to confront these "mentalistic images" with the reality of Don Fernando's actual political efforts. What is truly important and significant in understanding the Monarch is "to know up to what point the Catholic King bowed to circumstances in the evolution of his governmental role, and to what point he was an innovator within Spanish politics, economics, and society."[49] Vicens notes the gullibility of the biographers who have come before him, particularly in their uncritical acceptance of the chronicles. He counsels extreme caution and strict adherence to a statistical norm:

> . . .it is necessary to surround oneself with antiseptic procedures, that from the beginning will sterilize one's study from the germs of error and tergiversation contained in the same pristine narrations [the chronicles] that were concerned with the life and deeds of the Catholic King. It is necessary to steel oneself against any manner of suggestion, including those which seem most innocuous, such as those which appear in seemingly intranscendent documents. And that goes without saying for the contemporaneous chronicles, which are composed with such clearly propagandist hues that only on very few occasions do

they permit in their commentaries the flight of a glimpse of truth. It is necessary to find refuge in facts and dates, and even to doubt these if they are not supported by the overlapping security of historical documents.[50]

In addition, Vicens exemplifies the danger of topical versions of events which proliferate and undermine historical understanding. Historical convention has it that Fernando was given the throne of Sicily by his father, Juan II, in order to "add luster to his person so as to make him an attractive candidate for marriage with the sister of Enrique IV."[51] This version, which cannot be located in contemporaneous chronicles or documents, is found for the first time in Zurita's *Anales de la Corona de Aragón,* and "surrounded by the prestigious aureola that emanates from Zurita's work, has been reiterated once and again by Castilian, Catalán and Aragonese historians."[52] For example, two modern biographers, the Baron of Nervo (1938) and José Llampayas (1941) repeat the commonplace almost verbatim. Finally the convention reaches its apotheosis in Martínez Martínez:

> This attitude leads inevitably to the writing of paragraphs of debatable lyrical quality but of scarce scientific usefulness. For example, note here how the pen of Martínez Martínez enthusiastically glosses Zurita's affirmation: "don Fernando was elevated to the category of king by his father who ceded (!) the throne of Sicily to him. This action added interest to the figure of don Fernando who, thanks to the ingenious stroke of his cunning father, now was exalted with a royal crown which must have left a marvellous effect inasmuch as the neophyte king of Sicily was such a gallant young man. . ." etc., etc. in *Los amores de Doña Isabel de Castilla con Don Fernando de Aragón* (Valencia, 1944), pp. 30-31. In this way, almost with the same words, the idle historian goes about disseminating commonplaces that manner our vision of the past.[53]

The basic drawbacks of the "romantic" school of history, according to Vicens, may be summarized as the following: (1) An excess of essayistic philosophizing in contrast to a paucity of methodological training.[54] Vicens considers the statistical method as essential in order to establish historical certitude: "One datum may contain the truth, but what is more important, two hundred free us from error. The statistical method is essential in the determination of values, riches and mentalities. Without recourse to statistics by means of a detailed analysis of prices, salaries, political trends and cultural tendencies, it is impossible to understand anything. . . ."[55] (2) An impetuous, overt effort to make history reflect certain desirable norms, themes or ideologies.[56] (3) A reliance on the commonplace and on conventionalized statements transmitted and restated by generation after generation of historians.[57] (4) An excessive, often blind admiration for the narrations contained in the chronicles contemporary to the historical figures themselves. The constant recourse by historians to the mordant libels of the period which become repeated for generations until they establish themselves as "facts," deadens the effort for true historical understanding.[58]

Marañón's biographies are vulnerable to all of these criticisms of the contemporary, professional historian. In the first place, Marañón characteristically took the attitude that his work was properly a type of "medical archeology," an adjunct based on a stratum of well-explored incontrovertible historical facts. In his introductions Marañón typically excuses himself and begs the indulgence of historians. He makes no claim to writing another "history" of an already clearly examined phenomenon, but rather, is inspired to present a new explanation of well-known facts. Rather than history per se, Marañón asserts that he is offering the history of a certain passion, inhibition, or obsession. However, in deferring to a sense of supposed historical reality, a stratum of factual truth that he is convinced has been established by other historians prior to his incursions in the topic, Marañón permits himself the indulgence of repeating and taking for granted as incontrovertibly proven, "explanations" of the most general, popular and sophomoric nature. The following are a sample of such old, worn out conventions which Marañón accepts as "true." (1) Habsburg Spain was characterized by a national vanity, the Spaniards of that period had an inflated idea of themselves.[59] (2) One of the fundamental characteristics of the Spanish people from the initiation of decadence in Phillip II's reign is laziness.[60] (3) The psychological key to Spanish decadence in the 17th century is the loss of the spirit of sacrifice, of faith and generous ideals, in sum, the death of quixotism.[61] (4) The expulsion of the Jews in 1492 was "with out doubt, the most intelligent, and therefore, the least inhuman of all of all of the anti-Semitic persecutions known in history."[62] (5) Phillip II represented "severe, puritanical, withdrawn and bureaucratic Catholicism," while Don Juan de Austria represented a fusion of two types: the medieval knight and the sensuous, impetuous courtier of the Renaissance.[63]

Conventions such as the above are not valid explanations or even erroneous explanations of anything precise. They perhaps stimulate the general reader to consider history on a grand scale; they catch one's fancy but they have no objective, historical validity whatsoever.

Their purpose is "biographic" in the Marañónian sense of attempting to fulfill the criteria for a "humanistic art form substituting for the novel," and as such they reflect our observation that the inherent tensions between Marañón's dual goals—artistic value and historical validity—led to a result more satisfying to one's sense of art than one's understanding of history. The same evaluation must be reserved for Marañón's technique of characterizing his subjects through recourse to a dramatic opposite. Marañón's subjects invariably appear on the scene as paired antagonists: Phillip II vs. Antonio Pérez; Antonio Pérez vs. the Princess of Eboli; the Conde-Duque vs. his detractors; Tiberius vs. Agripina; Phillip II vs. Don John of Austria; asthenics vs. pyknics; the Don Juan vs. the *tímido* and so on.

Moreover, Marañón was not content to merely repeat the quintassential historical folklore of generations, he actively went about creating partisan themes of his own. Laín Entralgo points out that Marañón's entry into the field of history was guided by a "radical nobility of the soul"[64] consisting of an effort to sweep away the myths and legends that clung to his subjects in order to reveal their bare humanity. Upon first appraisal one would judge that Marañón's goals embody the essence of objectivity. As Marañón states in his prologue to *Antonio Pérez*:

> Here is the reason why we need disappoint those who seek in the pages that follow an apology for or a diatribe against Phillip II or an attempt to revindicate or intensify the historical condemnation that bears upon Antonio Pérez. When these figures are studied with humane criteria, the great monarch does not emerge in an aura of sanctity as his defenders would have, nor his minister besmeared with evildoing. Both were men, one immensely superior to the other, but both were made up, as we all are, of a mixture of good and evil whose proportions and reactive possibilities in life are only known by Divine Wisdom.[65]

Unfortunately, due to Marañón's artistic-biographic techniques, his dramatization of opposites, his romantic flights, his reliance on the libels of the times, his detailed accounts of lurid intimacies, his medical insinuations and the abundancy of moral, prescriptive judgments, the results are anything but objective. Examples are legion. Let us demonstrate how Marañón actually develops Antonio Pérez in relationship to Phillip II. The basic thesis is that from 1568 to 1578 Antonio Pérez was able to "completely capture the will of Phillip II."[66] Subsequently Pérez experienced "vertigo" upon finding himself

83

at the "peak of influence and power," leading to several poor decisions and his ultimate downfall.

How does Marañón validate his thesis? His utilization of probabilistic phrases is remarkable: "The impression that young Antonio produced on Phillip II must have been, from the beginning, extraordinary. . . .There is no doubt that the monarch preferred this type of soft courtier to the men of hard and warlike character."[67] Thus we are led to the argument that Phillip was captivated by Pérez because essentially he was a timid individual and his Secretary was able to play upon him and cultivate him.

> One need only read the apologies of his contemporaries, Porreño's for example, which dedicates a long chapter to "the rare and admirable prudence" of Phillip, to convince oneself that this was not a matter of authentic prudence, which is an active virtue, an intelligent, energetic and efficient containment of one's impulses, but rather a passive attitude of indecision, the daughter of his timidity hidden behind the rigid mask of omnipotence. It is not possible to call prudent, despite anecdotes which attempt to justify him, a monarch who gave all of his confidence. . .to a man of the moral qualities of Antonio Pérez. . . .[68]

Moreover, in 1568, although Phillip was only forty-one years old, "the portraits of this epoch give an unmistakable impression of his decline."[69] Marañón insinuates that the king is suffering from a natural psychosexual decline: "At this climacteric moment, when the naturally weakened will is shattered, Antonio Pérez appears at his side, young, brilliant, ready for any outcome, endowed with a marvellous facility to foresee the monarch's doubts and to resolve them."[70] Marañón even goes so far as to insinuate that Phillip may have been suffering from syphillis, although in his infinite "discretion" he does not mention the disease by its proper name, preferring the euphemism "an affliction that was running loose all over Europe during the time and which he might have inherited from Charles V."[71] Marañón notes that the above hypothesis "explains" heretofore enigmatic phenomena:

> . . .the interminable series of miscarriages suffered by his wives, the breaking out in pustules that Isabel de Valois underwent during their honeymoon, the anosmia with which Phillip was afflicted as a youth, the aged, prematurely toothless, open-lipped appearance of the king in his portraits. . .and that horrible corruption of his ulcerated, suppurating body during his last days. All of the above is difficult to explain simply by the gout.[72]

The argument abounds with other, impassioned, subjectivistic conjectures of Marañónian coinage. For example, Antonio Pérez's adulation and cultivation of the king "reminds us of the servility of the persecuted races, of which Antonio almost undoubtedly was a member."[73] Similarly: "Antonio Pérez did not understand up to what point he could go and up to where he could not pass in the exercise of his influence over the king. This lack of understanding of one's true situation. . .is a defect very typical of the Jewish race, and thus a cause of almost all of their misfortune."[74] With respect to Phillip's attitude toward Don John of Austria and Alexander Farnese, Marañón moralizes: "Phillip's hidden aggressivity toward his brother-in-law and toward his nephew, who, on the other hand, he loved sincerely, is one of the unforgivable sins of this monarch."[75]

The ironic, almost hilarious culmination of this tangled web of subjective conjectures is when Marañón, after commenting sarcastically on a number of fanatical defenders of Phillip II, observes: "Passion is also History, just as long as it is considered as an historical event and not as historical method."[76]

Marañón, despite his avowed aim of baring the fundamental humanity of his subjects, in the actual creation of his biographies, hurled himself into history like an impassioned, embattled cavalry charger. His caricature of Phillip II may be engaging, fanciful, even suspenseful reading, but its historical validity is dubious, to say the least. Finally Marañón is quite vulnerable to Vicens' criticism concerning the over-reliance on the chronicles and libels of the period. Marañón was fond of weaving the material from these sources into his biographies, endowing them with an anecdotal flavor, although on occasion, as in Chapter XV of *Conde-Duque*, entitled "The Witchcraft of Olivares," after having exploited their picturesque qualities, he would dismiss the libels as preposterous.

While in toto Marañón's biographies are unreliable for the professional historian, they have their place, perhaps not in the forefront of historical research, but as readable, speculative, specialized adjuncts. Indeed, certain subsections of Marañón's work have proved of value, such as his analysis of the Escobedo affair, his uncovering of new material dealing with the intrigues and trial of Antonio Pérez, his exhaustive bibliographies and faithful transcription of documents.[77] Moreover it seems inappropriate to belabor Marañón's inadequacies when in fact the biographer himself always affirmed his non-identity as a historian as well as consistently characterizing his oeuvre not so much as history but rather as the typification and development in history of some instinct or pathology. Among his many attempts to express his relationship to the historian, the following, expressed in his acceptance speech into the Real Academia de Historia, is perhaps the most poignant: "The contribution of the physician is just as essential as that of, say, the archeologist, in arriving at a total comprehension of history; and this consideration inspires me to present myself before you. I am not, nor do I wish to be, anything else than a physician; but because I am a physician so wholeheartedly, I want to be one in all of the possible dimensions of that role, and therefore, in the historical dimension."[78]

Finally, the assertion of a lack of relevancy in Marañón's oeuvre for subsequent historiography is a criticism that can be levelled in kind against all of the romantic-historical biographies of the period, not only the work of, say, Marichalar, Jarnés, Amezúa, but also of the stellar European biographers: Maurois, Ludwig, Zweig and others. The value of Marañón's biographies ultimately rests on their ability to pluck the heartstrings and engage the fancy of the general reader, a task which they accomplish with great effectiveness. In this respect Marañón's biographies stand at the forefront of the genre, not only in Spain but internationally: their dramatic strengths are on a par with other first rate, popular biographies in France, Germany, England and the United States; their weaknesses are symptomatic of all the biographies written with a mind toward the general public during this period.

Marañón's implicit historiographical assumptions

Let us turn to the question of Marañón's formal attitudes toward historiography. As we have noted earlier, at heart Marañón thought of himself more as a biographer than as a historian. This evaluation stands out clearly when we compare the various observations that he expressed with reference to the nature and evolution of biography, with his lack of interest in the theory of history. Despite Marañón's prestigious credentials as a scientist, he was not moved to discuss even the question of the scientific nature of history and the possibility of deriving historical laws, two prominent philosophic issues during his time. Indeed, as we have noted, Marañón was wont to seek the indulgence of his reader on the grounds that he was not an historian per se, but a naturalist or a medical historian. On the other hand, the endocrinological, morphological and clinical notions which he brought to bear on his biographies were, at least in Spain, uniquely Marañónian and not easily relatable to the mainstream of Spanish historiographical speculation. Hoddie terms him, "A unique writer in the utilization of his ideas on the relationship between individual temperament and historical actions."[79]

Of course, despite the fact that Marañón did not express himself at length on the philosophy of history, his utilization of biopsychological constructs as well as romantic and dramatic techniques constitute an implicit historiography. We have already discussed the effects of the romantic, dramatic, subjective element on Marañón's historical biographies. Laín Entralgo has attempted to distinguish the salient aspects of Marañón's implicit philosophy of history despite the fact that "Marañón was not nor did he want to be an historiologist, that is, a man explicitly devoted to describing in a philosophic manner what is history."[80]

Laín is able to distinguish five aspects:

(1) History reflects the radical seriousness of man's life.

(2) Historical events are not the reflection of a hypothetical "collective spirit." "They are the reflection of the free and creative spirit of the executor. Marañón is a determined personalist."[81]

(3) Historical events, originally personal and free, are determined in their concrete reality by the character of the protagonist, his environment and the temporal or epochal circumstances in which he lived.

(4) The human agents of history may be divided into two groups: the "representative men" (the major protagonists of a given period, all of whom are so comparable in terms of their historical depiction that they blur into each other) and the "non-representative men," the masses who paradoxically are the truly mutable ingredient of history.

(5) Despite frequent detours and pitfalls, history reveals that mankind, seen in his entirety, is progressing to situations in which there is less and less human suffering.

Aspect (1) clearly reflects Marañón's religious feelings, his Catholicism, as the example of this facet that Laín cites from Marañón certifies: ". . .in History the only protagonist is God. All others, each in his own category, are only retinues of personages assigned such and such a role; and when we are called on scene we often forget our lines."[82] Without in any way denying Marañón's sincere religious feelings, in our judgment this "aspect" had no significant impact on Marañón's interpretation of history. Nothing could be further removed from an eschatological view of history than Marañón's busy explanations of outcomes in terms of resentments, passions, aboulias, frustrations, anxieties, temperaments, humors, menopauses, climacterics, etc. The sentiments isolated in aspect (5) perhaps are also associable with an eschatological spirit as well as with Marañón's avowed belief in scientific progress. Marañón developed his argument for human progress in such essays as "El pánico del instinto," and "Crítica de la medicina dogmática," but these beliefs do not appear to have any measurable influence over the construction of his major historical biographies.

Aspect (4) touches upon a thematic current which had a deep emotive appeal for Marañón. Marañón's sympathy with the "average man" (the common man who by dint of his efforts is able to establish himself in society) is a sentiment which plays a major part in his writing of *Amiel*; it leads him to single out the Alcalde de Zalamea over Don Juan, Cervantes over Lope de Vega and motivates his penning of such a highly moving historical essay as "La medicina en las galeras en tiempos de Felipe II." Nevertheless, his major historical biographies, while they contain short headings such as "El Pueblo," are preponderantly concerned with prestigious or notorious public figures, typically those who were attracted to the Court. Marañón's *Antonio Pérez*, for example, emerges as a veritable gallery of illustrious Spanish grandees. The biographer's method, relying on such supports as portraits, chronicles, libels, epistles and other such documentation is simply inconsistent with the depiction of the average man or his lot in society. Moreover, despite his sympathies for the common man, Marañón was of the mind that history was determined basically by abnormal personalities. He judged that "biological biographies" involved with the investigation of personality, including its pathological aspects, are essential for the understanding of history because "if men were sane and sound, history, far from what it is, would be completely different. With some exceptions, it is those men who are endowed with somewhat more than a few grains of abnormality who we associate with the direct intervention of history. . ."[83]

In Laín's analysis the aspect that genuinely stands out as relevant to Marañón's historiography is "personalism," the determination of history by personalities who in turn have been determined, originally by their inheritance, soma and morphology, subsequently by environmental and temporal circumstances. What saves Marañón from an overtly neo-Tainian formulation[84] is his insistence on biopsychological explanatory concepts. As Marañón puts it, "The history of each of us, in sum, the great history of mankind is determined principally by that subhistory that may only be registered on apparatuses in physiological laboratories."[85] Marañón's explanation of historical processes in terms of biographical events is so consistent that Hoddie is led to judge that "Marañón almost never treats the concerns of the historian and those of the biographer as separate entities."[86] Moreover, Marañón's historical biographies are methodologically consistent with the principles that guided his other writings such as his literary criticism or biographies of artists and writers. In this case clinical observations and biopsychological constructs are applied to personalities of historical significance in order to correlate their external performance with their biological underpinnings, as well as to clarify erroneous popular myths and legends. Marañón customarily explained peculiar and problematic historical outcomes in terms of the intimate make-up of the historical protagonist—his resentments, sexual limitations, overpowering obsessions, or instincts. In turn Marañón characterized himself with respect to the historical discipline either as a "biologist historian," a "naturalist historian" or a "physician historian." Francisco López Estrada comments that the great figures treated by Marañón such as Tiberius, Enrique IV, the Conde-Duque and Antonio Pérez "appear on the scene as if they were patients in his charge; the books and other information that Marañón handles with extremely careful documentation complement this clinical technique which adopts itself naturally to historical investigation."[87]

Marañón's works, in their clinical aspect, emerge as a sort of "intrapersonal" biography. Not only is the biographer interested in his protagonist's deeds, he is even more interested in his protagonist's inner states, in the tensions, conflicts and contradictions which determined the protagonist's external course, in the inhibitions which prevented him from taking a sound or signal decision, in the obsessions which spurred him into a misadvised policy. For example, Marañón speculates on Phillip II:

> We already know quite well what happened in the kingdoms of Phillip II and in the universe which saw him grow and decline. But what happened in the heart of that man, who contemplated the most ghastly or most successful scenes in the drama of the world and in the dramas of his own soul without contracting a muscle of his face, perhaps only, when the emotion was tremendous, stroking his sharp-pointed beard? What women did he really love and to which was he united by cold reason of State? When he raised men towards him or when he poured upon them his indifference (as deadly as a beheading) or his punishment from which there was no appeal, what was there in his expression of superhuman justice or of passionate arbitrariness? That unlikely slowness before immediate danger, was it serenity,

> cold calculation or impotence? Perhaps a sort of abnormal gratification, of voluntary and painful ecstasy on the verge of the enigmatic? What happened to the live, burning flame of his faith in his hours of confrontation with God, alone with Him or through his confessors, when he had to choose between a father's love and his longing for justice, or between his duties as a Catholic and those of the King of Spain?[88]

The above passage is very characteristic of Marañón's biography. He dismissed "that which happened in Phillip II's reign" as the more or less successfully completed task of mere historians. Marañón's biography, in its insistence on the protagonist's subjective essence, often becomes a history of "what might have been if the protagonist had been destined differently" as well as a "what had to have been and could never have been altered just because the protagonist was so destined!"[89]

IV

BIOGRAPHIES OF ARTISTS
AND WRITERS

El Greco

As we have seen, Marañón first forayed into the field of literary criticism by applying his clinical experience, garnered from his medical practice, to the relationship between the fictional Don Juan and the biopsychology of Don Juanism. However, from the beginning, in his grouping together of fictional protagonists and actual artists within the same categories, Marañón was implicitly extending the suitability and lawfulness of his biopsychological criteria to the field of biography. There is a sequential and chronological expansion of Marañón's methodology to extra-medical concerns. He first emerges from a purely medical specialty in 1920 with his "Biología y feminismo," a lecture given at the Sociedad Económica de Amigos del País, Seville,[1] where he applies his knowledge as specialist to important sociocultural questions of the period, such as the rights of women to vote and to be gainfully employed. In 1927, Marañón further extends his methodology to biography in his article "Nuevas notas médicas sobre la pintura del Greco."[2] In 1927, he discusses the biopsychology of Casanova. In 1930, he describes his first historical figure, Enrique IV of Castile.

The sequence is clear: Marañón emerges from his specialty first as an essayist, using his scientific expertise to treat topics of political, social and cultural urgency, such as the rise of the feminist movement, the question of sexual education, the responsibilities of different age groups, etc. He next turns to the field of literary mythology—the Don Juan motif. Thereafter, he extends his competence to biography, first el Greco, then Casanova, Enrique IV, Amiel, Garcilaso, the Conde-Duque de Olivares, Tiberius, Antonio Pérez, etc.

El Greco

As we have seen in our survey and critique of Marañón's Don Juan theories, the doctor was encouraged to apply his medical theories to the Don Juan motif partially by the precedent that already existed for such a medical approach, remotely, in Armand Hayam and, directly, in Pérez de Ayala. Thanks to a great deal of work (some of which was done by Marañón himself) chronicling the changing cultural attitudes toward El Greco,[3] we see that a similar precedent existed for a medical approach toward the painter, affording the doctor a stepping stone from medicine to the field of biography. Even in the seventeenth century, El Greco's sanity had been questioned, and, in the romantic period, the "mad genius" label became the explanation for El Greco's peculiarities as an artist. This suspicion could not help arousing the professional interest of the doctor, particularly since Marañón had a close acquaintance with the city of Toledo and its folklore. Shortly after the turn of the century, El Greco became a figure to be rehabilitated and exalted by the members of the Generation of 1898, particularly Azorín and Pío Baroja. In 1912, Azorín wrote the prologue to Maurice Barrès' *Greco ou le secret de Tolède*. Similarly, a group of painters led by Ignacio Zuloaga campaigned in his favor. In 1902, an El Greco exposition was given at the Prado and, in 1908, appeared the pioneering and monumental work by Manuel B. Cossío, *El Greco,* which to this day provides the starting point for a study of the painter. Marañón was personally acquainted with the author and knew the book intimately. Although Cossío's book bears stylistic similarities to Menéndez y Pelayo's work in its orientation toward synthesis, its readiness to judge and evaluate subjectively, and its use of nineteenth-century rhetorical devices, it displays a certain thematic kinship to the spirit of 1898. For example, there is the motif of El Greco as crusader with a not unexpected parallel drawn to Don Quijote. Just as the Quijote vanquished the "pompous epic-heroic poems of its time,"[4] the "Entierro del conde de Orgaz" protested "the false and ostentatious compositions of the mannerists after Michelangelo, which were veritable romances of chivalry in painting."[5] El Greco's painting is said to serve as a model for all sorts of vanguard movements:

> . . .for symbolist, decadent, intimist and ethereal painters; for those of a nervous elegance and complicated psychologies; for those of allegorical mysticisms and enigmatic visions; in sum, for the infinite aspects of literary and pictorial neo-idealism. These movements discovered in the subtle spirituality of El Greco's neurotic figures and in the poetic transcendence which surrounds these figures, much that

was in accord with its general protest against the mute reproduction of reality, at once gross and empty of spiritual values.[6]

Moreover, there are aspects of Cossío's book that have direct relevance to Marañón's professional interest. Cossío claims that El Greco's painting represented the features of

> . . . the most genuine and enduring Spanish type of all times, which formed, especially in Castile and Andalusia, men who are melancholy, lean and angular; dry and hard in body and spirit like the arid plains and the granitic mountains in which they live . . . sullen and insolent in expression and movement . . . inclined toward fantasy. . . .[7]

During the same years in which El Greco was exalted by the Generation of 1898 and Cossío's book was published, a series of works appeared by various medical and scientific personalities, using a scientific format and a medical terminology, attributing either a physical or a mental pathology to El Greco.[8] In 1911, Goldschmidt and, in 1913, Beritens argued that El Greco suffered from myopic astigmatism. Beritens published photographs of El Greco's paintings with a purported correction of the myopic deformations. These photographs received great attention throughout Europe. David Katz, the distinguished gestalt psychologist, and M. Márquez came to the painter's defense. Katz rejected the astigmatism theory but only in favor of raising the old insanity charge: "perhaps the art of El Greco's last period is the result of a pathological personality and is a subject for the psychiatrist rather than the historian to study."[9] Thus, the old El Greco as "mad genius" notion was revamped and established on allegedly scientific grounds. Perhaps the scientific-pathological literature reaches its hilarious and pathetic culmination in the work of the Portuguese psychiatrist Ricardo Jorge. Jorge describes El Greco's heads as having deformations marked by "microcephaly, scaphocephaly, oxycephaly, stenocephaly, and plagiocephaly...."[10] El Greco is diagnosed as a paranoid and his work is an "aggregate of disease, vice, insanity, and crime."[11]

Marañón's first article on El Greco, in 1927, mentions the earlier pathological literature only to reject it, as well as all facile diagnoses.[12] Yet, no doubt this well-publicized body of pathological literature incited Marañón to enter the El Greco controversy with his own, much more profound application of scientific and medical criteria. Once having entered the field, as we shall see, Marañón's initial medical applications lead him to historical, psychological and esthetic speculations of a very broad scope.

El Greco

Marañón's writings on El Greco range in increasing complexity and exhaustiveness from a brief article in 1927, "Nuevas notas médicas sobre la pintura del Greco" to a full-length book, *El Greco y Toledo*, in 1958.[13] The 1927 article modestly pretends to be "provisional notes which might be modified or discarded, or on the other hand, might be broadened by confirming data."[14] Clearly Marañón left the door open for a more systematic treatment of El Greco that he already had in mind. The article itself protests explanations of El Greco's stylizations in terms of "anomalies in the vision or the mind of the great painter."[15]

Marañón, agreeing with the critic M.B. Cossío, considers that the peculiarities of El Greco's painting reflect "principally intellectual motives."[16] On the other hand, Marañón assumes that El Greco's iconography was based on real, contemporary models. In toto, El Greco's iconographic representations have a morphological similarity which permits the layman to identify the painter's works. Furthermore, the typical El Greco representation corresponds exactly to what, in medicine, is termed the asthenic type of individual. The correspondence is accurate to the point that one can even perceive a goitre in some of El Greco's paintings (e.g., "Los Tres Angeles"). The goitre is frequent in the asthenic, who often suffers from an inflamed thyroid gland that keeps him thin and accounts for his irregular motor performance. Marañón judges that a certain type of Jewish physique, common even to this day in Toledo, provided the physical reality for El Greco's representations. Once having established morphological correspondences with El Greco's paintings, the doctor attempts to relate the psychology of the asthenic type with the animation or lack of animation in El Greco's paintings. In other words, he judges that El Greco mirrored not only the morphology but also the typical mannerisms of the asthenic type.

> Another interesting point of view is the one which refers to the psychology of these asthenic individuals in relation to El Greco's painting. In general, the characters painted by this unique artist give the impression either of a static catatonic immovability or of agitation, restlessness, frenzy, and tormented energy. And the latter are, precisely, the psychological characteristics which in fact pertain to the majority of asthenic individuals. The nervous or pensive, unsociable and fanatic men and women painted by El Greco frequently look like pure schizoid archetypes: that is, they seem to be models of the temperament which usually conforms to the morphology of the asthenic type.[17]

Thus El Greco's "Apocalipsis" "looks like a conclave of frenzied, hyperthyroid subjects, who have been stylized to reveal their anguish, and who show the continuous trembling and agitated emotion peculiar to these sufferers."[18]

Marañón takes a final, bold plunge in an effort to find an explanation for El Greco's insistence on this asthenic type of morphology and its characteristic motor frenzy. He finds the explanation in a deep fixation of the artist. Marañón cites Rubens as a parallel example, an artist

> ...whose vision was, for many years, intoxicated with a female profile and female form which came out not only in almost all of his representations of women, but even in some of his portraits of men, and, on occasion, in his animal figures, as it would be easy to show. All of this occurred, no doubt, independently of the painter's conscious will.[19]

Although El Greco consciously used the asthenic type for "principally intellectual motives," the "blurring of the sexual traits" of El Greco's representations leads Marañón to believe that perhaps one basic model served as the fundamental archetype for El Greco's paintings, at least in terms of the artist's fixation. This allows him to speculate that "close to his field of vision—and who knows if also close to his heart—the artist had the living model of a young hyperthyroid woman, a frequent phenomenon in the Jewish race. This is the Virgin of the 'Jesús en la Cruz' in Madrid; the Santa Tecla and the Santa Inés of the painting in the chapel of San José in Toledo, etc., etc."[20]

There is a very notable omission in Marañón's article, that of the relationship of El Greco to the canons of Mannerism. What has implicitly occurred is that Marañón has preferred to explicate El Greco's iconography with reference to environmental influences and personal fixations rather than in terms of a primary art historical explanation: Mannerism. This is not surprising. We have seen that Marañón's approach to Don Juan entailed a collapsing of the classical-romantic categories of literature in favor of biopsychological and environmental criteria.

The 1939 lecture: El Greco's Orientalism

Marañón's second publication on El Greco is a prologue written in 1935 to his own translation of Alejandra Everts' *El Greco*. The basic goal of this curious prologue, apart from introducing Everts' book, is to emphasize El Greco's genius in terms of his racial and ethnic background. The critical position that El Greco was, as an artist, working within the Mannerist school, predominant during his life, is dismissed as superficial. Mannerism is equated with "European" elements in El Greco's art by Marañón. "This European aspect is the least complicated because it is, to sum up, pure art, and it can be measured according to the passive and exact standards of artistic technique."[21] In the following, Marañón specifically attacks the academic critics:

> Almost everything which could be written about El Greco has already been written. But if one discards the useless banalities, the academic criticism, and the decisive errors, all that remains of such a vast literature is that part which reflects the commentator's ethnic consciousness when confronted with the great universal suggestiveness of the work of this painter of tormented and infinite humanity.[22]

He seeks the genius and "universality" of El Greco in the complexity of the artist's racial and ethnic heritage. His evocations of what constitutes universality have a certain resemblance to Unamuno (*intrahistoria*) and to Carl G. Jung (collective unconscious).

> Men of a pure race are never universal. They may be great men, heroes, renowned artists, discoverers, or martyrs, but they do not possess that complicated network of antennae which binds the universal being to the origins of the cosmos. This network is only present in those human specimens which come from complex races, wrought by antiquity and by repeated racial crossing; races which are a melting pot of many lineages, in which the good and bad features of the millenial generations are distilled, and whose final product is the cosmic, almost divine sense of universality. . . . The brilliant work of these men of multiracial spirit, which fades into the background of History and into the labyrinth of blood mixing, is. . .the only genuinely universal work, and, as a result, only a very few men can understand it: it is understood by neither the clever nor the wise, but rather by those who possess the appropriate resonator for collecting the multiple and remote echoes of History.[23]

The overtones that we have cited in Marañón's 1935 prologue are more fully developed in a subsequent essay, "El Secreto del Greco," given initially as a lecture on November 9, 1939, at the Asociación de Amigos del Arte, Buenos Aires, the day after Marañón finished his series of talks on Don Juan. This material was later published, with some additions in order to strengthen the thesis, in the early editions of *Tiempo viejo y tiempo nuevo* and later in *Elogio y nostalgia de Toledo*.[24]

This lecture, which foreshadows Marañón's book on the subject, somewhat theatrically purports to uncover and explain two abiding "secrets" of El Greco: (1) The popularity of his work among the people in spite of a lack of official consecration. (2) The origin and basis of his peculiar iconography. In a sense, both secrets are explicated by reference to one phenomenon. El Greco was successful because he was a painter of Oriental temperament who reflected an Oriental, Semitic milieu that readily found a public constituency in the Oriental, Semitic community of Toledo and its environs. Marañón explains El Greco's popularity by posing two distinct religious poles in sixteenth-century Spain. One pole is the faith of the Counter Reformation, "a faith of triumphant controversy, of learned and unyielding theologians."[25] This religiosity, typified by the figure of Felipe II and the members of his court, Marañón judges to be severe, puritan, official, aristocratic, basically Occidental, associated with Central Europe. The other pole embodies the faith of the people, "ingenuous, compassionate and direct, a faith of recent converts who had been sermonized and convinced by apostolic activity; it was this faith which perhaps gave the purest forms of religiosity and which produced the most glorious spirits of our mysticism."[26] He describes this religiosity in terms of its "Oriental origin." Of course, the dogma of both varieties of religious faith was identical in the sixteenth century. Nevertheless, there was a difference in "the tone of religious emotion . . .and a difference, therefore, in esthetic preferences."[27]

This difference in religious constituencies explains the comment of Padre Sigüenza, the historian of the Order of *Jerónimos* whose comment Marañón judges reflected Felipe II's attitudes toward El Greco. Sigüenza comments about El Greco's work: ". . .saints are to be painted in such a way as to not take away the desire to pray."[28] Marañón judges that this opinion reflects the fact that "Felipe II found that El Greco's paintings were *not very religious*. No doubt this is what the personages who surrounded the monarch also thought. Those saints of El Greco's took away the desire to pray; they did not inspire devotion or the desire to kneel down before them. They did not echo their faith."[29] The puritan Catholicism of Felipe II found its best expression in painters who "painted Christ as a man, with a touching realism; they heaped on His flesh, which was the same as ours, sufferings which are like ours. This was done with such veracity that he who knelt before the image thought he was feeling the blood and sweat of martyrdom in his own flesh."[30] Evidence that El Greco was accepted by the people, however, is provided by the fact that, aside from exceptions such as the "Expolio" in the cathedral of Toledo or the "San Mauricio" in El Escorial, almost all of El Greco's religious work was scattered through the parish churches of Toledo and all through Spain. "While Felipe II knit his brow, the common people felt the religiosity of El Greco's pictures and, reversing the reaction of the monarch and his courtiers, they bowed and knelt before them, and prayer rose to their lips as a spontaneous impulse."[31]

The second secret of El Greco is intimately bound to the hypothetical reason for the painter's popularity in his own time. Marañón claims that a consternation with El Greco's elongated figures is an intellectual problem rather than a popular concern. The people accepted El Greco's iconography without any feeling of strangeness.

> A cultured man standing before these same figures would discourse on whether El Greco was insane, or whether he had a visual defect, or whether he had proposed to revolutionize his art. On the contrary, common people *understand God and supernatural beings as forms which may be different from the human figure.* In the same country where God is painted or sculptured with dreadful realism, there is an aspect of consciousness and sensibility—the aspect which looks toward the Orient—capable of experiencing the dehumanization of sacred images as a completely natural phenomenon.[32]

Thus, El Greco's peculiar stylizations served to separate the divine from the human in a way similar to Calderón's use of the *auto sacramental.* The populace, steeped in a Semitic religious orientation, not only accepted El Greco's stylizations as proper, but rather shared the painter's sensibilities without any conscious sense of dissonance. In other words, for the people, El Greco's religious paintings represented the category of the divine with perfect naturalness! Furthermore, Marañón attempts to reinforce his hypothesis of a fortunate encounter between an "Oriental Christian"[33] painter and a *converso* (recently converted) public, by seeking the origin of El Greco's stylizing techniques in Oriental concepts and methods. We have noted in the earlier efforts on El Greco that, at first, Marañón does not mention Mannerism at all; in 1935, he dismisses El Greco's Mannerism as a merely European, technical and superficial aspect. In 1939, Marañón is even more direct. Using as a support a despective remark that El Greco was reported to have made about Michelangelo,[34] he asserts that "Titian and Tintoretto's studios did not mean anything to him, aside from matters of technique. . ."[35] Besides, the elongation of figures, which could have been adopted either from Italian Mannerism or Byzantine art, is not the essential aspect of El Greco's style. In El Greco's art there is more than mere lengthening: "there is a vague trembling of flame and shadow, which is expressed not only in the design but also in the color; a tremulous zigzag, like a lightning-bolt or underground explosion. In short, there is a living element which has nothing to do with purely academic problems of esthetic standards."[36]

In explaining this "living element," Marañón has recourse, first, to his old theory of a real model—an asthenic woman, probably Jewish, whose psychology is reflected in the trembling effect inherent in El Greco's art. However, he adds a complementary explanation to this theory: ". . .in El Greco there is a deep inner anxiety, an unquestionable problem of the spirit, which he tried to resolve in his paintings."[37] This problem, naturally, is how to portray God, the angels and the saints without a human appearance. According to Marañón, El Greco solved the problem by using two techniques: flame and shadow. El Greco's art shows progressive stylization in representing divine figures with the use of flame. This tendency increases over the years. [38] Likewise, shadow is used to dehumanize and evoke the divine. Marañón quotes the psychoanalyst Otto Rank[39] to the effect that in many cultures, including the Orient, "the shadow, our shadow, is. . .the body's double; it is our soul which is projected outside us, and it is, therefore, sacred."[40] Marañón feels certain that El Greco, basically Oriental in outlook, painted his divine subjects in the same proportions as a shadow might appear at sunset.

> Their proportions are the same as those of our bodies when the sun illuminates us from behind—this is the sun's transcendent hour, and also ours. At that hour our shadows grow longer before us, with the limbs extended in a supremely expressive posture of aspiration; and out there, finally, is the little head, a brief gesture whose force is in what it symbolizes and not in its size. It is like the keystone of an arch, which we can hardly see due to its height, and which is, nevertheless, what holds the arch up simply by being there.[41]

In sum, Marañón claims that El Greco represented divine beings as "lights aggrandized by distance, shadows of lights which are their essential complements, flames produced by a mad interweaving of light and shadow"[42] and that El Greco's use of flame and shadow, particularly shadow, exposed an Oriental conception of the divine which was well received by the Spanish populace of the time.

Gregorio Marañón and Américo Castro: parallelisms

Of course, it was nothing new in 1939 to claim El Greco's affinities either with the Orient or with Spain. By 1939 controversies over the national temperament of El Greco had become somewhat of a commonplace in the art world. Harold Wethey provides us material and bibliography concerning a polemic between two groups of Greek art historians (beginning in the 1930s), those who supported the theory of El Greco as a Byzantine artist and those who claimed that the artist rejected his Byzantine heritage and adopted the coloring technique and style of the Venetian school under the influence of the Italian Mannerists.[43]

Similarly, a polemic ensued in 1929-1930 between August L. Mayer and Joaquín Pijoán of which Marañón was certainly aware.[44] Mayer claimed that, although El Greco "felt at home in Spain due to his conscious or subconscious awareness of the connections between Spain and the Orient,"[45] the religious aspect of Spain, typified by the earth-bound naturalism of Zurbarán's "San Bonaventura en el lecho de la muerte" (rather than the "Entierro del conde de Orgáz") "had nothing in common with El Greco's."[46]

For his part Pijoán, who had collaborated with Manuel B. Cossío on the *Summa Artis*,[47] a general history of art in Spain, rejoined that in Spain El Greco was so popular that not only did "nuns, priests and peasant folk kneel and worship in front of the ghostly figures of El Greco which did not have any tradition or miracle to boast,"[48] but El Greco's canvases were kept on the altars during the latest baroque and the neoclassic periods—a practice alleged to be directly at variance with other countries. Pijoán concludes that El Greco's art "expressed well the Spanish soul."[49]

In 1953, Alejandra Everts made her contribution on the side of Orientalism. In general, the topic of El Greco's Orientalism or Occidentalism has had a perennial enchantment.

One could make a case that Marañón's 1939 essay is an ingenious synthesis of the two opposing positions taken in the Mayer-Pijoán controversy. It has an added virtue in that it not only purports to demonstrate the lack of contradiction between an Oriental and Spanish sensibility, but it also sifts out and avoids the extreme and caricaturesque attitudes adopted in the Mayer-Pijoán polemic. Yet, Marañón's argument is more significant than would be a mere reconciliation. Indeed, there is a certain parallelism between Marañón's position and Américo Castro's general hypothesis that the sense of being Spanish formed in the sixteenth century involved both a surface separation from and opposition to Arabic and Jewish customs and attitudes, as well as an undercurrent of assimilation of these Oriental and Semitic orientations toward reality. For Castro, the prime agent of this undercurrent of assimilation is the new convert, just as for Marañón, it is the convert who naturally and unselfconsciously accepts El Greco's iconography.

Of course, the influence of Arabic and Semitic culture on Spanish Christendom had been studied long before the appearance of Castro's *España en su historia*, or even before the first of Marañón's writings on El Greco. For example, Julián Ribera traced the Arabic influence in Spanish music and poetry, and, in a study on Raimundo Lulio, went so far as to term the above figure a "Sufi Christian."[50] Gómez Moreno and his school came to similar conclusions vis-à-vis the influence of an Arabic esthetic in the field of architecture and archaeology.[51] Miguel Asín's book *La escatología musulmana en la Divina Comedia*[52] sought to prove the infiltration of Islamic conceptions of the afterlife (particularly those of the "Christianized" Arab mystic, Abenarabi) into the popular beliefs of Western Christendom. This work achieved international fame and aroused an intense polemic. In a subsequent work, *El Islam Cristianizado: Estudio crítico del "Sufismo" a través de las obras de Abenarabi de Murcia*, Asín traced the influence of Sufism in Spanish Christian mysticism and came to conclusions such as that the origin of the *alumbrado* movement must be understood, at least partly, with reference to a Moslem sect (the *Xadili*). Asín traces the influence of a primitive Christian-Oriental monachism around the time of Abenarabi (early twelfth century) both in its "influence on European Christian spirituality"[53] as well as "the influence that it also had on the spirituality of Islam."[54] Asín concludes: "Both lines would finally end up coinciding (parallel or perhaps tangentially) on Spanish soil, which was the setting, in this as in other aspects of medieval culture, for the most fruitful cultural interferences."[55]

The point is, however, that while there are a number of studies looking to the influence of Arabism and Semitism in the areas of Spanish art and mystic thought and imagery, Marañón's conception ought not to be merely lumped together with the others because it presents some rather radical departures, which tend to corroborate, in their limited way, some of Américo Castro's assertions. Indeed, some of Marañón's actual phrases bear a remarkable resemblance to similar sentiments (albeit in different contexts) expressed by Américo Castro in 1948 in his *España en su historia. Cristianos, Moros y Judíos.*[56] For example, in comparing the *cante jondo* (asserted to be a form of "semitic air"[57]) with El Greco's painting, Marañón claims the following:

> . . .the *cante jondo* and El Greco's painting are connected not only by their origin, their general direction, and their common flowering, but also by their technique and their expressive impetus. The melody of the *cante jondo* has *the same enigmatic arabesque* as El Greco's figures, the same boundless motifs, the same expressiveness of a hieroglyphic which aspires to transcend its own form, while knowing that it cannot achieve this.[58] (Italics mine)

Américo Castro uses a similar metaphor to describe the erotic theme in the *Libro de Buen Amor*: "The expressly erotic theme did not dare to present itself except disguised as a poetry of comic and burlesque elements, or in the religious *cantigas*, or in the narration and description of adventures with those evanescent paramours who weave in an out *like arabesques*."[59] A little further on, Castro asserts that the public airing of Juan Ruiz' woes reflects an "Islamic existential experience" characterized by "the oscillating and limitless arabesque which we have pointed out."[60] Américo Castro's terminology and perspective toward Juan Ruiz' *Libro de Buen Amor* and El Greco's "Entierro del conde de Orgaz" are very similar. For example, both the *Libro de Buen Amor* and the "Entierro" are judged in terms of an "inside" and an "outside," "reversibility," a "double-faced reality," etc. The *Libro de Buen Amor* is termed "an example of Christian-Islamic peculiarity" and the "Entierro," a "hādit" (Arabic narrative or tale, e.g., Old Spanish *nuevas*). (See p. 103). Therefore, it is valid, we judge, to point to the parallelism between Marañón's terminology with reference to El Greco and Castro's with reference to Juan Ruiz.

The correspondences are not only on the level of phraseology. Conceptually, Marañón approaches and provides reinforcement for Américo Castro's subsequent position in hypothesizing a popular Oriental consciousness composed primarily of converts which exercised a powerful influence on esthetic criteria during the Spanish Renaissance. I judge this to be the crucial point of parallelism between Marañón and Castro. For Marañón is not merely asserting that El Greco was an Oriental painter or that Spain was an Oriental country and, therefore, able to appreciate El Greco. He goes much further and deeper, claiming that Spanish religiosity in its affective and esthetic components can be broken down into two poles, the "puritan" and the "Oriental." Furthermore, the Oriental religious esthetic, as represented by the icons of El Greco, was recognized not as "Oriental" but as "Christian" by those who Marañón considered to be the natural and spontaneous constituency of El Greco during this period, the *converso* population. Marañón is hypothesizing, although he is unaware of the larger historical and existential implications which Castro was to later propose, that an Arabic and Semitic religious affectiveness and iconography was divested of its identification as Oriental, and assimilated into Christendom and incorporated into the Spanish identity via the agency of a large *converso* population.

The correspondence is even more remarkable when we reflect that, already in 1927, Marañón was speculating about the transcendent paradox involved in a Jewish constituency which perhaps provided the crucial model for El Greco's mystical representations. In comparison, in an article published in 1929, Castro declares ". . . mystical theology is an importation which comes to us from the North— from the Rhineland and the Low Countries. When the mystic-ascetic fervor is extinguished there, the splendid anachronism is developed here."[61] In discussing the question of an Arabic influence in Spanish mysticism in general and Asín Palacios' hypothesis specifically (the influence of Raimundo Lulio), Castro comments prophetically, "Whoever reads our study will perceive the historical dilemma which, in the present case, the Arabism hypothesis entails, at least until some facts or ideas are adduced which we do not now suspect."[62]

Castro's 1948 position is in sharp contrast. He claims with respect to Spanish mysticism that via "Sufi spirituality . . . we shall understand Santa Teresa's art, which gains nothing by being discussed with the commonplaces applied to universal mysticism, which have neither time nor country, color nor flavor."[63] With reference to El Greco, he asserts:

> What El Greco took was not Hispanic color nor tonality. His Toledan work reveals a "living-togetherness" (*convivencia*), a "cross-breeding" (*mestizaje*), produced by the alluring attracting of a life which was dense with values and with infinite perspectives. It is not a question of an Hispanic "manner," but rather of carrying a Hispanicizing process to the extreme.[64]

Finally, Castro judges the "Entierro del conde de Orgaz" to be a ḥādiṯ in the Arabic sense, inasmuch as it shares with Arabic consciousness a "reality which presents an 'inside' and an 'outside' which are reversible in themselves. The new effect, which is included in the terms which narrate it, serves as a double-faced reality, which can be perceived in either of its two faces, or, if one wishes, by shaping the container by means of the content, or vice versa."[65]

Marañón and Américo Castro

Of course, the fact that Américo Castro, in 1929, was disinclined to accept an Oriental influence in Spanish mysticism in no way discredits his later monumental efforts to explain the sense of a Spanish identity through a methodical comparison of the process of "living-togethernes" *(convivencia)* and "experiential awareness" *(vivencia)* among Christians, Arabs, and Jews as it developed and was altered in history. Nor do we entertain any illusion that Marañón was in a position intellectually or professionally to systematically expand upon his early insight. Nevertheless, the doctor did become quite aware of his *coup* in positing an Oriental, Semitic, popular base for El Greco, but not until *after* the furor caused by Américo Castro's 1948 *España en su historia.* Thus, in 1939, Marañón provides no bibliographical support for his Orientalism contention, but the 1956 book *El Greco y Toledo* is replete with citations supporting the influence of Jews, primarily recent converts, on figures such as Sta. Teresa and San Juan de la Cruz as well as the influence of Orientalism on the doctrine of the *alumbrado* movement, Counter Reformation in Spain, etc. Américo Castro is cited of course, as well as others who were hinting at such connections in the late 1920s and 1930s: Ch. Zervos, Marcel Bataillon, and Pedro Sáinz Rodríguez.[66]

Mannerism: Marañón vs. the art historian

At this point it is most interesting to compare Marañón's speculations with the views held by scholars in the field of art history. A favorable comparison would tend to reinforce and validate Marañón's theory of El Greco's popularity. An unfavorable comparison would weaken it. We shall be as concise as possible; references may be checked for more details.

Harold E. Wethey, in his recent, thorough study of El Greco's life and art, with reference to the painter's Cretan background, finds that certain "iconographic survivals are unmistakable in the artist's mature work in Spain, but some recent scholars have exaggerated the Byzantine thesis beyond credibility."[67] This is so because El Greco's "technique of painting is so completely Venetian and the assimilation of ideas so fully El Greco's own that these evocations from the artist's youth are barely perceptible to anyone except the historian in search of origins."[68] On the surface, Marañón's dismissal of the influence of Italian Mannerism on El Greco as superficial and merely technical stands in marked contrast to the scholarship of professional art historians. Art historians consider El Greco a Mannerist from the technical aspects of pose, morphology, space, design and some aspects of light. For example, Walter Friedlaender traces the influence of Michaelangelo's techniques on El Greco through the Mannerism of Parmegianino.[69] Wethey specifically traces the Mannerism in El Greco's mystical paintings done at Toledo. El Greco's "San Sebastián" "with his enormously long-limbed body might have been painted by Tintoretto himself, so completely is the picture in the style of the 'Miracles of St. Mark.' "[70] Wethey considers the elongation of proportions to be El Greco's most obvious Mannerist trait, "one that occurs in all schools of European Mannerism from the time of the early Florentines, Pontormo and Rosso Fiorentino, that is from about 1518 until the end of the sixteenth century."[71] The spacing of the "Expolio" with its "compression of the figures vertically and laterally"[72] falls into a Mannerist scheme. With respect to the "Entierro del conde de Orgaz," Wethey judges that it "marks the complete triumph of Mannerist design. . . .The general conception of the lower part of El Greco's 'Burial of the Conde de Orgaz' is anticipated by the negation of the early Florentine Mannerists and to some extent by Tintoretto's 'Crucifixion' in the Accademia at Venice and his 'Resurrection of Lazarus' in the City Museum at Leipzig."[73] El Greco's use of white light which contributes to the "eerie and spectral nature"[74] of his canvases is "typical of all Venetian painting of the sixteenth century. . . and closely approximates Titian's later style and also that of Tintoretto."[75]

On the other hand, El Greco is not to be understood as the typical Mannerist. On the contrary, Walter Friedlaender concludes that although in El Greco

> . . .the flame of original, true, and spiritual Mannerism again bursts into life with completely unprecedented vehemence. . .it should not be forgotten that this could happen only in the special circumstances of Toledo, that is, far from the specifically "modern" art movement of central Italy. . . .The flamboyant forms of his [El Greco's] later period can hardly be imagined in the Rome of the nineties.[76]

Similarly, Wethey attributes a good deal of El Greco's artistic peculiarities to the environmental circumstances of Toledo and the unique genius of El Greco himself. Just as Friedlaender remarked on "spiritual Mannerism," Wethey judges El Greco's mature compositions as the "ultimate expression of mystical Mannerism."[77] Tintoretto also partook of this mystical mode of Mannerism as well as the painter-theoreticians Paolo Lomazzo (who wrote *Trattato dell' arte della pittura,* Milan, 1584, a copy of which was listed in El Greco's inventory of 1614) and Federigo Zuccaro (who wrote *L'Idea,* Turin, 1607). Both Friedlaender and Wethey associate El Greco with a mode of mystic representation common also to Italian artists. For this reason, Wethey considers as unconvincing Hatzfeld's effort to correlate Sta. Teresa's written experiences with El Greco's representations. Nevertheless, both emphasize the religious and social temper of Toledo. Furthermore, it is noted that El Greco's art in certain respects is distinct from Mannerism. Tintoretto began in the sixties "the scheme of placing the chief figures far in the background, creating an unnatural depth leading to them."[78] This Mannerist device, which has been termed "funnel space," was never used by El Greco. Wethey judges that: *"The isolation of El Greco's figures and their disembodied detachment from earthly associations are El Greco's own conception and they have no exact analogues in Venetian art."*[79] The above judgment, which Wethey considered important enough to have printed in italics, is the one which corresponds most closely to Marañón's speculation of El Greco's use of shadow.[80] Although he finds the use of form, color and light is altogether consistent with Mannerist thought and art, Wethey nevertheless admits that El Greco puts these techniques to use in creating an "acutely unnatural appearance" which is "eminently his personal creation."[81] Wethey also finds it extraordinary that "during his mature Spanish years profane subjects held little attraction for El Greco,"[82] and he is surprised by the "lack of mythological themes during his Italian period, in view of the fact that he was a pupil of Titian, one of the greatest masters of classical subject matter in art."[83] Both comments would tend to reinforce Marañón's theory of the artist's personal fixation as well as the sharing of sensibility between artist and layman, who would have little knowledge of classical mythology. Wethey concludes:

> El Greco began as an artist of the Venetian late Renaissance, and his pictures of the Italian period show no divergence from that norm. In Spain he developed into a Mannerist of an unprecedented mystical nature, but one whose style is inconceivable without knowledge of the Italian forerunners in this artistic movement. It would be a mistake to attempt to catalogue every single work created by a great master according to narrow limits and rigid classifications. Nevertheless, to comprehend the art of El Greco one must understand not only its uniqueness but also the stylistic framework of the second half of the sixteenth century out of which it grew.[84]

From our brief survey, it is obvious that for the professional art historian, who uses, of course, stylistic rather than ethnic criteria, the question is complicated and ambiguous. From a hypothetical standpoint, to the degree that Mannerism and the Italian school in general are unable to account for El Greco's stylistic peculiarities, it is conceivable for Marañón's theory of Orientalism to fill the gap. On the other hand, the art historian would more likely point to El Greco's separation from Mannerism as a function of his own originality and genius. In addition, we must recall that art historians have detected Oriental motifs of a Byzantine origin in El Greco's work rather than the Mudejar peculiarities which Marañón has in mind. The only art historian whom I have located who actually incorporates Marañón's specific theory into his framework is Paul Guinard. This critic clearly reflects the hesitation and insecurity in claiming an ethnic consciousness as the substratum of an esthetic modality. However, Guinard, in commenting on realistic and unrealistic strains in El Greco, wonders: "Possibly—as ingeniously suggested by Dr. Marañón in a recent study—the Spanish genius, being half Semitic, half Celtiberian, takes dual and even contradictory forms at certain periods of history."[85] Guinard uses Marañón's theory in an unwarranted manner as if it were some magical, all-embracing and explaining formula!

El Greco y Toledo

Marañón published two more articles and a prologue, "Meditaciones sobre El Greco," in the 1950s before the publication of his full-length book, *El Greco y Toledo* in 1956. "El Greco otra vez," published in 1951 both in *La Nación,* Buenos Aires, and *Cuadernos Hispanoamericanos,* was written in response to Camón Aznar's study and collection of reproductions published in 1950. Here Marañón succinctly repeats his theories of 1939 as well as noting the more recent efforts of Goldscheider (1935), Cocteau (1943),[86] Juan de la Encina (1944) and the aforementioned Camón Aznar. Marañón is pleased with Juan de la Encina's noting of the relationship between El Greco and Sta. Teresa. He thinks that if Sta. Teresa "had painted, her depiction of Christ would have been very much like El Greco's, and his theology, if he had written about it, (perhaps he did and it has been lost) would be very similar to that of the marvelous woman."[87] In this article, Marañón also judges that, as with El Greco, Felipe II never really understood the genius of Sta. Teresa.

In 1956, in *Papeles de Son Armadans,* Marañón published "Las academias toledanas en tiempo del Greco." This article, which, except for the very beginning and a few word substitutions, is reproduced in the book *El Greco y Toledo,* is only nominally concerned with El Greco. Actually, it is an evocation of the academies, associations and poetry contests prevalent in Toledo during El Greco's day. Marañón considered it unlikely that El Greco attended these gatherings, made up mostly of "frivolous people" and "literary hacks."[88]

Marañón's book *El Greco y Toledo* (1956), the essential core of which was first presented as a "reception speech into the Real Academia de Bellas Artes,"[89] represents the culmination of the doctor's writings on the painter. *El Greco y Toledo,* thematically and conceptually, is basically a restatement of Marañón's earlier hypotheses, particularly those expressed in the 1939 lecture. There are numerous amplifications and some important additions, but the basis of the argument is essentially the same. Structurally and methodologically, *El Greco y Toledo* is modeled on earlier historical biographies, such as *El Conde-Duque de Olivares* (1936), *Amiel* (1932) and *Antonio Pérez* (1947). To a significant degree, *El Greco y Toledo* is not only a theoretical statement about El Greco's art and a psychologically oriented biography of the artist, but also an historical treatment of Toledo in the late sixteenth century. The subtitle of *Antonio Pérez: El hombre, el drama, la época* would not be an inaccurate description of *El Greco y Toledo.* The book has been thoroughly researched and the use of bibliographical references is very extensive, with special attention given to two important scholars on El Greco, Manuel B. Cossío and F. San Román, as well as to Camón Aznar. However, we shall not dwell here on the study of history per se, but rather focus on the continued development of the biographical, critical and speculative themes that were summarized in the earlier writings.

El Greco y Toledo is divided into eight chapters. In the first, "El proceso del genio del Greco," utilizing the commonplace of El Greco as genius, Marañón expands on an earlier theme. El Greco, who, as virtually every critic has remarked, was a second-rate painter in Italy, flourished in Spain because his "instinct" (here in a way reminiscent of Carl Jung, considered to be the creative gift of the artist) unerringly guided him to an environment more consonant with his Oriental roots and spiritual leanings. The second chapter, "El Toledo del Greco. La Ciudad, las mujeres, la vida intelectual," evokes the physical splendor of Toledo and corrects unwarranted impressions of its decadence in Felipe II's reign. Also, the various poetry contests, academies and associations are discussed. More substantially, Marañón tries to establish the human models for El Greco's female figures. He presents us with two women rather than the one Jewess of the 1927 article. One of the women is Jerónima de las Cuevas, the mother of

El Greco's son, Jorge Manuel. (Recently it was established that El Greco did not marry Jerónima.) Marañón, here at variance with Camón Aznar, claims that the famous painting "La dama del armiño" is a portrait of Jerónima. Marañón appears to be somewhat obsessed with this portrait. Once establishing in his mind that indeed it is Jerónima, he proceeds to associate the likeness with "many of the Virgins in the painter's vast production: in the paintings of Sagradas Familias, Anunciaciones, Adoraciones en Belén . . . ."[90] Furthermore, he finds her likeness in some of the male representations also, such as the icon of Jesus in "La Verónica" where "the eyes bring to mind those haunting eyes of doña Jerónima de las Cuevas."[91]

It is very difficult to deal with these subjective arguments, particularly when Marañón explains variations in the following way:

> If one were to use the anthropometrical techniques of police laboratories to examine El Greco's paintings, one would not be able to identify a single woman's head as being the same as any other. This is because the inner turmoil of the man who painted them underwent a perpetual ebb and flow, and because the model was a shadow, and like all shadows it was transformed with each appearance. But the empirical and sentimental eye of the spectator does not make a mistake, and it always sees the same woman, modified by a dream-like magic from one version to another.[92]

In this case, we must single out "sentimental eye of the spectator." Neither concurrence or disagreement with the above assertions can be found in the academic literature since, there, comparisons are made not only from alleged physical likenesses, but also in terms of poses, design, lighting, etc. Of course, Marañón proposes the above observations in order to reinforce his theory that El Greco was fixated on a certain morphological and psychological type.

While the virgins are claimed to be modeled on "Jerónima, a Spanish woman of old Christian [*cristiano viejo*] stock,"[93] the angels are modeled on "a common woman of Toledo, replete with Oriental features, also of an ancient race, but a new Christian [i.e. recently baptized]."[94] Finally, to confuse things even more, in the later years, in such works as "La Verónica" or "La Asunción," both the Christian and Hebrew features become "mysteriously mixed."[95]

The third chapter, "El Toledo del Greco: Los amigos, el mundo religioso," identifies personages painted by El Greco in his portraits, as well as the persons in his larger commissioned works such as the "Entierro del conde de Orgaz." A profile of the most important individuals is given as well as others, such as Góngora, of whom no portrait by El Greco has been identified. Marañón is very fond of subjectively projecting his feelings about the personages in question into the portrait itself. This is not surprising. Eugenio D'Ors, noted for his intellectualism, classicism and anti-mysticism, placed El Greco and Poussin on opposite ends in terms of "spiritualization."

> El Greco was, without a doubt, a painter for literati. His vindication was the task of Romanticism, when dynamism, ecstasy and mysticism, and the supremacy of passion triumphed. . . .In this situation, things lose their importance; and poets call—or rather have called—this loss of the importance of things: spiritualizing.

> But Poussin must be a painter for philosophers. . . for Poussin, spiritualizing things does not mean taking away their importance. On the contrary, it means appraising this import accurately and connecting it to others, thereby granting to all that supreme absolution of importance which is called equilibrium.[96]

Ortega y Gasset, in attempting to describe a nonutilitarian ethic, finds it convenient to use El Greco's "San Mauricio" as a model of an individual who "takes his own life and that of his legionaries and casts it away from himself, precisely because if he preserved it, it would not be his life. In order to rise to himself, to be loyal to himself, he has to completely throw himself into death."[97] Not unexpectedly then, Marañón is moved to judge, from the portraits, that El Greco painted Fray Hortensio de Paravicino not out of gratitude but "because of the delight in his rhetoric and the fervor which the famous preacher kindled in the masses,"[98] and that the portrait of the doctor Rodrigo de Lafuente is a "prototype of the magnanimous doctor, a bit of a skeptic, a philosopher, and somewhat of a poet, as one should be; and it is understandable that El Greco should get along well with him."[99] Two more notable appreciations of this sort: Marañón judges the shadowy nudes of "indeterminate" gender frequently in the backgrounds to be "oneiric images. . .which appear in many young or mature men's dreams, and which are related to the persistence of prepuberal experiential awareness, in which sex is still indeterminate."[100] Also, he concludes that "many of El Greco's great pictures have, unlike any other in Spanish painting, the edifying significance and scenography of the *autos sacramentales*."[101]

The fourth and fifth chapters, "El Toledo del Greco: Griegos, Judíos, Moros" and "Orientalismo y Misticismo del Greco," narrate the general situation of Jews and Arabs in Toledo, and particularly the resistance to conversion after 1492 and their support of the

Comunero uprising against Carlos V. Marañón presents evidence reflecting the widespread intermingling of Christians and Jews in documents such as the *Tizón de la nobleza*, a gibing *panfleto* describing the alliance between impoverished nobles and opulent Jews. Also, there is Lope de Vega's *La judía de Toledo,* where the fascinating Raquel casts a spell on the Christian monarch.

We have, in addition, a restatement of and expansion upon the hypothesis that the mysticism of El Greco, as well as the popular mysticism of the time, had an Oriental, fundamentally Semitic origin. A large bibliography is cited to furnish evidence for this hypothesis. For example, Marañón cites Asín Palacios' demonstration that Raimundo Lulio, who was deeply influenced by Sufism, in turn influenced Sta. Teresa and San Juan de la Cruz through the intermediary of Francisco de Osuna. He also cites Marcel Bataillon and Pedro Sáinz de Rodríguez to the effect that a great number of *iluminados* were *israelitas* and the majority, *judíos conversos.* The doctor concludes:

> It is true that the Oriental influence on mysticism should not be exaggerated, but neither can its importance be ignored. It was of sufficient magnitude to color Spanish mysticism and, of course, to explain why a great Cretan mystic and artist should choose to find the propitious atmosphere for his creation in Toledo.[102]

In addition, Marañón addresses himself to Hatzfeld's efforts in his article "Textos teresianos aplicados a la interpretación del Greco."[103] He agrees with Hatzfeld that both Sta. Teresa and El Greco "have an eidetic inclination in common; that is to say, both have the tendency to represent the supernatural by forms and colors which are visible to them in their imaginations of their experiences."[104] He adds that this "eidetic inclination" can be found in El Greco's "oneiric experiences . . . his dreams."[105] It should be mentioned that, separate from the correspondences Hatzfeld has in mind, Marañón considers an example of El Greco's eidetic powers his ability to reproduce from memory the likeness of Jerónima de las Cuevas who the doctor speculates had died or had been encloistered many years before. He considers excessive, however, Hatzfeld's assertion that "specific Teresian texts serve as a key for decoding certain of El Greco's secrets,"[106] although he does admit that "there is a mysterious correspondence among some interpretations which are common to them both."[107] The doctor judges that what El Greco and Sta. Teresa share most closely is their form of expression: "ineffable, halting, and, of course, anti-academic; therefore the approbation or condemnation of it is marginal to the usual criticism of esthetic values. Scholars may reject this form of expression while common people accept it enthusiastically. . . ."[108] This similarity, however, Marañón attributes to their common historical substratum. They are "contemporary flowerings of the same historical climate. . . ."[109] The academicians Wethey and Paul Guinard take a similar atttitude to Marañón. Marañón thinks it unlikely that Sta. Teresa ever met El Greco, as Hatzfeld seems to imply: "Sta. Teresa's wealth was placed far away from the pictures of the painter in vogue; and besides, painting did not interest Sta. Teresa. It did not interest her, as, in general, it did not interest any mystic. There is no pejorative judgment of any kind in what I am saying. The mystic, absorbed in prayer, lived apart from worldly concerns, even esthetic ones."[110]

The sixth chapter, "Evolución de la fama del Greco," traces the changing attitudes toward El Greco from his own time until the present. Although the survey is derived from the more complete studies of Manuel B. Cossío and Camón Aznar, Marañón makes some interesting and valuable additions to these commentaries, particularly personal reminiscences concerning the attitudes of Ignacio Zuloaga, José María Sert and Pérez Galdós. At first, Galdós, "in the flower of youth and very much influenced in his tastes by an exaggerated academicism,"[111] believed in the mental derangement theory. But by 1890, as evidenced by the novel *Angel Guerra*, Galdós had acquired a great love for El Greco's art. Marañón considers that for El Greco's art to be truly appreciated, not only did the history of art have to evolve from romanticism to impressionism to expressionism, but likewise

> . . .it has been necessary above all to experience the keen desire to interpret art which issues from the new psychological points of view, from the knowledge of hidden aspects of personality. Freud and the psychoanalysts are a result of this desire and not the cause, but nevertheless they are a distinguished and representative result. . . .the great popularity of El Greco's painting at present does not depend on mere admiration for the esthetic value of his work, but rather on the desire to interpret the psychological problems that the painter tried to explain on his canvasses.[112]

For this reason Marañón judges that Havelock Ellis was unable to come to terms with El Greco, because he was "stagnating in a pre-Freudian psychology, and. . .he could not see the significance of El Greco to the expression of thought."[113]

In addition, Marañón reiterates his argument, with abundant bibliographical support, that while El Greco may have suffered at the hands of certain official critics at the Spanish court, he was always popular with the masses. Marañón adds an anthropological criterion to his earlier assertions entailing a correspondence between the Orientalism of the artist and the Orientalism of his constituency. On the one hand, he judges it characteristic of the masses to readily accept "the representations of supernatural power in unreal images, bearing an absurd and often grotesque humanity."[114] On the other hand, "there is much more of a resemblance than is generally believed between the mystic and the innocent, primitive man than between the former and the cultured, pampered man."[115] Thus, often there is a correspondence in esthetic preferences between the superstitious man and the mystic, which is not to say that the mystic is superstitious or to debase mysticism in any way.

> What is a strange, or perhaps a ridiculous distortion, in the mind of the primitive man is, in the mystic, an occasionally delirious yearning for dehumanization. But it is still a question of the same yearning for the magical sublimation of the divine.

> Thus, the result is that the acceptance of El Greco's saints on the part of the people, in their pristine simplicity, coincides in part with the complex, elaborate predilection of superior spirits for this same divine iconography.[116]

The seventh chapter, "La irrealidad de la pintura del Greco y su sentido. La pintura ascensional," strives to interpret the mood of unreality and its corresponding techniques. Marañón reiterates his theories on the use of fire and shadow as techniques for imbuing mysticism. He notes that since his 1939 essay his theory of the shadow has taken hold. For example, Cocteau, in his book, comments upon and parallels Marañón in claiming that El Greco had the intuitive memory of what the shadow meant for the classical Greeks: the double of the soul. Similarly, but in a more general historical context, Marañón notes Américo Castro's assertion that the connection "shadow-soul" "lacks Latin or Romanic antecedents and must be related to the Oriental idea that the shadow has its own existence."[117] Marañón produces allusions to the "shadow-soul" connection in Bécquer and in an Andalusian ballad. In addition, Marañón discusses another aspect of El Greco's unreality, its oneiric quality. Marañón observes that:

> The ability to forget dreams, characteristic of the normal man, can be reduced or nullified by a type of deliberate 'cultivation of dreams,' that is, by reiteration and concentration on the intention and the act

of dreaming. Many creative people have accomplished this, by their own admission: in addition to the well-known stories of Stevenson and Richter, there are others, some very recent, like Stravinsky, who have used oneiric material for their creations. This material is conditioned by their will to dream, and sometimes by some stimulant or fantasy-altering drug.[118]

The doctor mentions but does not evaluate A. Perera's hypothesis that in El Greco's art a toxic element, hashish, may have had some influence. However, he does list some examples of the oneiric quality of El Greco's work: the nudes which have a vague intersexual character and are typical of adolescent dreams; the landscapes of Toledo, "which are all an imagined Sinai,"[119] and the strange "heaping up of human figures" that parallels many nightmares in which the individual dreams that he is being overwhelmed by humanity.[120]

Marañón also surveys and evaluates the various pathological interpretations of El Greco. The astigmatism theory is rejected because it fails to explain El Greco's systematic alteration of proportions in a dynamic, expressionistic way. Moreover, the X-ray techniques of R. Gilbert show that in several cases beneath a stylized figure there is an original sketch with normal proportions. Marañón approaches the insanity hypothesis primarily from a definitional point of view. Sanity is evaluated as a normative label which in a given society at a given time characterizes individuals who abide by the laws and mores of their peers. As history and mores evolve, so does the concept of insanity.[121] Moreoever, in each society there is an "ambiguous zone" in which "the great saints and great creators are found, and it is inevitable that they should be judged as eccentric, disturbed or demented by normal mortals."[122] Marañón considers that only the extreme case could be medically described as insane. He does not consider El Greco such an extreme or, for that matter, Santa Teresa. Rather, he argues along with Cossío that El Greco, like Góngora, was a revolutionary who broke with traditional canons. On the other hand, he finds an element in El Greco's art which does permit him to be *experienced* as mad.[123] Moreoever, Marañón does advance the thesis, in the form of an empirical exercise, that El Greco deliberately used some of the inmates of the Nuncio de Toledo (the insane asylum) as models for his saints.[124] This hypothesis has certainly received the most attention of all of Marañón's thoughts on El Greco. It must be recalled that Marañón never claims that all of El Greco's representations were modeled on the mentally disturbed. Quite to the contrary, he considers the females to be modeled either on Jerónima de las Cuevas or on an "Oriental Toledan woman." Marañón had photographs made of the current inmates of the Nuncio (he considers that "Toledo is, in a way, a still-intact biological relic)[125] who had been permitted to grow beards, and published them alongside the heads of several of El Greco's saints. The resemblances in some cases are startling, in others, less so. While "these experiments dealing with a strictly empirical morphology could not have more than a relative value,"[126] Marañón is convinced that El Greco used the inmates of the Nuncio as models. The academicians, while recognizing the ingenuity of the doctor, are skeptical.[127]

The final chapter, "La persona, la vida y la mujer del Greco. La Gloria," evokes the personality of the artist through reference to some salient points in his life. The establishment of the location and the reconstruction of El Greco's house by the Marquis of Vega Inclán (Benigno Vega) and Archer Huntington are also referred to. The last vision of El Greco that Marañón permits us is of a failed, quixotic mystic:

> His pictures, above all those of his last period, are desperate signs for coming to terms with God; they are frustrated signs, for God must be spoken to with an inaudible voice, like that of the mystics, but not with brushes in hand, even when one is a genius.

> But in this failure is the hidden secret of his glory: his heroic significance. For great heroes are not those who have conquered, but those who have fallen while attempting their dreamed-of feats, those chimerical and superhuman feats that transcend man's possibilities of realization.[128]

Amiel: the evolution of critical attitudes

Amiel. Un estudio sobre la timidez (1932) is Marañón's second full-length biography, the first to deal with a writer. It is preceded by and builds upon short biographical essays on Pasteur (1922),[129] El Greco (1926), and Casanova (1927), as well as the translation of Frederick Hardman's Peninsular Scenes and Sketches (translated as *El "empecinado" visto por un inglés,* 1926).[130] More specifically, it is substantially influenced by Marañón's first clinical biography, *Ensayo biológico sobre Enrique IV de Castilla y su tiempo* (1930),[131] with which the 1932 *Amiel* has both important parallels and differences in methodology.

In addition to the 1932 book, Marañón also published an article on the topic of Amiel with the same title as the book in the *Revista de Occidente*; an article in *La Nación* in 1938 entitled "La moral de Amiel y otras cosas (Crítica de críticos)" and a prologue to the 1944 Portuguese translation of fragments from Amiel's diary, "Todavía Amiel."[132] The *Revista de Occidente* article, foreshadows, in summary form, the basic material presented in the 1932 full-length book. The article also gives special attention to contrasting Amiel with Don Juan, undoubtedly in reaction to José Luz de la León's 1927 anthology of Amelian writings, in which this Cuban diplomat, who had been stationed in Geneva, concluded that Amiel was "a 'chaste Don Juan,' who enjoyed inflaming women's hearts, but who abandoned them once this was accomplished."[133] The 1938 *La Nación* article as well as the 1944 prologue contain interesting material referring to Marañón's personal orientation toward the Amiel "legend," both in its pre- and post-1923 phases. The above writings also refer to Marañón's effort to defend the Swiss professor from two extreme attitudes toward him: that of a lay mystic versus that of a frustrated misogynist.

Marañón has chronicled the changing atttitudes toward the diary, and more especially, toward the personality of Amiel. Attitudes toward Amiel ranged from initial indifference to subsequent praise and admiration. Before the publication of the *Journal Intime,* Amiel had impressed his Swiss and French colleagues, mostly in a negative manner, as a man whose professional and literary career, while not detestable, had not lived up to its potential. The poetry that Amiel published remains to this day mostly forgotten (with the notable exception of *Roulez Tambours,* a patriotic hymn).

However, upon the publication, posthumously, of the first volume of his *Journal Intime* in 1883, and the second in 1884, Amiel's art and sensitivity began to receive public acclaim, soon to make a significant impact, not only in France, but in Germany, Spain and the United States as well. Some critics were to point to the professor's moral philosophy, estheticism and mystical tendencies with praise, others, such as Mathew Arnold, praised his capability for precise literary criticism. In the main, however, the critics were struck by the depth of Amiel's introspective powers—his ability to bare and trace the aboulia that possessed him. Some twenty or thirty years later, however, with the publication of Bernard Bouvier's 1923 three-volume, unexpurgated edition of fragments of Amiel's *Journal Intime,* a wave of medical studies appeared classifying Amiel as a pathological type.

Marañón judges that the general impression during the first period of Amiel's popularity was that the Swiss professor was a sort of mystic and moral guide.[134] The doctor claims that in his youth "I saw Amiel's *Diary* alongside of the *Kempis* in the nun-like rooms of many schoolgirls."[135] He even confides that: "Around that time I was writing, like all young men, a diary which was no doubt very much in the style of Amiel's; and for the sake of brevity I made note of the balance of my three great preoccupations—love, study and time—with numbers from 0 to 40, like the scale of a thermometer."[136]

However, although there certainly was a current of criticism that singled out Amiel's mysticism,[137] from the first, the most influential and subtle critics considered Amiel a sick man, although suffering from a superior sort of illness. I stress this notion of the superior ill because it is precisely the orientation of Marañón, who preserves the diagnosis by establishing it on newer, biopsychological foundations. Amiel was compared with Faust and Hamlet, particularly the latter. Paul Bourget's extremely influential essay in 1884 set the tone. Curiously, Bourget contrasts Don Juan and Faust with Amiel who is termed the "modern brother" of Hamlet. Don Juan and Faust are example of "the tireless activity which drives the energetic man to change constantly, even while experiencing the raptures of love and the ecstasies of knowledge."[138] On the other hand, Hamlet and Amiel incarnate "the irresistible invasion of dream, which, even at the moment of drawing swords, of pouring the poison, and of furious combat, suddenly immobilizes the dreamer in a captivating hallucination, from which nothing will ever awaken him completely."[139] What Bourget does is to project onto Amiel one of the most preeminent nineteenth-century critical attitudes toward Hamlet: that of the will overpowered by the intellect.[140]

Ernest Jones has effectively traced and summarized the above critical attitude in a host of late eighteenth- and nineteenth-century authors and critics, including Henry Mackenzie, Herder, Goethe, Coleridge, Schlegel, Christian Semler, C.D. Steward, Sir Edmund Chambers, Konrad Meier and others.[141] Jones summarizes the view of Hamlet as representing "unduly developed mental activity" in the following way:

> Owing to his highly developed intellectual powers, Hamlet could never take a simple or single view of any question, but always saw a number of different aspects and possible explanations with every problem. A given course of action never seemed to him unequivocal and obvious, so that in practical life his scepticism and reflective

powers paralysed his conduct. He thus stands for what may roughly be called the type of an intellect overdeveloped at the expense of the will, and in the Germany of the past he was frequently held up as a warning example to university professors who showed signs of losing themselves in abstract trains of thought at the risk of diminished contact with external reality.[142]

For Bourget, Amiel is the living encarnation of the fictional yet archetypal Hamlet. Both are suffering from "the malady of the will," for both "thought replaces opium."[143] Yet, just as Hamlet's sickness is of the most majestic kind, a superior ill, a tax upon the superior sensibility, Amiel, whose malaise is indicative of the "deep malaise which torments the heart of the modern Frenchman,"[144] is likewise proof that "even during the most cruel moral sufferings, the soul can maintain its nobility and can agonize, like a beautiful and pure young woman, without any ugliness, without a blemish."[145]

As we have indicated above, from the very first, Bourget and others such as E. Caro and E. Scherer set the tone. Amiel suffered from a "malady of the will" or a "malady of the ideal," which were one and the same malaise, depending on your perspective: a crushing of the will or a hyperdevelopment of the intellect. In France, Charles du Bos followed this general tendency.[146] In Spain, Alberto Insúa termed Amiel a "Don Quijote of the Alps."[147] Salvador Albert, Rodó, and Ventura García Calderón compared him with Hamlet and/or Faust.[148] In Italy, A. Severino judges Amiel a martyr to idealism.[149] In the United States, Van Wyck Brooks wrote a book, *The Malady of the Ideal.* Amiel is one of the three main protagonists.[150]

For many, the malady of the ideal which Amiel suffered and painstakingly detailed was at the same time an ideal malady. Amiel was a noble martyr who had sacrificed himself at the altar of reason. As John Sheridan Zelie puts it:

> If he did not act himself in the literal sense in which we commonly speak of action, he did explore to the bitter end and the last analysis those subtle causes which paralyze the spirit and make action impossible. . . . Amiel had tracked down and isolated the germ of a malady which before him and during his lifetime had destroyed the power of many a spirit beside his own. . . . If to many his confession seems only a piece of spiritual pathology, let them stop to think that it has assisted in making the trouble more rare by interpreting it. . . .[151]

For Marañón, the above apologetics on behalf of the Swiss professor were mere myth-making. Nevertheless, we must bear in mind the affinities between the line of critics praising Amiel as suffering from a noble aboulia and Marañón's own conception of Amiel as plagued by a superior and masculine timidity.

The myth of the ideal malady was to be shattered by the publication of unexpurgated fragments of the *Journal Intime* that had been suppressed by the overly puritannical Fanny Mercier and E. Scherer, who sought to present Amiel in the "best" possible light.[152] Berta Vadier, another admirer of Amiel, in her biography of 1886, likewise was guilty of presenting the poet-professor with an apologetic criterion.[153] In 1923, Bernard Bouvier published a three volume recopilation of Amiel's diary, which, containing close to seventeen thousand pages, has never been published in its entirety and included material of a tone quite different than the earlier anthologies. In 1927, Bouvier published another volume dealing specifically with Philine, the one woman with whom Amiel had a single physical love episode.[154] Also in 1927, José de la Luz León published an anthology of unedited fragments in *Amiel o la incapacidad de amar*[155] containing, in addition, an essay judging Amiel to be a sort of Don Juan who conducted a never-ending search for the ideal woman.

Attitudes and particularly the tone of the critics substantially changed toward Amiel with the publication of material in which the Swiss professor, with excruciating detail, exposes his timidity toward women, his bewilderment at and denigration of his self-imposed celibacy, his moral and psychological inhibitions, his erotic obsessions which caused him to stay awake at night composing Priapic poems or reading La Fontaine and Ovid, as well as, as Edmond Jaloux terms them, "the most insipid and colorless verses of Parry and Gentil-Bernard."[156] Moreover, there were the profoundly callous and selfish aspects of Amiel. Edmond Jaloux is amazed at the insensitivity of Amiel toward Philine who wrote such ardent love letters to him and desired only to be his wife.[157] Marañón recounts the "procedure" that Amiel used to evaluate a conjugal candidate:

. . .he divided a sheet of paper in two columns: one for virtues and the other for defects, and each of the former or the latter was expressed by a grade, with a maximum of 6, as is the custom for grading licentiate examinations in Switzerland. Thus, in the right-hand column: beauty, 5 3/4; sensitivity, 4 1/2; imagination, 3 1/4; order and method, 4 3/4; dowry, 1 1/2. Everything was carefully evaluated. . .disposition, taste, memory, sobriety, subjectivity, and even certain qualities which he called algorithmic, although we do not know why. In the left-hand column the capital sins were recorded, with subdivisions, among which cardiac hypertrohy and atrophy were included. Afterwards he

> added up the two columns and compared them. He generally found
> that the left-hand column had the greater sum.[158]

In reaction to the publication of the unexpurgated material, the
fiction of Amiel as a "guide of consciences"[159] was demolished. Marañón confesses:

> I myself, who read the original *Diary* so often in my youth, a book
> which made me think so much and which perhaps influenced my ado-
> lescent spiritual attitudes so much; I myself, when I compare my
> Amiel of that time with the present one, react as if I had caught an ex-
> emplary, untouchable saint in the act of emerging from a brothel in
> the slums.[160]

Several pathological and medical studies, such as those by Miniconi
and Medioni,[161] were written purporting to classify Amiel's illness,
which was, of course, no longer considered "ideal." Joseph Haimovici, who is in the same camp of physicians and pathologists, nevertheless, summarizes well the manipulation of Amiel's excruciatingly
honest confessions to the self-serving ends of theoreticians of all
sorts. Pathologists attempted to validate and exemplify theories
which were little more that mere descriptive labels through recourse
to Amiel's confessions.

> Each time that a new theory, embellished with a strange new vocabu-
> lary, has appeared in psychiatry, it has been applied to Amiel. Thus,
> they have successively made him into a paranoid, a schizoid, a psy-
> chasthenic. . . .Each psychiatrist has adapted Amiel to his preferred
> theory. That was easy, for in his intimate diary one can find, in any
> case, justification for whatever one wished to prove.[162]

Marañón's interpretations, while on one hand motivated by the
depth and honesty of the newly-published Amelian fragments, as well
as by the negative medical diagnoses that these fragments inspired,
must be seen primarily as a biological and psychological defense of
Amiel against those who sought to use the Swiss professor as a pretext to publicize narrow, self-serving pathological classifications and
theories. He asserts: "We believe. . .that it is childish to want to make
Amiel into a sick man. Amiel was a physiological normal man, and
socially he was very ordinary; and—let us repeat—this is precisely the
reason why his life arouses our interest."[163] On the other hand, Marañón agrees with Medioni, who destroys the diagnoses of paranoid
and schizoid and has "called attention to the sexual origin of his
[Amiel's] strange psychology and behavior."[164] In other places, Marañón asserts, "Amiel's ethical significance has declined, it is true, but
for that very reason his significance as an invaluable human docu-

ment has risen"[165] and in a similar vein, "what has happened is that he has emerged from the confines inhabited by schoolboys, by spinsters and by bourgeois liberals, holdovers from the past century; and, with his soul laid bare and without arbitrary disguises, he interests all men. Now what captivates us is not his false exemplariness but rather the genuine facts about him."[166]

Thus, Marañón's interpretation of Amiel was written partly in reaction to what he considered an inappropriate utilization of Amiel's confessions for morbid diagnoses. Just as his earlier biography was partially motivated by the desire to save Enrique IV from an implacable legend of impotence,[167] the biography of Amiel seeks to escape the confining labels of "mystic" or "misogynist" and proclaims the Swiss professor an archetype of superior timidity. The biography of Amiel is no panacea, the subject emerges as a defeated human being, but his profile as traced by Marañón is substantially more complex and subtle than the silhouette projected by those physicians who came before.

Nevertheless, while Marañón protested the "tyrannical" pathologies of the post-1923 Amelian critics and in contrast created a "benevolent" and complicated pathology, it should not be concluded that Marañón was able to escape the fatal penchant for mere labeling that characterized personality studies during this period, and which was always a capital ingredient in the doctor's approach. He was imprisoned within a cell, perhaps within a wider confine than his predecessors, but a cell, nevertheless, plastered with labels like *supervarón* (supermale), *supertímido* (supertimid), *superdiferenciado* (superdifferentiated), etc. Nor was Marañón any less free from *a priori* motivations than his predecessors. His Amiel serves well as an antithetical foil to his Don Juan. As we shall see, Marañón's goal to project Amiel as a prototype of timidity marked by superior masculinity has been strongly condemned by several critics who followed him.

Marañón's theory of the supertímido

Amiel. Un estudio sobre la timidez, is not a biography in the traditional sense. This feature was immediately realized. For example, in a book review in the *Indice crítico* it is observed that *Amiel* "is not a biography. . . .The work in question is really an essay about timidity, for which the author has chosen Henri-Frédéric Amiel as the subject, considering his case to be much more complex and to have more

121

Theory of the *Supertímido*

abundant data than that of any of his current patients."[168] It is characteristic of Marañón's biographies that certain biopsychological features are emphasized because of their alleged power to explain the essentials of the personality of the individual in question. Hence the biography of Enrique IV centers around the sexual vicissitudes and the aboulia of that monarch, *Amiel* is subtitled *Estudio sobre la timidez, El Conde-Duque de Olivares* is subtitled *La pasión de mandar,* and Marañón claims that his biography of Tiberius is really the history of a resentment. What is most notable in *Amiel* is the concentration on the professor himself and his woman friends to the relative exclusion of the environment. This narrow focus is in contrast to Marañón's usual procedure, which even in the early *Enrique IV* devotes much effort to detailing the sexual, religious and moral customs of the period in question. The lack of environmental detail is attributable to the fact that Marañón is dealing with a non-Spanish figure and had relatively little interest in detailing the peculiarities of Geneva or the Germanic or even the puritan influence on Amiel, in contrast to Paul Bourget and Van Wyck Brooks. Marañón writes in a prologue to the French translation of *Amiel*:

> . . .to the astonishment of those who are mesmerized by documentation and by environmental detail, I have not wanted to visit Amiel's neighborhood, to read his manuscripts, to touch his personal effects, and to meet his friends until after having said all I had to say about him. I have done the right thing. Documents and environment are merely anecdotal when a soul as alive and complete as that of the author of the *Diary* is within our reach. By means of documents and environment, we try to reconstruct, from the outside, the souls which have vanished from our sight. If the soul is alive, as is that of the author of the *Diary* in the pages of his mammoth notebook, then everything which is anecdotal—Geneva—only serves to distort its original, naked reality.[169]

This was hardly Marañón's procedure with reference to Olivares or Antonio Pérez. His other full-length biography on a non-Spaniard, *Tiberius,* is quite replete with environmental detail, yet understandably so, due to the remote, classical topic and the role of Tiberius as head of state. The net result of Marañón's concentration on Amiel as *supertímido* is that the Swiss professor stands out starkly as a prototype of a certain class of personality, more so than his alleged opposite, Don Juan, who even in Marañón's criticism, has his historical variations. This effect of concentration is further enhanced by the format of the biography, which, after a preliminary survey of the chronologically changing attitudes toward Amiel, proceeds to lay down a theory of different grades of sexual timidity which is then deductively applied and exemplified in the remainder of the book. The prototypical starkness in *Amiel* is related to another explicit motive for writing the book: to present some important facts about the nature of sexual timidity and to console and comfort any reader who may be suffering a condition analogous to that of Amiel. It must be borne in mind that the success of *Amiel* with the public has less to do with the specific conclusions about the Swiss professor than with the psychological theory of timidity exalting the timid individual and with the material intended to sexually educate. No wonder that Marañón, who had good reason from his clinical experience to be concerned with sexual education in Spain, takes pains to make it clear that "real" timidity does not exist in an individual sexually incapacitated because of an organic condition.

> . . .in the clinic, when we examine patients who complain of the weakness of their instinct, their state of calmness or anxiety when they tell us about it is useful as a guide to the organic or purely neurotic basis of their abnormality. The truly timid personality is, as I have indicated, the one whose sexual apparatus is theoretically perfect or nearly so, but whose functioning is inhibited, impeded or made impossible by the false awareness that the patient has of his alleged incapacity.[170]

Indeed, much of the fourth chapter of *Amiel* is an exposition on sexual education and a plea for reform, on the one hand, chastizing the inculcation of lies by moralists and doctors in the interests of sexual hygiene, and, on the other, condemning the "barbaric" expectation that condemns as "shameful and incomplete males those who are not capable of sexual activity from the age of fifteen or so."[171] Also noted is the adolescent's intense preoccupation with his body. The adolescent is vulnerable to what Marañón terms the "the volumetric idea of sex." This "sexual mythos" has harmed many men, instilling in them a false belief that they are suffering from some organic anomaly or defect, or more frequently a "consciousness of the smallness of the genitalia."[172] These false beliefs may lead to "an authentic inferiority complex."[173]

While the above material is marginal to the thesis of a *supervarón*—this category of timidity is contrasted with the category of the *supervarón* as exemplified by Amiel—it is important in understanding the popularity of the book itself as well as Marañón's motivation in writing it. We recall that Marañón is writing in 1932 during the period when he helped establish, along with Ortega y Gasset and Pérez de Ayala, the Agrupación al servicio de la República, an organization conceived with the goal of establishing an outlet where the expertise of intellectuals, professionals and scientists could be made available to the Republic. During this period, Marañón offered professional advice and even political exhortation to society in the various prologues and literary works he penned as well as the lectures he gave in various places.[174] Specifically, with respect to *Amiel,* the hope and consolation that Marañón offers for the *tímido* (timid personality) is in sharp contrast to his condemnation of the Don Juan ruled and damned by his unsublimated instincts. In opposing Amiel to Don Juan, not only is a conceptual paradigm established, but an affective one as well. Furthermore, Marañón's feelings toward sexual, and ultimately, social lifestyles are circumscribed and defined in the biography, ranging from repugnance toward Don Juan to compassion both for Amiel, the *supertímido*, and the great contingent of ordinary neurotics. Implicit in *Amiel* is a double-pronged plan of action. On the one hand, Marañón seeks to neutralize the effects of Don Juanism in order to liberate Spanish society in general and foster scientific pursuits. On the other hand, he seeks to socially and sexually educate the young in order to prevent their succumbing to typical, hazardous misconceptions. Moreover, he attempts to influence an adult group that has incorporated a false belief of socio-sexual inferiority.

We have noted above the compassion of Marañón both for the *supertímido* and the ordinary *tímido*. Nevertheless, although both types are worthy of compassion, there is a great theoretical divide between the two categories. Amiel belongs to the *supertímido* category, which, in contrast to the typical *tímido's* "authentic inferiority complex," is marked by a "superiority complex."

How is it that a conscious (or unconscious) awareness of either one's inferiority or superiority can lead to the same behavioral result: timidity or the incapacity to love? In order to answer this question, Marañón refers to his theories of sexual development as expounded in *La evolución de la sexualidad.*[175]

Marañón discovered, independently of Freud, through his endocrinological research, the undifferentiated sexuality of the infant.[176] This discovery reinforced Marañón's contention that sexual evolution basically involves the conditioning of the instinct to attach itself to more and more differentiated objects. Marañón, like Freud, has a notably extroverted, object-oriented theory of sexuality.

In outlining the evolution of the sexual instinct, which is, as we have noted, not an evolution in the basic instinctual energy or capacity, but rather, a development in terms of the specificity of the instinct-satisfying object, Marañón describes four stages:

1. The stage of the "undifferentiated object" where the instinct searches blindly for any individual irrespective of sex. This occurs in certain species of animals and in certain sexual phases of the child.

2. The stage of "shameless, generalized sex" or "absolute polygamy" where the object of attraction is the opposite sex at large and without differentiation. This is the normal life stage for most animals and of "undifferentiated men" such as all authentic Don Juans.

3. The stage of "group monogamy" or "conditioned polygamy" where the attraction involves a certain group or type of individual of the opposite sex characterized by similar morphological and psychological qualities. This is perhaps the most common stage in human sexual evolution since the rigors of pure monogamy are exacting. In this stage it is typical in the West for a man to have a wife "to share his social position and public affections, and a series of casual mistresses to calm the undifferentiated instinct."[177] This sort of polygamy really reduces itself to "a simple exercise of variations on the same theme."[178] Marañón claims that he is convinced that "the extramarital affair is a pretext to renew one's taste for the same basic model; it is similar to the case of the gourmet who, proud of his own cuisine, from time to time visits one restaurant or another in order to affirm, away from home, his conviction that nowhere does he fare as well as at his own table."[179] The phrase reminds us of Alejandro, the main protagonist in Unamuno's *Nada menos que todo un hombre,* who when confronted with his adultery by his wife, exclaims, "And now, after this rustic appetizer, I shall better appreciate your beauty, your elegance and your pulchritude."[180]

4. The "individual or genuinely monogamous stage" where the instinct attaches to one sole object-member of the opposite sex. The third and fourth stages, but particularly the fourth, characterize the essentially virile man.

Two important considerations that pertain to *Amiel* as a treatise on sexual and social education should be mentioned here. First, according to Marañón, puberty is not to be seen merely as a period when sexuality is awakened in the adolescent, but mainly as a stage characterized by "the determination of the sexual object."[181] For example, the coquettishness of a girl that typically appears at this time "is basically. . .one more attempt to accentuate sexual differentiation, and as a result it aids in the choice of a specific heterosexual love object."[182] The second consideration is that Marañón judges that the fourth and final stage of sexuality, genuine monogamy, has been obstructed by old-fashioned social traditions. Marañón claims that pure monogamy presents an almost insurmountable difficulty "as long as the restraints of the old morality and social prejudices remain, and as long as preparation for marriage consists of a long engagement, which is a compromising situation for young people, and sometimes for the reputation of the woman. . . ."[183] Marañón applauds the loosening of the social structure, permitting more freedom for the sexes to seek out differentiated mates in contrast to the reliance on arranged marriages oriented toward economic needs. "The direction which modern sexual behaviour is taking, in the sense of a loosening of restrictions on men and women's premarital acquaintance with each other, will surely facilitate the discovery of the ideal mate."[184]

In his own, peculiarly radical way, Marañón proclaims the usefulness of freeing the instincts and permitting them to develop. He notes the views of "timorous people. . .who shudder at an imagined disappearance of the family because of changes in the mores of family life and because Governments, as is now the case in Spain, are including divorce in their laws. . . ."[185] Marañón judges these fears to be completely unfounded. He considers that the family may shed its "solemn patriarchal structure and turn into something which is more flexible,"[186] but its perennial endurance is unquestionable: ". . .nothing *fundamental* will happen to the family either now, or ever."[187]

Application of the model of the supertímido *to Amiel*

Having sumarized his theory of sexual evolution, Marañón applies it deductively to Amiel. Amiel is placed within the fourth stage. He exhibits the striving for the ideal of a genuine monogamy. Although Amiel falls within the category of the *supervarón,* his personality is characterized by a certain malady to which this type of man is susceptible: sexual timidity due to a "malady of the ideal" or "fetishism of the ideal." Other similar individuals who have suffered the same ill are Leonardo da Vinci and Angel Ganivet. Marañón assumes several different perspectives in order to demonstrate that both Amiel's "supervirility" and "fetishism of the ideal" determined his timidity. Amiel's malady is analyzed in terms of its genesis and morphology, and to a lesser degree, its environmental determinants.

In terms of the genesis of the "fetishism of the ideal," Marañón invokes the Oedipus complex. He observes that, in a certain number of men, at a tender age the image of the mother powerfully fixes itself, conditioning the sexual instinct to the point that it will not attach itself to women other than those who closely resemble the mother. If the individual cannot discover such a woman, he will run in vain from one experience to another. Marañón quotes several items from Amiel's diary pointing not only to the Swiss professor's love for his mother, but reciprocally, his hostility toward his father. He also notes that Berta Vadier's biography of Amiel reflects the same situation: the mother defending the son against the hostility and violence of the father. An added factor in Amiel's case was his sickly childhood. According to Marañón, this organic weakness predisposes the child not only to an "overevaluating of the mother" but to "timid reactions when confronted with the difficult moments of life." The typical mechanism is to compensate for one's physical weakness with heroic daydreams. (We recall Amiel's erotic readings and poetry.) Marañón also considers it plausible that "an unpleasant experience during infancy"[188] may have contributed toward Amiel's aversion to physical love. The fact that Amiel seemed to be terrified that physical contact would dampen his sentimental fervor is deemed an "idea of infantile origin."[189]

The above observations lead to a series of considerations on sexual education that are most valuable inasmuch as they reflect Marañón's understanding of the newly discovered psychological effects of infantile traumas. Marañón attempts to reconcile the psychological realities of infantile sexuality with the traditional mores of his society as reflected in his own education and background. The following tensions give us a glimpse of the challenge for Marañón, in the Republican Spain of 1932, of being a Catholic liberal and scientist who desired very much not to be accused of heterodoxy. On the one hand, Marañón applauds the "great intuition" of the psychoanalysts who have demonstrated the genesis of many psychoses in maturity as the result of an "inopportune exposure. . .to the sight. . .of physical love."[190] Socially indignant, he takes a radical psychological point of view: ". . .when I enter those wretched dwellings of the poor, in which the same bed harbors the children's innocent sleep and the parents' nights of love, I am irritated by the subtle injustice that this cohabitation entails even more than I am by the inequality with which sustenance and material comforts are distributed."[191] In addition, the doctor attempts to reconcile psychological investigations of traumas with the dogma of Mary's virginity by pointing to the psychological value of this belief:

> The dogma of Mary's virginity, the glorification of motherhood to the point of cleansing it of all male participation, is no doubt one of the ideas which can most positively influence a child's mind, and one of the most exalted symbols of the prestige of femininity. Until the time when life reveals the simple truth to the child, I think that it is extremely important that he should see the greatness of the creative act, which should not be deformed but rather divested of its pagan components; for, without a doubt, when those components are coldly considered they have the appearance of a violation.[192]

On the other hand, Marañón is horrified by the lies that are perpetuated to camouflage sexuality and procreation. The net result of this sort of tactic is infirmity, and he agrees when Amiel himself asserts:

> An essential part of education is to initiate the young person in the area of sexual rights and obligations. I possessed, to a great extent, all of the gentle instincts, all of the most noble aspirations, and all of the tendencies toward virtue, but nevertheless I have seen my existence thwarted because of not having had either direction or advice, support or initiation, in things which concern Eros.[193]

Thus, Marañón proposes a tense and difficult course, a middle path between too early a revelation of sexual knowledge and the suppression of that knowledge altogether.

> On speaking of sexual education we have often said "never use deception." This is right, but let us permit that these thorny truths, whose hidden fruit can only be savored in maturity, make their appearance as late as possible and as delicately as possible, and not in a premature way, conveyed by a brutal impression of the senses.[194]

From a morphological point of view, Amiel displays "all of the signs of a perfect and strongly accentuated virility, once he overcame the childhood stage of weakness and false, transitory effeminacy. . . ."[195] Marañón offers a good deal of analysis of paintings of Amiel as well as supporting testimony from female admirers and critics to the effect that physically Amiel was considered very masculine. In terms of his behavior, Marañón judges that Amiel directly opposes the inferior *tímido* who systematically flees from women because they are mirrors that implacably reflect his own inferiority. The superior *tímido* on the contrary, "seeks. . .female company continually: it seems that all of his vital activity is directed towards the never completed investigation into an ideal prototype of the opposite sex."[196]

Reciprocally, for Marañón, the conduct of many women toward Amiel is most revealing. Several chapters are spent describing the personalities and behavior of the women—Philine, Fanny Mercier,

Berta Vadier, Egeria—who loved Amiel during and after his life. Only one, however, Philine, had a single consummated sexual experience with Amiel. Marañón judges that: "The feminine instinct perceives and appraises, with a very keen intuition, the quality of a man's sexual component, independently of his physical ability for love."[197] Toward the typical *tímido,* women characteristically respond with pity or rejection. In contrast, the behavior of Amiel's lovers, their loyalty for long periods (for Fanny Mercier and Berta Vadier, permanent fidelity), their desire for marriage, bear evidence of Amiel's stature as a *supervarón.* Marañón asserts: "This category of the ideal is what the instinct of woman—at least, that of an important type of woman—values and rewards in a man, rather than the extent of his physical strength."[198]

Finally, from the environmental perspective, the puritanism of Geneva during this period reinforced the psychological and organic disposition of Amiel and provided a philosophic superstructure for him to rationalize his self-imposed celibacy.

For Marañón, the clearest incident that reflects both Amiel's "superior" timidity and his malady of the ideal is the often-commented reaction he had after making love to Philine.[199]

Amiel finally is deflected from his instinctual ideal out of a haunting, obsessive curiosity, but after making love to Philine, he does not react like the typical *tímido* as Marañón has clinically observed this type, experiencing a "liberation from a sort of slavery"[200] and reorganizing his life on a more normal social and sexual basis. Nor does he create an erotic embroidery as would Casanova in his memoirs. On the contrary, only one-half page of the lengthy diary is devoted to the occurrence, this material expressing the confirmations of the Swiss professor's anticipations. Marañón quotes the salient passages:

> For the first time, I have been successful in love, and frankly, in comparison with what the imagination fancies and promises, the actual event is not very extraordinary at all. At least three-quarters of sensual pleasure is in desire, or, more precisely, in the imagination. Its poetry is worth infinitely more than its reality. In the last analysis, I am astonished at the relative insignificance of this pleasure, about which so much fuss has been made.[201]

Amiel does not feel any great elation or even any particular sense of transcendence in the occurrence because "for the markedly typical man, the great amorous adventure is only one episode among the rest of life's activities. For him, the loss of his virginity does not represent anything transcendental, because without realizing it he has a deep awareness of his capability. After the happy occasion, his manhood has not increased even one mite."[202]

Here then, is Amiel's sickness: He has engaged in a momentous transaction. "What he gains by living for ideal categories is achieved at the expense of a total loss of his physical, heterosexual life."[203]

What Marañón has done is to revive and defend the traditional belief of Amiel as suffering from a malady of the ideal which is at the same time a noble, superior malady. Marañón judges the earlier conceptions of this ideal malady, based on the expurgated editions of the *Journal Intime,* as mere myth-making. In contrast, Marañón adjusts the notion to a biopsychological schemata. He "modernizes" it, as it were, by translating it into biopsychological terms. Amiel's aboulia is now seen as noble in terms of the subject's ability to be faithful to a genuine monogamy. He is a *supervarón.* On the other hand, Amiel is a sick *supervarón* because the "ideal" that he pays lasting homage to is none other than his mother—which makes, socially, for a rather unproductive relationship in mature life!

Amiel is disappointed by his one involvement with Philine. This confirmation of his anticipations is of course unrealistic: "A ridiculous deception, because love cannot be understood in one day, as he supposed with true professorial presumptuousness. On the contrary, love requires at least the thousand and one nights of the legend simply for one to be initiated into its secrets."[204] Amiel is anxious to allay his doubts about the worthwhileness of his celibacy and making love to Philine serves to stem his doubts and permits him to pursue his ideal, at least for a while.

The ideal woman that Amiel seeks is, as Marañón puts it, a "phantom." Amiel writes:

> Happy is the man who finds an energetic and pure wife, for she is the companion of his nights and days, the support of his youth and old age, the partner in hardship, the echo of his conscience, the balm of his sufferings, his prayer and counsel, his repose and aura. In her the husband finds uncorrupted Nature, the incarnation of poetry, the tranquilizer of his anxiety, the realization of his dreams. Genuine marriage is a prayer, a cult, a religion, because it is nature and spirit, contemplation and action at the same time; it visibly participates in the eternal plan through work, fertility, and education.[205]

Yet, what Amiel never learned was that an ideal woman is not found by luck, but is the result of one's own efforts. Matrimony is the product of "everyday sacrifice, of risking the future of one's own heart for it in a risky game of chance."[206]

Why did Amiel fail to learn this truth and instead prefer to aimlessly search for a magical woman? Because his mother was a magical and all-important figure to him. "The mother appears from time to time in his *Diary,* above all as death approaches; she is like a religious ideal, like something superhuman that, by dint of being inside the soul, hardly needs to be named to be venerated."[207] Try as he might, Amiel could not completely give up this relationship in which he was loved innately, without having to make any effort or prove himself, for a dangerous intimacy with any one of his several "lovers." Therefore, he imposed a distance on his relationships, in the meantime, searching relentlessly for the "ideal," a chimera originating in unearned, innate maternal love. In the end,

> All of his attempts to find the female ideal having failed, his senses now calmed, he turns again in his old age to a pure recollection of his mother, who was, without his realizing it, the starting point and conclusion of all his investigations into love.[208]

Critics of Marañón's theory

Marañón's thesis of Amiel as a *supervarón* and *supertímido* aroused an immediate controversy, significantly centering not around the legitimacy of utilizing the diary to diagnose the personality of Amiel, but rather on the validity of the diagnosis itself. The two main critics who confronted Marañón in a polemical manner, F. Oliver Brachfeld and Juan Pablo Muñoz Sanz, did so in order to substitute their own psychological diagnoses of Amiel.[209]

Oliver Brachfeld, in *Polémica contra Marañón,* applies his general critique of Marañón's sexual theories by criticizing *Amiel* on three basic grounds. First, Brachfeld accuses Marañón of practicing, "a type of primitive psychoanalysis, one that is not well guided and consequently badly assimilated, which comes to take the place of the usual intersexual interpretation. . . ."[210] Whereas Marañón discussed Enrique IV's timidity in terms of a "preconceived theory of intersexual states,"[211] he now has recourse to explanations of an entirely different order—those of Freudian psychoanalysis. We have already dealt with this criticism in a more general way in our survey of Marañón's theoretical foundations, noting the eclecticism involved. His tendency is to base himself on established morphological theories, such as those of Kretschmer, or biological theories of intersexuality, such as those of Magnus Hirschfeld and Goldschmidt. Yet, there is a very strong effort in his work to incorporate the psychoanalytic ex-

131

planations into his formal, basically classificatory, biological system. Marañón is profoundly ambivalent toward Freudianism, which leads him, in some instances, to harshly criticize Freud, in others, to explain away his theories as commonplace and well-known, although reformulated in a new jargon. Yet, on many occasions he reserves enthusiastic praise for Freudian theories and actively associates his own work with them. Furthermore, one must bear in mind that Freud himself, the celebrated leader of the psychoanalytic school, usually receives the brunt of Marañón's harshness. When the doctor is critical of Freud, it is often on moral grounds, and there is a strong affective component involved. Rarely do we find any emotional criticism of Rank or Stekel, and more often than not, there is, both intellectually and affectively, an acceptance. Obviously, it was easier for Marañón to publicly applaud lesser-known disciples rather than the founder himself (although Marañón does support Freud on several occasions). It is quite significant that he reserves his highest praise for Rank while, at the same time, he quotes only the early, Freudian work of this psychologist.[212]

In truth, Marañón's eclecticism can be traced, in his writings at least, as far back as *La edad crítica* (1919), and his concurrence with and disapproval of psychoanalytic theories runs through his *Tres ensayos sobre la vida sexual* (1926), and his lectures on intersexuality leading to the publication of *Los estados intersexuales en la especie humana* (1929).[213] By 1930, the date of publication of *Enrique IV*, Marañón's attitudes toward and partial acceptance of psychoanalysis were clearly formulated. Thus, there is no real validity in the assertion of a change in orientation on the part of Marañón in *Amiel* as compared to *Enrique IV*. Even Oliver Brachfeld notes, thereby contradicting himself in the process, an hypothesized psychoanalytic explanation on the part of Marañón for Enrique IV's behavior in inciting the adultery of his wife with the man for whom the monarch allegedly had an "abnormal predilection." Marañón cites and praises Stekel's studies (as he did on the same grounds in the earlier *Tres ensayos sobre la vida sexual*), claiming they support his own observations. On the other hand, we must recognize that there is very little reference to psychoanalysis in *Enrique IV,* especially as compared to *Amiel* in which the Oedipus complex plays a notable part in the analysis. Even the example that we have cited above is termed "another important argument supporting the thesis of the King's homosexuality,"[214] which merely reinforces the morphological diagnosis: "a hypogenital constitution" characteristic of "intersexual males, who are organically inclined. . .toward the abnormal practice of love. . . ."[215]

However, the reason that the utilization of psychoanalysis is meager in *Enrique IV* in comparison to *Amiel* is not really because of a total change in orientation, but because, for Marañón, Enrique IV reflects a sexual timidity based on primary organic and instinctual inferiority. Marañón asserts: ". . .the facts which we can gather about his biology permit us to judge him, with certainty, to be a schizoid with sexual timidity. . . ."[216] Because, for Marañón, Enrique IV was so clearly inferior constitutionally, he did not need or utilize theories of psychological development to explain the monarch's behavior. A developmental approach was nonessential. For Marañón, Enrique IV's behavior has a consistency which singularly contrasts with the peculiar inhibitions that so bemused the doctor during his student days when he assiduously read Amiel.

I do not believe that Marañón substantially developed a psychoanalytic orientation between the years 1930-1932; he already had a solid understanding of psychoanalysis dating at least from 1919. The explanation for the relative emphasis on psychoanalysis in *Amiel* is to be seen primarily in terms of Marañón's needs for a theory that would explain the historical development of Amiel's personality, as well as the separation between Amiel's constitutional "superiority" and behavioral inhibitions. Thus, the extended use of psychoanalysis in *Amiel* versus the limited use of this theory in *Enrique IV* reflects the psychological subtlety of Amiel's personality. Another important element, rather than a theoretical change, is the development by Marañón of a more varied and flexible biographical-analytic technique. Pedro Laín Entralgo points to this:

> In his first monograph on a historical subject—the *Ensayo biológico sobre Enrique IV*—he feels obliged to give an explanation to his possible critics. "What do you, a physiologist, have to do with History, one asks in a case like this. . . .I have not really claimed. . .to write about History in the strict sense of the word. . . .I have only wanted to throw the light of recent progress in the physiology of personality and human instincts onto the bodies and souls. . .of a distant king and some of those who accompanied him in his passage through life." Two years later, in *Amiel* (1932), the doctor-historian has found his approach, and he now speaks of his study with complete certainty. Now he knows how to situate himself, as a historian and as a man, before types like Casanova or Amiel, whose testimonies about themselves are no more than "desperate and endless attempts to confer dignity upon their failure to overcome themselves."[217]

Critics of Marañón's Theory

A third element was probably the changing social climate in Spain. The establishment of the Republic permitted and even encouraged a certain radicalness in approach, particularly when applied to a Swiss Protestant rather than some Spanish figure more likely to stir passions. Certainly in the field of politics, Marañón was at his most radical during this period. His professional support of socialist causes and his affiliation with the Unión General de Trabajadores resulted in his appointment, along with Unamuno, Pérez de Ayala and Ortega y Gasset, as a deputy in the Spanish Parliament.[218]

The second aspect which Brachfeld finds untenable is that Marañón has misapplied psychoanalysis to Amiel.

> Marañón—who in this book becomes a psychoanalyst, but one who has understood Freud very badly—seems not to understand the great truth of the Adlerian thesis: it does not matter whether a real inferiority exists or not if the feeling, the sensation and the awareness of it exist. Even if the individual only has this feeling, he will act as if he actually possessed a perceptible inferiority. . . .[219]

The problem here is that Marañón does not really integrate, except in a superficial, narrative way, psychoanalysis with his own model. The Oedipus complex serves to explain the unconscious nature of Amiel's ideal—the mother—but the behavioral consequences of such an over-dependence on and over-identification with the mother are not explored. On the contrary, Marañón makes a special effort to present Amiel as "unfeminine although he was worried about his masculine identity"[220] and neglects the consequences of Amiel's hypothesized over-dependence on his mother in childhood by consistently stressing Amiel's virile and autonomous adherence to an ideal of monogamy in adulthood. The Ecuadorian writer, Juan Pablo Muñoz Sanz, who in 1936 compiled an anthology of Amelian fragments as well as a psychological theory of his own, clearly saw this gap in Marañón's theory between Amiel as a child and Amiel as an adult: Marañón has emphasized only the post-pubescent stage of Amiel's timidity, and has discovered two etiologies for the same disease; for when dealing with timidity he explained it using Freudian theory."[221]

As I have treated earlier the vicissitudes and contradictions in Marañón's theoretical foundations, I shall not dwell on this aspect here. At this point, it is more important for us to note *Amiel* as a good example of Marañón's eclectic approach to literary and biographical subjects, and particularly to note the full-fledged use of the Oedipus complex to explain personality.

The third aspect that Brachfeld criticizes is Marañón's opposing of Amiel to Don Juan. Inherent in Brachfeld's criticism is a rejection of the categories of "inferior timidity" and "superior timidity." Brachfeld asserts in a 1942 book on the inferiority complex:

> Here we are not in the presence of any "inferior" or "superior" timidity, and these attitudes cannot be explained, using the ingenuous materialism characteristic of Marañón, by the "quantity of instincts" in one or the other type. In this way we would never manage to explain the observed cases of timid individuals who turn into Don Juans. . . . Deep inside the timid person, whether he be timid due to a deficiency or an excess of male traits, and also inside the Don Juan, there is always the same, very real sensation of insecurity and incompleteness.[222]

Marañón, both in his 1932 *Revista de Occidente* article and in the book-length biography, goes to some length to deny the assertions of Thibaudet, Leon Bopp, José de la Luz León and others who conceived of Amiel as a Don Juan. According to Marañón, Amiel is not a Don Juan for the following reasons:

(1) Amiel was characterized by a

> . . .fear of ridicule. . .when confronting women, each time that the imminence of sexual union approached. It was not the fear of physical failure possessed by the individual who is timid because of impotence, but precisely the fear of ridicule which characterizes the very differentiated man. Physical love requires an absolute inhibition of any criticism of the love act. It is evident that, especially for the male, this act is replete with critical moments, ones which are inevitably prosaic and sometimes touched with absurdity, if considered with cold reason instead of when under the influence of desire, which idealizes everything and stops at nothing.[223]

On the other hand, "The characteristic thing about Don Juan is precisely not being acquainted with this specific fear. . . ."[224]

(2) Amiel's love affairs lasted for long periods of time. Don Juan, as Zorrilla brilliantly describes, detains himself with one woman only for the briefest possible period of time.

(3) Don Juan is an expert "public relations" man. As Marañón ingeniously puts it: "during the day he intentionally and meticulously concerns himself with overwhelming other men in order to gather the submissive admiration of the females as a nocturnal reward. . .he plays with both sexes like a clever billiards player, caroming his ball off the man in order to hit the woman."[225] On the other hand: "The exact opposite occurs with Amiel, who was awkward, unpolished, not a sportsman, and without a single one of the external qualities

that would have attracted the attention of passersby when he walked along the streets of Geneva on the way to his class or during his Sunday strolls along the sunny banks of the lake."[226]

(4) The women that are attracted to Don Juan are sexually anonymous, undifferentiated. Amiel's women were perhaps not as flamboyant, pretty or well-dressed, but the love they expected from the Swiss professor was far from instinctual. On the contrary, "a Fanny, a Philine, or a Berta certainly did not expect to find sensual pleasure in Amiel, but rather consolation of the spirit, intelligence and protection."[227] Marañón claims Amiel's relationship with his lovers contains a slight analogue with the psychoanalyst and his patient.[228] More specifically, Amiel took the part of confessor, not in the mechanical sense, "like that of the perfunctory type who functions as guilt's mailbox,"[229] but in the "deeply human sense of an intimate unburdening of the conscience to a stronger conscience that is able to sympathize with and purge one's guilt. . . ."[230] This type of relationship demands:

> . . .for unalterable biological reasons, that the receiver be a profoundly virile man, and it is, therefore, a rigorously specific act. As a result, no one imagines that religious confessors could be women. And for this same reason, confession is an act of much greater transcendence and usefulness for women than for men. Confession is, then, basically an homage to the most exalted qualities of manhood, which are the sense of and capacity for justice and moral integrity.[231]

In conclusion, let us note that not only is it asserted that women are biologically unequipped to be confessors (or judges), but just as the notion of the noble malady of the ideal was redeemed, Marañón is here indicating that Amiel represents to some degree the archetype of the priest, a powerfully virile man with a superior constitution who maintains a disciplined celibacy for religious ideals. As a prominent Catholic liberal, Marañón is interested in justifying the priesthood on scientific grounds, very ingeniously interweaving arguments for denying women a place in the priesthood and for continuing to idealize the priest as a superior individual.

Oliver Brachfeld comes to the defense of those who characterize Amiel as a Don Juan, by applying Adlerian theory to the controversy. As we have seen, the idea of superior and inferior *tímidos* is rejected. All inferiority complexes are traced to the same fundamental disorder. On the other hand, Amiel and Don Juan represent two different behavioral reactions to the same disorder.

Amiel and *Don Juan* are simply the opposite poles of the same mental ailment, of the same unhealthy anxiety and fixed idea. They over-value the conquest of women, as in general they overvalued all phys-ical contact with them. Except that the reaction of one is to retreat from this overvalued figure, while the other believes he can prove his superiority to her—being incapable of desiring normal *equality* because of his feelings of inferiority—by scoring the maximum num-ber of victories: the record.

Amiel is the Don Juan *in nuce,* the Don Juan *en potencia;* he is the Don Juan who—if we are permitted to use a mathematical compar-ison—has a negative sign but the same numerical value. And Don Juan is the Amiel who, instead of compensating normally for his inhibition—which is a true psychic-mental defect—*overcompensates* by means of aboulia.

Muñoz Sanz, without the adherence to Adler that Oliver Brach-feld maintains, also rejects the notion of a *supertímido,* at least as personified by Amiel. Muñoz Sanz judges: "as far as Amiel's superior psyche is concerned, what we see is a neutralized virility rather than a sublimated one."[233] Concerning Marañón's own motivation in ex-alting Amiel, Muñoz Sanz waxes ironic:

Marañón's is a book which proves the possibility of sustaining a very debatable thesis by means of scientific talent, preparation and author-ity, even when what is concocted is an elegant and liberal utopia.

Thus, Marañón's subsequent interpretations combine abundant clinical data, exact psychological symptoms and delicate cosmic and mesological nuances in a single melting pot, and as a result we are given a myth. Marañón's is a veritable refining process, which uses adjectives as the precious metals for molding a new psychological type, the supervirile, timid individual—superdifferentiated—me-diocre, who is born—oh surprise!—out of the dust of a clay idol: Amiel.[234]

In sum, Muñoz Sanz judges that "Marañón's moralistic criterion takes precedence over his psychological or biological models."[235]

I am in agreement that Amiel is analyzed not for his own sake, but for an ethical yield. As an exercise in apologetics, *Amiel. Un estudio sobre la timidez* has an imaginative brilliance and is the pro-duct of a subtle, albeit superficial, synthesis of many disparate cur-rents: biology, psychoanalysis, socio-sexual education, religion, etc. One conclusion is that to sacrifice one's sexual instincts for an ideal is the mark of genuine biological manliness. Hence, the en-forced celibacy of the priest for a religious ideal and the unswerving loyalty toward one's wife of the industrious man lie on steadfast biological grounds. Also the torments and resentments of many *tímidos*, both "superior" and "typical," who suffer from sexual inhibition are redeemed. They should not envy and attempt to emulate the flamboyant rake, for the blessed meek are truly superior men. Finally, as we have seen, tightly woven into the narrative are a large number of observations and prescriptions concerning social and sexual education which strive to reconcile tradition and religious orthodoxy with certain psychological speculations relevant to child-rearing that were accepted as facts in the 1920s.

In conclusion, let us note that since the 1923 publication of unexpurgated fragments of the *Journal Intime,* emphasis has been preponderantly placed on diagnosing the personality of Amiel himself. As noted, Marañón's thesis is born out of reaction to the pathological studies before him. Likewise, F. Oliver Brachfeld and Muñoz Sanz form their theories out of reaction to Marañón. The line continues unabated: Clara Campoamor in her 1949 introduction to the Losada edition of the *Diario íntimo* rejects the hypothesis of timidity: "what is seen is misogyny: a fear of, or physical repulsion towards, women. . . ."[236] Oreste D'Aló terms Amiel an "intellectual prude."[237] Perhaps a fitting culmination to this situation occurs in a recent book, *Le journal intime* by Alain Girard. Here, the poor, harried author issues an amazing utterance capitulating to all the critics at once in a sweeping accession!

> All of these analyses are adequate, and each contains a large measure of truth. Whether the subject is tagged with the label of malady of the ideal, or whether one calls it aboulia, dissolution of the self, super-differentiated timidity, Oedipus complex, inability to love, or any other name, the malady suffered by Amiel all his life is one.[238]

Garcilaso de la Vega

Gregorio Marañón has three writings on Garcilaso. His first effort was an essay written while in exile in Paris in 1940, entitled "Garcilaso, natural de Toledo." This essay has been anthologized in *Elogio y nostalgia de Toledo.* The second essay, entitled "El destierro de Garcilaso de la Vega," was first published in *Finisterre* in 1948 and then anthologized in *Españoles fuera de España.* Both of the essays cover the same basic material: ambivalence in Garcilaso in reference to his poetry, exile and religious sentiments. Thus, there is much overlap between the essays, although the 1940 work focuses somewhat more on a general analysis of Garcilaso's personality, while that of 1948 dwells in more detail on Garcilaso's exile and the military episode in which he died. In addition to the above, in 1957 Marañón wrote a prologue to Antonio Gallego Morrell's *Antología poética en honor de Garcilaso de la Vega*, where he addresses himself to the historical factors influencing the attacks on Garcilaso by Cristóbal de Castillejo and other traditionalists.

In contrast to criteria such as morphological diagnoses or constructs involving instincts utilized by Marañón in earlier works, the analytic tool invoked here is ambivalence. In 1940, the same year as the publication of his first essay on Garcilaso, Marañón wrote an article in *Estampa*, Buenos Aires, describing ambivalence as he understood it. In this article, Marañón first describes the term as Bleuler (a disciple of Freud) designated it, ". . .that state in which two opposing tendencies act on the spirit and make it hesitate in its judgments and in its decisions."[239] However, Marañón, in a way characteristic of his classificatory, descriptive and judgmental approach, does not address himself to the dynamics of ambivalence as a psychological mechanism nor to the function of ambivalence. Rather, he compares ambivalence with doubt and univalence and associates these three terms with personality types, particularly in connection with a pleasurable or amorous situation. That Marañón uses ambivalence (as well as univalence and doubt) to describe personality styles is very clear in the following remarks:

> These three states of mind sum up all of the human types. It can be said that doubt occupies the central position between the other two. If the sense of doubt is very strong, it impedes action. If the sense of action is stronger than doubt, then the action is carried out. If the man of action is univalent, he will pursue two distinct goals with equal strength.

> When confronting any classification of mankind, the human spirit is apt to assign an intellectual or moral category to each group. Which one of these three types, then, is the best? . . .For effectiveness, the best is the resolute man. Intellectually, the best is the man who doubts. And morally, the best is, perhaps, the ambivalent man. Ambivalence actually indicates an abundance of love. To the ambivalent man everything agreeable seems deserving of his preference, and, in the same way, everything bad seems unworthy of his attention.[240]

Thus, doubt is associated with intellect, univalence with action and ambivalence with sensitivity and love. Marañón defines doubt as "a suspension of one's reasoning powers; an inhibition, therefore, of the spirit, from which timid acts or a complete paralysis of action will result."[241] Although the doctor does not mention Amiel, we would expect that the Swiss professor would well typify an extreme condition of doubt.

Univalence is the mark of the "resolute man" or the "one-dimensional personality." This type of individual, "faced with two paths which are open to him, with two possible objects of his pleasure or his love, neither hesitates nor pauses between the two but instead firmly chooses one of them."[242] Marañón judges Michelangelo, Lope de Vega, Titian and Beethoven to be examples of this type.

Finally, ambivalence is

> . . .a craving for all of the possibilities, because the soul finds all of them to be worthy of its time and its enthusiasm. . . . Therefore its perplexity does not arise from doubt but from anxiety. Other times the heart justifies one of the choices and the mind the other. This is extremely common; in the life of the ambivalent person the dissociation between emotion and reason is a frequent conflict.[243]

Personalities which exemplify ambivalence are Schubert, Bécquer, Chopin, and, of course, Garcilaso de la Vega.

Having defined ambivalence according to Marañón's usage, and having charted out its relationship to doubt and univalence, we are now in a position to survey this notion as applied to Garcilaso's *Primera égloga,* his attitude toward the *Comunidades* uprising and even to his religious feelings. Furthermore, as we shall see, when Marañón applies the concept of ambivalence to Garcilaso, he actually hypothesizes that two distinct, opposed and complimentary personalities reside in the soul of the poet.

In interpreting Garcilaso's *Primera égloga,* Marañón asserts that the poet's ambivalence is reflected in the "dynamics of his [Garcilaso's] multiple personality."[244] In real life, Marañón claims, Garcilaso solved what would have been a violent conflict between duty toward wife and children and love for Isabel Freyre, in a way completely natural and spontaneous to his "ambivalent soul." As Marañón puts it:

> He had his children by his wife, and the Portuguese woman provided him with his illusions. This coexistence of two feelings, which it is customary to consider as presenting an incompatible situation for the heart and for morality, is, however, perfectly natural in people of this psychological type. As a result, the obstacles which society and ethics set against the double attitude produce a deep disturbance in these individuals, for they naively interpret the criticisms of puritanical types as being unjust and arbitrary.[245]

Similarly, the oscillations of a multiple (in this case, double) personality are evident in the parallel and complementary laments of Salicio and Nemoroso. For a long time it was thought that Salicio spoke for the poet and that Nemoroso could possibly be "various other personalities, principally Fonseca, the husband, since Salicio complains harshly of the betrayal of Elisa (Isabel) just as Nemoroso, with infinite tenderness, laments her death."[246] Currently, no one doubts that Salicio and Nemoroso are one person, Garcilaso de la Vega, who, with two distinct names, evokes complementary feelings of love, jealousy and resentment, and mourning.[247] However, whereas "this license is not exceptional in pastoral poetry," in the case of Garcilaso, "the double personality assumed by the author has a deeper significance than that of a simple rhetorical device."[248] Marañón claims that Garcilaso, the ambivalent man par excellence, achieves a much deeper sincerity in his poetry than would result from a mere remote and exterior reconstruction of the husband's hypothetical feelings of sorrow upon the beloved's death. On the contrary, Garcilaso's powers of identification are so strong that he actually introjects the husband into his soul. Part of Garcilaso becomes the husband and dialogues with the resentful, abandoned lover. "The husband is introjected into the poet, and both express their tender discord over the same love, with the same anguish."[249] The concrete, esthetic result of the psychological processes of introjection and confrontation is the *Primera égloga,* a touching exposition of jealousy and despair that has always struck readers by its integrity and authenticity.

Marañón finds a similar "civil war in the soul"[250] in Garcilaso as a consequence of the uprising of the *Comunidades.* Writing in 1940, in exile in Paris, Marañón observes that,

> It is in civil wars that one-dimensional personalities discover a propitious environment, the normal result of which is fanaticism; this type of individual believes that he possesses the whole truth and, therefore, he is capable of fighting his own brother to the death. The latter, in turn, believes that truth is on his side. But the ability to identify with the antagonist's position, which the one-dimensional man is unable to do, is characteristic of the man of complex soul. The latter type is not necessarily neutral. He may serve the side which seems best to him with unequivocal loyalty, but he always reserves, deep within him, a touching and liberal indulgence toward those who fight against him.[251]

Marañón judges that Garcilaso fell into disfavor and was exiled for a short period by Carlos V because he witnessed and was party to a secret marriage that met with royal disfavor. The marriage between Garcilaso's nephew (whose father, Garcilaso's brother, had sided with the *Comuneros*) and Doña Isabel de la Cueva, the royalist, Duke of Alburquerque's niece, was interpreted—and rightly so—as a symbolic gesture of deference to the *Comuneros*. For this reason, Garcilaso was punished by the emperor:

> Garcilaso's gesture cannot only be interpreted as showing kindness and love for his brother. Both feelings would have been compatible with his absence at the wedding. If he went, it is because he was moved to do so by the element of truth that his anti-*Comunero* attitude conceded to the *Comuneros*. In sum, it was a liberal gesture. Salicio remained faithful to Carlos V, but Nemoroso received the *Comunero* with open arms.[252]

Although Garcilaso maintained a steadfast loyalty toward the emperor, he was imbued with a "generous inner ambivalence" that marks the superior individual. He could not help but be sensitive to and even introject the *Comunero* cause that divided the loyalty of his family.

Finally, although cautiously, Marañón detects a similar "fluctuation" in Garcilaso with respect to religious feeling. Garcilaso's lack of allusions (with one minor exception) to religious motifs is well-known. That Garcilaso was not a believer is difficult to conceive given his background and education. The lack of religious themes is explained by the fact that "All of Garcilaso's work was done in the flower of his youth and passion; that is, under conditions in which the soul is normally distracted from transcendental concerns."[253] On the other hand, Marañón judges it possible that Garcilaso may have been influenced by the religious turmoil of the period, noting that "Garcilaso and Juan de Valdés were friends, judging by a sentence of the latter in his *Diálogo de la Lengua,* although we cannot judge the extent of their relationship."[254] In addition, two of Garcilaso's Italian friends, Jerónimo Seripando and Mario Galeoto, were involved in religious questions.[255] Seripando attempted to reconcile orthodox Catholicism with a reforming spirit and Galeoto, to whom Garcilaso dedicated his Sonnet XXXV, was at a later date jailed by the Inquisition. Marañón concludes: "It is, then, possible that his religious faith also had its Salicio and its Nemoroso. But this is merely conjecture."[256]

Nevertheless, Marañón explains some of the attacks on Garcilaso by Cristóbal de Castillejo and other kindred, traditionalist spirits as reflecting "politico-religious motives."[257] Marañón points to the tremendous hostility between "*Comuneros* and supporters of the imperium, or advocates of the feudal caste system and Europeanists."[258] Garcilaso, because he was loyal to the emperor while his brother was one of the leaders of the *Comunero* faction in Toledo, was a notable and resented figure. Nor was his theme of "pagan love" accepted by the traditionalists who suspected him of heterodoxy, as evidenced by Cristóbal de Castillejo's demand that Garcilaso be investigated by the Inquisition.

Francisco de Quevedo

Marañón's several writings on Quevedo[259] all pertain to what the doctor has termed the "legend of Quevedo," the tale that Quevedo was imprisoned for having slipped satirical verses under the dinner napkin or plate of king Felipe IV. Marañón's interest in the matter is connected with his evaluation of the Conde-Duque de Olivares. The biography of the Conde-Duque, as are the other biographies by Marañón, is motivated by a desire to puncture myths and clarify fixed, negative assumptions. In the specific instance of the Conde-Duque, Marañón desires a "revindication of Felipe IV's great and unfortunate minister. . . ."[260] Dámaso Alonso, pointing to Marañón's goal of revindicating Olivares, while not denying the plausibility of the doctor's hypothesis about the Quevedo incident, judges that it displays "the partial sympathy towards Olivares with which [Marañón] judges Quevedo."[261] Marañón, in the third edition of the biography of Olivares, answers: ". . .I wish to object that none of my arguments has been refuted, and that this idea of mine about the imprisonment of the great poet not only was prior to my interest in the Conde-Duque, but it was also one of the factors that moved me to study Felipe IV's minister in depth."[262]

Whatever the case may be, Marañón's interpretation of the incident, which is found in all of his writings on Quevedo, points to the personal role of the king in Quevedo's imprisonment. Without entering into the details, let us summarize the interpretation: Marañón considers that Quevedo has been idealized by the legend of a hero who perceives the mounting administrative corruption in Spain and boldly lets the king know about it through the stratagem of satirical verses. ". . .the legend has arisen from this: Quevedo valiantly dares to tell the King the truth and the latter and his favorite, infuriated, order him to be exiled."[263] However, to idealize Quevedo in such a way is to falsify the facts, inasmuch as the poet, at least through 1636 (Quevedo was imprisoned in 1639), had an excellent relationship with the Conde-Duque maintained by his constant and

143

Francisco de Quevedo

insistent adulation of the *Valido*. For example, Marañón says of Quevedo's comedia *Como ha de ser el privado* (1627),

> . . .it is such a cynical defense of Olivares, that it produces an anti-pathetic reaction on the part of the reader. One by one [Quevedo] defends him against the same charges that a short time later he was to hurl against the minister. It is impossible to explain, without grave damage to Quevedo's dignity, how the author of this play could later be the enemy of his idol. Without a doubt, it was for this reason that he arranged for the play to disappear, and it has remained hidden for three hundred years. It is extremely interesting to read it as a docu-ment, but not as a literary work, for as the latter, it could not be more mediocre.[264]

Moreover, during this period when tremendously accusatory and very concrete satires were circulating around the court, even suppos-ing the "childish action" or "prank" that has been attributed to Que-vedo, it would never have merited such a harsh punishment as several years in prison. Marañón cites evidence to the effect that Quevedo was punished for maintaining some sort of contact with the agents of Richelieu. That the king, personally, ordered Quevedo punished is implied by, among other things, the fact that when Don Juan Chu-macero asked for Quevedo's pardon in January 1643, after the fall of Olivares, it was still denied until June. Once liberated, Quevedo asked for an audience with the king and was denied. On the other hand, all of Olivares' enemies "were immediately freed and reassured with a pardon or with new favors. . . ."[265]

Benito Pérez Galdós

Marañón has several writings on Galdós,[266] all of which are rem-iniscences, evoking the novelist as Marañón saw him as a child and later as a physician. Marañón was in attendance at the time of Gal-dós' death. On several occasions, Marañón treats Galdós' friend-ship with Menéndez Pelayo, an admirable relationship, Marañón judges, forged in spite of ideological differences. We shall discuss this aspect of Galdós in more detail in our treatment of Menéndez Pelayo. Here we shall confine ourselves to a survey of Marañón's evocations of Galdós.

"Galdós íntimo," originally published in *El Liberal* in 1920, shortly after Galdós' death, reveals the writer's lightheartedness and childishness during his last months. In turn, Marañón is stimulated to recall how, as a child, he viewed the novelist's reticence and re-straint in the world of letters as compared to his spontaneity with children or ordinary people. In addition, Marañón recalls Galdós' interest in and talent for art, which led him to do some illustrations for the *Episodios Nacionales.*

"Un profeta de España" in *Raíz y decoro de España* (1933) draws parallels between Galdós' philosophy of history (as articulated shortly before his death) and the ferment of Republican Spain in 1933. Marañón judges that the Republic represents not the destruction of Spain as some believe, nor a utopian hope, but a new, yet-unknown phase of Spanish history, replete with the typical tremors and dislocations involved in the readjustment of national institutions. Marañón claims that Galdós was party to the same general phenomenon several times, and this partially explains the continued publication of the *Episodios Nacionales.* In one of his last insights, Galdós told Marañón:

> On three occasions I have thought I was finished with my history of Spain. The last time was when my life had no more to give. I always believed that a stage of Spanish life had ended, and I was always obliged to resume my history. Because, in history, today's flower is the seed of the future. Because today's existence is the same as that of the past and the same as always. Living with the awareness that one is alive is no more than repeating the past and dreaming of the future.[267]

The passage is applied to current events to the effect that the Spanish Republic is not an iconoclastic rupture with the past but a link in the great chain of historical evolution.

"Galdós en Toledo," published in *Elogio y nostalgia de Toledo* (1941), is the result of several articles on Galdós published in *La Nación* in 1940. In this nostalgic essay, Marañón evokes topics and memories such as Galdós' relationship with his secretary, José Hurtado de Mendoza (rather like Feijoo's relationship to Sarmiento, the "luminary" and his "shadow" or "double"), Galdós' deep, nonceremonious sense of religion, his affability with the nuns in Toledo, his walks and visits through the medieval city, his discussions with Manuel B. Cossío and his ambivalence toward El Greco. (Galdós was somewhat affronted by El Greco's disregard of the classical norms of proportion.)

The article, "Aparece en Inglaterra la traducción de una novela de Galdós," published in *Efemérides y comentarios,* nominally a discussion of the English translation of *La de Bringas,* continues the nostalgic vein, focusing on Galdós as a man of the people, who if he had any affectation at all, "one could say that it corresponded to a fully executed attempt on his part to be the prototype of the common man."[268]

The Generation of 1898

Marañón has written a good deal about the significance of the Generation of 1898. His basic position is that the critics have forgotten that the Generation of 1898, besides realizing a literary, philosophical, ethical and existential renewal in Spain, also accomplished a political and above all, scientific renewal.[269] Marañón finds it an object of reproach that "the commentators of the Generation of 1898. . .absorbed in their interest in its literary aspect, forget what is most important: its scientific influence."[270] Such considerations lead Marañón to the judgment that a figure like Santiago Ramón y Cajal represents not a precursor of the Generation of 1898 as most critics would represent him, but rather "because of his age, his political and social concerns, the particular tone of his Hispanicism, his literature, and the nature of his scientific work, he is, perhaps, the purest representative of the Generation of 1898."[271] However, we shall reserve further considerations of the Generation of 1898 in its scientific aspects as well as Cajal's relationship to the Generation for a later, more penetrating appraisal in our survey of Marañón's general tracing of the growth of an experimental methodology in Spain. In this section, I shall merely survey Marañón's writings on the figures which have more conventionally been considered *noventayochistas*: Unamuno, Baroja, Azorín and the Machado brothers.

Virtually all of Marañón's writings on the above figures are occasional literature: speeches commemorating an entrance into the Real Academia, newspaper articles inspired by the publication of a new book, evocations, necrologies and the like. Thus, Marañón's opinions and judgments in this area are interesting and valuable, not because they apply any particular methodological or critical approach, but rather because they are spontaneous, subjective impressions that reflect his personal relationship with several major figures of the Generation of 1898.

Marañón has several articles on Unamuno.[272] In 1930, in a very brief, virulent statement, he defended Unamuno from certain "stunted spirits," "worms" and "cockroaches" suffering from "mental nearsightedness" who, taking advantage of the fact that Unamuno was in exile, were maligning him. In 1955, Marañón wrote an article on Unamuno's life in France during exile (1924-1930). Shortly after

Unamuno's death, Marañón wrote three articles paying homage to the philosopher. His tone is rather apologetic, particularly with respect to Unamuno's religious attitudes. In one article, he claims that Unamuno was "a vigorous, pure and religious man."[273] In another article, he asserts that Unamuno's "mysticism defended him against the Spanish rightists, which was the supreme paradox of his life, but at the same time a repetition of what always happened to all Spanish mystics."[274] It is typical for Marañón to "apologize" for figures whom he admired yet whose orthodoxy was in question. The doctor takes a similar stand toward Roberto Novoa Santos.

Among Marañón's writings on Pío Baroja,[275] we have the reception speech accepting the Basque novelist into the Real Academia Española. Under the rubric of justifying Pío Baroja's acceptance of membership in the Academy, he arrives at some penetrating observations about the novelist and his use of language. Marañón quotes the following statement by Baroja on the relationship between spirit and style:

> I think that what must happen here is similar to what happens in a portrait, which is better as a portrait (not as an artistic work) the more it resembles what is depicted, and not the prettier it is. Thus, the simple, humble and careless man will achieve perfection in a simple, humble and careless style, and the rhetorical, high sounding and Gongoristic man in a rhetorical, high sounding and Gongoristic style. Let the tall man look tall, the thin man, thin, and the hunchback, hunchbacked. This is as it should be. The cosmetic altering of snub noses is all right for beauty institutes and other places specializing in esthetic farces, but not for style.[276]

Marañón considers the above passage to be the key to the novelist's literary esthetic and, in part, to his psychology. It is evident that, for Marañón, Baroja is that one and the same "simple, humble and careless man" that he described, and his excellence as a writer stems from his capacity to project his spirit with a proper style devoid of "theatrical, manipulated and insincere exploits which are later related to us by historians as if they were real events. . . ."[277] He confides that upon reading some of Baroja's criticism of Galdós, he would close the book in ill humor. Yet on further reflection, he realized that,

> In each of Pérez Galdós' novels there is a thwarted dramatic work; in several that were later performed. . .the dialogue is the same as in the original version. It is a dialogue that was meant to be spoken on stage when it was written; the same thing could have occurred with the rest of the novels. Baroja, on the other hand, is essentially antitheatrical

and in the human, genuine account that he presents in his books it is precisely in the dialogue that he achieves his greatest precision and realism.[278]

Baroja's world, Baroja's dialogues, partake of an exactitude undistorted by theatrical artifices. The detail is so fine that even the "irregularities" [*incorrecciones*] are captured. Of course, most of these "irregularities" will be, at a later date, standard Spanish, since, "popular speech, fortunately, is always in the vanguard of literary language."[279]

Marañón rejects the associating of Baroja's work with the picaresque novel. The doctor has a deep repugnance for the picaresque based on moral grounds. He judges that the moral of the picaresque novel reflects the profound cynicism of the historical epoch in which it was written. Since it expresses a justification of wrongdoing, it is a menace:

> The appalling thing about this literature is the fact that it adorns all types of villainy—robbery, fraud, the failure to keep one's word and other crimes—with such a subtle charm that it excuses everything and ends up justifying everything. It is obvious that one can be a scoundrel while still possessing a certain skill that induces others to pardon one's roguery. But in the picaresque novel, the rogue is something more than a likeable rascal: he is always the intelligent, clever, witty protagonist, before whom all obstacles vanish; in sum, he is the hero.[280]

On the other hand, Baroja describes these

> . . .same fringes of Spanish society that served as the landscape for our rogues; but he does it in a sense that is not, perhaps, optimistic but implacably honest. None of his shadowy characters show signs of heroism, none triumph in life or die tranquilly in bed, the victor over a good-hearted, simple soul by means of his roguery, which is what always happens in the picaresque novel. Baroja's work is sad, but it is frequently exemplary.[281]

In addition, Marañón rejects Pío Baroja's claim that the Generation of 1898 did not really exist as such. He proceeds to outline his theory of what a "generation" constitutes. It is not a group of persons born during the same period partaking in a determined, common enterprise. Rather, it is the consequence of implacable historical, cultural, and above all, biological factors that determine the peculiarities of a given nation during a given period. "A generation is simply a section of humanity which, when first seen from a distance, appears to be defined by a certain number of outstanding figures, who stand out like the sections of the sea that are delimited by high reefs."[282]

The most representative individuals in the nation during this period symbolize the so called "generation":

> The simple, biological fact of the contemporaneous existence of a few representative men, this alone, imprints a particular character on the life of their time, a character that they symbolize without being aware of it. And frequently, without their intending it, a radical change in the course of human events results from their moment. The fateful, historical aspect of this enterprise, in its deep biological sense—that is, what is independent of the deliberate intention of those who represent it—causes them to not be exactly aware of it. For this reason, sometimes it is the very representatives of it [the generation] who deny its existence with the utmost sincerity.[283]

In addition to the reception speech, Marañón has written "Baroja," an article published in *Hoy*, Mexico City, in 1937, composed under the stimulus of Baroja's return to Spain after a brief exile. Here Marañón judges the Basque novelist's three basic attributes to be: 1) His love for humble and ordinary people; 2) His bittersweet humor; 3) His love for adventure and romance. In this article, Marañón makes a rather inaccurate prophecy—that, of Baroja, Azorín and Valle-Inclán, it will be the latter "whose mark on Hispanic thought will be erased most quickly."[284]

The article "Pío Baroja vuelve a su casa de Vera," published in *Efemérides y comentarios,* recalls a visit that Marañón, Julio Caro Baroja (the novelist's nephew) and others paid to Baroja at his summer home in Navarra.

In a manner similar to his praise of Baroja, Marañón claims in a lecture given in 1941, "Sobre Azorín," that Azorín has taught Spain two things: "the lesson of simplicity and that of curiosity."[285] Particularly interesting are Marañón's comments on Azorín's style which he feels is very instructive for the scientist:

> The scientific writer, above all. . .learned about precision and responsibility in language from Azorín's prose. These qualities are necessary for describing what the naturalist observes or what the thinker intuits. When Azorín depicts a landscape or a human being there is an echo of the man of science, an echo of what is best and most enduring in the naturalist's work. In his first books, the pleasure with which he describes an insect or an old woman in mourning, or the humble interior of a village house, reminds one of a naturalist who, fortunately for us all, missed his calling.[286]

Thus, for Marañón, Azorín represents, as does Cajal, the application of "a different, precise, exact, diaphanous language"[287] in order to come to terms with the circumstances of modern life. Azorín and Cajal helped to bring down the rhetoric characteristic of the period immediately before them, which impeded the communication of genuine emotion and, above all, hindered clarity of expression and therefore was a grave drawback to both science and scholarship.

In an article in *Efemérides y comentarios* entitled "Cumpleaños de Azorín," Marañón celebrates the occasion with superlative praise for Azorín's *Don Juan*. One of the reasons for Marañón's prophecy that the novel of the future will be like Azorín's is that in this interpretation of Don Juan there is completely lacking a rebellious or demonic component. Marañón applauds this fact, although at the same time conceding "Azorín's almost seraphic interpretation had never appeared before."[288] He concludes:

> The demonic element seemed to be the indispensable component of the *Burlador*. But here Azorín's Don Juan, who is a genuine Don Juan, is presented as an angel. . . . Azorín's discovery is that his Don Juan, and probably others, loved his fellow creatures; and he loved women who were in need of loving out of sheer goodness, almost out of charity, and not because of any lustful impulse.[289]

Other various writings

In addition to the titles surveyed under the various headings that we have established, there are a large number of single, occasional writings that Marañón has penned. I shall briefly mention the most notable of these. In addition to the aforementioned reception speech for Pío Baroja, Marañón also gave the speeches welcoming Pedro Laín Entralgo (1954) and Camilo José Cela (1957) into the Real Academia.[290] In the former speech, Marañón surveys and pays homage to Laín Entralgo's *La generación de 1898, Historia de la medicina* and *La antropología en la obra de Fray Luis de Granada*. In the latter speech, Marañón focuses on Cela's "travel books" (Marañón was an avid reader and great collector of this genre), going so far as to place the *Nuevas andanzas y desventuras de Lazarillo de Tormes* within that category. In addition to the speech, Marañón also prologues the fourth edition of *La familia de Pascual Duarte*, commenting, among other things, on the phenomenal popularity of the book as well as the meaning of human (as opposed to divine) justice.

Among the lectures, we have one on Rubén Darío, filled with reminiscences and intimate anecdotes, in which Marañón discusses the often egotistic intercourse between Darío and Spanish figures such as Unamuno and Baroja; also there is a lecture paying homage to Maurice Legendre.[291]

Biographies of Artists and Writers

Among the articles are short compositions on Arniches, Casona, Salaverría, Emilio Castelar, Ortega y Gasset, Astrana Marín and others.[292] In addition, Marañón wrote a number of articles on French figures of prominence: Descartes, Victor Hugo, Cocteau and Paul Valéry.[293] Prologues on literary topics that ought to be mentioned include the introduction to books by André Gide, Gabriel Miró, Sta. Teresa, Francisco de Icaza, *Clarín,* Lope de Vega and others.[294]

V

BIOGRAPHICAL HISTORY OF THE EXPERIMENTAL, INDUCTIVE CONSCIOUSNESS IN SPAIN

Marañón and the "problem" of Spanish science

Marañón's chronicle of the development of Spanish science as well as of a corresponding empirical, naturalistic philosophy is, in terms of its motivation, partially a response to several virulent polemics concerning the nature and goals of Spain. Specifically, Marañón's survey of Spanish science is framed by an earlier polemic, described by him as taking place between the *krausistas* (e.g., Azcárate) and the *tradicionalistas* (e.g., Menéndez Pelayo),[1] over the relative worth of Spain's contribution to Western science from the sixteenth century to the present. In addition, Marañón's history reflects his position within the political-cultural-scientific controversy, current in his generation, over the need to Europeanize Spain (or vice versa, the need to Hispanicize Europe).

Pedro Laín Entralgo, in his *España como problema,* notes the relevance of programmatic Europeanization for Marañón's generation. While this notion became frequently expressed around the turn of the century by men such as Joaquín Costa and, in his early phase, Miguel de Unamuno, in reality, "those Spaniards were not intimately familiar with Europe: they knew a lot of literature, a little philosophy, some theology, in Unamuno's case, and very little positivist science. Basically, they were provincial readers, but not truly knowledgeable about Europe."[2] Without concerning ourselves with the absoluteness of Laín's statement about the Generation of 1898's total understanding of Europe, we readily agree with him that, at least with respect to science, the situation begins to change around 1905 with the appearance in Spain of a generation of thinkers, theoreticians and scientists who had achieved at least part of their intellectual and professional formation in European universities. This is the generation of Ortega y Gasset, Eugenio d'Ors, Ramón Pérez de Ayala, Américo Castro, Salvador de Madariaga, Julio Rey Pastor and Gregorio Marañón.

In 1906, Ortega y Gasset, the main public advocate of the concerns of this generation, laments the fact that there is no "disciplined science"—science in Spain is a product of exceptional individuals—"monoliths. . .wholly formed beings who are born without precursors, by spontaneous generation. . . ."[3] In contrast to Germany, science here is "a very personal event and not a social action."[4] Ortega's conclusion is bleak:

> Our science, therefore, will always be undisciplined, and as such, showy and daring; it will attain certainty by leaps and not step by step; at one moment it will get its wanderings in step with universal science, and then it will remain behind for centuries. Spanish science has always been barbaric, mystical and errant, and I presume that it will remain so.[5]

In 1908, however, Ortega casts his lot with pedagogical reform, asserting that the problem of Spanish science can be solved by education (which is associated with Europeanization):

> The Spanish problem is, certainly, a pedagogical problem; but what is genuine and characteristic about our pedagogical problem is that we first need to educate a few men of science, to awaken even a glimmer of scientific concern. Without this previous labor, the rest of our pedagogical action will be futile, impossible, without meaning. I think that something analogous to what I am saying might be the exact formula for Europeanization.

He pleads that young Spaniards be given the opportunity to prove themselves in science:

> There is no science in Spain, but there are a good number of fervent young men who are ready to dedicate their lives to scientific endeavor. . . .It is necessary to make life and work possible for them. . . . They only wish to live modestly, but nevertheless adequately and independently; they only wish to be granted the tools of their profession: teachers, libraries, travel grants, laboratories, archive service, protection of publications.[7]

In conclusion: "If we believe that Europe is 'ciencia,' we shall have to symbolize Spain by 'inconsciencia';"[8] the way to make Spain more European is to educate her so as to elevate her from a state of inconsciencia to ciencia.

The "Problem" of Spanish Science

During these same years, Marañón was actually practicing science in the same manner advocated by Ortega, in 1908 receiving the Martínez Molina prize, which had been withheld since Ramón y Cajal had won it, and in 1910 earning his *doctorado* in Medicine with honors. Marañón left at once for Germany to continue his studies under the direction of Paul Ehrlich, one of the initiators of modern medical chemistry. In that same year, Ehrlich perfected salvarsan (606), a drug extremely effective in combating syphilis. Marañón's first book, *Quemoterapía moderna según Ehrlich. Tratamiento de la sífilis por el 606*,[9] introduced Ehrlich's techniques into Spain. Marañón was never to abandon his role as publicizer of European science in Spain nor his efforts for educational reform in the sciences and, above all, medicine, in terms comparable with Ortega y Gasset.

Yet, Ortega and Marañón occupy extreme positions within the same reforming, Europeanizing movement. Ortega, from the first, almost in his adolescence, took the position of radical and iconoclast, gibing figures like Unamuno, Joaquín Costa and Cánovas del Castillo, whom Marañón greatly admired as an historian. Ortega treats the *Restauración* after the first Spanish Republic (1874) with, as Laín puts it, "a merciless analysis."[10] With respect to politics, Ortega refers to the *Restauración* with terms like "senility," "disintegration," "behavior of ghosts." Ortega is particularly hard on Cánovas: "The *Restauracion*, gentlemen, was a panorama of ghosts, and Cánovas was, gentlemen, a great corruptor; or as we would say now, a professor of corruption."[11]

On the other hand, Marañón did not enter the political aspect of the movement for renewal and Europeanization until a much later date, after he had accomplished a sizable amount of theoretical research in endocrinology and physiology. In 1920, he published his first major non-medical essay, advocating women's suffrage.[12] Also, in the same year, Marañón criticized the Spanish government's debarment of foreign physicians.[13]

Furthermore, Marañón was sentimentally and affectively, although not intellectually, tied to the nineteenth century, to figures like Galdós, Menéndez Pelayo, Cánovas del Castillo, even Campoamor, of whom he claims in his speech receiving Cela into the Real Academia, "I like the same Campoamor whom Cela abhors; and I like him precisely because simple, common people understand his verses well, people who also deserve their ration of poetry and who naturally cannot understand that of the surrealist poets."[14] A clear example of Marañón's nostalgia and affinity toward these figures appears in "Aquella España." Speaking of the *Restauración*, he observes:

> . . .within that isolation, and a tone of modest provincialism which was permeating the entire nation, it can be assured that the soul of a people has seldom achieved such plenitude, such a profound fulfilment of what it should be. . . . Perhaps there was nothing of extraordinary greatness in the Spain of that time. But there were many things of discreet dimensions, necessary for the normal flow of existence, which were no doubt perfect.[15]

In the following, the doctor glorifies *casticismo*:

> There were, in short, universal men like Menéndez y Pelayo, who was not inclined toward any school or tendency aside from his integral Catholicism. Nevertheless, by his very universality he was profoundly Spanish. Then as always this paradox presents itself: the truly universal men are the most radically *castizos,* just as those who make a profession of being citizens of the universe are really small-town folk.[16]

Julián Marías has well captured the spirit of Marañón within the movement toward Europeanization: "Marañón was, of course, a man 'of the past,' but he had not stayed behind 'in the past.' For that reason he was a builder, always ready to bridge gaps, just as he had neither the time nor the disposition to 'pontificate.' At one and the same time he had avoided insularity and mummification."[17]

In Marañón's history of Spanish science, there is an insistent defensiveness, and this aspect is fundamentally attributable to the doctor's response to very strong pressures, not only upon him, but within him. This is quite evident in his attempt to apologize for Menéndez Pelayo. On the one hand, he harshly criticizes the poligrapher's *La ciencia española* as a basically politically-oriented pamphlet against the *krausistas*; on the other, he exalts Menéndez Pelayo personally as an example for Spanish science. Similarly, but on the anticlerical side of the polemic, Marañón apologizes for Ramón y Cajal's pointing to religious intolerance as a cause (among many) of Spanish scientific backwardness, claiming it was endemic to Cajal's intellectual milieu and, therefore, not really intensely felt. In other words, merely an anticlerical convention. At the same time, he defends Cajal's right, and even duty as a Spanish intellectual and patriot, to make such pronouncements. As we shall see, Marañón engages in polemic with relish, but he rarely sets out to "hurt" anyone. His attitude is defensive; his goal is to rise "above" the conflict, his need: to identify, from the past, individuals like himself who succeeded in achieving a scientific orientation without relinquishing their identity as *hombres castizos.*

As a Catholic scientist and intellectual, as a constant advocate of Spanish science and of reform, on several occasions Marañón came into sharp contact with conservative elements. He responded to these pressures with deference, with a tactical sagacity and with an impassioned defense, often in the same essay, lecture or prologue, joined in a subtle, ambivalent fusion. He was a highly effective introducer of scientific literature into Spain. Among his prologues are introductions to books by Iwan Block, Pavlov and Malinowski.[18] His prologue to Malinowski, "Notas a un libro de antropología sexual," is a eulogy to the sexual habits of Melanesia. Wistfully, the clinician notes the superiority of the islanders in terms of morality by comparing their mental health with the sexual aberrations inherent in Western life:

> . . .there is one sure indication of their superiority, which Malinowski later dwells upon: sexual perversions do not exist among the inhabitants of these islands. Onanism, sadism, homosexuality, and bestiality are hardly known; they are not plagues, as they are among us, but rather sporadic and very rare diseases which only affect some degenerate individuals.[19]

Moreoever, Marañón was not only a bearer and publicizer of foreign theoretical and scientific thought in Spain, he often was obliged, by virtue of his role as clinician and naturalist, to effect moral decisions. As I have earlier stated, among other issues, he actively campaigned for women's rights to vote and to be gainfully employed. Later in this chapter, in dealing with Feijoo, I shall survey his arguments for artificial insemination, which, in view of the conventional premise of the period of a "maternity instinct," are a model of scientific as well as common sense. Nevertheless, the conclusion the doctor arrives at runs counter to traditional Spanish ethics.

Primarily due to his role as innovator and publicizer of scientific advances and theories, Marañón was extremely sensitive to criticism. As we have seen, he habitually assumed the role of public defender: protecting Enrique IV from the charge of impotence, El Greco from the accusation of insanity, Amiel from pathological diagnoses, etc. Here, however, the charges that Marañón addresses himself to, against figures such as Vives, Feijoo and Cajal, are basically a lack of patriotism and irreligiosity—charges that were directed at times toward Marañón himself.[20]

The defensive stance becomes even more exacerbated in a book like *Españoles fuera de España,* reflecting Marañón's response to the criticism which he received due to his switching of allegiance from Republican to Franco Spain as espoused in *Liberalismo y comunismo,* a pamphlet that his political antagonists have claimed served as a sort of passport back to Spain for the exiled physician.[21]

It is my observation that Marañón's chronicle of Spanish science, while polemical and combative, reflects a process of projection and identification. He projects into the past and "solves" in the past the polemics engaging him in the present. Often, it is perfectly legitimate to operate in such a fashion, for the causes of Spain's backwardness in science have a longstanding history. Similarly, Marañón is motivated to seek in the Spanish past the roots of his professional identity, particularly the environmental and psychological elements of that identity. For example, his identification with Feijoo's struggle to establish self-confidence through science and experimentalism, while filled with doubts and premonitions, is not only movingly described by Marañón, but exemplified as an object lesson in the eternal struggle between reason and superstition in the psyche. As we shall see, this projection of scientific-moral issues of the present into the past and the identification of (and with) the great, isolated scientific figures in Spanish history leads to sound, concrete results when conducted on a sophisticated basis, with proper qualifications and reserve, and where there is an actual situational concordance between past and present. The outstanding example is *Las ideas biológicas del Padre Feijoo.* Other works, such as the articles on Luis Vives and Menéndez Pelayo, are less valuable for they are less formal, less well-researched, more subjective and self-serving, more commemorative and rhetorical.

Pedro Laín Entralgo, in his article on Spanish science for the *Diccionario de historia de España* (*Revista de Occidente*), subsequently published in *España como problema,* summarizes the position of the most important evaluators of the "problem" of Spanish science since the 1876-1878 polemic between *progresistas* and *tradicionalistas*: Cajal, Unamuno, Ortega, Américo Castro and Gregorio Marañón.

The positions of Unamuno (in his later phase) and Américo Castro, both of whom balanced Spain's great artistic achievements in a compensatory manner with her scientific paucity, find only minor, remote and infrequent echoes in Marañón's writing. This is to be expected, for Marañón, as a scientist, was sensitive to the implication in their arguments that, for historical reasons, the Spaniard was incapable of scientific research. Laín summarizes the implication of Américo Castro's thesis:

> The peculiarity of the Spanish Middle Ages—eight centuries of life set in the future, of living together with Arabs and Jews—would have made genuine Spaniards inacapable of the vigorous reliance on present reality demanded by science. The Spaniard would see the world more according to what he and the world "can be" than according to what one and the other "are."[22]

Marañón did not accept any implication that Spain was permanently restricted from scientific expertise, but rather, he consistently advocated that an energetic educational drive and plentiful economic funds would rehabilitate Spanish science.

Ramón y Cajal, in his well-known *Reglas y consejos para la investigación científica* (1897), after reviewing various explanations for Spain's modest scientific achievement, concludes: 1) Spanish science has not produced a notable number of contributions, not because of any racial or geographic reason, but because of historical circumstances. Thus, with proper education, the Spanish scientific dilemma can be overcome. 2) The basic cause (aided by circumstances such as the Inquisition, an aristocratic disdain for mechanical work, etc.) for the paucity is Spain's intellectual isolation which she imposed upon herself as a consequence of the Counter Reformation.[23] Marañón wholeheartedly embraces both of these points, although he criticizes Cajal for what he judges to be an over-evaluation of the role of the Inquisition in the paucity of Spanish science. (See p. 171 and p. 212.) Ortega y Gasset, as we have seen, is in this same line and Marañón quotes approvingly Ortega's assertion that Cajal's triumphs are not able to signify "a source of pride for our country: they are rather an embarrassment because they are accidents."[24] The above statement by Ortega provides us with one of the keys to Marañón's approach to the biography of Spanish scientists. With respect to Spanish history, Marañón strove to refute any apology for Spanish science. As we shall see, Marañón was led to vigorously attack both Menéndez Pelayo's attempt to glorify Spanish scientific achievement and the *leyenda negra* notion entailing an European misrepresentation of Spanish science as a part of the general, bigoted attack on Spain that was initiated in Protestant countries as a consequence of religious strife. On the contrary, Marañón purports to demonstrate that the great Spanish scientists were outstanding figures who sagaciously imposed their scientific genius on an environment either devoid of encouragement or actively hostile to them.

Marañón's vision of the history of Spanish science emerges, not quite as "monolithically" and isolated as Ortega would have us believe, but rather, romantically and dramatically, as a succession of illustrious figures, a select minority, handing down the light of an experimental consciousness from age to age, burdened with the immense charge of maintaining reason and objectivity in a sea of superstition.

Huarte de San Juan and Luis Vives

Two of these illustrious figures who accomplished pioneering scientific work, far in advance of their time, are Huarte de San Juan and Luis Vives. In 1933, Marañón gave a lecture at the Ateneo de Pamplona, "Notas sobre Huarte," published that same year in *Cultura Navarra* and in *Cruz y Raya* and subsequently, in 1940, in *Tiempo viejo y tiempo nuevo* with the title "Juan de Dios Huarte (Examen actual de un examen antiguo)."[25] Marañón comments on the notable events in Huarte's life and surveys some of the physician's theories in his *Examen de ingenios,* particularly pointing out their relevance to contemporary science. For Marañón, one of Huarte's major achievements was his ability to transcend his university background and education (Huarte attended the University of Huesca) so that he was able to advance a step beyond the theological, abstract, authoritarian approach to medicine and science. While Marañón observes that even in Huarte's work the abstract predominates over the naturalistic and the "biology of observation"[26] is hidden within "the tangled jungle of the theological and philosophical concepts of his time,"[27] nevertheless, behind all of this is an admirable talent for naturalistic observation and a "sure biological instinct."[28]

Huarte's *Examen de ingenios* starts out from the traditional theory of the four temperaments—choleric, melancholic, phlegmatic and sanguine. Arturo Farinelli, in his study, *Dos excéntricos: Cristóbal de Villalón—El Dr. Juan Huarte,* argues, as does Marañón, that the emphasis is on naturalistic observation, once the traditional theoretical explanation is accepted. "Just as his [Huarte's] spirit, all clarity and concision, rejects any metaphysical thesis. . .he abstains from philosophizing on the primary elements of man's nature, which he accepts without discussion, as he accepts the theory of temperaments which he found in his course of investigation as proven and unquestionable."[29] Thus, the *Examen de ingenios* is primarily a practical manual, applying certain theories and speculations on different personality types to such matters as the criteria used for selecting a profession, philosophies of child rearing, types of behavior demonstrated at different ages, etc. In addition, Huarte attempts to educate his reader in evaluating a person's character from the peculiarities of his physique.

It is instructive to contrast the atttitude toward Huarte of Marañón, the medical scholar, with that of Farinelli, the scholar-philologist, particularly since both wrote their studies during the same period, although under vastly different political circumstances. Farinelli's study is colored by his apprehensions concerning the rise of Fascism in Italy and elsewhere. In general, Marañón finds much scientific substance in the *Examen de ingenios*, locating precedents for certain twentieth-century speculations on characterology, both individual and national. Farinelli is in general agreement with Marañón concerning the efficacy, for their time, of Huarte's methods and procedures:

> . . .the work as a whole resists the devastating effect of time through its method and its crystalline procedure of clarifying the truth and constructing, not with fantasy and conjecture, but rather with deep meditation, a system of science. It deserves to be placed among the best, most characteristic and original [works] produced by the Spanish genius in its best century.[30]

Nevertheless, concerning the details and substance, Farinelli is convinced of "the fallacious and worn-out nature of some of the fundamental doctrines of the *Examen*."[31]

Let us cite some examples of the divergent positions of Marañón and Farinelli. Marañón applauds Huarte's exposition of personality variations as a function of national background, climate and age. Indeed, Marañón's psychological-moral observations in "El deber de las edades" (1927), and "Los deberes olvidados" (1933) are notably similar to his interpretations of Huarte's speculations on the "proper" behavior of different age groups. According to Marañón, Huarte associates chastity, charity and humility with the child; malleability and passivity with the early adolescent; violence and rebellion with the young man; prudence, creativity, comprehension and tolerance with the mature adult; and wisdom with the senior adult.[32] In his own "El deber de las edades" a similar series appears, although in a tone more exhortational than speculative. Marañón concludes that "each age has a duty, as does each sex, and as does being a father or being a son. . . ."[33] Duty and morality are to be aligned once more with the natural requirements of the human organism. The foremost duty of the child is obedience; that of youth, rebellion; that of manhood, austerity; that of old age, adaptation. Here, in a sense, is the logical (or rather, biological) conclusion to the visionary *hombre de carne y hueso*! For allegedly, these prescriptions are derived, not from social or political contract, but from the natural constitution of man.

Farinelli, on the other hand, is utterly skeptical of such extrapolations by Huarte (and hence, by extension, of Marañón):

> . . .the theory of temperaments and humors, already developed in antiquity, which passed with few alterations to the doctors and other learned people of Huarte's time;. . .the idea that there are indications of our most intimate being and our individuality which can be perceived exclusively in the physical world, seems exceedingly fanciful and fallacious to me. However, such indications and signs were seen with clarity by the author of the *Examen,* in view of his new system, organized according to the variety of temperaments and abilities, a system which constitutes the axis and foundation of his doctrine.[34]

Furthermore, Farinelli is fearful of the racism inherent in any national or regional characterology.

Marañón is enthused with Huarte's attempt to correlate temperament with nation and region on the basis of differences in climate and customs.

> How are the uncomplicated Basque and the amiable Andalusian, or the sensual Catalonian and the lean, austere man of the two Castiles, supposed to be the same? The diversity of the sections that form our Spain is profound, biological; in this diversity is the reason for its perpetual restlessness and originality, but also the reason for its eternal reappearance in history and its irrevocable unity![35]

In the above paragraph, Marañón is partially responding to the politico-cultural demands of various regionalists during the Spanish Republic. Farinelli, in his apprehension, explicitly associates such psychologizing with fearful racist theories that had become prominent in the 1930s:

> . . .my natural disposition leads me neither to studies of psychological analysis nor of physiology harmonized with philosophy, nor to the acceptance of Huarte's dogmas and axioms as acquired truths and experiences. I am a decided enemy of the racial theories on man's spiritual make-up, and I consider the allotment of superiorities and virtues to be sick and demented. Such an allotment is . . . made with stupid arrogance by modern theorizers who presume to construct a scientific work in addition to manuals for perfecting the species.[36]

161

Similarly, Marañón applauds Huarte's judgments on the relationship of personality to physical appearance, gesture and dress. This is no surprise inasmuch as Marañón, in 1937, was to publish both *Psicología del gesto* and "Psicología del vestido y del adorno," where, despite the addition of relationships comparable to the work of Whilhelm Stekel (e.g., the sexual meaning of the shoe and the hat), ideas appear which are very similar to Huarte's speculations. Farinelli, on the other hand, considers as passé, as well as capricious, "all the credence granted to man's physical powers and the judgment on the thickness and color of the hair. . . ."[37] The contrast between the two critics is attributable not only to different professional and scholarly orientations and even to different political circumstances in Spain and Italy during the 1930s, but, in addition, points to Marañón's consistent tendency to select for evaluation those authors with whom he had a close affinity in terms of both personality and subject matter. He ranges through the Spanish scientific literature of the past seeking out and developing bonds and concordances, establishing a tradition in which he can situate himself.

Keeping in mind this zeal for seeking historical precursors in order to explain his own identity as a scientist in Spain, we are in a better position to comprehend Marañón's deeply emotional conclusion to his essay on Huarte:

> Huarte's book is an exceptional event in Spanish science. . . . And it is fitting that we should demonstrate that we, his brothers in science, continue to hear his voice in our restlessness before the mystery of life and in our inextinguishable faith in Spain.[38]

In 1940, Marañón wrote three articles for *La Nación* (Buenos Aires) on Luis Vives, commemorating the centenary of the Spanish thinker. In the same year, several other Spanish thinkers paid homage to Vives with their contributions, including Ortega y Gasset and Eugenio d'Ors. Marañón's initial 1940 articles are entitled "Gota y humor del maestro," "Teoría de la sobriedad," and "El intelectual desterrado."[39] These three articles, with slight additions and, in the case of the last two, changed titles, respectively, "La lección de la sobriedad" and "Patria y universo del intelectual," are anthologized in *Luis Vives (Un español fuera de España)*, in 1942.[40] In addition, two new writings round out the above anthology, "Margarita" and "El doctor melifluo." A French version of the latter of these two new essays, "Le Docteur Melliflu," is to be found in *Vives: Humaniste Espagnol*,[41] an anthology of essays also containing contributions

The Experimental Consciousness in Spain

by Eugenio d'Ors, Juan Zaragüeta, Tomás Carreras y Artau, Pierre Jobit and Vicente Genovés. The French version of the above essay is probably the original, inasmuch as it was published in 1941. In addition, the five writings on Luis Vives were published together with essays on Garcilaso and on the emigration of Spanish intellectuals to France, in *Españoles fuera de España* (1947).[42]

Marañón's five writings cover various aspects of Vives' personality, thought and social life. The articles most germane to our reconstitution of Marañón's historical development of the Spanish scientific consciousness are the following: "La lección de la sobriedad," a commentary on Vives' experimentalism via a survey of the Spanish thinker's prescriptions on mental hygiene; "Patria y universo del intelectual," a revindicatory essay, very typical of Marañón, defending Vives, as he had Feijoo in 1934, from the charge of lack of patriotism; and "El doctor melifluo," primarily an account of Vives' association with the Sorbonne (and to a lesser degree, Oxford University) where a large number of Spanish expatriates, such as Juan Martínez Siliceo, Juan de Celaya, Padre Victoria and others, were studying or teaching. Marañón judges that Luis Vives represents for Spain "the first successful attempt of an intellectual attitude replete with empirical significance—or better, experimentalist. His influence can be situated in the line of that which was to be exercised by Bacon and Descartes, although in a different category."[43] Ortega pays homage to Vives in a similar vein, proclaiming his modernity as an anticipation of the later, more substantial work of Bacon and Descartes.[44]

Marañón applauds Vives' attack on the "pseudodialecticians" which he compares to *La derrota de los pedantes,* written two centuries later during a similar crisis, by another Spanish émigré, Leandro Fernández de Moratín, guilty only of "an excess of love for Spain."[45] Thus we are led to Marañón's acknowledgment that Vives, as well as his close friend, Erasmus of Rotterdam, was critical of many aspects of Spanish intellectual life—and with justice. Vives objected to the mediocre books that were being published in Spain, stating that he would not be content until he was certain that in Spain at least a dozen publishers existed to edit and propagate only the best authors. Only in this way have the other countries been able to "clean themselves of barbarism."[46] Vives yearned for the day when Spain would have many universities like the one in Paris. Marañón defends Vives' right to criticize Spain as the "duty" peculiar to the intellectual. He compares Vives with Cajal in this respect. Of the Generation of 1898, "Cajal was the harshest in his judgments."[47] The doubts expressed in his own day about Vives' patriotism, and even his orthodoxy, are lamentable, and moreover a tragic index of the morale of the country. Marañón judges that the weakness or strength of a nation is measurable in terms of its openness to the criticism of its intellectuals. As long as Spain retained its consciousness of its greatness, "its talented minds could tell it the truth, sure that in the truth it would find a spur to perfection and not a reason for depression and anguish, and much less for anger."[48] But when a nation begins to collapse morally, she becomes like a person who is sick and yet prefers the "merciful lie" or the "choir-boy who swings the censer."[49]

Marañón judges that one of the reasons why Vives did not return to Spain was because of his "intellectual rebelliousness, his painful consciousness of his Spain which was irritated by the very depth of his love."[50] When he was asked to come to the University of Castilla la Nueva to occupy the chair which Nebrija, by his death, had just left vacant, Marañón detects a profound ambivalence in Vives. On one hand, there is his love for Spain and his sense of duty. On the other:

> He imagined his life with a Complutensian professorship: the routine preparation of classes; the struggle with the organized barbarism of the students, clothed in that roguish cynicism which for Spaniards has always been a prior and plenary indulgence toward all misdeeds. He felt the daily contact with the pedants of the faculty as a physical discomfort under his skin. Perhaps he would be, in time, the outstanding figure of the university, the flower of the Spanish spirit. But at the expense of how many wasted hours, how much useless effort spent in the patient lubrication of the thousand small wheels of the official teaching mechanism, of the contacts with the Royal Court and the Church and the invisible monster of the environment, which little by little conquers us and concludes by binding us, without our realizing it, to its plebian sadness![51]

Whether or not the above actually fits Vives' feelings at that historical moment, it is a rather clear indication of Marañón's antipathy toward the University, its environment and its officialdom, as administered in the present as well as the past. Marañón deals with this topic in its historical aspects again, with more detail, in his studies of Feijoo and Casal. For Marañón, at least with respect to medicine, a university background meant adherence to an abstract authoritarianism that was the death of all diagnosis or therapy based on genuine observation.

With respect to the theoretical side of Vives, rather than grappling with the psychological theories of the thinker, these having been treated in some detail already by others (Vives has been frequently termed the "father of experimental psychology"),[52] Marañón prefers to comment on the lesser-known speculations and dicta on personal hygiene. These are evoked because they likewise represent "one aspect of Vives' experimentalist concern, the echo of which was not to be heard until several centuries later; an aspect little studied by his commentators."[53] The lessons on personal hygiene are to be found in the *Exercitatio linguae latinae* [*Ejercicios de lengua latina*], nominally a manual of Latin composition dedicated in 1538 to prince Felipe, son of Carlos V.[54] Not that Vives practiced these dicta himself. He was suffering gravely from the gout when he wrote these exercises and was to die within a few years.

Marañón in his evocation is, of course, following Azorín, who in *Lecturas españolas* glossed this same material, arriving at a typical Azorínian conclusion: "Vives feels an intense love of small things. . .he has felt, perhaps better than anyone else, the eternal poetry of the small and the commonplace."[55] Marañón evokes a wide range of Vives' precepts on topics such as the proper lighting for reading, how to protect oneself from mosquitoes, proper diet, how to treat insomnia, and the rating of different varieties of wine, beer, and water according to the criteria of digestion. Nevertheless, despite Marañón's contention that this material reflects Vives' experimentalism, there emerges no systematic comparisons, varying of experimental conditions, interest in measurement and quantification—in short, no real experimental attitude. We must wait until the eighteenth-century Feijoo (who had available the work of Roger Bacon, 1561-1626, upon whom he so heavily relied) in order to appreciate a true experimentalism with techniques involving measurement and systematic variations of experimental conditions.

Vives, on the other hand, has been judged an empiricist on the basis of his mastery of the techniques of subjective introspection and observation. The most valuable and original part of Vives' psychological masterpiece, *De anima et vita* (1538), deals with the laws of memory and forgetting, these being arrived at through introspection. Thinkers as early as Samuel Coleridge and the nineteenth-century Scottish philosopher, Sir William Hamilton, as well as modern historians of psychology have consistently pointed to Vives' fundamental contribution to the law of the association of ideas.[56]

165

Huarte de San Juan and Luis Vives

Yet, in contrast to the subjective, introspectionist empiricism at work in *De anima et vita,* the dialogues in the *Exercitatio linguae latinae* are simply a compilation of traditional teachings for the young or guidelines drawn from the experience of a well-traveled, active, Renaissance mind.

Let us turn to the other two essays for a moment. "Gota y humor del maestro" is a discussion of Vives' own temperament in terms of his physiology. Vives' "sober" sense of humorism is related to his arthritic condition that manifested itself in various physical symptoms such as the gout. The relationship is one of frustration transcended:

> The arthritic is apt to be a man who is eager and hungering to live, but at the same time subject to limitations in the satisfaction of his appetite and to chains forged by his own vital exuberance. Thus originates the very human and productive oscillation between the 'wanting to' and 'not being able to' characteristic of the arthritic, which is often resolved by the formula of humorism.[57]

Marañón masterfully evokes the regal and intoxicating descriptions of all varieties of meats, sauces, fish and wines upon which Crito, Simonides, Democritus, Escopas and others discourse with gusto, again in the *Exercitatio linguae latinae.*

"Margarita" is a profile of Vives' renowned wife, Margarita Valdaura, whom Marañón terms "la mujer patria" inasmuch as she allegedly provided the sustenance which permitted Vives to endure his self-imposed exile from Spain.

> Woman is so close to the earth's quintessence that she herself is the mother country: wherever she may be, she is, at the same time, a part of the distant homeland and a creation of a new land. And the man who is united by love to this quintessence assuages his nostalgia and directly experiences the enigma of unmediated life.[58]

Margarita is said to be the model for Vives' famous *Institutio foeminae christianae* [*Formación de la mujer cristiana*].[59] In Marañón's interpretation, Margarita emerges as a sort of maternal guardian, a self-abnegating comforter of her husband in trial and illness whose one peccadillo is her zeal for cleanliness which results in her constant tidying of Vives' desk, much to the scholar's dismay. Poor Vives! "A man who is absorbed in his work is always, for the intelligent woman, somewhat of a son."[60] The profile, quite similar to the doctor's evocation of Pasteur's wife,[61] is suspiciously reminiscent of a stereotyped impression of the domestic life of the contemporary "absent-minded professor."

Other contributions to the study of sixteenth- and seventeenth-century Spanish science

In addition to the works that we have already surveyed, Marañón's engagement with Spanish science and medicine of the sixteenth and seventeenth centuries is rounded out with three additional contributions: "La literatura científica en los siglos XVI y XVII" (1953), "Cisneros y la Universidad de Alcalá" (1956) and "Servet. Psicología de una heterodoxia" (1954).[62]

"La literatura científica en los siglos XVI y XVII" is basically a compendium, a listing of prominent figures in Spanish medicine, natural science, mathematics, etc., written for the reference book *Historia general de las literaturas hispánicas.* Inasmuch as the article is fundamentally a reference document that is now out of date,[63] I shall not survey it, except for the long introduction on the black legend aspect of the polemic on Spanish science that will be discussed later. (See p. 170.) The lecture on Cisneros is a brief commemorative piece on the writer and his mission as founder of the University of Alcalá de Henares.

The curious, moving lecture on Servet applies the psychological constructs of ambivalence and timidity or inferiority complex to Servet's political-religious behavior. Marañón notes that in Servet's trial for heresy conducted by the Calvinists, facts came to light which have been little considered by the biographers of the ill-fated theologian and physician. In this trial, Servet admitted to a self-imposed chastity due to an organic, physical peculiarity which in no way hindered his sexual functioning but which embarrassed him and caused him to shy from sexual relationships with women. At the same time, when he would be questioned on why he didn't marry, by his behavior he led people to come to the conclusion that he led a rather libertine life. For Marañón, these admissions are indicative of a deepseated timidity in Servet with its comparative analogue: an overwhelming resentment. The timidity-resentment diagnosis elucidates for Marañón, on the one hand, his sullen, withdrawn ways as in a famous incident where he arrogantly arranged a meeting with Calvin in order to polemicize with him, and then failed to appear. Marañón notes that behavior of this sort led contemporaries such as Melanchthon and Stupanius to doubt Servet's mental stability.

Marañón goes so far as to imply that Servet's heterodoxy is attributable to a great extent to this resentment (together with the "spirit of the times" which fostered doubt). Marañón makes this implication by noting that Servet seemed on several occasions (as when his brother, a clergyman, came from Spain to plead with him) to yearn to return to the Catholic fold, but always, in the end, held back. Marañón uses phraseology reminiscent of his study on Amiel. Servet emerges as a theologian tormented by "interminable nights of forced chastity."[64] In the following passage, Marañón brings himself as close as he chooses to a thesis asserting Servet's theology to be substantially determined by his timidity and resentment: "During those years he might have gained salvation, but his theological disquietude did not let him be. During those nights, tormented by the agitation of his imagination and by his self-imposed chastity, he reverted to his delirium. Out of this grew, little by little, his *Christianismi Restitutio,* a heretical book rendered almost ineffectual by its disorder and confusion. . . ."[65]

Moreover, Marañón analyzes Servet's bizarre behavior toward Calvin that brings him directly to Geneva, to his implacable enemy, immediately after escaping from an Inquisitorial cell in France. Marañón judges that, while much has been discussed with regard to this phenomenon, in terms of religious and political motivations, these orientations are not adequate.

> This [explanation] must be sought in Servet's active disposition, in his emotional life, and not in the incidents of his social life. By focusing the problem in this way it becomes evident that Servet's great tragedy, his obsession with Calvin, was driven and justified by a dark passion—but one of immense unsettling effectiveness—timidity.[66]

In the last four months of his life, sought after by the authorities, he was driven straight to Calvin "who was the attraction of his delirious soul."[67] This was fatal for Servet. He was cruelly prosecuted by Calvin, recanted and was burned at the stake.

Concerning Servet's famous and disputed discovery, the circulation of the blood, Marañón observes that the insight does not appear in one of Servet's medical works, but in the *Christianismi Restitutio* because "the perfect understanding of circulation was only important as an argument in the resolution of a theological problem—that of the formation of the soul, infused into the blood by God. Therefore it was necessary for blood, and its mechanics and mixtures in the organism, to be understood accurately. . . .In his time, only an ardent theologian, not an anatomist, would have discovered pulmonary circulation."[68]

The Experimental Consciousness in Spain

The vindication of Fray Benito Jerónimo Feijoo

Feijoo is the stellar figure in Marañón's scientific pantheon, the first of the experimentalists with whom Marañón became preoccupied. Marañón's research, dating from the early 1930s in preparation for his entry speech into the Real Academia Española in 1934, was highly productive. His identification with Feijoo was not only fertile in its own right, but led him to cultivate a number of other eighteenth-century personalities such as Casal, Sarmiento, Pablo de Olavide and Jovellanos.

Marañón judges Feijoo to be an extraordinary individual, one of a very small group of illustrious and productive thinkers of the eighteenth century—a man who, in his approach toward the utilization of knowledge and the search for truth, was far advanced for his time.

Marañón depicts an "heroic" and "glorious" Feijoo. Indeed, in 1941, in exile in Paris and with the Spanish Civil War and his antagonism toward the Republic (see his *Liberalismo y comunismo*) very much on his mind, Marañón goes so far as to make Feijoo's situation paradigmatic for his own: "What is essential in the great friar is his Spanish significance . . . .However, in his own time he was called unpatriotic, because he knew how to adopt an intelligent attitude in times of national misfortune."[69] But this is not a late development. Marañón closely identified with Feijoo from the first edition of his *Las ideas biológicas del Padre Feijoo* in 1934.

The epithets "glorious" and "heroic" are expressed in direct reaction to Menéndez Pelayo's depiction of Feijoo as ". . .vain, to the point of lessening national glories in order to make his own stature more conspicuous; a reader of secondary rather than original sources; a man of 'extremely bad taste.' "[70] Marañón, while on the one hand paying homage to Menéndez Pelayo's scholarship and critical powers, feels, in this instance, that he has mistreated Feijoo, and in the process, overly esteemed the scholarly and scientific contributions that were produced in Spain during the eighteenth century. "Menéndez Pelayo, in his study on Feijoo in the *Heterodoxos,* energetically contradicts the reality of Spanish intellectual decadence during this stage of our history, in order to diminish the reformative significance of the Benedictine's writings."[71]

The situation is particularly serious for Marañón because Menéndez Pelayo directly connects his defense and justification of Spanish scientific output in the eighteenth century together with, in inverse ratio, a devaluation of Feijoo's contribution toward the general pursuit of science.

Marañón is troubled by Menéndez Pelayo's spirited defense of Spanish science, although it is undoubtedly inspired by the critic's "admirable patriotism," as well as, unfortunately, "the prejudice...of not recognizing the inferiority of absolutist Spain in contrast to the liberal Spain of the last third of the nineteenth century."[72] Similarly, Marañón inveighs against those (such as Julián Juderías) who claim that Europe's lack of appreciation of Spain's scientific output is but another aspect of the general black legend that Spain has suffered at the hands of Europe. On the contrary, claims Marañón, echoing Feijoo, more often than not "foreigners have been the ones to bestow a just appraisal on illustrious Spaniards, forgotten or disparaged by their own countrymen."[73]. This has been the case, for example, with Vives and Calderón. Let us recall Feijoo's famous remarks on the subject two hundred years earlier:

> From this and other examples which I could quote one may surmise the injustice of that common Spanish complaint, so frequently heard, that foreigners, envious of our nation's glory, endeavor to belittle it and darken it as much as they can. No such accusation could be farther from the truth. I protest that I have no knowledge of any illustrious Spaniard, celebrated either for military or literary feats, who has not seen himself more lauded by foreign authors than by our own. Those who try to lessen the glory of illustrious Spaniards are the Spanish themselves. . . .[74]

Thus, Marañón is led to conclude that the invocation of the black legend with respect to science is merely a "pretext for inaction."[75] This myth has created a "reaction of rhetorical nationalism detrimental to the creative effort, the latter a more difficult task than uttering invective against occult powers."[76] Marañón cites the eminent Spanish mathematician, Rey Pastor, who has noted the creation of a special genre of "vindicatory literature, in which a large number of books are cited, and in addition there is a recital of the editions published, of the Latin panegyrics accompanying each one, of everything, in short, which is external to the book. The only thing which the vindicators do not tell us is the content, which is precisely what would interest us most."[77]

These attempts by Menéndez Pelayo and others are in vain. While Menéndez Pelayo was able to cite eight to ten illustrious names from the eighteenth century, Marañón, echoing Ortega's remarks in "La ciencia romántica" (1906),[78] recalls that the scientific level of an epoch is not measured by "the height of the solitary peaks in the desert" but rather by "the average level of the surroundings."[79] As measured by the above index, the eighteenth century was so scant that much admirable work, such as that of the mathematician Hugo de Omerique, who was praised by Newton himself, was not divulged in Spain, even in the great universities of Salamanca and Oviedo, until many years later. Symptomatic of the depressed cultural situation was, for Marañón, the success of Torres Villarroel.

> There might have been a great isolated mathematician; but at the University of Salamanca the chair of this science was unoccupied by both teacher and disciples, and finally it was won, amidst the cheers of the multitude, by a gutter rascal—dedicated to exploiting his reader's foolishness with absurd astrological almanacs—like Torres Villarroel.[80]

He also reminds us that the Inquisition "maintained its zeal for the purity of the faith with such a conscientious inflexibility, that the new ideas of science suffered a dangerous quarantine by censure...."[81] The doctor laments that "There is no science book which is slightly open and bold, or simply original, that is not read today just as it was expurgated by the deletions of the Holy Office; and in many it is necessary to reconstruct the original text around the rigors of censorship and the vacillations of the author, panicked by the threat of the dungeon."[82]

Furthermore, of the figures that Menéndez Pelayo cites, several, at least in the field of medicine, in Marañón's estimation are much less worthy of positive regard than they would naturally appear.

Concerning the doctors, Solano de Luque and Martín Martínez, whom Menéndez Pelayo praises highly, Marañón judges the first to be "a mere practitioner, whose work has absolutely nothing worth remembering"[83] and the second, "only an enthusiastic anatomy teacher, but without the slightest hint of originality and without any possible comparison to the admirable Spanish anatomists of the fifteenth and sixteenth centuries."[84]

With respect to the defense of Spanish science in the eighteenth century, Marañón concludes:

> It is not, therefore, an unpatriotic exaggeration to speak of the obscurity of science in Feijoo's time. The truth is never unpatriotic. By recognizing it in this case, the remarkable stature of Feijoo's work becomes more evident, an authentic glory for Spain. The truth also reveals the stature of those who accompanied him in his movement

of renewal and those who supported him in high places with their favor and their fervor.[85]

As we have indicated, Marañón equally rejects the other side of Menéndez Pelayo's position, the personal criticism of Feijoo. It must be noted that Menéndez Pelayo wrote two books in which Feijoo figures significantly. In the early *Historia de los heterodoxos españoles,* Marañón judges that Menéndez Pelayo is clearly disturbed "when Feijoo destroys *milagrerías* and superstition, and when he becomes enthused with the experimental method and struggles to throw open the windows of Spanish culture so that light from abroad might come streaming in."[86] Moreover, the doctor notes that there is a certain agreement by Menéndez Pelayo with the charge of antipatriotism that was hurled against Feijoo in his own time. Menéndez Pelayo states: ". . .it seems that he put an excessive determination into contrasting the inferiority of the Spanish intellectual level with his own stature. This was Feijoo's approach when he wrote under the spell of French ideas. I repeat that I shall never forgive him for these sins against Spanish science."[87] On the other hand, in the later, *Historia de las ideas estéticas en España,* Menéndez Pelayo discusses Feijoo with a much more enthusiastic tone. However, due to the greater diffusion of the *Heterodoxos,* the first judgment has prevailed. Feijoo typically has been relegated to a subordinate position in Spanish letters and considered "a pleasant disseminator of vast but not solid learning; an entertaining writer and intelligent polemist, and nothing more. This is a notorious insult to the truth, for quite another rank is appropriate to him, and it is a much higher one."[88]

In order to counteract the negative evaluations surrounding this figure and, also, inasmuch as a more specialized interpretation of Feijoo's scientific output is necessary to parallel the numerous "general critiques" which Marañón cites,[89] the goal of the *Ideas biológicas del Padre Feijoo* is expressed as an interpretation of Feijoo's medical and biological ideas "with modern criteria. . .in order to rigorously appraise all that represented involuntary rashness and error in the exuberant abundance of his essays; and all that represented solidity, insight, rebelliousness against the fading present, and renewal of the culture of his time."[90]

The attitude of Marañón toward Feijoo is somewhat that of a son toward a spiritual progenitor. As we have indicated earlier, Marañón's empathy for Feijoo is quite intense and productive. He is not loathe to point out Feijoo's mistakes on certain points of fact, usually mistaken beliefs that the poligrapher shared in common with his age,[91] but on basic issues and developments, Marañón points to Feijoo with deep admiration and pride as an innovator and "padre maestro." In one essay, he proclaims his discipleship: "I, his remote disciple, in the love of truth and of Spain; and in the expectation and the faith that tradition, liberty, and rank will someday be compatible. . . ."[92] In a notable chapter in his book, our critic movingly narrates the struggle in Feijoo of reason to gain ascendency over irrationality supported by superstition. His general attitude toward myth is quite similar to that of Feijoo. Marañón shared with others in his generation the notion that "myth" was to be disentangled. Thus Don Juan is a "false myth" or a "false symbol." The doctor's biographical technique is offered as a procedure which is able to clarify myths, such as the supposition of Amiel's incapacity to love, Enrique IV's impotence, El Greco's insanity, etc. Carlos Clavería notices a similar (although more ambivalent) attitude toward myth in Ramón Pérez de Ayala. Clavería traces the philosophic roots of this notion to the renowned nineteenth-century philologist, Max Müller, via the intermediary of Julio Cejador y Frauca.[93] Max Müller associates myth with "a world of illusion" and claims that mythology "no doubt, breaks out more fiercely during the early periods of the history of human thought."[94] Mythology has the linguistic function of being the "dark shadow which language throws upon thought, and which can never disappear till language becomes entirely commensurate with thought, which it never will."[95] Man is destined to "live in the very shadow of myth, . . .because we all shrink from the full meridian light of truth."[96] Both Feijoo in the eighteenth century, who associated myth with superstition, popular beliefs, *milagrería,* etc., and Marañón in the twentieth, who views myths as obfuscations of a biopsychological reality, would be substantially in accord with the above statements.[97]

In addition, there is a strong identification with Feijoo's situation as a Catholic scientist, completely orthodox and patriotic, yet embroiled in conflicts and polemics thrust upon him by outsiders who questioned his religious sincerity and patriotic ardor. Marañón does not consider that the polemics directed at Feijoo, in some measure, merely reflect a prevalent literary genre of the eighteenth century. On the contrary, again revealing his empathy for Feijoo, he "takes them to heart." He is profoundly repelled by the attacks. No wonder then that he reacts with a determination to clarify the real situation when Menéndez Pelayo goes so far as to revive some of the polemics which "have passed to posterity justly crushed by silence and by the polemical art of the Benedictine monk."[98]

For Menéndez Pelayo, Feijoo, although certainly a prominent eighteenth-century figure, egotistically downgraded the achievement of others in order to aggrandize himself. In opposition, Marañón proclaims Feijoo as "The Saint Christopher of Culture," the symbol of the continuity of culture in Spain during a particularly critical epoch. He is one of the "great isolated titans entrusted with seeing that the line of continuity of civilization is not broken."[99] The great cultural and political tragedy for Spain and, indeed, for the whole world is that the genius, the intellectual, is not born to direct society but rather to "completely exonerate it from effort and from responsibility."[100] For this reason, the cultural hero becomes one only at the expense of great torment, "at the expense of being a martyr." Feijoo was such an individual: ". . .he knew how to transmit the treasure of our genius and our culture over the void of several decades of ignorance, while the everpresent curs harassed him from all sides."[101]

Thus *Las ideas biológicas del Padre Feijoo* is not only a scholarly survey of Feijoo's biological and medical ideas, but also, in its own peculiarly impressionistic and dramatic fashion, a biography of Feijoo that reflects Marañón's intimate identification with the Benedictine monk. It is most notably biographical as an account of the emergence of the critical and experimental attitude in Feijoo. There is a certain similarity here between the stark opposition, experimentalism versus superstition, and the theme of civilization versus barbarism, so frequently evoked in the novel and essay of nineteenth-century Latin America. In Marañón's work, however, this opposition and conflict appear not only on the social level as a struggle between Feijoo, the educator, and the ingenuous multitude in dire need of guidance. The conflict is advanced one step further. It is found to subsist deep in the mental processes of Feijoo himself. Contained in a chapter entitled "Una batalla consigo mismo" are some of Marañón's most moving and dramatic pages, narrating the eternal struggle between "the two halves of a single soul, the rational and the instinctive, put face to face without any warning."[102] This struggle is exemplified in an incident which Feijoo, with admirable honesty, permitted his readers to share.

One autumn night while Feijoo looked out the window of his cell, he was confronted with a huge phantom. This was the supreme moment. Feijoo, the implacable denier of apparitions, found himself confronting his own irrationality.

He who goes about destroying superstitions one by one comes to a point, perhaps on a day when he is alone, when he is face to face with the last one. Upon penetrating it with the sword of reason, he feels the pain in his own soul, because the last misconception was also his, and he believed in it without knowing it. This is a terrible moment, which all men who have pursued phantoms or injustices have experienced, and which our great Quijote of the eighteenth century was also to experience![103]

For an instant, Feijoo capitulated to his own "other" self, ready to run from the cell "and not return until daylight were to enter." The monk imagined the sensation in Spain that his conversion would cause. But none of this was to happen. "The experimental spirit of the man rose in revolt against the superstitious Spaniard and faced the phantom—'not without some fright,' he writes—and he coldly began to investigate. . . ."[104]

The phantom was nothing more than a projection of his own shadow carried and enlarged by the autumn fog. This projection is also a psychological one, permitting the monk to overcome himself and comprehend the essential nature of his paradoxical antagonist: human irrationality. Already "the master of his experience," Feijoo works out the scientific details of the apparition. "After the dangerous test in the nocturnal silence of the monastery, phantoms were never to disturb him again."[105]

On Feijoo's alleged afrancesamiento

Having pointed to Marañón's interest in Feijoo's biological and medical ideas, not merely in themselves as abstractions or advances in the ongoing development of science, but rather as a function of Feijoo's engaging and open personality, I am now in a position to clarify his stand on the questions of Feijoo's alleged afrancesamiento and religious unorthodoxy. We must realize that apart from the objective merits of Marañón's arguments, the critic takes positions that have the positive value for him of permitting him a closer and deeper identification with Feijoo.

Marañón protects Feijoo from the charge of radical (i.e., atheist) afrancesamiento, on the one hand, by denying any great debt on the part of Feijoo to the French Encyclopedists, and on the other, by proclaiming that Feijoo was "predestined" to renew Spanish science, that is, his rational, critical and experimental spirit was the result basically of personality and motivational factors that can be traced to his formation in youth, rather than to bookish or scholarly influences.

On Feijoo's Alleged *Afrancesamiento*

Marañón readily admits that in Spain the "analyzing spirit of the eighteenth century began to influence the prominent men and the aristocratic minorities with the advent of the Bourbon dynasty."[106] The eighteenth century is characterized at its core by a "definite imitation of Gallic as well as English attitudes: the Academies were copies of those of France and England, Phillip the Fifth's ministers modeled themselves on the French royal court, and the first rationales for experimentation by Bacon and his followers were translated."[107] Yet, although in Europe the French Encyclopedists, whom Marañón consistently terms a "sect," perhaps provided "the boldest and above all most flamboyant imprint on the general awakening of men's souls,"[108] the Spanish cultural renewal should not be identified with this French movement inasmuch as, in Spain, "The eighteenth century represented an eagerness for human enlightenment and for the serene and profound contemplation and exploration of things; in a certain sense it was an antitheological reaction, but not atheistic."[109] Marañón proposes that parallel cultural movements sprang up in the nations of Europe during the eighteenth century, marked by a "criterion of experimental rationalism" which manifested itself under the governance of a common "historical climate." Marañón deplores the tendency of critics such as Menéndez Pelayo to equate a general eighteenth-century striving for learning, material well-being, education, etc. with heterodoxy under the rubric of *Enciclopedismo* or Freemasonry.[110] Specifically, with respect to Feijoo, Marañón asserts: ". . .it is clear that we must designate Feijoo as the first Spanish Encyclopedist; and so he is called by many of his commentators. But the eighteenth century was, in its cultural significance, much more than that admirable but nevertheless limited, passionate and sectarian enterprise represented by the works of Diderot and his collaborators."[111] Marañón approves of Montero Díaz's comment that Feijoo is "an encyclopedic spirit, which means, precisely, an anti-Encyclopedist spirit."[112] As may have been indicated from our survey above, the way to decipher this cryptic distinction is to equate encyclopedic spirit with a general eighteenth-century movement toward science and experimentalism and anti-Encyclopedist spirit with a philosophic position opposed to radical political stances or manifest religious skepticism. However, in my judgment, Marañón oversteps himself when, having noted the French and English influence in eighteenth-century Spanish science and intellectualism, he claims, "But in Feijoo, contrary to what has been said, these influences are difficult to find, and he gives us the impression—and in this lies his greatest interest—that his revolutionary gesture arose as a spontaneous impulse, born of the 'historical climate,' by a type of contagion which operates in the transcendental moments of civilization. This contagion spreads from a few souls to other distant ones, carried by subterranean currents whose course is impossible to follow. Yes, he was very universal, but also spontaneous, and very, very Spanish."[113] This appears to us an exaggeration which is unnecessary to validate his "predestination" notion and appears dissonant with respect to other parts of his study where Feijoo's devotion to Bacon is surveyed and evaluated, as well as his profound indebtedness to the Journal of the French Jesuits of Trevoux. Marañón even notes Feijoo's pained exclamation of 1739: "The tremendous delay in receiving books from France is very damaging to me."[114] The debt of Feijoo as a poligrapher to foreign sources is abundant, as the work of Gaspar Delpy and of Charles N. Staubach clearly show.[115]

I note the above, not as a curious aberration or lapse contradicted in other sections of his study, but as a peculiar, consistent tendency. For example, as we have seen earlier, Marañón argues that Don Juan, psychologically speaking, is an exotic, Italian importation, and that while El Greco may owe something to Italian (particularly Venetian) Mannerism, his genius stems from his Oriental roots. These assertions are dogmatically made by Marañón despite the fact that in each case substantial research exists to disprove them.

At any rate, Marañón records two anecdotes in which Feijoo as a youth, by using himself as a subject of an experiment, refuted the beliefs that one could not eat anything after drinking hot chocolate and that one should not sleep after taking medication to purge oneself. For Marañón, these incidents, inasmuch as they are "the source of his [Feijoo's] future attitude,"[116] provide evidence that Feijoo was predestined by the "historical climate" and above all, by his own "inner life"[117] to be an experimentalist. And all of this occurred long before he had read "the Encyclopedia, or the books of Lord Bacon, from whom almost everyone claims he copied his doctrine and his experimental attitude."[118] This theory of historical and psychological determinism in the case of Feijoo has had a widespread popularity among subsequent critics of the Galician monk, a reflection of the profound impact and popularity of Marañón's study. For example, Jean Sarrailh accepts these arguments.[119] Moreover, the anecdotes, together with their interpretation, find their way into Pérez-Rioja's *Proyección y actualidad de Feijoo*.[120]

Marañón offers other interesting psychological observations on

Feijoo. He judges him to have been a frustrated physician since medicine was for him "more than a subject of interest, a real obsession."[121] Marañón concludes:

> It could be affirmed, without fear of erring, that inside the austere clergyman and the admirable essayist there was a great frustrated physician. Of the several "doubles" that we all have hidden in our personalities, no doubt one of the most common is that of "the other calling;" and when the social pursuit chosen is not the one which corresponds to the strongest inclination, that other one, the true vocation, remains alive, although suffocated in our soul, and it annoys us and troubles us. . . .[122]

This passage is specially revelatory of the closeness with which Marañón has identified with Feijoo and of the manner in which he has engagingly projected his own feelings and self-estimation toward his lifework in order to arrive at an ingenious interpretation of Feijoo's worldly interests.

James Hoddie, Jr. has carefully traced the evolution of Marañón's attitude from an initial position where "Marañón did not regard favorably the participation of the physician in non-professional activities"[123] to a more enlightened position focusing on the complexity of a man's personality which is too fertile and unbounded to be restricted, and ultimately, deadened, by the concentration on one mere area of specialization. Diversity is the necessary tonic for a well-developed mind. Furthermore, the need to diversify is especially intense for the scientist because of an unconscious sentiment:

> . . .the man of science, even the one of genius, experiences the ephemeral nature of his scientific work. And the instinct of immortality, which is alive within all human beings of superior category, turns its anxiety for survival toward artistic creation. This creation, when it is sublime, abides forever in men's memories.[124]

As Hoddie puts it, Marañón considers that "Men of science are impressed by the fact that the name of the creator of a great work of art survives as long as the work itself, while a scientific discovery soon becomes the anonymous instrument of everyone's thought."[125] Marañón not only applies this observation to himself, implicitly, but, explicitly as well, to Cajal's literary production, which is alleged to have served "the subconscious aspiration for the work wrought by our hands to endure, united to our names; for so it happens with the literary creation, the painting, the monument or the sonata, but not with the scientific book."[126] In addition, this notion of the diversity of the mind is applied to the psychological problems of professionalism in *Vocación y ética*.[127]

Very closely associated with the charge of Feijoo's alleged *afrancesamiento* has been the claim made by many critics that the latter used a language saturated and plagued with Gallicisms and neologisms taken from Latin and that even his syntax displays a marked French influence. Marañón reviews what had become, by this time, a rather broad dispute. Critics such as Menéndez Pelayo, Vicente de la Fuente, Pardo Bazán, Pí y Margall and Araujo Costa judged Feijoo's language negatively either because of his alleged "French terms," his Latinisms or his stylistic incapability for *belles lettres*. Others such as Montero Díaz, Morayta and Laborde praised Feijoo's clarity and precision. In truth, the question of Feijoo's stylistic and linguistic characteristics as well as his philosophic ideas on language and rhetoric is a complicated one which has generated a good deal of recent bibliography. It has become increasingly clear that in order to avoid distortion Feijoo must be evaluated within the milieu of which he was a part.

Antonio Rubio and F. Lázaro Carreter have pointed to the fact that Feijoo himself criticized the usage of certain Gallicisms. As early as 1726, Feijoo protested and satirized certain "impassioned lovers of the French language who, preferring it for having great advantages over Spanish, ponder its charms, exalt its excellences, and, unable to endure even a brief absence of their beloved language, pepper their conversation with some words they have usurped from it, even when they speak Spanish."[128] Yet, this was so early that the Real Academia de La Lengua, which had recently been founded, did not react. Feijoo also attacked excessive *cultismo*, particularly in his *Justa repulsa* against the *Reflexiones crítico-apologéticas* of Rodrigo Soto y Marne. In return, he was attacked for his Gallicism and *cultismo* by Salvador José Mañer and Domingo Pargas Zuendia.

Clearly, the problem of the excessive influence of the French language was a topic for polemic and debate in the eighteenth century, not restricted to the style of any one author, and as Lázaro Carreter has seen, was another instance reflecting Spain's "violent attempt to survive in a totally hostile political and cultural environment."[129] Lázaro Carreter observes that "the threat represented by French gave occasion to the awakening of natural defenses which, although they crystallized on the one hand in rigid formalistic purism, acquired an effective and active role on the part of Feijoo or Capmany, who were true defenders of the language."[130]

Marañón's attitude within this debate is most revealing because he finds himself in circumstances similar to Feijoo's. The doctor, in a profound understatement, guises himself as a "mere scientist" and claims: "I will not be so daring as to add my opinion to the rhetorical battle."[131] Yet, on the other hand: "I do not mind his Gallicisms, his unusual usage or his provincialisms. As for his innovations: not only do I not mind them, but they delight me."[132] Marañón speaks with the impatience of a scientist frustrated by the Academy's timid response to his attempt to introduce into the dictionary new words like "ambivalencia." (See note 239 for Chapter IV.) He explains that Feijoo, among other things, was involved in a task which he and other scientists are constantly confronted with:

> This necessity of speaking clearly to everyone and of dealing with scientific subjects not written about in Spanish until then. . . . This is the same thing which we men of science, especially biologists, must do now. A modern psychiatrist, for example, necessarily must Hispanicize a large number of Germanisms; without them he would have to give up writing in our language.[133]

Marañón simply cannot be bothered with a linguistic philosophy that would deny the coining of Spanish equivalents of foreign technical words. Such a philosophy is unable to make any effective or sentimental demand upon him, and in practice, it would be a pure hindrance. Here again, he identifies Feijoo's situation in the eighteenth century with his own. He concludes that "what is typical in Feijoo's language is that it is an essentially scientific language, in which the only allowable elegance is clarity. . . . In this didactic sense I venture to repeat that Feijoo is the creator in Spanish of scientific language. . . ."[134]

Angel del Río, in a book review of Marañón's *Ideas biológicas,* although still adhering to the position of earlier critics who claimed that Feijoo was guilty of an abuse of Gallicisms and of rigidity in his construction, maintains that ". . .Marañón was basically right . . .one can clearly see his relationship as a prose writer with other typically modern authors."[135] Lázaro Carreter is also substantially in agreement. The effort to keep up with the French in terms of scientific nomenclature is attributable to the innovative spirit of Feijoo and the neologisms of Capmany. Feijoo rejected *cultismo,* as did the Real Academia de la Lengua, but the procedures used by the poligrapher and the Academy were quite different:

> One can appreciate how Feijoo concurs with the Academy in the attempt to free the language from the excesses of *cultismo*. But he differs totally with the Academy in his procedures. The most effective Academic remedy is, as we have already seen, the standardization of the language. In Feijoo, on the contrary, we observe that same dynamic conception of the language that was held by the Spanish treatise writers of the Golden Age. . . . For the *padre maestro*, the language is always mobile and elusive, and it escapes all attempts at standardization. For that reason, he rejects the role which is assigned to dictionaries, considering it useless and fanciful.[136]

Since the publication of Marañón's book, a number of critics have formed opinions on the essence of Feijoo's style. Entrambasaguas and J.L. Marichal have pointed to the intimacy and familiar tone of Feijoo, noting that the author openly takes the reader into his confidence.[137] Entrambasaguas, as did Marañón, compares Feijoo with Azorín and also with Leandro Fernández de Moratín. It also should be noted that Marañón himself dwells in the same literary community as Feijoo (and Azorín as well). Marañón and Feijoo have in common not only an all-embracing scientific curiosity, an involvement in the same sort of topics, a subjective, confidential style which liberally utilizes anecdote and imaginative, often picturesque language, a clear and direct technical approach involving a rectilinear narrative structure, but a true relish for polemic and disputation as well. It is revealing, in this respect, that Marañón is not sensitive to the fact that Feijoo actively invites polemic and rebuke in his work, but rather, in his empathy, he leaps into the fray and comes to Feijoo's defense as if he were the polemicizer himself, judging the persons and issues in terms of true and false, right and wrong.

The charge of Feijoo's heresy

Just as in the case of Feijoo's lack of patriotism, as alleged by his polemicists, Marañón defends the monk against the charge of heretical tendencies or lack of sincere religious faith. He comments that the three favorite charges leveled against Feijoo in his own time were that he "lacked originality," and that he was "unpatriotic and a heretic." The charges are closely related to each other for, if it could be proved that Feijoo were an Encyclopedist in the manner of Diderot, all of the charges would then be validated. Marañón notes that not only Feijoo's contemporaries but also several nineteenth- and twentieth-century critics doubted Feijoo's religious sincerity.

The Charge of Feijoo's Heresy

In his own time, priests such as Tronchón, Torreblanca and fray Luis de Flandes, offended devotees of Raimundo Lulio, whom Feijoo had criticized, attempted revenge by spreading "malevolent suspicions."[138] As an outgrowth of Feijoo's famous denunciation and explanation of the "miracles of the flowers of San Luis," the monk earned the wrath of the Franciscans, culminating in what Marañón judges to be an infamous accusation by Padre Soto y Marne. Finally, Feijoo was involved in a minor incident with the Inquisition over the interpretation of some innocent writings of his concerning "the confessor's conduct with respect to authorizing or not authorizing the attendance of young ladies at dances and at the theater."[139]

On the other hand, in the nineteenth century, without the tone of violent accusation, but rather with a "sympathetic ear" for meanings between the lines, Pí y Margall judged that Feijoo's many protests of his faith and orthodoxy were motivated more by "calculation than by conviction."[140] Likewise, Montero Díaz points to an "inner conflict which evidently must have arisen in his soul."[141] Morayta, the author of a book on Feijoo highly praised by Azorín for its nonsectarianism (the author was an ardent liberal), asserts: "Feijoo did not want to decatholicize Spain; but let us forthrightly maintain that if he had so intended, he would, at any rate, have begun in the way that he did."[142] Marañón is completely opposed to this line of thinking, be it accusatory or merely evaluative. He states categorically:

> Feijoo wrote a great deal and he overflowed onto his pages with a unique candor, in which the least of his theological anxieties would have been clearly visible. My reading of his thirteen volumes has been slow, and repeated over many years, and it has never given me the impression of witnessing a disillusioned conscience. . . ."[143]

Marañón points to an important goal of eighteenth-century experimentalists throughout Europe, the separation of philosophy and theology from experimental science. As I.L. McClelland puts it:

> Once that separation could be achieved. . .once the study of the meaning of man and his place in the world of the spirit could be treated as one kind of specialization, and the restricted study of his body and his place in the physical universe as another, then tensions produced by tying the results of modern experiment to the apron-strings of old authorities would automatically be removed.[144]

Yet, that separation took an inordinately long time (one may argue that it still has not been totally achieved). Descartes experienced the tensions that McClelland speaks of in proposing as proof of

Man's existence (and ultimately, of God's existence) nothing but the fact that Man knows that he thinks. In the past, criteria for such questions were theological and Descartes himself, bowing to the established custom, attempted to prove that his theory was theologically sound. Similarly, Feijoo often quoted the Jesuits at Trevoux "when he was attacked on grounds of orthodoxy."[145] Nevertheless, the goal was to make experimental science independent of theological rectitude, not to be used as a weapon against the acceptance of religious belief or religious phenomena, not at least on the part of Catholic scientists, but rather to be utilized as an independent medium of the confirmation of the divine. St. Thomas had already overtly separated faith from reason and had proposed a number of rational arguments for the existence of God independent of the mightier argument of faith itself. Feijoo was working on a much more mundane level. As Marañón puts it:

> The preoccupation with miracle must be. . .fundamental in the strict believer; for him the destruction of false miracles is equivalent to enhancing the transcendence of the real ones. And this was Feijoo's attitude; he surely did not feel the slightest fear for his faith when he brandished his experimental criticism against the religious fables which here and there sprang up on Hispanic soil.[146]

Our critic judges the nineteenth-century attempt to seek out a skeptical Feijoo to be a consequence of the politico-intellectual struggles of liberals and conservatives.

> If his philosophic attitude has ever aroused suspicions, it has been, a long time after his death, beause of the puerile eagerness of the nineteenth century liberals to add the Benedictine to the retinue comprising their faction; or else, because of Catholics themselves: these Catholics of ours, faithful to their instinctive vigilance against everything which means a free and active intelligence.[147]

Marañón's defense of Feijoo's religiosity and the natural and harmonious relationship of his religious beliefs and scientific goals has been widely accepted by major critics. Sarrailh, for example, accepts the arguments completely:

> Marañón, in his book on Feijoo, is right when he observes that if indeed the Benedictine monk is 'the most genuine representative of eighteenth century Encyclopedist criticism,' he does not, therefore, fail to conserve 'all of the Iberian characteristics, including the most strict orthodoxy.' It is necessary to study him, then, 'with complete independence from the general trend of French *enciclopedismo.*'[148]

Others, however, such as Arturo Ardao and Raquel Sajón de Cuello, specifically oppose Marañón, returning to the critical line of Pí y

The Charge of Feijoo's Heresy

Margall and Morayta. Sajón de Cuello judges:

> If the learned Benedictine did not appear as an *afrancesado* in the sense that the word later was used, he was, on the other hand, the point of departure of the future *afrancesamiento*. This explains his rapport with the European Enlightenment, his strong links with eighteenth century rationalism, and the consequent wavering of his faith.[149]

Marañón himself took extraordinary precautions to make perfectly clear his own philosophic position on the relationship between faith and science. In the very first chapter of the *Ideas biológicas,* entitled "Ciencia y superstición," Marañón presents an apology for science claiming that "the man who is gifted with true wisdom is always, whether he wants it or not, confronted with divinity. Fleeing it only leads to falling into the superstition of science itself and, as a result, ceasing to go forward, going endlessly in circles.[150] Marañón asserts that the history of human progress can be reduced to the struggle of science against superstition. Superstition is termed "faith in the absurd, typical of primitive man."[151] Science, however, is "faith in things which can be demonstrated by means of the reasoning or experimentation which characterizes civilized man."[152] Thus, science is a form of faith also, characterized by an "unsatiable desire to transcend."[153] This "desire," while it results concretely in the "rationalization of the absurd," at the same time leads us to "a limitless, mysterious world, at whose door our 'why?' will call out in anguish, without receiving any answer other than one word: 'God.' "[154]

The biological and medical theories of Feijoo

Having reviewed the criticism of Feijoo, defended him from the twin charges of *afrancesamiento* and heterodoxy or skepticism, and also, in the process, having outlined some of the psychological characteristics of the Galician monk, particularly an innate curiosity and experimental outlook, Marañón proceeds to survey, systematically and in detail, the basic biological and medical theories of Feijoo. This survey is enlivened and endowed with a dramatic flavor through Marañón's abundant use of anecdote and his psychological speculations concerning Feijoo, which he does not abandon even in discussing technical matters. Contributing to the dramatism is an evaluation of Feijoo's "successes" and "mistakes" which produces the impression that Marañón is tallying a transcendental account book on Feijoo's contributions to Spanish thought and science. In addition, we must note that Marañón has admirably sorted out the numerous letters and essays of Feijoo, categorizing them into a coherent body of material. Menéndez Pelayo and others had judged that Feijoo really did not have a set philosophic criterion toward the world, but rather that "his curiosity caused him to wander not only from fact to fact, but also, at times, from criterion to criterion."[155] Marañón demonstrates that, at least in the case of medicine, "it cannot be denied that the ideas of the *padre maestro* were fit and elaborated into a definite system."[156] This demonstration was no easy task, since in Feijoo's work no definite and finished outlines appear. Rather, his thought is dissolved in his essays, letters and polemics, all of which are substantially circumstantial literature. Marañón characterizes his task in the following way:

> The essayist. . .upon dying, sometimes leaves the substance of his philosophy intact, but without a visible structure, like a puzzle whose pieces are all present but jumbled in a heap. Then another person—another essayist—is the one who takes charge of lovingly and patiently putting each piece in its place.[157]

Feijoo's cardinal tenet was the judgment that medicine is not an infallible science, nor a determined philosophic system, but rather an imperfect science in the mere beginnings of its evolution. Since no abstract system will be adequate to the circumstances of healing and curing patients, the only "rational criterion for the clinician is the observation of Nature and the appraisal by experimentation of what is observed."[158]

During Feijoo's time, doctors and medical philosophers could be divided into two major groups: the *dogmatics* who subscribed to the teachings of some accepted authority, Hippocrates, Galen, and so forth, and the *skeptics* who were greatly in the minority, such as Martín Martínez, author of the *Medicina scéptica*, and who advocated experimentalism. These two groups were in fierce opposition. The skeptics were forced to prove that their skepticism referred only to the body of medical practice and not, as they were accused by figures such as López de Araujo, to theological considerations.

Feijoo's curiosity and interest extended to a countless variety of topics such as the theory of infections, hysteria, the chemical reactions of love, giants and dwarfs (both mythical and factual), bestiality, personal hygiene, heredity, the theology and morality of medicine, psychiatry, and many others. Among his most notable conclusions was his theory that epidemics are caused by "extremely minute insects," which Marañón judges to be an embryonic bacteriological theory of epidemic infections.[159] Feijoo judged that most examples of bewitched individuals were simply cases of melancholy and hysteria usually associated with sexual perturbations. He was much interested in the power of suggestion and claimed that he had astounding success in treating patients, including the demented, through the proper use of voice, gaze, and general comforting.[160] With respect to the sexual nature of illness in women, Marañón considered notable his aphorism stating "the Proteus of illnesses is no doubt hidden in the female uterus."[161]

With respect to the moral and theological problems presented by medicine, Feijoo made splendid use of his tolerance and common sense. Concerning the question of whether it was acceptable for women to be aided by men during labor, he concluded,

> Two lives depend on performing this service well: that of the mother and that of the fetus; and for the latter not only its temporal [life] but its eternal one as well. Does not a matter of such supreme importance deserve to have all excessive modesty abandoned in its favor? It is all right, I say, for a woman to sacrifice her own life because of modesty. But why should a mother sacrifice that of the innocent fetus?[162]

This sort of moral-medical consideration appears frequently in the clinical practice, and hence writings, of Marañón himself. In an article on artificial insemination written in 1932, Marañón analyzes the question with good sense, in accordance with his belief in a powerful, innate maternal instinct in women. Marañón provides a striking example of the advantages of biopsychological constructs as applied to morality, one being their powerful situational flexibility. Logic leads Marañón to judge that a doctor should accept for treatment either "a married couple that, although having the biological potential, does not succeed in producing offspring because of a mechanical impediment,"[163] or its variant "when because of the proven sterility of the husband both partners ask the doctor to perform artificial insemination with another man's semen."[164]

Marañón concludes: "When both partners are in agreement, the doctor should not have the slightest objection with regard to his professional conscience as to the solution of the problem. This would be a variation of adopting a child with which the couple will live."[165] This seems radical from the point of view of traditional morality but is clearly logical from that of an ethic which considers and weighs the intimate needs of mankind. We notice in the case of a "single woman who might want to be a mother without experiencing the act of physiological insemination by a healthy and potent man"[166] the biological-moral pros and cons more or less balance each other:

> The solution of this case is left to the doctor's conscience. We think that we would resist the idea of granting these maternal *desires* to the woman, and in this case we would advise her to adopt a child or else to run the risk of becoming pregnant by a casual lover. Perhaps this repugnance toward the idea of artificial insemination for a single woman is a question of the present moment and is changeable with the passing of time.[167]

In the area of reform, Feijoo outlined a series of important suggestions. These more or less fall into three basic categories:

1) Inasmuch as illness and disease are a function of the constitution and temperament of the patient, to a large extent, medicine must be meted out according to the personal requirements of the patient. Feijoo strongly protested the practice of medicine which avoided a systematic observation of the patient and relied instead on medical axioms or the aphorisms of Hippocrates, Galen, and so forth. Similarly, Feijoo rejected the prohibition of certain foods to patients on axiomatic grounds. Diet should not be accomodated to "theoretical biases, but rather to the observation of each case and to the very instincts of the patient."[168] Feijoo was guided by the following aphorism: "There is no food so good as to be good for everyone, nor is there any so bad as to not be good for someone."[169]

2) Feijoo pleaded for a sharp curtailment of prescriptions and other medicinal treatments. Feijoo was very much aware that illness has its own natural process of evolution. It is usually this natural process that prevails, not medicine. Therefore, a doctor, as Marañón puts it, should "reduce his function to helping the healing power of Nature."[170] Feijoo accepted the utility of a very small number of medicines: "cinchona for tertian fever, opium for pain, mercury for venereal disease, ipecacuanha for dysentery, valerian for hysteria."[171] He considered worthless all of the celebrated compounds with alluring epithets like Agua Angélica and Jarabe Aureo as well as any other prescription which did not fully detail the ingredients. He decried the practice of some doctors who, "in order to become more respectable and even more expensive, pretend to have special remedies which they prescribe with an air of mystery; usually these prescriptions do not contain anything special at all."[172] He condemned the so-called "major cures" which had been advocated by Galen: purges and blood-letting. Likewise, he condemned the "miraculous" cures performed by countless practitioners in touch with the supernatural that were (and continue to be) the plague of honest medicine.

Theories of Feijoo

On the other hand, Feijoo was ambivalent toward the alleged universal efficacy of water (and/or wine) as a curative, particularly as espoused theoretically by the picaresque "water doctor," Vicente Pérez.[173]

3) In the area of medical training and conduct, Feijoo advocated that theological and philosophical systems of medicine, particularly Aristotelianism, not be taught in favor of instilling the methodology and techniques of medicine itself. Feijoo favors a clinical rather than a classroom orientation. Marañón outlines the three "very precise propositions" that Feijoo laid down in his plan for the reform of medical education. "It must be begun, he says, with a complete study of anatomy and physiology, followed by the examination of pathology, symptomatology and therapeutics. The cycle will finish with the study of hygiene and the understanding of the optimum regimen for the prevention of illness."[174] Feijoo advocated the recruiting of foreign expertise, particularly French surgeons, to upgrade the quality of Spanish medicine. On the other hand, he cautions his public against a large number of charlatans from other nations "who came to Spain then thinking that their foreignness alone gave them proof of competence in a country of ignoramuses."[175] With respect to professional conduct, Feijoo decries the "expedients which are used by doctors to disguise their failures,"[176] such as claiming the sickness, which originally had been hidden, was now in the "open field" or accusing the patient of excesses such as "any ridiculous trifle at all which the orderlies report, like rinsing his mouth, changing his shirt, removing his arm from under the sheets, cutting his nails, etc."[177] Likewise, Feijoo is outraged by what Marañón terms "medico-pharmaceutical knavery,"[178] the concert between doctors and pharmacists.

Marañón is so impressed by and devoted to Feijoo that he claims of his own book *Crítica de la medicina dogmática* (1954),

> These admirable ideas of Feijoo's on therapeutics have been annotated and expanded on by me, without exceeding his orthodoxy by even one iota, in a little book which has had universal acclaim, no doubt because of its adherence to Feijoo's ideas. I bestow this laurel, which is hardly mine, on the memory of the great Benedictine monk.[179]

Devotion notwithstanding, Marañón concludes that some of Feijoo's judgments must be placed in the debit column. The most important of these is Feijoo's rigid attack against what he termed the "exterminating aphorism" of Hippocrates, stating, "By doing everything according to the dictates of reason, you should not, therefore, change to another treatment; on the contrary, you should continue what you approved from the beginning."[180] While it is true that a dogmatic adherence to this, or any other aphorism, can cause great harm, Marañón judges that Feijoo's merciless attack reflects his lack of confidence in doctors as well as his conviction that the physician himself should adopt a skepticism, which Marañón believes could undermine his faith in medical effectiveness. Marañón asserts: "It was, no doubt, an error for Feijoo to confuse the consciousness of medical uncertainty with the lack of faith in the doctor. . . .The truth is that this Hippocratic rule is admirable, because it assumes the doctor's rational faith in his science and therefore the certainty that he will not change his criterion each time the course of the illness does not follow the usual pattern, something which occurs quite frequently. Without this principle there would be no Medicine."[181] A similar overstatement is Feijoo's rejection of blood-letting. This technique did have its merits in certain instances, even as late as 1918-19, "when antibiotics were still not dreamed of; the only patients with bronchopneumonia that we can be certain were saved by medical treatment were those who were bled in time."[182] In addition, Marañón lists a number of "common misconceptions" in which Feijoo believed.[183] Some of these beliefs, accepted by all in the eighteenth century, give a hilarious glimpse of a society coming to rely on a newly-found interest in detailed observation, an embryonic phenomenology, yet burdened with the ponderous tradition of a mythological and superstitious past.

Thus, Feijoo did not believe in the existence of the hippopotamus, which was for him another specimen of the mythological bestiary. Yet, his close observations led him to accept the existence of a dog able to pronounce up to thirty German words, "although not perfectly"! He believed that tigers flee the sound of the lyre and that King Philip of Macedonia died because his flesh turned into lice as well as that the cock in its old age lays an egg.[184] Feijoo's most notable lapse into superstition, according to Marañón, was his belief in the Fish-man of Liérganes.[185] He not only accepted this tale but went out of his way to explain it scientifically and publicize it. Marañón devotes a separate and admirable chapter to the Fish-man which well deserved to be published as a separate essay under the same title, "Historia Maravillosa del Hombre—Pez y su Revisión Actual," in *Revista de Occidente*. Indeed, the material has an independent coherence and unity although it fits perfectly into *Las ideas biológicas del Padre Feijoo.* The chapter is somewhat reminiscent of Azorín's best anecdotal-critical essays, although here the material is built on a scientific rather than subjective, impressionistic foundation. Marañón introduces the topic by reviewing references to amphibious men in the past, as in Pliny, Pedro Mexia, and the *Quijote.* He then proceeds to narrate the tale as it was first presented by the Marqués de Valbuena and others, ingeniously separating out the "fabulous" elements that had been taken from earlier folkloric and mythological material and appended to a rather ordinary tale of a child whom the doctor diagnoses as a Cretin probably suffering from ictiosis (a disease inflicting scaliness on the skin) and who was lost in Galicia and found several years later at the port of Cádiz. Marañón finds it instructive indeed that an educated and enlightened woman like Emilia Pardo Bazán added to the Fish-man account the following apocryphal material: "and adhering to them [the scales] were algae, seaweed, and minute, delicate shells."[186] He observes that "This superimposition of the algae and the shells by a person of such superior intellect, one who was several decades removed from the monster, shows what the collaboration of plebian minds, contemporaneous to the marvel, would have been capable of."[187]

Feijoo believed that it was possible to breathe under water and, hence, was predisposed to accept the Fish-man for several reasons, the basic ones being: 1) since corpses of drowned persons revealed no water in their lungs, it was commonly inferred that lungs were able to function beneath the water; 2) the human fetus lives without breathing in an aqueous state while in the uterus of the mother, thereby permitting conjecture that under some other mysterious and abnormal conditions a human could conceivably survive in a liquid environment. In addition, Marañón detects an innate fear and admiration for the sea in Feijoo, a monk cloistered in a monastery "surrounded by four high mountains, which not only closed him in on all sides but also oppressed him; and who could only see the stars which were directly above him."[188] This easily led him astray.

> . . .let us notice that the miracles of rationalization of the absurd which were achieved by the great writer on solid land were wanting when he found himself face to face with the mysteries of the sea. He always speaks of the ocean superstitiously and ignorantly. Without a doubt, he did not often bathe, since he did not know how to swim. He had the idea that sea water was not only salty but also foul-smelling.[189]

Most revealing is the fact that among all of the polemics and attacks written against Feijoo, with one exception, none of them criticized him for his false belief, but rather, usually attacked him for his insights. Marañón draws a moral from the tale: "A strange attitude toward his lucid, experimental mind! And very instructive, because it shows us once more how truth and error can exist together in the weak intelligence of mankind, even in the loftiest examples."[190] These are among Marañón's finest pages in the anecdotal-scientific vein. In a moving narrative, executed in high, dramatic style, he presents a profound object lesson on certain psychological and cultural curtailments upon the free reign of reason.

The influence of Feijoo and his colleagues in their own time

Marañón devotes several chapters to commenting on the lasting influence and results achieved by Feijoo. While Menéndez Pelayo observed that in his own day "Feijoo became an oracle. . .the enthusiasm of his admirers bordered on fanaticism,"[191] physicians as a professional group reacted with violence toward him. This is clear even in the nineteenth century in the medical histories of Chincilla and Hernández Morejón who "treat him as a simple agitator and intruder into Medicine."[192] Nevertheless, Feijoo's impact was considerable on the profession. Under his influence, and under the direction of Martín Martínez, the Sociedad Regia Sevillana, established in 1697, and judged by Marañón to be the first Spanish academy, was strengthened and achieved its maximum impact. Seven years after the publication of the first volume of the *Teatro crítico* and "surely on account of the storm which was stirred up by the writings of the monk in the professional and scientific consciousness of our doctors,"[193] the Academia de Medicina de Madrid was founded. The following year marked the establishment of the Academia Médica Matritense which was destined to become the Real Academia de Medicina. One of the articles in the statutes of this Academy proclaimed Feijoo's slogan, "Observation and Experience as a medical ideal." (Marañón judges that the statutes were probably composed by Pedro Sarmiento.)

Around the middle of the eighteenth century, a number of medical colleges were established which bore the influence of Feijoo's thinking, specifically at Cádiz, Barcelona, Madrid, Santiago de Compostela, Burgos and Málaga. Feijoo was influential in the establishment of the Real Sociedad Vascongada de Amigos del País (which was accused of Freemasonry because of the contact established between some of its members and Jean-Jacques Rousseau). In addition, Feijoo was able to put an end, at least temporarily, to the earlier-mentioned "miracle of the flowers of San Luis" as well as the "rite of the bull of San Marcos" in Extremadura.

Marañón rounds out his study with several customary chapters devoted to a physical and morphological description of Feijoo, a medical history of his ills (Feijoo was sickly as a youth) and a description of his old age and the specific causes of his death.

In addition, he devotes considerable attention to Feijoo's colleagues who were very essential in his effort toward renewal: specifically a chapter each is devoted to Martín Martínez, Gaspar Casal and Padre Sarmiento. Martín Martínez, who for a long period was one of the physicians to the royal court, since he was an authority with the proper medical credentials, served (as did to some degree the French surgeon D'Elgar) to legitimize Feijoo's ideas among physicians. This, for Marañón, explains the reason behind Feijoo's extremely enthusiastic defense of Martínez's *Medicina scéptica* which is judged to be even more aggressive than Feijoo's defenses in his own behalf. It is thought that at that time (1725) Feijoo had never met Martínez, the beneficiary of his *Apología del scepticismo médico*. As Marañón puts it:

> ...one guesses that his basic aim was to cover himself with the banner of a respectable man of science and to establish a firm position under his protection for the battle that he had planned and almost decided on. His lack of academic degrees compelled him to do so. This, in my judgment, is the meaning of the strange irruption of Feijoo onto the literary scene, at the age of fifty, and on the arm of a professor of medicine with whom he had nothing in common.[194]

He finds that, as a result of this first opportune association, "in the medical treatises of the first volume of the *Teatro*, the influence of Martín Martínez's doctrines is clearly observable; these doctrines ended up being halfway measures when compared to Feijoo's."[195] Marañón also describes Martínez's most important work, the aforementioned *Medicina scéptica*, written in the form of a dialogue between a "Galenic practitioner, a chemist, and a Hippocratic or skeptic practitioner, the latter representing the voice of don Martín himself."[196] While the work praises the virtues of clinical observation and experimentalism, with respect to style it does not shine; Marañón characterizes it as "full of confused ideas, pedantic and artificial."[197]

On the other hand, Marañón has nothing but praise for Gaspar Casal, of whom Feijoo was a very intimate friend. (In contrast, the Galician monk had a cordial, but merely professional relationship with Martínez.) Marañón does not doubt that Casal was "the foremost Spanish doctor of his time: cultured, independent of spirit, an incomparable observer, a profound meditator on what he observed, heedful of concurring with universal science, and finally, a genial precursor of one of the most fertile branches of present-day biology, vitaminology."[198] He laments the fact that Menéndez Pelayo did not include him in his defense of Spanish science and finds it curious that Feijoo himself, although he considered Casal a first-rate physician, was rather sparing in commendation. Marañón sets out to rehabilitate and exalt Casal in the same way that he elevates Feijoo himself. In addition to the chapter devoted to Casal in *Las ideas biológicas,* where he points to Casal's naturalistic and clinical precision in describing the disease *pellagra,* in a conference entitled "Los amigos de Feijoo" (1937), later published under the same title in *Vida e historia* (1941), Marañón points to Casal's education background as one of the reasons behind his success. Casal did not go to one of the universities which at this time were extremely corrupted (Marañón enjoyed pointing out that the likes of Torres Villarroel, "a rogue from the street,"[199] was able to obtain a chair in mathematics at Salamanca), thereby avoiding the dogmatism and vacuous theories being laid down in these institutions. In this lecture, Marañón also discusses Casal's relationship to the polemics revolving around Feijoo. Casal was consistently prudent and withdrawn. Marañón attributes Casal's silence, despite his friendship with Feijoo, to a rejection of Feijoo's "anti-medical extremism and his quickness to judge the classical authors of our science."[200]

In 1959, Casal's masterpiece, *Historia Natural y Médica del Principado de Asturias,* thanks mostly to Marañón's efforts, was republished for the first time since 1900. Marañón, of course, wrote the prologue to the book. Finally, in 1960, he had prepared a speech, "La humanidad de Casal," which was given posthumously at the Real Academia de Medicina. In this lecture, Marañón expressed his well-merited satisfaction concerning the number of studies that had been composed to honor Casal's bicentenary. Contributors included Pedro Laín Entralgo and R. Sancho de San Román.[201]

Finally, a separate chapter is devoted to Padre Sarmiento, who, like Casal, appears in the aforementioned "Los amigos del Padre Feijoo." Marañón judges Sarmiento's role to be that of the "shadow" or "double" of Feijoo. Sarmiento was Feijoo's agent in Madrid. He devotedly provided Feijoo with books and instruments, gave him bibliographical advice, read his manuscripts, and, in regard to achieving ecclesiastical approval for the publication of Feijoo's books, had complete authority to "erase, change or add"[202] anything that seemed suitable to him. Marañón judges Sarmiento to be "a marvel of erudition, a very keen observer and an almost monstrous worker."[203] Sarmiento wrote a good deal,[204] yet he published only the two-volume *Demostración Críticoapologética en defensa del Teatro crítico universal.* Sarmiento's reluctance to publish has usually been considered as evidence of excessive humility, but Marañón notes that he was an extremely antisocial, withdrawn, moody individual. Sarmiento even says of himself:

> Who might there be that, having some information about me, has not heard, at the same time, a thousand stories, stupidities and false imputations against me? I am, as is amply attested by all, a ridiculous man, a hypochondriac, difficult, sullen, stubborn, unbearable, curt, severe, uncommunicative, melancholic, unsociable, ungoverned, obstinate, intractible, unpolished, inurbane, discourteous, coarse, unmanageable, willful.[205]

Marañón judges that Sarmiento suffered from an inferiority complex:

> I have the impression that Sarmiento's kindness, which was very great, coincided with an extraordinary conception of himself; and that it was this attitude of disdainful superiority which secluded him in his cell. There is nothing either in his papers or in his life which might convince us of a basic modesty. There is rather that other attitude, which many times passes for modesty, which consists of not doing what everyone else does, of renouncing beforehand what others eagerly desire, precisely to place oneself in a position of initial advantage with respect to the fortunate or the ambitious man. He who tells us 'I have not wanted to be anybody special' is apt to give us the impression of a much greater arrogance than does the puerile vanity of the one who says 'I have been somebody special.'[206]

Marañón's general opinions and particularly his diagnosis of Sarmiento's personality are restated in "Los amigos del Padre Feijoo" and also in a lecture given in 1948 at the Biblioteca Nacional entitled "El siglo XVIII y los Padres Feijoo y Sarmiento." In this 1948 lecture, Marañón laments that he had intended to write a biography of Sarmiento but that his papers were lost during the Spanish Civil War.[207] Although in 1948 he still had hopes of realizing that goal some day, the biography was, unfortunately, never undertaken.

The influence of Marañón's work on Feijoo on subsequent scholarship

Las ideas biológicas del Padre Feijoo is probably the work by Marañón which has had the most enduring impact on academic scholarship in the field of Spanish arts and letters. (However, its implications for the history of science have been superseded.) This is so despite the fact that it is not, strictly speaking, a work of literary scholarship. Certainly, Marañón's *Don Juan* has been the most widely read and controversial of his essays, and I have noted earlier its catalytic effect, its tendency to cause other essayists and critics to define or redefine their ideas on the *Burlador* in reaction to Marañón's position. Nevertheless, *Don Juan* remains marginal inasmuch as it has never been accepted in substance by academic critics or scholars. Marañón himself comments on the unusual fate of his *Don Juan*:

> My book on *Don Juan* has the characteristic that all of the critics have claimed that it is balderdash. The unanimous attitude of the critics has been negative, no doubt because the book contradicts the fundamental notion of Don Juan which men universally share. . . .Yet be it through disdain on the part of men or understanding on on the part of women, the fact is that my *Don Juan* has been the book that has outsold all my others, both within and outside of Spain.[208]

The impact of *Las ideas biológicas del Padre Feijoo*, while more specialized and situated in a less explored area of Spanish intellectual history, has been substantial indeed, although as we shall see, recently his work has been superseded by historians of science, such as J.M. López Piñero, Julio Caro Baroja, Luis S. Granjel and others. (See p. 198.) The first reviews were most laudatory. Angel del Río comments that Marañón "puts into application a varied repertoire of methods—science, erudition, a deep sensibility—in order to study, or rather, revindicate, one of the most eminent figures of eighteenth century Spain."[209] G. Cirot, in his review, stated, "It constitutes one of the most serious contributions to our understanding of eighteenth century Spain, of which Feijoo was one of the intellectual giants, although not the only one."[210] Similarly, Santiago Montero Díaz found:

> The most profound significance of this monograph does not reside in its rigorous, erudite documentation, nor even in the precise criticisms revealed in some of the opinions, but rather in an intimate sense of renewal which causes it to be one of the bases for all subsequent reappraisals of Feijoo's significance for Spain.[211]

Gaspar Delpy in his well-known book, *Feijoo et l'esprit européen* (1936), noting that his research on Feijoo began as early as 1914, is gratified and encouraged by Marañón's work: "In 1934, a physician of world renown, Dr. Marañón, demonstrated that both in medicine and biology, Feijoo, a true forerunner, achieved remarkable insights. That demonstration. . .has encouraged us and inspired us in our work."[212] Delpy attempts to demonstrate, just as Marañón had done two years earlier, that Feijoo is not a mere poligrapher, a uniter of disparate knowledge, for "the course of his varied work is unifed by a brilliant, authoritative intelligence."[213] Jean Sarrailh is deeply indebted to Marañón and to Gaspar Delpy as well. The chapter in *La España ilustrada de la segunda mitad del siglo XVIII* entitled "Hacia un nuevo espíritu científico" adopts Marañón's argument that Feijoo and his group were involved in a dramatic sociocultural struggle to supplant authoritarianism and dogmatism with experimentation and clinical observation. It also relies heavily on Marañón for facts.

Pérez-Rioja, who has compiled the most complete bibliography of Feijoo available, points to Marañón's preeminence in the field which has led to much of the later research:

> Dr. Marañón, in his well-known study on Feijoo, as well as in lectures or monographs that are less-known, not only has given us a solid analysis of the biological and medical theories of the author of the *Teatro crítico*; he has suggested for us a variety of lines of thought which are worthy of future elaboration. . . .Among other things he has the merit of having suggested new areas of research or at least, of having interested numerous Spaniards in the study of Feijoo.[214]

Pérez-Rioja himself is usually in agreement with Marañón's judgments, albeit making interesting interpretations of his own as, for example, his relating of Feijoo's zeal for renewal to the professional vocation of the monk: "In this missionary sense of literature, a tack which he undertakes with the patriotic impulses of a conquistador, perhaps lies the fundamental characteristic of Feijoo's literary personality. . . ."[215]

Similarly, a survey of the various articles in *Fray Benito Jerónimo Feijoo y Montenegro: Estudios reunidos en conmemoración del IIº centenario de su muerte (1764-1964)* published by Universidad Nacional de la Plata, treating Feijoo's personality and his scientific speculations, bears evidence of Marañón's premises.

Among the ideas which were, at least partially, in the air before Marañón, but which the doctor solidified and clarified and actively promulgated so that they have withstood the tests of time and scholareship, at least until the "new wave" of scholarship in the history of science, are the following:

1) The characterization of Feijoo's efforts as "the struggle of experimental common sense against dogmatism lacking in intelligence,"[216] behind which is the assumption that Feijoo's transcendence is attributable to his pursuit of truth and struggle against error. Therefore, it is pertinent to point to Feijoo as a systematic thinker (amply demonstrated at least in the area of medicine) rather than a mere compiler of facts.

2) Feijoo is part of a select group of "torch bearers" who maintained culture and learning during a period of widespread ignorance, attempting, whenever possible, to initiate renewal and establish new institutions for the dissemination of knowledge. Sarrailh notes that Ortega y Gasset laments the misfortune of Spain's having passed over the "enlightened century;" Eugenio d'Ors, on the other hand, claims, "Spain was realized in the eighteenth century. In this country the *settecento* was everything."[217] Yet, Sarrailh accepts Marañón's conclusion as his own:

> Neither one nor the other. The truth lies between these two antithetical attitudes. Doctor Marañón, an excellent analyst of Feijoo and his time, is the one who seems to express the facts most accurately when he writes: 'Spain, perhaps did not join the encyclopedist movement on a national scale, which on the other hand, everywhere appears to have been an attitude adopted by the elites. Yet she did have, as always, her isolated titans charged with maintaining the continuum of civilization.' Let us convert those titans into giants and accept as a whole, for the conclusion of this study, the judgment of Marañón.[218]

3) Feijoo practiced experimentalism and "skepticism" in the scientific sense, yet he was totally orthodox, traditionalist, and patriotic. We have noted earlier Sarrailh's adherence to the above; even Paul Hazard, independently, comes to the same conclusion: "Feijoo was equally at home in the traditional and in the modern worlds. . .he was profoundly Christian."[219] According to Hazard, Feijoo judged: "It was not the Church's dogmas that dwarfed the intellect and hindered the march of Science; it was the usurping authorities, spurious Aristotelianism, for example, that had paralysed the Spanish mind, and even now, in the middle of the eighteenth century, was doing its best to keep it under its benumbing spell."[220]

Despite the strong influence that Marañón has exercised and continues to exercise on the history of Spanish science and Feijoo's particular contribution within it, our critic's work has been supplemented and supplanted to a great measure by extensive, rigorously scholarly work performed by professional historians of science

Marañón's Influence on Feijoo Scholarship

working in academic settings. The professional, "scientific" evaluation of the history of science, pursued by persons specifically trained in this discipline, is a relatively new phenomenon in Western scholarship. One index is the recency (and paucity) of specialized chairs in the History of Science established at major Western universities. In Spain, professional training in this field (as contrasted by sporadic works written by full-time physicians and scientists) dates from the 1950s and particularly the 1960s. The scholarship that it has produced is associated with such journals as *Archivo Iberoamericano de Historia de la Medicina y Antropología Médica* (also called *Asclepio*, Madrid, established 1949), *Boletín de la Sociedad Española de Historia de la Medicina* (Madrid, established 1960), and *Cuadernos de Historia de la Medicina Española* (Salamanca, established 1962). In 1963, the Actas del I Congreso Español de la Historia de la Medicina appeared. This has been an ongoing event. Researchers associated with this new wave of investigation in the history of science include figures that I have mentioned earlier (López Piñero, Caro Baroja, Granjel) as well as others, not only in science but in the history of economics, philosophy, ideas, politics, etc., such as J.F. Prieto Aguirre, V. Peset Llorca, L. García Ballester, R. Marco Cuéllar, J.M. Morales Meseguer, E. Portela Marco, J.R. Zaragoza Rubina, Olga V. Quiroz-Martínez, J. Reglá, J. Nadal, P. Vilar, A. Domínguez Ortiz, S. García Martínez, R. Ceñal and M.L. Terrada Ferrandis.[221]

As a result of the investigation of the above researchers we are now able to chart the development and vicissitudes of Spanish science with such a wealth of detail as to overwhelm and render obsolete earlier generalizations that were at the same time catchy dramatizations in the interest of creating lively biography (e.g., empiricism vs. dogmatism, encyclopedism vs. authoritarianism, etc.). For example, it would be inconceivable for a contemporary researcher such as López Piñero to become enthused or even preoccupied to any degree with the notion of the "predestination" of scientists—a concept which so swept Marañón and Sarrailh in their understanding of Feijoo. Indeed López Piñero proclaims the obsolescence of the whole so-called method of the "eminent figures." With respect to Feijoo himself and Marañón's treatment of the Benedictine, López Piñero is equally definite:

> For a long time the studies of Marañón on Feijoo and the noble passion that the illustrious physician and historian felt toward this figure, imposed upon him the role of fundamental renewer of Spanish science. Subsequent research has introduced decisive qualifications

upon Feijoo's image. Today we know that Feijoo was only a great and intelligent propagator of this resurgence. The renewal at the properly scientific level is attributable both to forerunners and contemporaries of the illustrious Benedictine. The labors of these renewers is known to us thanks to the studies of Quiroz, Ceñal and Mindán in the area of philosophic thought, and to the recent work of Granjel and his colleagues and Peset Llorca, with respect to the medical and biological sciences.[222]

One of the results of the work of López Piñero and the others that I have alluded to has been a more accurate charting of the development of Spanish science, not so much in terms of personalities (although one of the outcomes of professional history of science has been the discovery of numerous, heretofore forgotten, Spanish scientists), but more importantly, as a reflection of the ongoing development of theories, hypotheses, constructions, empirical verifications, practical applications and so on. In terms of methodology, the net result has been to sweep aside the "romantic" (in Vicens Vives' sense, see p. 80) dramatizations of scientific "titans," or the vision of a struggle between science and blind superstition in favor of a more neutral, scientific, data and document-oriented topography of Spanish science. The similarity on the one hand, between developments in the history of science and, on the other, the developments in general historiography and the methodology of biographical studies that we have evaluated in Chapter III are striking indeed. This is not unexpected, for both fields reflect the ongoing trend of history to become a social science rather than to remain one of the humanities. Persons such as Vicens Vives and López Piñero are more interested in the objective (often quantifiable) analysis of documents and data than, as Marañón had envisioned in the 1930s, creating a "humanistic substitute for the novel."

Additional writings on Feijoo and others in the eighteenth century

In addition to his main effort, *Las ideas biológicas del Padre Feijoo,* with its many ramifications and general observations on the intellectual history of the eighteenth century, Marañón has given many lectures and penned numerous essays, articles, and prologues on Feijoo and other important and lesser-known figures of the eighteenth century. I have already noted Marañón's additional writings on Casal and Sarmiento.

In 1933, in anticipation of *Las ideas biológicas,* the material on the Fish-man of Liérganes was published as a separate article with the title "Revisión de la historia del hombre-pez" in *Revista de Occidente*. Moreover, in 1934, Marañón gave his entrance speech into the Real Academia Española entitled "Vocación, preparación y ambiente biológico y médico del Padre Feijoo." Marañón confesses that in preparing the topic of Feijoo for his entrance speech he was struck by the value of Feijoo's scientific speculations and their relevance. So engaged did he become in the subject that the result was *Las ideas biológicas del Padre Feijoo,* and, since he had to forgo bringing the bulky manuscript,[223] the speech "Vocación, preparación y ambiente biológico y médico del Padre Feijoo" is a summary and synthesis of the book!

In 1934 Marañón gave a lecture at the Real Academia Nacional de Medicina entitled "Nuestro siglo XVIII y las academias." In 1935, the lecture was published as an article entitled "Más sobre nuestro siglo XVIII" in *Revista de Occidente.* In 1941, it was published in his book *Vida e historia.* This lecture combines a summary of Marañón's observations on scientific developments in Spain during the eighteenth century as expressed in *Las ideas biológicas* with a good deal of new material concerning the social decadence in Spain—the problem of beggars, the over-subscription of clerical professions, the abandonment of the land, and so forth. Marañón describes Menéndez Pelayo's *La ciencia española* as nothing but "guerrilla warfare and oratorical denunciations,"[224] claiming that the nineteenth century critic was actually interested primarily in struggling "against the Europeanizers, Azcárate, Sanz del Río, the hated *krausistas* and those related to them."[225] On the other hand, Cajal's observations are the product of a more constructive analysis: 1) Spain is "intellectually backward" but not "decadent"; 2) the scientific output in Spain has been relatively stable and has maintained itself at the same level since the sixteenth century; 3) however, in order to produce a great scientist such as Galileo or Newton, it is necessary to reach a high general intellectual level in the country so that the genius may be supported in his intellectual growth; 4) Spanish scientists in general have been oriented toward the practical, their "deplorable theoretical poverty"[226] has been a severe handicap; 5) science is not really in a state of decrepitude in Spain, but rather exists as an embryo *in potencia.*

In his essay, Marañón's antipathy toward Torres Villarroel, at least as a scientist, reaches its height. He calls Villarroel a "rascal, bamboozler and liar to the point of cynicism, who has achieved an honorable reputation because he wrote with indubitable charm, although it is always easy to be witty when one is irresponsible."[227] As for his scientific output, a typical example is an incredibly long-titled monograph on a corpse that the rabble claimed to have seen sweating.[228]

Marañón's most recent lecture, given at the Biblioteca Nacional in 1948, is entitled "El siglo XVIII y los Padres Feijoo y Sarmiento." I have already mentioned the material in this lecture that deals with Sarmiento. In general, the lecture is stimulated by Paul Hazard's then recently published *La Pensée européenne au XVIIIe siècle; de Montesquieu a Lessing.* Marañón reacts to the fact that Hazard does not mention any Spanish forerunners of the rationalism and empiricism typical of the eighteenth century. Nor even is Erasmus mentioned, whose influence, for Marañón, was "principally Spanish."[229] Erasmus and Vives are considered by Marañón as genuine precursors of the "liberal" spirit of the eighteenth century. Both figures were suspect by the church. Erasmus was eventually deemed heretical and Vives "did not enjoy the favor of official Spanish Catholicism."[230] This accounts for the fact that, on the one hand, Erasmus was never mentioned by Feijoo and, on the other, that Feijoo, "who was constantly inspired by Vives, cites his name much less than his thoughts."[231] Thus, the influence of Erasmus and of his colleague and friend, Vives, still has to be detected between the lines in the eighteenth century, just as that scholarly necessity has been practiced in regard to the seventeenth century by Bataillon, Américo Castro and others. Vives does not really come out into the open in Spain until the nineteenth century, after being cultivated by foreign thinkers and finally by Spanish liberals. Paul Hazard's neglect of Erasmus and Vives as progressive thinkers is exacerbated, according to Marañón, by the fact that both were more or less "orthodox" (in spite of the condemnation of Erasmus). Marañón implies that the inclusion of Catholic precursors of experimentalism such as Vives and Erasmus would be dissonant with Hazard's characterization of the eighteenth century as a period during which Christianity "stood on trial," "the God of the Christians was impeached," "religion was reduced to the affirmation of the evidence of God, the Supreme Being, and to belief in final causes."[232] Marañón criticizes people like Paul Hazard who "consider as one of the typical features of the century what he calls the open trial against the God of the Christians. With this criterion, exciting books can be written. But it is not true."[233] At any rate, Marañón is implacably opposed to a vision of history which considers the French Revolution to be the inevitable consequence of a chain of social and ideological advances in the eighteenth century.

In 1934, Marañón published a profile of Feijoo for *La Razón*, Buenos Aires, and in 1938, in *La Nación,* in an article entitled "Feijoo en Francia," Marañón praises Gaspar Delpy who, in his book *Feijoo et l'esprit européen*, has "realized, in an insurmountable way, a study integrating the cultural significance of Feijoo into the mechanism of European civilization."[234] In an undated lecture (probably 1949 according to the editor of the *Obras completas*) given in Peru, entitled "Una mañana en una celda," Marañón evokes some of Feijoo's speculations concerning the new world and, in particular, his defense of the *criollo*.

In 1955, Marañón published "Evolución de la gloria de Feijoo,"[235] basically a restatement of his survey of critical approaches to Feijoo as well as a reiteration of his standard defense of the Galician monk. In addition, Marañón penned several prologues dealing with Feijoo or closely related topics. In "Enciclopedismo y humanismo," Marañón contrasts these two stances, condemning the former as an inheritance from the eighteenth century and a "plague of the nineteenth."[236] He contrasts the personality of the humanist with that of the encyclopedist in polemical terms, reflecting his earlier struggles to protect Feijoo and others from the charge of encyclopedist:

> The Encyclopedist measures his knowledge by the number of things that he is acquainted with. Knowing a lot does not matter to the humanist; rather he is only interested in knowing what is essential in order to understand what is incomprehensible. Apart from its quality, the encyclopedist's knowledge is expansive, extroverted; that of the humanist is concentrated and introverted. The encyclopedist aspires to induce men to admire him. The humanist merely seeks to take his stand with regard to his proper worth, and to cause others not to admire him but rather to learn from him. The encyclopedist smacks of a pedagogue and the humanist, a teacher.[237]

"La razón conduce inexorablemente a Dios," published as a prologue in 1949 and later anthologized in *La medicina y nuestro tiempo* under the title "Milagros y milagrerías," describes Marañón's attitudes toward the pseudo- and authentically miraculous in terms comparable to Feijoo's stance.[238]

Let us turn now to a series of studies by Marañón spun off directly from the research involved in the preparation of *Las ideas biológicas* or indirectly as the consequence of Marañón's active dissemination in various public forums of his ideas on the eighteenth century.

"Vida y andanzas de Don Pablo de Olavide" is a lecture given in 1959 at the Peruvian embassy in Spain. In 1960, it was published in an anthology entitled *Seis temas peruanos*. The lecture is a profile of Olavide, a prominent and picturesque Peruvian *criollo* who was put on trial for "heresy, atheism and materialism" in the most famous Spanish inquisitional process of the eighteenth century, and who is mentioned once or twice in the 1933 *Las ideas biológicas*. Marañón is perturbed by some "distortions" and legendary aspects of the trial which led to its evaluation, particularly in France, as a manifestation of religious oppression in Spain. He asserts that it is a grave mistake to interpret Olavide's condemnation as theologically motivated as did some followers of Voltaire in Spain and France. ". . .the true meaning of the punishment, was principally civil and, in large part, an expression of the wretched passion of envy. . . .The accusation and sentencing of Olavide. . .did not have a religious significance but rather only a religious appearance in order to cover up a political purpose."[239] Olavide, engaged in a conflict with the Capuchin order over an important project that he headed, intended to colonize the Sierra Morena. This conflict was further exacerbated by the envy and antagonism of many Spaniards associated with the court. The Inquisition, "already weakened and powerless to confront power wielders as in times of past splendor,"[240] was used as an instrument to punish Olavide.

Olavide was condemned to eight years reclusion in a convent and his assets were confiscated, but it was not long before he managed to escape to France. Marañón feels that even the inquisitor-general and certainly Carlos IV intervened in order to facilitate his escape, both being convinced that he had been treated unjustly. Marañón judges that Olavide was not a particularly revolutionary individual, although at the time of the French Revolution, "it is possible that, when the uprising began, he had the illusion, like so many others, that a greater justice, so agreeable to the humanitarian ideals of the time, might arise from that popular movement.[241] Marañón here follows Menéndez Pelayo who accepted at face value Olavide's palinode, the celebrated and extremely popular, *El evangelio en triunfo o historia de un filósofo desengañado*. Marañón agrees with Menéndez Pelayo that the book is extremely deficient in terms of its literary worth; its value lies in the palinode, the genuine rejection of once-held cynical and frivolous attitudes: "The important thing is that in this book a man publicly corrected his behavior; and not because of fear or desire for profit, but rather because of loyalty to his fellow men."[242] Sarrailh holds otherwise, concluding, as did Morel-Fatio, that the book was no more than a "passport" for returning to Spain and that the personal or biographical part detailing impiousness and rebellion is the only serious material in it.

> Therefore, what should we think of that retraction, about which such a fuss has been made, in that book of his, *El evangelio en triunfo* which has been correctly called a "total palinode" by the same French Hispanist [Morel-Fatio]? We believe, as he does, that it was simply a subterfuge to be able to return to his beloved Spain and receive some help and favors from the monarch. In it we find a striking picture of the pleasures and vices of those times in which Olavide and his friends, because of their exceptional perversity, engaged, such as insulting religious and divine law. We find a faithful evocation of a scandalous life whose substance was composed solely of orgies, pharoah games followed by quarrels, duels and sometimes by deaths; by the reading of irreverant books and by licentious conversations. . . .Just as this whole personal part of the book vibrates with sincerity and even with a badly disguised nostalgia, so the long catechistic tracts. . .are marked by a cold and insipid quality.[243]

On the other hand, Richard Herr points out that while "the exiled author betrayed a conscious attempt to appeal to the recent Spanish fury against the Revolution. . .and was catering to the prejudices of the audience he was writing for and hardly, as many readers have thought, attempting to give an honest account of his own early life and friends,"[244] nevertheless, Olavide no doubt did feel genuine revulsion at "witnessing Christian churches turned into temples of Reason where Marat and Pelletier occupied the niches from which Saint Peter and Saint Paul had been removed in disgrace."[245]

Aside from the question of the authenticity or conventionality of the biographical material in *El evangelio en triunfo*, it appears that Marañón was very much influenced by his estimation of his own exile in his evaluation of the book. This becomes obvious when we interpret the "lecture" on the virtues of "rectification" which follows the literary evaluation of *El evangelio en triunfo*.

> Life's repertoire is full of examples of people who way into maturity or old age take refuge in a deplorable error, both for their own conscience and for others, because of not wanting to take the serious step toward rectification which is much more heroic and naturally more effective than the classic "maintain and do not make amends [*mantenerlo y no enmendarlo.*]"[246]

The fact is that Marañón's pamphlet *Liberalismo y comunismo* (1937), a vehement rejection of his former affiliations with the Republic, has been accused likewise, by José Bergamín, of being a "passport," a palinode, so that the author might be able to return from exile in France to Franco Spain. In this pamphlet, Marañón accuses the extremist elements of manipulating and corrupting the liberals. From this time forward the terms "liberal" and "liberalism" become highly charged terms for Marañón and assume a certain cryptic air. Marañón on several occasions continues to proclaim his liberalism, yet he now describes it as a form of consciousness and a personal life-style and shuns any usage of the term in connection with political movements of any sort. At any rate, it is clear that he is referring to his own situation, implicitly, in his acceptance and moral approval of Olavide's palinode.

A similar ambivalence is expressed toward the term, liberal, in the lecture entitled "Jovellanos" (1958), an "outline" (as Marañón terms it) of Jovellanos' attitude and relationship toward the Jesuits, of his method of working through the academies rather than the universities,[247] and of possible reasons behind his exile and his fundamentally anti-romantic personality. Marañón is perturbed that certain "eternal excesses that sterilize Spanish thought"[248] are still being discussed: namely, the alleged conservatism or liberalism of Jovellanos. Marañón judges that Jovellanos was a realist who "declaimed, with reason, against the utopian reformers who on some occasions achieve nothing with their preaching and on others only manage to disturb the masses."[249] Marañón asserts that Jovellanos was "a man of genius and a liberal,"[250] hastening to add:

> I know that you will not understand by liberal the individual affili-
> ated to a political party, which could even have seemed just another
> act of heterodoxy. He is instead the man who, because of his instinc-
> tive reactions, his culture, both traditional and modern at the same
> time; and because of his moral greatness, loved liberty as long as it
> could be compatible with the social order: the true liberal who bases
> himself on understanding between men, whatever their ideas and pas-
> sions might be.[251]

Having created such an heroic archetype, a man who is not only a "liberal" but a transcendental individual who ought not to be eval-uated in terms of mere political epithets, Marañón finds it not at all difficult to identify with Jovellanos! ". . .and for my part, I say, that if I could aspire to so much, I would have wanted to resemble, even re-motely, Jovellanos."[252]

Two prologues, "La historia moderna de España" (1954), and "El afrancesamiento de los Españoles" (1953),[253] penned to introduce, respectively, Jean Sarrailh's *L'Espagne éclairée de la second moitié du XVIII siècle*, and Miguel Artola's *Los afrancesados*, are of interest here due to the judgments they bring to bear on the general characteristics and tendencies of the eighteenth century. Marañón's commendation of Sarrailh in his prologue is only half-hearted, particularly when we consider the praise that the French critic heaps upon him in the book itself. We gather from the wording that Marañón did not want to overly associate himself with Sarrailh. He calls the rector of the Sorbonne "a liberal and a foreign writer, although full of love for Spain; and necessarily there are many nuances of the extremist Spain of that time, and the Spain of the present, in the aftermath of a civil war, with which he cannot agree."[254] Although he judges Sarrailh's work a "fundamental work,"[255] the grounds upon which Marañón bases this evaluation are: "his erudition is conclusive and exhaustive; and this would be enough to make his book irreplaceable, even for those who might think in a different way than the author."[256] Certainly, one of the things which he did not enjoy, particularly with the Spanish Civil War still on his mind, was Sarrailh's pointing to the French Revolution as the occurrence which jolted the Spanish political balance and began reforms. Sarrailh judges that while the elite (Jovellanos, Cabarrús, Pérez Rico, etc.), prudently or violently were asking for "enrichment of the nation by means of the labor of *all* of its sons, by the rational exploitation of land which, even up to our time, has been distributed and badly cultivated, and by the suppression of abuses and of social inequality,"[257] nothing came of this until 1789.

> Outbursts of anger begin to be heard against the great landowners and against the idle rich, but these become muted in proximity to the throne, nor do they ever encompass the monarch. It is necessary first for the great upheaval of the Revolution of 1789 to occur for discussion to turn to political matters where the principle of an absolute monarchy might be questioned.[258]

In "El afrancesamiento de los españoles," Marañón attacks Artola's thesis, which he laments has become a sort of historical dogma: "the French Revolution was the natural—even normal—outgrowth of the spirit of the eighteenth century, that is to say, of the cult of reason, of the spirit of enlightenment. . . ."[259] According to Marañón, the classical form of this dogma considering the French Revolution as the culmination of the Enlightenment is as follows: "It is claimed that the intellectuals took advantage of the freedom that was granted to them by 'benevolent despots' in order to study and publish the works that led to the encyclopedist movement and later to the Revolution, thus bringing to completion an ongoing, evolving trend."[260] He considers the above "dogma" to be patently dangerous inasmuch as it implies that "the desire for liberty and self-determination, which constitutes the normal goal of human evolution, are subversive desires; or that revolutions are natural episodes of normal evolution."[261]

Marañón goes on to propose some observations on the nature of revolution (and naturally, civil war!). The physician claims that a revolution "is always a retrograde event."[262] Revolutions have only indirect and tenuous relationships to intellectual movements. They are "rather than a political event, a pathological accident, an explosion of three passions that prey on civilization: resentment, envy and masochistic fury."[263] Of these three "eternal subterranean motor forces,"[264] the first two are created by civilization itself. Both are the inevitable *verso* of the *anverso* of progress. The third element, "masochistic fury," is described in rather Jungian terms as "an ancestral energy that civilization has not and perhaps never will dominate."[265] In times of peace, these passions are repressed, but when peace is ruptured: "The resentful sectors of humanity, envious or cruel, which encompass three-fourths of our species, take advantage of the outbreak of freedom to remove their masks and surge into the streets."[266]

Let us note that Marañón does not really deal with the question of the outbreak of specific revolutions, but instead offers some rather bleak, ahistorical speculations on the reasons behind the extreme violence associated with revolution, these being a function of repressed feelings and deep-seated instincts which are part of the human makeup.

In sum, as we see from our survey of the many public statements and writings on Feijoo and other figures of the eighteenth century that were produced as a result of the critical success of *Las ideas biológicas del Padre Feijoo*, Marañón became a very active researcher, theoretician and publicizer in the field of eighteenth-century studies, most willing to actively disseminate ideas in prologues, newspaper articles, and, above all, lectures to the general public. He brought to the field of literary scholarship the same sort of technique and delivery that he would use for a scientific talk on a topic of general public interest. The doctor was an active campaigner in the sciences, he courageously took the public forum repeatedly in order to advocate certain ethical stands on such questions as women's rights and sexual education. The public and polemical habits known to operate in the scientific and cultural arena are transferred to the field of literary scholarship and criticism in the form of the lecture: a genre in which Marañón was most effective, combining a strong, usually polemical thesis, a direct delivery displaying both the organization and the research of the scientific paper and the anemity, wit and moving imagery of the speech.

Marcelino Menéndez Pelayo

Marañón's biographical chronicle of the development of Spanish science picks up again in the nineteenth century with Menéndez Pelayo. Marañón has four writings[267] on Menéndez Pelayo: "Recuerdos de Menéndez Pelayo," a speech given in 1954 and published in *Efemérides y comentarios,* under the title "Se celebra el centenario de Menéndez Pelayo," a prologue to the *Epistolario* (between Menéndez Pelayo and "Clarín"), entitled "Aquella España" and subsequently published in *Ensayos liberales* with the title "Dos vidas en el tiempo de la concordia," and, finally, there is a little known study, "Menéndez Pelayo visto desde su precocidad," written for a facsimile edition of the critic's secondary school and university assignments and prizewinning essays.

Marañón does not approach Menéndez Pelayo with the systematic attention that he dedicated to Feijoo. Rather, his observations on the nineteenth-century scholar are set within a narrative dominated by nostalgic reminiscences and devoted mainly to the attempt on the part of the adult Marañón to grasp and comprehend, in an articulate way, the essence of Menéndez Pelayo's genius, which he had accepted and known implicitly as a child. For a detailed, systematic analysis of Menéndez Pelayo, we must turn to Pedro Laín Entralgo who isolates and rigorously analyzes the qualities that define the nineteenth-century scholar: Catholic, Spaniard, modern intellectual, historian and artist.[268]

Marañón judges Menéndez Pelayo to be a scientific percursor of the Generation of 1898. The criteria here are not the ones that we have handled earlier: experimentalism, clinical and naturalistic observation, and the rejection of authoritarianism. The judgment is more subjective, pertaining to Menéndez Pelayo himself as an incarnate example of the systematic and exhaustive scholar and researcher.

I have registered Marañón's vigorous rejection of Menéndez Pelayo's judgments on Feijoo and other figures in the eighteenth century. Here, in his contributions specifically on Menéndez Pelayo, Marañón presents an apology for the man himself—but not without reviewing the weaknesses of *La ciencia española,* again, associating them with the personality of the critic himself. Having first prepared the reader by noting that, according to his remembrances, as a youth Menéndez Pelayo was able to scan a four-hundred-page book in half an hour, Marañón goes on to claim that *La ciencia española* was the product of "hasty readings."[269] Whereas Menéndez Pelayo could cover a prodigious amount of material in the humanities, due to his background, which permitted him to intuit the relevant material and discard the chaff, the same was not true of the many sciences where his expertise was scanty, if existent at all. In addition, the poligrapher was dealing here almost purely with secondary sources: "...he lacks a rigorous eye, but he does ply us with the names of dozens and dozens of Spaniards which like a waterfall overwhelms us in order to demonstrate that during all of the periods of our national existence, and in every scientific sector, we had numerous, outstanding figures."[270] Moreover, there is a deficiency due to the underlying motive for the composition of the book: to defend Spanish science from the *krausistas*. Thus, the style is hampered by "the grandiloquence of an orator rather than a writer."[271] Finally, in his essay in the facsimile edition of the student works, Marañón notes that Menéndez Pelayo's juvenile work in mathematics was of a lesser caliber than his achievements in other fields. It is observed that the precocious student won prizes in every field except geometry and trigonometry. In the following, Menéndez Pelayo's comparative lack of interest in mathematics is attributed vaguely to his father:

> ...without a doubt he would have won in Geometry if not for the circumstance that his father, a professor in this field, was a member of the examining panel. Nevertheless, it is evident that this circumstance fully coincides with his lack of interest in mathematics. This apathy for and less aptitude in mathematics and the natural sciences on the part of Don Marcelino is revealing; it permits us to explain another one of the qualities of his work...the incomplete information, and above all, the incompleteness in critical orientation in the mathematical and biological disciplines that we find in one of his most popular and praised works, *La ciencia española*.[272]

It is at this point that Marañón praises Menéndez Pelayo's *personal* scientific example in perhaps the most curious of the doctor's redemptive arguments, for here he revindicates the scholar personally in spite of his objection to a body of the scholar's work. It is not on account of Menéndez Pelayo's patriotic but inexact apologies that he extended "enduring services to Spanish science,"[273] but rather by his "own example as a researcher and scholar."[274]

Marañón goes on to argue, as he does in many other places, that the Generation of 1898 is really characterized "not so much by its thinkers, writers and artists, as by its scientists."[275] The immediate antecedent of the scientific contributions of the Generation of 1898 is found in the figure of Menéndez Pelayo. His "excusable exaggerations" as an historian are compensated by "his efficacy, which generated true science. A good portion of nineteenth century research was born from the seeds planted by his hands."[276]

Marañón's exaltation of Menéndez Pelayo as an example of Spanish science is brought into relief by his enthusiastic narration, both in the 1939 lecture and the 1954 speech, of Menéndez Pelayo's relationship with Galdós.

> His political opposition to Galdós, who at that time was undergoing the epoch of *Gloria* and *Doña Perfecta,* that is, the most acute moment of his liberalism. . .was not sufficient cause to dampen their intimate friendship. Quite to the contrary, the continual political and ideological controversies seemed, by dint of their intensity, to consolidate the bond of mutual affection and esteem that they professed for each other.[277]

The cordiality and friendship between these two ideologically opposed figures was assimilated by the young Marañón, who knew both of them, as a profound object lesson in tolerance, in the ability to respect a contrary ideological position. Indeed, this sort of openness is an essential prerequisite of the scientific orientation and, perhaps, in the phrase "[Menéndez Pelayo] extended enduring services to Spanish science," Marañón is, in part, alluding to a personal debt of gratitude. As he put it, "Of the moral lessons served to me in youth, none can compare to the example of loyal tolerance bequeathed to me by such remarkable teachers."[278]

In 1954, Marañón attempts to indicate the contradictions that he perceived in Menéndez Pelayo's work through recourse to the notion of a "multiple personality." There is not just one Menéndez Pelayo just as there is not just one Góngora, Garcilaso, fray Luis de León or Unamuno. On the one hand, there is the Menéndez Pelayo pictured as inflexible, archconservative and moralistic, the facet that most Spaniards have conventionally come to associate with the scholar. "Many Spaniards consider him a rigid, fanatical paladin of his beliefs and of his illusions about Spain."[279] Yet, on the other hand, there is the warm, tolerant Menéndez Pelayo as manifested in the scholar's active friendship with Galdós and his support of Galdós's acceptance into the Real Academia.

Pedro Laín Entralgo reacts negatively to this concept.

Are there, then, two Menéndez Pelayos, one an inquisitorial traditionalist, the other a tolerant neoliberal? In evocation of Solomon's dictum, need we split into half our noble critic, one for the inquisitors and the other for the free-thinkers? In my opinion, such a bloody hemisection is unnecessary.[280]

Laín sees a continuity and internal consistency in Menéndez Pelayo, based, once again, on the factors that best define his being: Catholic, Spaniard, modern intellectual, historian and artist. On the other hand, Menéndez Pelayo's life and scholarly work does go through stages, but this is due to the process of growing to maturity rather than the governance of a multiple personality.

> The man remains himself. The basic coordinates of his existence as well. . . . There was no "conversion" from one way of being to another, qualitatively different one, but rather successive "refinements" of a being in accord with his native temperament which in itself was the outgrowth of his early education. . . . This is the key that permits us to understand the course of his biological growth.
>
> Nevertheless, the ongoing vitality with which this sequential sense of maturity is earned is not an obstacle for his biographer's need to distinguish diverse stages in his development. In the first stage Menéndez Pelayo appears as a polemizing historian: he is the writer of *La ciencia española* and *Historia de los heterodoxos españoles.* In the second stage Don Marcelino is the mature historian, at a peak represented by the publication of his *Historia de las ideas estéticas.*[281]

In 1959, after reviewing Menéndez Pelayo's regrets over his critical excesses in the *Heterodoxos,* Marañón answers Laín Entralgo in the following manner, focusing on a profound transformation that governed Menéndez Pelayo's transition from youth to maturity:

> No doubt there are not two Menéndez Pelayos, but rather, one who evolved. Yet I believe that we lessen his glory by not properly emphasizing the difference between the "juvenile, prudish," and sour critic and the expansive and compassionate Menéndez Pelayo of his maturity. For this profound transformation is just as much a creature of his genius as his books.[282]

Santiago Ramón y Cajal

Whereas the cordial relationship between Pérez Galdós and Menéndez Pelayo stirred Marañón as a youth, the contribution of Ramón y Cajal to Spanish scientific thought, both in its theoretical aspect and as applied to the cultural, political and moral problems of the epoch, could not but fail to exercise a powerful influence on Marañón's professional development and orientation. Nevertheless, Marañón appears somewhat distant from the histologist. He never

211

was a disciple of Cajal, nor a researcher in histology, but, rather, forged a reputation for himself, on his own, in endocrinology, due to his research on the secretion of the glands, the action of hormones and the relationship between glandular functioning and such matters as sexuality and sexual determination, heredity, emotion, morphology, psychological characteristics and the susceptibility to disease. One senses a latent rivalry which occasionally makes itself apparent, usually under the rubric of the question of Spain's backwardness.[283] The relationship of Marañón to Cajal is not entirely unlike the relationship of the Generation of 1898 to Galdós, although nowhere does the physician criticize the histologist with that lack of cordiality or disrespect that characterizes, say, Unamuno's or Baroja's invective against Galdós. Moreover, Cajal differed from Marañón in certain other respects. Cajal's willingness to attribute, at least partially, the problem of Spanish science to religious intolerance, as well as his insistence on the notion of the "lazy" Spaniard, or his plan to send Spanish professionals out of the country to be trained, was not well received by Marañón and points to a difference of attitude and temperament with reference to two basic virtues in Marañón's pantheon: religious orthodoxy and patriotism. Although Marañón has championed Cajal as a man of the generation of 1898 because of, among other things, his *españolismo,* here and there one can perceive a certain antagonism to Cajal beneath the surface of an ardent, laudatory rhetoric.

Marañón has written several pieces on Ramón y Cajal.[284] Most of these, however, are circumstantial, commemorative works. In addition, Marañón has penned several brief profiles of a number of Cajal's followers in which he often alludes to the master.[285]

In 1934, the year of Cajal's death, Marañón was moved to pay homage to the histologist in a speech delivered at the Real Academia Nacional de Medicina. In commenting on Cajal's thoughts on love and sex, Marañón notes the histologist's "enthusiastic apology for conjugal love, based on friendship and companionship,"[286] as well as his conviction that "Man's instincts veer toward polygamy with such tenacity and vehemence that they cannot be interpreted other than as physiological forces."[287] This line of thinking appears, of course, with great elaboration in *Amiel* and it is, as well, one of the assumptions behind Marañón's negative judgment concerning Don Juan. Marañón notes that Cajal, like many other Spaniards during that time, was preoccupied by Don Juanism. Once Cajal confided to Marañón that he judged the Don Juan type to be attracted to the military because of, among other factors, the inherent mobility in that way of life.

Marañón's most fundamental contribution on the Spanish histologist is his speech, "Cajal," given upon his entrance into the Real Academia de Ciencias Exactas, Físicas y Naturales in 1947. The speech was then published that same year, with some additions, under the title *Cajal, su tiempo y el nuestro*.

Writing precisely fifty years after Cajal's first presentation (which was subsequently revised five times) of the *Reglas y consejos al investigador científico*, Marañón glorifies the scientist as an "insuperable archetype of the scientist and teacher."[288] Cajal was a genius who emerged, not out of a "hostile environment, but rather the lack of one."[289] Other kindred spirits who were preparing a Spanish scientific renascence were Oloríz, the anatomist and anthropologist, Carlos María Cortezo, a clinician, and Alejandro San Martín, a surgeon who, unfortunately, was frustrated as a physiologist due to a lack of facilities. Cajal was formed, professionally, out of a tradition which, although dominated by "illustrious figures, particularly among the naturalists," nevertheless, with respect to experimental science, was "notoriously inferior to what was the norm in the other great countries of Europe."[290] In the thirty years that preceded Cajal, only one figure stands out, the controversial Letamendi, who, according to Granjel, initially overwhelmed Pío Baroja and, ultimately, repelled him.[291] Gonzalo Lafora vehemently attacks Letamendi; Marañón, on the other hand, attempts to moderate.[292]

In a parallel study of Spanish psychiatry, Marañón traces the evolution of therapeutic techniques from a therapy practiced by charismatic, "almost quixotic practitioners"[293] to a disciplined and rigorous clinical science. The profile of Jaime Vera, psychiatrist and socialist candidate near the end of the century, emerges as a sort of hagiographic portrait:

> I saw him, a few days before his death, lying on an uncomfortable bed, blind and almost removed from this world, with his hat on and dressed as if he were going outside. He was still receiving patients and they felt relieved just by the touch of Don Jaime's hand, almost frozen already by death, upon their heads.[294]

Sanchís Banús exemplifies the emergence of modern psychiatry: ". . .he was an exemplary archetype of the post-war [World War One] generation: an enlightened mind, thorough learning, a natural sense of devotion to science. . . ."[295]

Within this "almost sterile environment," Cajal, on the strength of his genius, was able to impose himself. An "explanation" of the phenomenon of Cajal's existence in Spain has been the object of rather assidous discussion. Marañón utilizes the commonplace of "genius" in order to account for Cajal. This notion is perhaps attributable to Gonzalo Lafora. Cajal himself had composed a number of pithy sayings on genius, not unlike Gracián in tone.[296] Shortly after his death, in 1935, his disciple, the histologist turned clinician, Gonzalo Lafora, uses the genius notion in an article entitled "La influencia de la personalidad y el carácter de Cajal sobre su obra." Here Cajal's memories as expressed in his *Recuerdos de mi vida. El mundo visto a los ochenta años,* and his letters are utilized in order to prove from a theoretical point of view that just as in art,

> . . .in science there exists both predictable inspirations and genial intuitions, and when the latter are not present with all of their antecedent dispositions and inherited genial qualities, then the so-called scientist is no more than a scientific *worker,* but in no sense a *genius* of science.[297]

The conclusion, after a survey of such criteria as Cajal's "hereditary factors," "qualities of spirit and character," "esthetic tendencies," and a mental talent entailing "analytical-synthetic qualities," is that Cajal was a genius, at least in the manner that Kretschmer defined the personality type in his *Geniale Menschen* (1929). (Lafora also discusses the notion of genius in Kant, Segond, Claude Bernard and J. Picard.)

Marañón seems to have taken the notion that genius is the result of an optimum interaction between personality and environmental and temporal factors, either directly from Kretschmer, or through the intermediary of Lafora. (Upon reflection, the notion does not fit very well into his assertion in the same work that Cajal rose out of a "sterile medium.") This interaction is formally termed by Lafora, following Kretschmer, a "sociological juncture." The genius is the product of:

> . . .the coincidence of certain individual psychic dispositions, generally inherited, together with favorable circumstances in the environment that not only facilitate its development but react favorably to its production, creating an exalted environment: a so called *sociological juncture.*[298]

It is interesting to note that in 1952 Laín Entralgo published a moving lecture entitled *Cajal y el problema del saber,* covering much of the same ground as Lafora, but often interpreting the same remarks from Cajal's memoirs, not as a reflection of the histologist's genius, but rather of his developing comprehension of the world and of "the understanding that the scientist Cajal had of himself."[299] Here Cajal emerges as a perfect example of the Catholic intellectual as outlined in Laín's "Hacia una teoría del intelectual católico."[300] Cajal's intellectual prowess was composed of equal parts of intimately fused veneration and skepticism. This is so because "Pure veneration, without the appearance of skepticism, is religious piety and not scientific principles. . . .Yet pure and unvarnished skepticism, without a trace of awe, is not a genuine scientific perspective, but rather mere intellectual libidinousness or cynical arrogance. . . ."[301] Laín Entralgo rejects that notion of genius which attempts to separate the illustrious or productive individual from the rest of the species.

> Don Santiago did not become an actual "genial scientist" until he saw the nervous cells as morphological units and on that basis conceived the anatomical and functional organization of the axon; which is to say that intellectual genius sometimes can be acquired by means of the adequate and energetic exercise of intelligence. On the other hand, he became a "professional scientist" even as a youth upon his return from Cuba, in 1875, when he resolved to devote himself to the scientific knowledge of the human body; which is to say. . .that the scientist is he who dedicates his life to intellectually understanding something that men have thought worthy of science. Let each dedicate himself according to his own capacity; both the Cajal subsequent to 1889 and others, performing with the minimal standards of a book worm or laboratory rat, are rather accesory phenomena when seen from a formal, psychological and social perspective. One or the other, the eagle-man or the ferret-man, are no more than specialized versions of the generic, *homo sapiens*.[302]

Related to the claim that Cajal was a genius who transcended his environment is Marañón's assertion that Cajal must be included within the Generation of 1898, since by virtue of his political and social ideas, and above all, his scientific work, he is one of the leading representatives of that group. Marañón argues that the commentators of the Generation of 1898, unduly involved in literary concerns, have forgotten the scientific renewal that was a part of the achievement of 1898. Marañón considers this laxity worthy of reproach, a quite understandable bitterness, since our physician-critic has made the effort to bridge the gap between science and art, and would expect in return, some critic trained primarily in literature to make the same effort from that discipline. Unfortunately, Marañón does not really build upon his plea for Cajal's inclusion in the Generation of 1898, as well as a re-evaluation of the scientific aspect of that generation.

Santiago Ramón y Cajal

Most critics have more or less neglected both Marañón's plea and his reproach. The doctor merely limits himself to noting in the first place that,

> ...the generation of 1898 represents a noble critical reaction to a grave national crisis; a reaction that won over almost all of those Spaniards who felt a sense of responsibility toward their country and their times. It was, therefore, more than the mere posture of a literary group.[303]

Furthermore, the term "Generation of 1898" is a "dangerous expression because it tends to circumscribe a profound and complex national event to a limited group of men, principally a handful of artists. This is the cause of the unending discussions that have gone on concerning the existence, works and tendencies of that so-called generation."[304] Of these discussions, "Laín Entralgo's excellent book is the most recent and most comprehensive example."[305]

Clearly, Marañón, probably expecting the allegiance of his younger colleague, who so often could be relied on, was hurt by Laín Entralgo's neglect of Cajal in his *La generación de 98*. Laín, in his several writings on Cajal, consistently terms him an "eminent precursor" of the Generation of 1898, classifying him in the generation of the *Restauración,* along with Menéndez Pelayo, Oloríz, Julián Ribera, Hinojosa and others. Laín claims this group was guided by a "sense of quixotism toward scientific work" which it passed on to its successors: Menéndez Pidal, Asín Palacios, Altamira and others.[306] However, Laín does expose on several occasions the similarities between Cajal and the Generation of 1898. On the other hand, Luis S. Granjel takes Marañón's suggestion much more seriously, leading him to formalize the similarities between Cajal and the Generation of 1898. The most important of these, in Granjel's judgment, are: the publication of manifestos on the need for regeneration around the turn of the century, a "crisis of morale," a rejection of the rhetorical style characteristic of the preceding period, a nostalgic exaltation of the Golden Age, or rather, the period before Ferdinand and Isabella, a love for the small villages and countryside of Spain, the cultivation of the theme of womanhood and love, the evasion of the historical present "through the medium of fantasy." If we can be convinced of their existence, these are rather substantial and profound similarities! Nevertheless, Granjel using the chronological criterion, ultimately does not accept Marañón's assertion either.

> The judgment of Dr. Marañón contains a slight inexactitude that we need to rectify; chronologically Ramón y Cajal cannot be included in the group of men that form the Generation of 1898 because he is

twelve years older than Unamuno, the oldest member of that Generation. . . .[307]

In his prologue to G. Díaz-Plaja's *Modernismo frente al noventa y ocho,* Marañón goes to bizarre lengths, claiming that Manuel B. Cossío and Cánovas del Castillo (if only he hadn't been assassinated in 1897!) should also be associated with or included in the Generation of 1898. These figures display all of the rhetorical and stylistic artifice of the late nineteenth century.

In addition to the question of Cajal's *noventayochismo,* Marañón goes on to survey the nature of the histologist's social-political ideas, as well as the pedagogical impact he had upon Spain. Curiously, Marañón is basically critical toward Cajal's well-known review of the supposed causes of Spain's backwardness. We have noted earlier that Marañón accepts Cajal's tenets that Spanish scientific paucity was the consequence of historical circumstances, primarily her isolation, and that this state could be remedied by means of special efforts. (See p. 158.) Here, however, Marañón chastises Cajal for taking up the ridiculous myth of the Spaniard's laziness and for accepting the speculation, which he considers "an absurd superficiality that should be disregarded,"[308] that the expulsion of the Jews and Moors permanently affected Spain's finances and agriculture. Moreover, Cajal's belief that Spain's isolation has been based on her geographical location and the proud and haughty nature of the Spanish people Marañón deems, "two so-called causes that now seem ingenuous to us."[309] Pride is a commonplace; every nation in her moment of greatness has been accused of pride. Witness, for example, the British. And as for geographical position, Spain during the Golden Age was the political center of Europe. Nor has it ever been located far from the more recent centers of power, Paris or London.

Actually, what Marañón does is to steer his speech to a topic expressed in several other writings[310]—his own pet explanation for Spain's backwardness, the weakness of the university. "In sum: the ill can be detected in the University. All else is merely accessory and circumstancial."[311] Cajal saw this, but his cure, to europeanize the professors by having them trained outside Spain, is not the answer. The real culprit is the institution of the *oposiciones,* against which even Cajal, although he was humiliated in this ordeal, "hardly emitted minor protests against such a huge anachronism."[312] This "cancer" must be eliminated among other reasons, because it encourages students to specialize in *oposiciones* rather than in science, because it

217

encourages "scientism," a reliance on the outer garb of science—journals, books bibliographies, schematisms, graphic demonstrations, filmstrips, conferences and congresses, etc., and because it eliminates highly qualified personnel who for various reasons are not able to present themselves or win an *oposición*.

Marañón divides Cajal's pedagogical influence into three spheres: histology, the total field of medicine and the sphere of culture in general. Laín Entralgo adds his voice to this view:

> Cajal has exercised influence on the historical existence of his compatriots in two ways. In the first place, as the direct outcome of his teaching career and his establishment of professional groups. . . .Secondly, because of the exemplary prestige of his name, because of what can be called in Sorel's sense, "the myth of Cajal." There are few episodes in the history of contemporary Spanish science that are so filled with incentives than those effected by the mythical halo that surrounds the name of Don Santiago.[313]

Cajal's impact on histology has been overwhelming. Only one chair existed in histology when he entered the field. By 1922, dozens of illustrious followers occupied chairs in this discipline all over Spain. Marañón concludes: "In each of the medical schools in Spain almost invariably the most competent and modern professor is the one of. . . contemporary normal or pathological histology."[314] This is an important example for Spanish science and Marañón pleads that the government attempt some policy to retain Spanish scientists within the country because it is "the catalytic influence of a teacher. . .which perhaps Spanish youth need more than the students of any other country."[315]

Cajal's impact was felt throughout the field of medicine. He encouraged others by his example; his work led to the granting of new funds for laboratory equipment, research and training and, above all, became widely known through the intermediary of his disciples, who spilled over into other fields. For example, the clinicians, Achúcarro, Gayarre, Lafora, Sacristán and Villaverde, were initially histologists. With respect to Cajal's general influence on culture, Marañón points to the popularity of the *Reglas y consejos* and of the *Recuerdos*. He judges that the best part of the *Reglas y consejos* are those elements in the book which point to the scientist's ongoing development of his vocation and not the abundant dicta on the necessary psychological and moral qualities that the scientist must possess or the hypotheses on the causes of Spain's limited contribution to experimental science. "The best of the book is its juvenile, exuberant, even inexpert quality—

that generous sense of inexperience that the years later erase but which permit a not yet mature person to reap the fruit of many arbitrary but useful aspects of youth."[316] The *Recuerdos* appear to enthuse Marañón less, precisely because, since they are memoirs, they exaggerate the presence of the scientist. Marañón detects "a certain, perhaps not conscious tendency of the author to overesteem his own actions, a failing, however, that has affected almost all of the memoirs that have ever been written."[317] He has expressed his dislike for memoirs and his enthusiasm for confessions for similar reasons.

> I do not like memoirs. They may be useful for the historian but usually they tell us nothing about the protagonist, except for his vanity. On the other hand, I am attracted to confessions, in which we do learn the nature of the man even when he does not tell us the truth. In memoirs, throughout the succession of events, we find, hypertrophied, the personality of the author. In confessions the universe is seen as an exact microcosm by means of the soul that records itself.[318]

In addition, Marañón surveys Cajal's literary works, the *Cuentos de vacaciones* and the *Charlas de café*. As we have indicated earlier, the doctor believes that Cajal was motivated toward literary creation by his survival instinct in its most profound, sublimated aspect, "the desire for immortality." Perhaps some of Marañón's most interesting comments pertain to Cajal's style. Cajal and Azorín, each in their own field, reacted against the "rhetorical flatulence" of the period immediately preceding them. Yet, Cajal went too far in his attack on rhetorical excess, considering it a powerful cause of Spain's scientific backwardness. Cajal himself, "the pure scientist, almost a puritan, who considered himself. . .as a moral enemy of grand rhetoric,"[319] could not help but write, not only to describe, but in order to "create the word itself. . .an invincible temptation for scientists at all times.[320] Our critic perceives in Cajal's scientific literature a "repressed rhetoric" that was finally to find full fruition in pure literature.

Marañón's remarks on Cajal are particularly interesting because his own style often combines the "technical" and the "esthetic." The doctor himself characterizes the essay in the following manner, ". . .the able intermixture of literary and scientific elements. It is an amphibious genre that non-specialists are able to enjoy because of its agreeable appearance stripped of rigorous technicalities. . . ."[321] Francisco López Estrada remarks:

> I call the essay literature that is truly compromised, compromised because it must satisfy two criteria: rigor in science (whether the

theme be medical or historical) and literary impact. Marañón took up a tradition that is opened with Feijoo, that wavers during Romanticism, and strengthened in its scientific aspect by Ramón y Cajal, flowers splendidly and definitively in the generation to which Cajal belonged.[322]

This fused style has produced some remarkable and peculiarly Marañónian images. We have for example: "pleiad of naturalists, physiologists, medical historians and investigators," "Spain undergoing a long diet of the critical faculty," "the pious recipe," "the goal of progress is not in the infinite but in our own navel," "verbal orgasm." Certain modern poets are termed "astronomers of the soul." Some of the words used in Marañón's vocabulary are borrowed from other languages, as *el stress;* others are newly coined such as *arqueología médica*, and *seudología.*

Here is another characteristic passage:

> The newspapers are inspired by a freakish monster which is called currency, a monster which among other things, suffers from a sight defect that I don't know what opthalmologists might call: it consists of an incapacity to appreciate the true color and exact dimensions of things. What currency judges to be black sometimes turns out, upon hindsight, to be white as snow; what was once thought to be large may be a grain of sand, and so on.[323]

Other interesting usages peculiar to Marañón are his euphemisms and invectives. He was accustomed to the prestigious role of passing judgment, mediating and establishing precedents on new moral questions (or old ones) arising out of technological advances in his specialty or allied fields (for example, artificial insemination). On the other hand, Marañón was the type of liberal who achieved his aims from within the establishment. Hence, he developed a number of "psychological" methods for influencing public opinion, combining tact, applied invective, self-righteousness, exhortation, and euphemism. We have, for example, an appeal to guilt: "What is important in discussing the question of artificial insemination is to do so with clarity and seriousness, always with decency, without permitting ourselves to be swayed by a pharisaical and Calderonian sense of morality."[324] The following euphemisms for homosexuality and heterosexuality are obviously used for tactical reasons: ". . .the fact that the lack of differentiation of the instinct, so typical in Don Juan, allows for the possibility of *straying from the right path,* which is quite common (and reality demonstrates most unexpected examples of such cases) does not exclude the fact that many Don Juans in real life follow *the true path* biologically speaking, without ever straying from it."[325]

(Italics mine.) The same type of euphemism appears where he substitutes "law of instinct" for copulation.

In short, Marañón bears evidence of the same sort of stylistic peculiarities in his essays that our critic detected in Ramón y Cajal.

CONCLUSION

As I have shown in my analysis of Marañón's professional career as it developed over time, it is necessary to distinguish between any enduring significance that our critic might have, from his short term impact on Spanish literary criticism, biography and history.

Marañón's impact in his own time was indeed substantial. From the criterion of size of readership, he was extremely successful in the above-mentioned fields for a number of reasons. He was a highly recognized and esteemed medical researcher before he became interested in the humanities and social sciences. His approach was eclectic and flexible so that, although he lost in consistency, he was able to enrich his repertoire of biopsychological constructs, when necessary, with material taken from psychoanalysis or Adler's individual psychology. He was careful with his documentation and able to organize and evaluate extensive bibliographies. Moreoever, Marañón introduced a dramatic element into his essays and biographies. He consistently expressed himself in a polemical manner. He very rarely elected a topic in order to do neutral, objective analysis. Usually, he took to the field either to defend someone against the specific criticisms of others or to refute anonymous, damaging legends that had sprung up around a well-known figure. This is the case in his writings on Feijoo, Amiel, Casal, Quevedo and others. Occasionally, most notably in the case of Don Juan, he took the field with an aggressive stance. The flexible utilization of scientific constructs, combined with a dramatic, polemical presentation, expressed in a direct, often anectodal and imaginative style was a recipe (or perhaps prescription is the better term) for Marañón's success as a popular critic, not only in print but in the lecture hall before the general public as well.

The evaluation of Marañón's long-lasting significance is a task that is less clear-cut. Here again one must distinguish between and balance the claims that Marañón makes upon his appraiser by virtue of his massive, extensively-read output—that is, impact in one's own time to some extent *equals* significance—and the fact that all of his works in each of his preferred fields, criticism, biography and history, to a greater or lesser degree have been superseded. Marañón is clearly a significant intellectual figure of pre- and post-Civil War Spain.

Yet his contemporaries and those who followed usually read and analysed his work to debate it, or even to fulminate against it. This is not only the case of his *Don Juan*, which Marañón himself claimed was his most extensively read and most widely rejected book, but all of his other major works as well: *Amiel, El Greco, Feijoo, Tiberio, Olivares, Antonio Pérez*, and so on. (*Feijoo* has clearly suffered somewhat less from erosion.) The fact is that Marañón leaves no recognizable school of disciples or followers. Indeed, because his approach was so eclectic, so open to new scientific constructs and to major revisions, it is not genuinely possible to identify a coherent, integrated, unified, parsimonious system or methodology which could have served as his legacy to later critics. In this sense Marañón resembles his close contemporary and erstwhile colleague in the service of the Spanish Republic, José Ortega y Gasset (the former was born in 1887, the latter in 1883), who despite his obsession with scientific rigor and systematization, was not able to bring these qualities to plenitude in his own works. Yet the contrast stands: Ortega, more than any other Spanish thinker of his time, succeeded in leaving a legacy, and above all, a group of followers who applied his basic position to a wide range of disciplines and topics. Moreover, some of Ortega's basic works—I think of *Meditaciones del Quijote, España invertebrada, La deshumanización del arte* and *La rebelión de las masas*—have worn well with time in comparison to those of Marañón.

Nevertheless, the contribution of Marañón to the intellectual history of Spain is unmistakable. Whereas Ortega y Gasset was trained in philosophy and in the humanities, from which he pursued the ramifications of various advances in the sciences, Marañón, from the vantage point of science, embraced the humanities. Marañón was the major intellectual figure who brought into Spain and applied to various aspects of Spanish thought or life such basic scientific theories as the concept and function of hormones, Kretschmer's method of morphological analysis, psychoanalysis (as expounded more by Freud's disciples than by the founder himself) and Adler's notion of the inferiority complex and the will to power. And, of course, not only did Marañón apply promising scientific conceptualizations of man to arts and letters, but to law, psychology, education, history, mores, customs and general culture as well. For example, his pre-Civil War positions on artificial insemination, on women's rights and on sexual education were notable, exemplary social advances which, when set against the intellectual background of the times,

223

displayed a noteworthy sense of entlightenment. Thus Marañón, particularly during the fertile, possibility-laden years of the 1920s and early 1930s was part of the Spanish intellectual cutting edge; he was a forerunner and a breaker of new ground, not only in science but in society. As a physician he earned for himself a reputation in society as something of a thaumaturge; among the Spanish intellectual sector he became something of a hero, a liberal defender of progress in Spain, mostly in the areas of culture, education, law and the like, but even going so far as to occasionally pursue his ideals in political contexts.

In 1926 Marañón was briefly jailed by Primo de Rivera's regime for an alleged conspiracy (which he denied) to overthrow the government, and subsequently, during the Republic, he headed, together with Ortega y Gasset and Pérez de Ayala, the intellectual group "in the service of the Republic." Perhaps at this moment he was at the height of his prestige.

However, the Spanish Civil War and the Second World War had a deleterious effect upon our critic, one which in my opinion truncated his intellectual growth, and hence, the enduring significance of his work. In 1937 he wrote an inflammatory, propagandistic pamphlet, *Liberalismo y comunismo,*[1] which served him as a sort of passport to return to Franco Spain. His case, and the pamphlet that he wrote, reneging his earlier support of the Republic, is not unlike that of Pío Baroja. Marañón's output was much reduced as a result of the Civil War and World War and its aftermath. With the exception of one major work, on a clearly "safe" topic, *Antonio Pérez*, most of Marañón's books after 1945 were in fact collections of essays written earlier and/or works that had in part a concealed purpose: to rationalize or justify his return to Spain and his participation in the Franco regime as one of the major "house" intellectuals. Marañón had the devil of a time rationalizing himself as a liberal who at the same time was a supporter of Franco, and books such as *Ensayos liberales* (1946) and *Españoles fuera de España* (1947) display evidence of his discomfort and contorsions. His ludicrous critique of those who would "praise" the French Revolution bears a similar stamp. More importantly, the voice of Marañón as a social critic and social innovator was markedly curtailed. Where before the Civil War he would concern himself with such questions as the reform of the universities, women's rights, artificial insemination, etc., after assimilating into the Franco regime he tended to restrict himself mostly to historical topics such as Garcilaso de la Vega, San Martín, the three Vélez, the mysteries of San Plácido, Antonio Pérez, and so on. The sense of Marañón as a personal exemplar, a scientist of moral fiber willing to speak out frankly on issues that he believed were significant, was lost, and in its stead was substituted the image of a consecrated, "approved" intellectual who often represented the government when it needed to present an enlightened image at scientific and medical meetings, cultural events, conferences and conventions, *homenajes*, openings of institutions and installations, and other commemorative activities.

Marañón's major contributions within the fields of interest to us in this study are his literary writings on Don Juan, El Greco, Amiel and Feijoo, and his full-length historical biographies, *Enrique IV, Olivares, Tiberio, Antonio Pérez, Los tres Vélez,* which expose his biographical theories and methods and his historiographical assumptions. As Marañón himself has noted, his work on Don Juan had the curious fate of being influential in the paradoxical sense that it has served as a catalyst for those critics determined to oppose our critic's aggressive condemnation of the Burlador. However, seen from the perspective of Spanish intellectual history, the Don Juan writings represent an early, major attempt in Spain to apply scientific (biological and psychological) criteria in a massive way to a literary phenomenon which at the same time was a popular legend considered worthy of social emulation by a certain sector of Spanish males. Whatever the absolute value of the Don Juan writings, either from literary or scientific criteria, their historical significance is assured.

The biography of Amiel, written in part to exalt the Genevan professor as an archetype antithetical to Don Juan, was quite popular during the years immediately before the Spanish Civil War. This biography was a novel defense of Amiel, a figure who had aroused the interest of many Spaniards, Unamuno among them, and who, after the 1923 and 1927 unexpurgated editions of his diary, was being persecuted by a band of self-seeking pathologists. In addition, *Amiel* was of great interest at the time because in it Marañón addressed himself to certain sociosexual problems and certain aspects of sexual education. He attempted to combat conventions equating timidity with a lack of manhood. However, with the outbreak of the Spanish Civil War, and, subsequently, the Second World War, interest in Amiel and the nature of his plight waned considerably. Currently, Marañón's biography is read almost strictly by specialists interested in Amiel. Nevertheless, the work is considered essential reading

225

among this group inasmuch as the general critical approach continues to entail an analysis of Amiel's personality and his illness.

Marañón's writings on El Greco, particularly his full-length biography, have enjoyed sustained popularity among the public. In 1955, *Life* magazine even published the famous series of photographs matching the heads of several El Greco saints with inmates of the insane asylum at Toledo. Yet, the situation here is not unlike that of the Don Juan writings. While art critics and art historians, particularly Spaniards such as Camón Aznar, have expressed their admiration for Marañón's good taste and insights, the doctor's critical speculations, judgments, and above all, terminology, have been marginal in their impact, at least with respect to academic art criticism. For example, terms such as oneiric vision, shadow, flame, shadow-soul and others have had little significant play in the art world. On the other hand, Marañón's speculations concerning the popularity of El Greco among the *converso* population of Toledo and other areas of Spain, contain striking parallels with Américo Castro's general thesis on the situation of the *conversos* and their relationship to other Spaniards. Further research on the question of El Greco's constituency during his own time would be of value in the clarification of the more general hypothesis of an alleged assimilation of a disguised Semitic and Arabic consciousness in Spain during the fifteenth and sixteenth centuries.

Marañón's procedures for writing biographies were not restricted to figures relating to arts and letters, but were transposed to history as well. Thus, while Marañón did not consciously devote himself to the methodology of history per se, his biographies of historical protagonists contain within them an implicit historiography. Marañón accepted the common early twentieth century assumption that the novel was "moribund" and he conceived of the biography as a proper humanistic substitute for that dying genre. Thus, within the ongoing debate concerning history as art or science, Marañón comes down squarely in favor of the former. Moreover, he shared with other well-known Western biographers what has been variously called the "intuitive" (Garraty) or "romantic" (Vicens) notion that there is a key to the personalites under consideration which, when exposed, could reveal their innermost character. What distinguished Marañón's biography, procedurally, from those, say, of Stefan Zweig, Emil Ludwig, André Maurois or Lewis Mumford, was the biopsychological construct as the proper "key." Thus, his biographies can be regarded in part as clinical or case histories. Marañón eschewed the lack of documentation and almost total adherence to fictionalization that was characteristic of some Spanish novelist-bibliographers such as Antonio Marichalar, who blithely invented dialogue, innermost thoughts and even events. Marañón attempted to arrive at a certain balance or compromise: on the one hand, providing for the general public stylistic amenities, a sense of melodrama and chic gossip (often under the guise of disposing of earlier legends or myths), on the other, providing the scholarly documentation normally associated with serious, objective history. Nevertheless, professional historians such as Francisco Tomás Valiente, Jaime Vicens Vives and Charles Howard Carter have expressed serious objections to Marañón's work because he was unwilling or unable to address himself to anything other than the personalities of his subjects. In part because Marañón was an avowed "personalist," judging that history is determined by personalities who in turn are previously determined by hereditary and morphological factors, he was unable to effectively evaluate what in fact were the policies, the structures or the administrative characteristics of the regimes in which the subjects that he described served. There is lacking any evaluation of the effectiveness of rule, nor any description of the relationship between Marañón's biographical subject and the actual power structure of the times. For example, Marañón alleges that Olivares' great passion was to "rule," which is fine and well, but he takes a fatal unexamined leap, assuming that because Olivares craved power, he actually exercised it, not only relatively, but as a so-called "dictator." As Vicens points out, Marañón's historiography has the drawbacks of excessive philosophizing (at the expense of methodology and the use of objective, particularly statistical, data), an attempt to make history reflect his desired outcome, and an over-reliance on commonplace, conventionalized assumptions transmitted by generation after generation of historians.

Marañón's contributions on Feijoo and allied figures have had more critical success and enduring significance, although here, ironically, due to the nature of the figure studied, the biography of Feijoo has been less popular with the general public than the writings on Don Juan, El Greco or Amiel. Marañón's ability to find a general coherent position in Feijoo with respect to medicine and his defense of Feijoo's religious orthodoxy but scientific skepticism have been substantially accepted by most critics. In short, Marañón's *Las ideas biológicas del Padre Feijoo* has become a standard reference work in the field. This is not entirely unexpected, for Marañón brings to his study of Feijoo two important assets which he was not able to

227

mobilize in his studies of El Greco, Don Juan or Amiel. First, he is able to utilize his biopsychological approach to analyze Feijoo's personality and he is also able to bring to bear his scientific expertise in the evaluation of the worth of Feijoo's own scientific ideas. Marañón the biographer discusses Feijoo's "obsession" with medicine and his struggles with his own irrationality. Marañón the medical expert refutes Menéndez Pelayo's objection that Feijoo's work has no real scientific coherence. Finally, the doctor deeply identifies with Feijoo as a person and is able to empathize with the monk's situation as a Catholic scientist. During this same period, Ortega calls for and produces a biography of Goethe, *desde dentro*. In contrast to his studies on Amiel or El Greco, Marañón is able to produce such a biography of Feijoo.

Marañón's characterization of the monk as a member of a professional elite charged with maintaining cultural and intellectual standards during a difficult period in Spanish history has fared less successfully; it has been supplemented and partly superseded by the research of professional historians of science such as J.M. López Pinero, J. Caro Baroja, L.S. Granjel and many others. These historians of science, because of the wealth of detailed research that they have brought to the development of Spanish science, have swept aside the notion of "eminent figures" who guided the scientific progress of the nation or who maintained the light of wisdom in a dark epoch. Just as in the case of "romantic" biography and history, "romantic" history of science, with its dramatizations of empiricism vs. blind superstition, of experimental "titans" and "torch bearers" has been forced to cede before the ongoing trend of history to become a social science based on natural, objective and document-oriented data. Moreover, one of the by-products of the new history of science has been to bring to light numerous personalities who contributed to Spanish science, and whose existence made possible the achievements of better-known figures such as Feijoo and Casal.

In my first chapter I have cited Rof Carballo's description of Marañón as a "Great Individual" in the Jungian meaning, a man who represented Spain in a traditional, stoic, hermetic sense, and who also represented the new Spain: one that analyzes without fear and without apprehension about the truth. My own concluding view of Marañón is somewhat less exalted. Rof has clearly captured the essential and enduring quality of Marañón's work: he is a bridge, an amphibian, a transitional figure. He is a bridge between the arts and the sciences, between the novel and the historical biography. He brings into Spain, applies to Spanish intellectual life and permits to take root many scientific notions and theories developed elsewhere. He was the perfect catalyst; he provided thought-provoking, controversial analyses from a scientific orientation of artistic, literary or cultural topics of great interest to Spaniards. He played a prominent social, pedagogical and even quasi-political role in both pre- and post-civil war Spain.

Yet, Marañón was just as much the victim of his contradictions as he was their synthesizer or surpassor. This is evident not only in his public life, which is markedly different after the Civil War in terms of fecundity, but also in the compromises that he forced upon himself between popular art and objective science in his biographies and historical works, between impartial analysis and an outraged sense of morality in his Don Juan writings, between his neutral artistic or scientific appraisals and his pre-arranged ideological position in his work on El Greco or Feijoo.

NOTES

Introduction

[1]Gregorio Marañón, "Contestación al discurso de recepción en la Real Academia Española, de Don Pío Baroja," *Obras completas*, II [Discursos], (Madrid: Espasa-Calpe, 1966), p. 318. Henceforth Marañón's *Obras completas* will be abbreviated *O.C.*

[2]Francisco Javier Almodóvar and Warleta, Enrique, *Marañón o una vida fecunda*, (Madrid: Espasa-Calpe, 1952).

Chapter I.

[1]Charles Binet-Sanglé, *L'epilepsie chez Gustave Flaubert* (Chronique médicale, 1900); Charles Binet-Sanglé, *La maladie de Blaise Pascal* (Annales médico-psychologiques, 1899); Charles Binet-Sanglé, *La Folie de Jésus*, 4 vols. (Paris: Maloine, 1908-1915).

[2]See Roberto Novoa Santos, *La indigencia espiritual del sexo femenino* (Madrid, 1908).

[3]Max Simon Nordau, *Degeneration*, introd. by George L. Mosse (New York: H. Fertig, 1968).

[4]Pompeyo Genér, *Literatura malsana: estudios de patología literaria contemporánea* (Barcelona: J. Llordachs, 1900).

[5]Havelock Ellis, *Views and Reviews* (London: 1932), quoted by John A. Garraty, *The Nature of Biography* (New York: Alfred A. Knopf, 1957), pp. 111-12.

[6]*Ibid.*, p. 112.

[7]Sigmund Freud, *Totem and Taboo,* trans. by A.A. Brill (New York, 1927); Sigmund Freud, *Wit and Its Relation to the Unconscious,* trans. by A.A. Brill (New York, 1916); Sigmund Freud, *Leonard da Vinci: A Psychosexual Study of an Infantile Reminiscence,* trans. by A.A. Brill (New York, 1910); Sigmund Freud, *Moses and Monotheism,* trans. by K. Jones (New York: Alfred A. Knopf, 1939); Otto Rank, *Art and Artist,* trans. by C.T.

Notes

Atkinson (New York, 1932); Ernest Jones, *Hamlet and Oedipus* (New York, 1949).

For an introduction with a substantial bibliography on Freudian literary criticism, see Frederick J. Hoffman, *Freudianism and the Literary Mind,* 2nd ed. (Baton Rouge, Louisiana: Louisiana State University Press, 1957).

[8]José Ingenieros, *La psicopatología en el arte* (Buenos Aires: Editorial Losada, 1961).

[9]José Ortega y Gasset, *Goethe desde dentro* in *Obras completas,* IV, 4th ed. (Madrid: Revista de Occidente, 1957).

[10]José Ortega y Gasset, "Ni vitalismo ni racionalismo," *Obras completas,* III, 4th ed. (Madrid: Revista de Occidente, 1957), pp. 270-82.

[11]W.B. Cannon, *Bodily Changes in Pain, Hunger, Fear and Rage* (New York: Appleton-Century, 1929).

[12]Gregorio Marañón, *La doctrina de las secreciones internas: Su significación y sus aplicaciones a la patología* (Madrid: Corona, 1915), p. 40.

[13]James Hoddie, Jr., "Gregorio Marañón, Historian and Man of Letters," unpubl. Ph.D. dissertation, Brown University, 1965, p. 53.

[14]Gregorio Marañón, *La doctrina de las secreciones internas,* p. 41.

[15]*Ibid.*

[16]*Ibid.*

[17]Pedro Laín Entralgo, *Ocio y trabajo* (Madrid: Revista de Occidente, 1960).

[18]Hoddie distinguishes Marañón's notion of *bisexualidad* from *intersexualidad* in the following way: *Bisexualidad* refers to the normal coexistence of two sexual natures, one dominant, the other dormant, in the same organism. On the other hand, *intersexualidad* is used to refer to cases in which sexual differentiation is imprecise. (James Hoddie, Jr., *op. cit.,* p. 85).

[19]*Ibid.,* p. 72.

[20]Gregorio Marañón, "Acerca del problema de la intersexualidad (Réplica a un artículo del doctor Oliver Brachfeld)," *O.C.,* IV [Artículos], p. 224.

[21]Pedro Laín Entralgo, *op. cit.,* p. 239 quoting Gregorio Marañón, *La edad crítica* (Madrid: Siglo Médico, 1919).

[22]Gregorio Marañón, *Gordos y flacos: Estado actual del problema de la patología del peso humano, O.C.,* VIII [Ensayos], pp. 396-398.

[23]*Ibid.,* p. 77.

[24]James Hoddie, Jr., *op. cit.,* p. 57.

[25]*Ibid.*

[26]*Ibid.*

[27]José M. Sacristán, *Genialidad y psicopatología* (Madrid: Biblioteca Nueva, no date).

[28]See note number 122 for chapter IV. Lionel Trilling, in a brilliant essay, has refuted the belief that mental illness is the condition which permits the artist to tell the truth. ("Art and Neurosis," in William Phillips, ed., *Art and Psychoanalysis* [New York: The World Publishing Co., 1963], pp. 502-38.)

[29]Gregorio Marañón, "Los estados intersexuales en la especie humana," *O.C.,* III [Conferencias], p. 167.

[30]*Ibid.,* p. 170.

[31]*Ibid.,* p. 171.

[32]James Hoddie, Jr., "El concepto de la labor del historiador y biógrafo

Gary D. Keller

en las obras de Gregorio Marañón," *Bulletin Hispanique,* Vol. LXIX, Nos. 1-2 (1967), pp. 106-21.

[33]Oliver Brachfeld, *Polémica contra Marañón* (Barcelona: Editorial Europa, 1933). This book, the outcome of a well-known polemic between Marañón and Oliver Brachfeld conducted in the periodical, *El siglo médico,* has been almost systematically neglected by critics dealing with Marañón. Despite the exaggerated hostility toward the Spanish physician, Oliver Brachfeld's book contains fundamental criticisms.

[34]*Ibid.,* pp. 51-52.

[35]Gregorio Marañón, "Los estados intersexuales en la especie humana," *O.C.,* III, p. 167.

[36]*Ibid.,* p. 168.

[37]Pedro Laín Entralgo, *op. cit.,* p. 236.

[38]Juan Rof Carballo, *Medicina y actividad creadora* (Madrid: Revista de Occidente, 1964), p. 313.

[39]F. Oliver Brachfeld contrasts the positions of Marañón and Freud toward infantile sexuality in the following way: "Marañón interprets the undifferentiated autoerotic mechanism of the child's libido as 'indifferently hetero- or homosexual;' Freud has interpreted it as indifferently hetero- and homosexual. . . ." (*op. cit.,* p. 124).

[40]Gregorio Marañón, "Veinte años de endocrinología," *O.C.,* I [Prólogos], p. 87.

[41]Gregorio Marañón, "La endocrinología y la ciencia penal," *O.C.,* I, pp. 569-70.

[42]Luis S. Granjel, *Gregorio Marañón: Su vida y su obra* (Madrid: Ediciones Guadarrama, 1960), p. 123.

[43]Gregorio Marañón, "La endocrinología y la ciencia penal," *O.C.,* I, p. 570.

[44]Sublimation is described by Freud as the modification of the aim and the change of the object of an instinctual drive occurring under the governance of social valuation. ("Anxiety and Instinctual Life," *New Introductory Lectures on Psychoanalysis,* trans. by James Strachey [New York: W.W. Norton and Co., 1964], p. 97).

[45]Oliver Brachfeld, *op. cit.,* p. 40.

[46]Robert C. Bolles, *Theory of Motivation* (New York: Harper and Row, 1968), p. 90.

[47]*Ibid.,* pp. 90-91.

[48]Oliver Brachfeld, *op. cit.,* p. 43.

[49]For a bibliography of current pyschological literary criticism see footnote number 59 for chapter II.

[50]Pedro Laín Entralgo, *Menéndez Pelayo* in *España como problema* (Madrid: Aguilar, 1957), pp. 79-80.

[51]Oliver Brachfeld, *op. cit.,* p. 48.

[52]For an explanation of *individuation* see the glossary in Carl G. Jung, *Memories, Dreams, Reflections,* recorded and edited by Aniela Jaffé (New York: Vintage Books, 1961), pp. 383-84. We shall record only one of the several explanations offered: "I use the term 'individuation' to denote the process by which a person becomes a psychological 'in-dividual,' that is, a

separate, indivisible unity or 'whole.' " (*Ibid.*, p. 383).

⁵³Juan Rof Carballo, *op. cit.*, p. 323.

Chapter II.

¹The following are devoted in their entirety to Don Juan: "Psicopatología del donjuanismo," *O.C.*, III, pp. 75-94; "Gloria y miseria de Villamediana," *O.C.*, III, pp. 545-69; "Notas para la biología de don Juan," *O.C.*, IV, pp. 75-94; "Don Juan en París," *O.C.*, IV, pp. 521-24; "La vuelta de don Juan," *O.C.*, IV, pp. 1059-1060; "Vejez y muerte de don Juan," *O.C.*, IV, pp. 1065-1074; "Les origines de la légende de Don Juan," *Revue Hebdomadaire* (Paris, January 1939), pp. 263-287; "Los orígenes de la leyenda de don Juan," *Revista de la Universidad de San Francisco Javier*, IV (1939), p. 197 (trans. of article in *Revue Hebdomadaire*); "La leyenda de don Juan," *Cuadernos de Adán*, No. 1 (1944), pp. 25-51; "La vejez de don Juan," *O.C.*, I, pp. 437-44; "Más sobre don Juan," *O.C.*, I, pp. 547-50.

Also, the following, in which various of the above articles are anthologized: *Don Juan. Ensayos sobre el origen de su leyenda*, 9th ed. (México-Buenos Aires: Espasa-Calpe, 1960); *Don Juan et le donjuanisme*, essais, traduits de l'espagnol par Marie Berthe Lacombe (Paris: Stock, 1958); *Don Giovanni. Tre saggi sull' origine della leggenda* (Milano: Gentile, 1945); *Don João. Ensaios sobre a origen da sua lenda* (Porto: Tavares Martins, 1947); Oscar Mandel, *The Theatre of Don Juan* (Lincoln, Neb.: University of Nebraska Press, 1963).

In addition, the following have substantial material dealing with Don Juan: *La edad crítica* (Madrid: Siglo Médico, 1919); *Ensayos sobre la vida sexual*, *O.C.*, VIII; "Historia clínica y autopsia del caballero Casanova," *O.C.*, IV, pp. 131-148; *Amiel*, *O.C.*, V [Biografías], pp. 165-288.

²We shall cite the following editions: Georges Gendarme de Bévotte, *La légende de Don Juan, son évolution dans la littérature des origines au romantisme*, 2 vols. (Paris: Librairie Hachette, 1911); Víctor Said Armesto, *La leyenda de Don Juan* (México-Buenos Aires: Espasa-Calpe [Colección Austral], 1946); Ramón Pérez de Ayala, *Las Máscaras. Obras Selectas.* (Barcelona: Editorial AHR, 1957); Ramón Menéndez Pidal, *Estudios Literarios*, 6th ed. (México-Buenos Aires: Espasa-Calpe [Colección Austral], 1946); Otto Rank, "The Don Juan Figure," trans. Walter Bodlander in *The Theatre of Don Juan*, ed. Oscar Mandel (Lincoln, Neb.: University of Nebraska Press, 1963); Ramiro de Maeztu, *Don Quijote, Don Juan y La Celestina*, 6th ed. (México-Buenos Aires: Espasa-Calpe [Colección Austral], 1948); Gonzalo R. Lafora, *Don Juan, Los Milagros y otros ensayos* (Madrid: Biblioteca Nueva, 1927); Francisco Agustín, *Don Juan en el teatro, en la novela y en la vida* (Madrid: Editorial Paez, 1928).

³For a bibliography of Don Juan versions, analogues and criticisms, see Armand E. Singer, "A Bibliography of the Don Juan Theme," *West Virginia*

Gary D. Keller

University Bulletin, 1954, with supplements, 1956, 1958, 1959 in *West Virginia University Philological Papers.*
For critical surveys and commentaries, see: Georges Gendarme de Bévotte, *op. cit.,* Oscar Mandel, ed., *op. cit.*
[4]Georges Gendarme de Bévotte, *op. cit.,* II, p. 178.
[5]Pérez de Ayala treats Weininger with the curiosity and distance we might expect of a humanist. Nevertheless, this treatment in connection with Don Juan by Pérez de Ayala must have been eye-opening and stimulating to Marañón who was well-acquainted with Weininger's theories from a clinical point of view. Weininger's work itself can be understood as an attempt to formulate mathematically the conditions of sexual attraction between men and women, parting from the theories of intersexuality of Magnus Hirschfeld, who hypothesized a varying element of masculinity and femininity in each individual.
[6]Already in 1919, Marañón had made some allusions to Don Juan (e.g., attracts the female rather than is attracted by her) in a basically technical work, *La edad crítica.*
[7]Gregorio Marañón, *O.C.,* III, p. 77.
[8]*Ibid.*
[9]*Ibid.,*
[10]*Ibid.,* p. 75.
[11]*Ibid.,* p. 78.
[12]*Ibid.,* p. 80.
[13]Marañón often uses the term *sublimación,* as for example in "Los misterios de San Plácido," where he hypothesizes that all mysticism, heretical or orthodox, is the consequence of the sublimation of sexuality. The psychodynamic process of sublimation, the question of how sexual energy suffers displacement and transformation, does not find comment by Marañón.
[14]Gregorio Marañón, *op. cit.,* p. 83.
[15]*Ibid.*
[16]*Ibid.,* p. 71.
[17]*Ibid.,* pp. 71-72.
[18]*Ibid.,* p. 83.
[19]*Ibid.,* pp. 83-84.
[20]*Ibid.,* p. 83.
[21]Ramón Pérez de Ayala, *op. cit.,* p. 1472. See p. 1505 for an interesting comment on the genesis and chronology of this "Don Juan as passive seducer" observation. Pérez de Ayala observes that both he and Marañón arrived at the same conclusion independently in 1919.
The concept itself has had a varied history. Ortega y Gasset accepted it: "Don Juan is not the man who makes love to women, but the man whom women make love to." ("Amor en Stendhal," *El Sol,* August 24, 1926, cited by Gonzalo Lafora, *op. cit.,* p. 30.) Ramiro de Maeztu, of course, hypothesized the opposite, Don Juan as the incarnation of activity. Gonzalo Lafora, as on several other occasions, ingeniously tries to reconcile the opposition: "Don Juan is not a passive lover, as several essayists have described him, nor is he a melancholic individual who lets himself be seduced by women.... He is sheer sensual force and erotic intuition. He is moved as if he were

excited by an unquenchable thirst for pleasure which never satisfies his ideal. When women pursue him is when his reputation as a restless lover has already created a halo for him. Now women respond to his renown, to his marvelous spell, to his supposed extraordinary attractiveness. . . . Don Juan, therefore, has two periods: a first one in which he seeks out women and conquers them by his effort and ability alone, and a second one in which women seek him out, attracted by his reputation as a skillful lover." (Gonzalo Lafora, *op. cit.,* pp. 51-52.)

22Gregorio Marañón, *op. cit.,* p. 85, citing Ramón Pérez de Ayala, *Las Máscaras.*

23Ramón Pérez de Ayala, *op. cit.,* p. 1503.

24Gregorio Marañón, *op. cit.,* p. 549.

25*Ibid.,* p. 77.

26*Ibid.,* p. 78.

27Georges Gendarme de Bévotte, *op. cit.,* I, p. 4.

28Gregorio Marañón, *op. cit.,,* p. 78.

29*Ibid.,* p. 79.

30Georges Gendarme de Bévotte, *op. cit.,* I, p. 3.

31Gregorio Marañón, *op. cit.,* p. 86.

32*Ibid.,* p. 87.

33Gregorio Marañón, *O.C.,* I, p. 440.

34*Ibid.*

35Gregorio Marañón, *O.C.,* III, pp. 550-51.

36Miguel de Unamuno, *Teatro Completo* (Madrid: Aguilar, 1959), p. 861.

37Jacinto Grau judges that Unamuno did not understand the essential Don Juan because the figure was too close to his heart: "Unamuno. . .never understood, or refused to ever understand Don Juan; this is essentially the same as his attitude toward Nietzsche, whom he always ignored or abused, because Nietzsche was a part of him and, deep down, he envied him, probably without ever confessing it to himself. . . ." (Jacinto Grau, *Don Juan en el tiempo y el espacio: Análisis histórico-psicológico* [Buenos Aires: Editorial Raigal, 1953], p. 23.)

38Miguel de Unamuno, *op. cit.,* p. 858.

39*Ibid.,* p. 863.

40Gregorio Marañón, *El Greco y Toledo, O.C.,* VII [Biografías], p. 504, citing J. Lhermitte, *Mystiques et faux mystiques,* Paris, 1952.

41Gregorio Marañón, *O.C.,* III, p. 87.

42Ramiro de Maeztu, *op. cit.,* p. 76.

43Gregorio Marañón, *O.C.,* III, p. 87.

44*Ibid.*

45*Ibid.*

46*Ibid.*

47 *Ibid.,* p. 82.

48C.S. Lewis, "Hamlet, the Prince or the Poem?" Annual Shakespeare Lecture of the British Academy, *Proceedings of the British Academy,* XXXVIII (1942), 7-9.

49Henri Matisse, "Notes d'un peintre sur son dessin," *Le Point IV,* XXI (1939), 14, quoted in *Art and Illusion: A Study in the Psychology of Pictorial*

Gary D. Keller

Representation, by E.H. Gombrich, the A.W. Mellon Lectures in the Fine Arts, 1956 (National Gallery of Art, Washington: Bollingen Series, XXXV, 1956), p. 115.

[50]For a survey of the problem see the following two works by Norman N. Holland: *Psychoanalysis and Shakespeare* (New York: McGraw Hill, 1964), and *The Dynamics of Literary Response* (New York: Oxford University Press, 1968).

[51]Cf., L.C. Knights, "How many Children Had Lady Macbeth?" (1933), in *Explorations* (London: Chatto & Windus, 1951), for an incisive criticism of the tendency by critics to treat fictional protagonists as if they had an existence apart from the literary text.

[52]Ramón Pérez de Ayala, *Las Máscaras* cited by Gonzalo Lafora, *op. cit.,* p. 25.

[53]Gonzalo Lafora, *op. cit.,* p. 25.

[54]Francisco Agustín, *op. cit.,* pp. 98-99.

[55]Ramiro de Maeztu, *op. cit.,* p. 89.

[56]Corpus Barga, "Don Juan y los doctores," in *El Sol,* December 18, 1926. See also by the same author, "Don Juan y los placeres renanos," *Revista de Occidente,* IX (1925), 374-381.

Gonzalo Lafora opposes Corpus Barga's criticisms in "Las psiconeurosis de situación," *El Sol,* December 17 and 24, 1926 and "Sobre el problema de Don Juan," *El Sol,* December 21, 1926.

[57]Jacinto Grau, *op. cit.,* pp. 27-28.

[58]Salvador de Madariaga, *El Hamlet de Shakespeare, ensayo de interpretación* (Buenos Aires: Editorial Sudamericana, 1949).

[59]Curiously Grau's remarks are contradicted by his own efforts. (We recall the subtitle of Grau's book, *Análisis históricopsicológico.*) For example, Grau observes: "The very profusion of versions of Don Juan, and the continuing and increasing interest that he goes on arousing, clearly prove that the true personification of this character is based on something alive, on something with deep roots in man's nature. What I am going to attempt to do is observe this living element and consider it in depth. . . ." (Jacinto Grau, *op. cit.,* p. 39.)

In truth it is perfectly possible to achieve a psychological literary criticism (sometimes termed metacriticism or infracriticism) without negating the formal aspects of a literary opus. Indeed, there is a school of critics who pursue a psychological interpretation of formal aspects such as sound and metaphor as well as character and meaning. See: Simon O. Lesser, *Fiction and the Unconscious* (Boston: Beacon Press, 1957), Ernst Kris, *Psychoanalytic Explorations in Art* (New York: International Universities Press, 1952) and especially, Norman N. Holland, *The Dynamics of Literary Response* (New York: Oxford University Press, 1968).

[60]Gregorio Marañón, *O.C.,* III, p. 86.

[61]*Ibid.,* p. 550.

[62]Gregorio Marañón, *O.C.,* I, p. 437.

[63]Gregorio Marañón, *O.C.,* III, p. 71.

[64]Ramiro de Maeztu, *op. cit.,* p. 102.

[65]*Ibid.,* p. 103.

[66]*Ibid.,* p. 105.

[67]Gregorio Marañón, *O.C.*, III, p. 79.

[68]*Ibid.*, p. 70.

[69]*Ibid.*, p. 71.

[70]For a classification of the generation of 1898 according to the anarchic-aristocratic category, and the generation of 1914 according to the aristocratic category, see: Gonzalo Sobejano, *Nietzsche en España* (Madrid: Gredos, 1967).

[71]Gregorio Marañón, *O.C.*, IV, pp. 883-84.

[72]*Ibid.*, p. 884.

[73]*Ibid.*, p. 885-86.

[74]Gregorio Marañón, *O.C.*, III, p. 545.

[75]The belief that Marañón implacably diagnosed Don Juan as a homosexual has entrenched itself so widely and deeply as to have become a topical assumption. For example, in the necrology written by Esteban Salazar Chapela, the author, with a vulgarity that reflects his (political) antagonism toward Marañón, repeats the conventional "wisdom": ". . .his astounding declaration that Don Juan Tenorio was an effeminate man. . . it must be recognized that the theory enjoyed a certain galling originality." (*La Nación*, July 17, 1960). In this country, Emile Capouya, although he knew Marañón first hand, finds it easy to simplify the critic: "In a now-famous essay, Gregorio Marañón. . .asserts that Don Juan's promiscuity is a mask for homosexuality and impotence." ("Apropos of Don Juan," *The Nation*, August 29, 1959.) This is an extreme irony. Ought we expect another Marañón to combat the new myth which has sprung up like a head of the Hydra? Although the technical complexity of Marañón's theory makes it vulnerable to distortion, the invariable tagging of Don Juan as homosexual is peculiar and revealing. It would seem that there is a lesson to be learned in the popularity (albeit distorted) of Marañón's theories with the layman. Perhaps the likes of Don Juan must receive his punishment if all will be well with the gentry. In Tirso's time one could empathize with the boldness and find relief in the condemnation of Don Juan at the same time. Currently, the religious punishment is not satisfying enough. Here, perhaps, is the reason why so many have gleefully accepted Don Juan as a homosexual. Ortega y Gasset indicates something along these lines: ". . .men can be divided into three groups: those who think they are Don Juans, those who think they have been, and those who think they could have been but did not want to. The latter are the ones who are inclined, with worthy intentions, to attack Don Juan and perhaps to decree his demise." ("Para una psicología del hombre interesante," *Estudios sobre el amor* [Madrid: Espasa-Calpe, 1964], p. 44.) Also, Emile Capouya, although he too misreads Marañón's theories, has an ingenious explanation for this popular belief: "The Counter Reformation dressed Don Juan in the gaudy robes of its most pressing fears. Our own age, so much more timid and tacit, undercuts the entire question of the necessity for revolution by declaring that the revolutionary is a defective. Lenin, Stalin, Hitler, Mussolini—our era has suffered so much from the actions of outsize personalities that it is ready to condemn out of hand any unorthodoxy, any originality, any exuberance, any protest." (Emile Capouya, *loc. cit.*).

[76]Miguel de Unamuno, *op. cit.*, p. 859.

Gary D. Keller

[77] Gregorio Marañón, *O.C.*, III, p. 551.

[78] Gonzalo Lafora, *op. cit.*, p. 29.

[79] *Ibid.*, p. 33.

[80] *Ibid.*

[81] Gregorio Marañón, *O.C.*, III, p. 549.

[82] Gregorio Marañón, "Los estados intersexuales en la especie humana," *O.C.*, III, p. 174.

[83] Gregorio Marañón, *O.C.*, III, p. 517.

[84] *Ibid.*

[85] *Ibid.*, p. 546.

[86] *Ibid.*, p. 547.

[87] *Ibid.*, p. 552.

[88] Joaquín Casalduero, *Contribución al estudio del tema de Don Juan en el teatro español* (Northampton, Mass.: 1938), Smith College Studies in Modern Languages, Vol. XIX, Nos. 3-4, pp. 45-46.

[89] For example, much of Ortega y Gasset's work was originally published in serial form in newspapers; many of Pérez de Ayala's *Las Máscaras* were originally reviews of actual theatrical productions; Marañón gave an enormous number of public lectures and wrote a sizable number of newspaper articles; Madariaga wrote a "guide" to the reading of Don Quijote and attempted to contrast the national character of the Spanish with the French and English, etc.

[90] Gregorio Marañón, *O.C.*, III, p. 553.

[91] *Ibid.*

[92] *Ibid.*

[93] *Ibid.*, p. 557.

[94] *Ibid.*, pp. 556-57.

[95] *Ibid.*, p. 554.

[96] *Ibid.*

[97] *Ibid.* In contrast to Marañón's speculations about mysticism where he judged as early as 1939 ("El secreto del Greco") that Semitic elements played an important part, there is no speculation as to the historical development of the Spanish sense of honor, either in its social or literary aspects. In our commentary of Marañón's interpretation of El Greco, we have compared the doctor's attitude toward Spanish mysticism with the position of Américo Castro. However, a similar comparison with respect to honor between the doctor and the historian is not productive. See Américo Castro, *De la edad conflictiva* (Madrid: Taurus Ediciones, 1961). Also H. Th. Oostendorp, *El conflicto entre el honor y el amor en la literatura española hasta el siglo XVII* (La Haya: G.G. Van Goor Zonen's U.M.N.V., 1962).

Julian Pitt-Rivers, "Honor and Social Status" and Julio Caro Baroja, "Honor and Shame: An Historical Account of Several Conflicts," in *Honour and Shame: The Values of Mediterranean Society*, J.G. Peristany, ed. (London: Weidenfeld and Nicolson, 1965), writing from an anthropological and sociological perspective, criticize Marañón for negating the sentiment of "honor" in Don Juan. Pitt-Rivers asserts: "Marañón is another writer who fails to perceive that Don Juan is a man of honor. . .and that the theme of the play is, precisely, a critique of this theory of honour—a fact which

238

Notes

is surely congruent with the circumstance that the author was a priest" (p. 110). Julio Caro Baroja asserts: ". . .the figure of Don Juan needs to be explained in sociological terms, and not in terms of psychology or psychopathology. . .the simple figure of the *burlador*, as drawn by Tirso de Molina, and even that of the *infamador* of Juan de La Cueva (1543-1610), who possibly took the character of Leucinio from reality, fit into a well-defined social structure independently of what may be argued from a psychological point of view for or against the realism of these characters and of the moral view which we may hold of those who take pleasure in deceiving and dishonouring others" (p. 113).

Apart from their opposition, they have much in common with Marañón in terms of approach. Marañón interprets Don Juan as a "faithful reflection" of a "real" body and character type. Caro Baroja and Pitt-Rivers interpret Don Juan as a "faithful" reflection of a "real" social type.

98See the notes and introduction by Francisco A. de Icaza to Juan de la Cueva, *El infamador* (and other plays) (Madrid: Espasa-Calpe, Clásicos Castellanos, 1941), pp. XLIV-XLV, for a criticism of the conventional assumption that Leucinio provides an antecedent and model for Don Juan Tenorio.

99Gregorio Marañón, *O.C.*, III, p. 554.

100*Ibid.*

101Cf. Frederick Robertson Bryson, *The Point of Honor in Sixteenth Century: An Aspect of the Life of the Gentleman* (New York: Columbia University, 1935); Curtis Brown Watson, *Shakespeare and the Renaissance Concept of Honor* (Princeton, N.J.: Princeton University Press, 1960); George Fenwich Jones, *Honor in German Literature* (Chapel Hill: University of North Carolina Press, 1959).

102Hugo Albert Rennert, *The Spanish Stage in the Time of Lope de Vega* (New York: Dover Publications, 1963), p. 130ff. (First published in 1909).

103Gregorio Marañón, *O.C.*, III, p. 554.

104*Ibid.*, p. 557.

105Marañón merely says the following: "The relationship between Machiavellianism and Don Juanesque love is worthy of a more thorough study, which I cannot undertake here." (*Ibid.*)

106See Victor Said Armesto, *op. cit.*, chapter III. Said Armesto makes an effort to demonstrate that, although the first knowledge we have of the *Burlador* is 1630, the play may have been written before 1615.

107Gregorio Marañón, *O.C.*, III, pp. 557-58.

108*Ibid.*, p. 559.

109*Ibid.*

110*Ibid.*

111Marañón cites Arturo Farinelli, "Cuatro palabras sobre Don Juan y la literatura donjuanesca del porvenir," *Homenaje a Menéndez y Pelayo* (Madrid, 1899), I, pp. 205-22 in his bibliography. The same Farinelli article has been reprinted in *Divagaciones hispánicas* (Barcelona: 1936), II, pp. 206-35 and *Ensayos y discursos de crítica literaria hispano-europea* (Rome, 1925), Vol. II.

112Victor Said Armesto, *op. cit.*, p. 20.

113Gregorio Marañón, *O.C.*, III, p. 554 and p. 557.

Gary D. Keller

[114]Ramón Menéndez Pidal, *op. cit.,* p. 92.

[115]*Ibid.,* pp. 92-93.

[116]*Ibid.,* p. 93.

[117]Menéndez Pidal gives us a summary of the play: "A Count named Leoncio, who is corrupted by the doctrines of Machiavelli, and who does not believe in eternal life, finds a skull on passing through a cemetery. He kicks it scoffingly, saying to it: 'if after death you can still understand me, come to supper with my other guests.' When Leoncio sits down to have a lighthearted supper with his friends, a bony monster appears at the door, and, after futile attempts to repulse him, he sits down at the table, assuring the guests that he is also invited. To the astonishment of all, the skeleton declares that he is Count Leoncio's grandfather, who has come to demonstrate the immortality of the soul to his grandson; finally he carries the ruined Count off with him." (*Ibid.,* pp. 90-91.)

[118]Gregorio Marañón, *O.C.,* III, p. 558.

[119]Georges Gendarme de Bévotte, *op. cit.,* I, p. 6.

[120]Gregorio Marañón, *O.C.,* III, p. 558.

[121]While it is clear that in general the artistic versions—with significant exceptions, for example, Unamuno, Henry de Montherlant, etc.—have not neglected Don Juan as rebel, a substantial evaluation along this dimension of the long line of Don Juan plays, poems, novels, etc., is beyond the scope and limitations of this book. For general surveys see the earlier cited works of Joaquín Casalduero, Georges Gendarme de Bévotte and Oscar Mandel.

It is interesting to note that Ortega y Gasset has doubts about the depth of the rebelliousness of Don Juan Tenorio and Don Luis Mejía in Zorilla's drama. Commenting on the overwhelming popularity of Don Juan Tenorio over any other Spanish play, Ortega wonders "whether there is the degree of irrevocability of authentic tragedy, in the *Don Juan Tenorio,* that there is in Tirso's *El Convidado de Piedra,* or even in the Duque de Rivas' *Don Alvaro.* In sum, if Don Juan 'ended badly,' would we Spaniards go so willingly every year, during those melancholy autumn days, to hear and see 'Don Juan'? Would 'Don Juan' be so popular?" (*Obras completas,* V, 4th ed. [Madrid: Revista de Occidente, 1933-1941], p. 246.) The following observation we feel points out the useful contribution that psychology is able to make to literary criticism, for Ortega finds it necessary to explain *Don Juan Tenorio* on the basis of a distinction between "real" and "rhetorical" existence: "does it mean that all that they [Don Juan and Don Luis] were—atheists, insolent, concerned only about themselves, lacking forethought—they really were not 'in reality', but rather. . .metaphorically; that their lives were a rhetorical exercise?" (*Ibid.,* p. 245.) Of course, Ortega does not question the existence of a rebellious or defiant component in the *Don Juan Tenorio.* Rather he questions the nature of that component: Does it have not only an external, rhetorical veracity but likewise an internal, psychological veracity?

[122]Georges Gendarme de Bévotte, *op. cit.,* II, p. 264.

[123]*Ibid.,* p. 249-50.

[124]Ramón Pérez de Ayala, *op. cit.,* p. 1318.

[125]The image of Don Juan as rebellious angel or Satanic being was a commonplace during this period, occurring in the writings of Pérez de

Notes

Ayala, Américo Castro, Gonzalo Lafora, Jacinto Grau, etc., although *not* in Marañón (Don Juan as psychopath) or Maeztu who speaks of the "superhuman power" of Don Juan. Jacinto Grau (*op. cit.*, p. 42) associates the image of "rebellious angel" with the critique of Pí y Margall who "focuses on the Catholicism of Don Juan." See Francisco Pí y Margall, *Opúsculos* (Madrid, 1884).

[126]Ramón Pérez de Ayala, *op. cit.*, p. 1319.

[127]Américo Castro, "Don Juan en la literatura española" (Prólogo) in *Cinco ensayos sobre Don Juan* (Gregorio Marañón, Ramiro de Maeztu, José Ingenieros, Azorín, Ramón Pérez de Ayala) (Santiago de Chile: Editorial Cultura), p. 15.

[128]*Ibid.* Américo Castro, as Jacinto Grau twenty years later, emphasizes the environment in which Don Juan was created, therefore, judging that clinical observations are invalid. "Don Juan was created in an environment that is essential to him, because he only functions in connection with that environment. Tirso, Molière, or Byron may have varied Don Juan's milieu, but they have never divested him of it, because then their character would have ceased to live. When I read those diatribes on Don Juanism, and I see that there are people who, in order to analyze what Don Juan is, bring clinical experiments into the picture, I cannot repress my astonishment." (p. 16). Castro also disagrees with Marañón's observation that the fisherwoman Tisbea falls in love with Don Juan even before he speaks. Castro asserts: "Tisbea falls in love in the most classic and normal way: a woman seeing an illustrious man perform acts of heroism, risking his life." (p. 16 ff.).

[129]*Ibid.*, p. 17.

[130]Ramiro de Maeztu, *op. cit.*, p. 95.

[131]José Ortega y Gasset, *Obras Completas*, III, 4th ed. (Madrid: Revista de Occidente, 1957), p. 178.

[132]Jacinto Grau, *op. cit.*, p. 27.

[133]*Ibid.*, p. 42.

[134]Salvador de Madariaga, *De Galdós a Lorca* (Buenos Aires: Editorial Sudamericana, 1960), p. 178. The above is a re-edition of *Semblanzas literarias contemporáneas* (Madrid: Biblioteca Cervantes, 1923).

[135]*Ibid.*

[136]*Ibid.*, prologue (unpaged).

[137]Salvador de Madariaga, "Don Juan and Don Juanism," trans. by Lloyd D. Teale in Oscar Mandel, ed., *op. cit.*, p. 647.

[138]*Ibid.*

[139]*Ibid.*, pp. 648-49.

[140]*Ibid.*, p. 649.

[141]Emile Capouya, *op. cit.*

[142]See Otto Fenichel, *The Psychoanalytic Theory of Neurosis* (New York: W.W. Norton, 1945), pp. 243-44.

[143]Otto Rank, *op. cit.*, pp. 626-27.

[144]Gonzalo Lafora, *op. cit.*, p. 20.

[145]*Ibid.*, p. 19.

[146]*Ibid.*, p. 20.

[147]*Ibid.*, p. 21.

241

Gary D. Keller

148 F. Oliver Brachfeld, *Los sentimientos de inferioridad* (Buenos Aires: Editorial Siglo Veinte, 1942), p. 126.

149 Francisco Agustín, *op. cit.*, p. 99.

150 Juan Rof Carballo, "El problema del seductor en Kierkegaard, Proust y Rilke," *Entre el silencio y la palabra* (Madrid: Aguilar, 1960), p. 120. An earlier version of the above essay in *gallego* is to be found in Xuan Rof Carballo, *Mito e realidade da terra nai* (Vigo: Editorial Galazia, 1957).

151 *Ibid.*, p. 120.

152 *Ibid.*, p. 144.

153 *Ibid.*

154 Albert Camus, *The Myth of Sisyphus and Other Essays*, trans. by Justin O'Brien (New York: Vintage Books [Random House], 1955), p. 54.

155 *Ibid.*

156 *Ibid.*, p. 56.

157 Gregorio Marañón, *Don Juan, O.C.*, VII, p. 203.

158 *Ibid.*, p. 189.

159 Roberto Novoa Santos, "Biopatología de la estigmatización mística," *El advenimiento del hombre y otras conferencias* (Madrid, 1933), p. 131, cited by Luis S. Granjel, *Baroja y otras figuras del 98* (Madrid, 1960), p. 282.

160 *Ibid.*

161 Gregorio Marañón, *Don Juan, O.C.*, VII, p. 189.

162 *Ibid.*

163 See Roberto Novoa Santos, *Patografía de Santa Teresa de Jesús* (Madrid: 1932).

164 Gregorio Marañón, *Don Juan, O.C.*, VII, p. 190.

165 *Ibid.*, p. 191.

166 James Henry Hoddie, Jr., "Gregorio Marañón, Historian and Man of Letters," Ph.D. thesis, Brown University, 1965, p. 195. Marañón actually claims the following: "Neither I nor anyone else could assert that he directly copied him [Villamediana] when he wrote the *Burlador*. I do not want to dispute with the scholars. But I do assert that the excitement of these typically Don Juanesque events must have made an impression on the great writer, that expert on the human soul; and it must have contributed to the process of creation of his immortal character. In the final analysis, if I were pressed to say who was the first living Don Juan, I would not hesitate to answer that it was Villamediana." (*O.C.*, III, p. 564.)

167 Gregorio Marañón, *O.C.*, III, p. 560.

168 *Ibid.*

169 A check of Corominas' *Diccionario crítico etimológico de la lengua castellana* reveals that Corominas relates etymologically "tener" and "tenor" but does not mention the surname, *Tenorio*.

170 See Narciso Alonso Cortés, *La muerte de Villamediana*, Valladolid, 1928. Emilio Cotarelo y Mori, in *El conde de Villamediana* (Estudio biográfico-crítico con varias poesías inéditas del mismo, Madrid: Sucesores de Rivadeneyra, 1886), speculates that Villamediana was killed on orders from the king because of his illicit love affair with doña Isabel de Borbón, the queen.

171 Gregorio Marañón, *O.C.*, III, p. 572.

172 Gregorio Marañón, "Vejez y muerte de don Juan," *O.C.*, IV, pp. 1065-1074.

[173]Gregorio Marañón, *O.C.*, I, p. 440.

[174]Gregorio Marañón, *O.C.*, I, p. 548. For more material on the female counterpart to Don Juan, see Gregorio Marañón, "Psicopatología del donjuanismo," *O.C.*, III, pp. 75-94.

[175]*Ibid.*

[176]*Ibid.*

[177]Also published in Gregorio Marañón, *Don Juan et le donjuanisme, essais*, traduits par Marie Berthe Lacombe (Paris: Stock, 1958).

[178]In *Correo Literario Madrid*, IV, No. 80 (1953) circumstances of Gregorio Marañón's trip to Brazil are noted, including the fact that he spoke on Don Quijote, Don Juan and Faust at the Casa de Cervantes.

[179]Gregorio Marañón, "Don Quijote, Don Juan y Fausto," *O.C.*, III, p. 957.

[180]José Goyanes Capdevila, *Tipología del Quijote* (Madrid: Aguirre, 1932), p. 30.

[181]Gregorio Marañón, "El libro más español," *O.C.*, I, p. 528.

Chapter III.

[1]Vicens Vives identifies the crisis of 1898 as especially Castilian (rather than Catalán) and claims that this crisis was "overcome by an act of nationalistic will, peculiarly unconnected to history, except in the cases of the academics associated with Menéndez Pidal and Gómez Moreno." Jaime Vicens Vives, *Aproximación a la historia de España*, 3rd ed. (Barcelona: Edit. Vicens-Vives), p. 21.

Vicens neglects to mention Rafael Altamira. Moreover, I reject his allegation that Ortega had no genuine involvement with history. Vicens claims that Unamuno and Ortega approached the Castilian soul by means of their own subjectivism, thereby producing an "unreal Castile." While this may be true, it does not preclude a genuine interest in history and historiography, albeit not characterized by the rigorous scientific and statistical procedures of later historians.

[2]A history of Spanish historiography taking up where Sánchez-Alonso's *Historia de la historiografía española* leaves off, is sorely lacking at this time. The following list of contemporary historiographical materials does not presume to exhaustiveness, but rather, encompasses those works that I have found to be of value in attempting to evaluate the evolution of contemporary Spanish historiography. Rafael Altamira y Crevea, *Proceso histórico de la historiografía humana* (Mexico: El Colegio de México, 1948); Guillermo Araya, *Evolución del pensamiento histórico de Américo Castro* (Madrid: Taurus Ediciones, 1969); Américo Castro, *Dos ensayos* (Mexico: Edit. Porrúa, 1956); Américo Castro, *España en su historia. Cristianos, moros y judíos.* (Buenos Aires: Edit. Losada, 1948); Américo Castro, *La realidad histórica de España* (Mexico: Edit. Porrúa, 1954); John E. Fagg, "Rafael

Gary D. Keller

Altamira," in *Some Historians of Modern Europe: Essays in Historiography*, ed. Bernadotte E. Schmitt (Port Washington, N.Y.: Kennikut Press, 1942); Manuel García Morente, *Ideas para una filosofía de la historia de España* (Madrid: Univ. de Madrid, 1943); Léon E. Halkin, *Initiation à la critique historique* (Paris: Librairie Armand Colin, 1953); James Hoddie, Jr., "El concepto de la labor del historiador y biógrafo en las obras de Gregorio Marañón," *Bulletin Hispanique*, XLIX, 1-2 (1967), 106-21; Edmundo O'Gorman, *Crisis y porvenir de la ciencia histórica* (Mexico: Imprenta Universitaria, 1947); José Ortega y Gasset, *Historia como sistema, Obras completas*, VI, 5th ed. (Madrid: Revista de Occidente, 1961); Jorge Pérez Ballestar, "Ideas para una ordenación metódica de la historiografía," *Estudios de Historia Moderna*, III (1953), 1-24; Claudio Sánchez-Albornoz, *España, un enigma histórico*, 2 vols. (Buenos Aires: Edit. Sudamericana, 1956); Claudio Sánchez-Albornoz, *Españoles ante la historia* (Buenos Aires: Edit. Losada, 1958); Benito Sánchez Alonso, "Epílogo," *Historia de la historiografía española*, III (Madrid: Consejo Superior de Investigaciones Científicas, 1950); José Luis Romero, *La historia y la vida* (Buenos Aires: Edit. Yerba Buena, 1945); José Luis Romero, *Sobre la biografía y la historia* (Buenos Aires: Edit. Sudamericana, 1945); Jaime Vicens Vives, "Al cabo de tres años," *Estudios de Historia Moderna*, III (1953), pp. v-viii; Jaime Vicens Vives, *Aproximación a la historia de España*, 3rd ed. (Barcelona: Edit. Vicens-Vives, 1962); Jaime Vicens Vives, "Estructura administrativa estatal en los siglos XVI y XVII," *Eleventh International Congress of Historical Sciences, Rapports*, IV (Stockholm: Almqvist and Wiksell, 1960); Jaime Vicens Vives, *Historia crítica de la vida y reinado de Fernando II de Aragón* (Madrid: Consejo Superior de Investigaciones Científicas, 1952); Jaime Vicens Vives, "Presentación y propósito," *Estudios de Historia Moderna*, I (1951), i-xii; Jaime Vicens Vives, "Progresos en el empeño," *Estudios de Historia Moderna*, II (1952), v-vii.

[3]José Luis Romero, *Sobre la biografía y la historia*, p. 21.

[4]For an extensive bibliography concerning the impact of psychology on biography, see the following two works by John A. Garraty: "The Interrelations of Psychology and Biography," *Psychological Bulletin*, LI (1954), 569-82; and *The Nature of Biography* (New York: Alfred A. Knopf, 1957).

[5]John A. Garraty, *The Nature of Biography*, pp. 125-26.

[6]Gregorio Marañón, "Las mujeres y el Conde-Duque de Olivares," *O.C.*, II, pp. 139-140.

[7]*Ibid.*, p. 140.

[8]*Ibid.*

[9]See for example the appreciation in Gonzalo Torrente Ballester, *Panorama de la literatura española contemporánea*, 3rd ed. (Madrid: Ed. Guadarrama, 1965), p. 438.

[10]Antonio Marichalar, *Riesgo y ventura del Duque de Osuna* (Madrid: Espasa-Calpe, 1930), p. 276.

[11]Agustín G. de Amezúa y Mayo, *Isabel de Valois*, vol. I (Madrid: Gráficas Ultra, 1949), p. xiv.

[12]Gregorio Marañón, "Las mujeres y el Conde-Duque de Olivares," *O.C.*, II, p. 139.

[13]Gregorio Marañón, *Vocación y ética y otros ensayos, O.C.*, IX, p. 329.

[14]Gregorio Marañón, "Médicos poetas," in *Idearium de Marañón*, ed. Alfredo Juderías (Madrid: Edit. "Cultura Clásica y Moderna," 1960), p. 215.

[15]*Ibid.*, p. 214.

[16]John A. Garraty points out that "Maurois, while still dependent upon the one insight that 'will suddenly illuminate a character,' was, by the fifties, convinced of the value of thorough scholarship, and even of footnotes. His later biographies, such as his studies of George Sand and Victor Hugo, were far more substantial than anything he had produced in the twenties." *The Nature of Biography*, p. 148.

[17]Jaime Vicens Vives, *Historia crítica de la vida y reinado de Fernando II de Aragón*, p. 8.

[18]John A. Garraty, *The Nature of Biography*, p. 129.

[19]Emil Ludwig, *Genius and Character* (New York, 1927), cited in John A. Garraty, *The Nature of Biography*, p. 131.

[20]John A. Garraty, *The Nature of Biography*, pp. 130-131.

[21]Stefan Zweig, *The World of Yesterday* (New York, 1943), cited in John A. Garraty, *The Nature of Biography*, p. 131.

[22]André Maurois cited in John A. Garraty, *The Nature of Biography*, p. 131.

[23]André Maurois, *Aspects of Biography* (New York: Frederick Ungar Publishing Co., 1966), p. 71.

[24]*Ibid.*, p. 70.

[25]*Ibid.*, p. 46.

[26]*Ibid.*, p. 47.

[27]John A. Garraty, *The Nature of Biography*, p. 126.

[28]*Ibid.*, p. 138-39.

[29]Gregorio Marañón, "Las mujeres y el Conde-Duque de Olivares," p. 139.

[30]Gregorio Marañón, "Prólogo," to Nicolás Ruiz, *Obras selectas* (Madrid, 1947), p. xiii, cited in James Hoddie, Jr., "El concepto de la labor del historiador y biógrafo en las obras de Gregorio Marañón," p. 109.

[31]James Hoddie, Jr., "El concepto de la labor del historiador...," p. 109.

[32]The original passage follows: ". . .pero un libro de ciencia expurgado de todo dogmatismo, transido de humanidad, limpio de datos que no tengan una razón interpretativa, inmediata, del alma del biografiado; aun cuando sean falsos: que la verdad se compone también de mentira; porque ésta, la mentira, es siempre el reverso de una verdad; y el reverso, si es neto, nos permite, a veces, identificar la moneda mejor que el anverso confuso y semiborrado." Gregorio Marañón, "Las mujeres y el Conde-Duque de Olivares," p. 141.

[33]John A. Garraty, *The Nature of Biography*, p. 129.

[34]John E. Fagg, "Rafael Altamira," p. 6.

[35]Marañón discusses the "black legend" explicitly in his prologue to J. Pérez de Barradas, *Los mestizos de América*. See, Gregorio Marañón, "Sobre el problema de la raza," *O.C.*, I, pp. 761-67.

[36]Benjamín Jarnés, *Sor Patrocinio* (Madrid: Espasa-Calpe, 1929), pp. 11-12.

Gary D. Keller

[37] Agustín G. de Amezúa y Mayo, *Isabel de Valois,* vol. I (Madrid: Gráficas Ultra, 1949), pp. x-xi.

[38] Gregorio Marañón, *Tiberio. Historia de un resentimiento, O.C.,* VII, p. 14.

[39] James Hoddie, Jr., "El concepto de la labor del historiador y biógrafo en las obras de Gregorio Marañón," p. 118.

[40] Francisco Tomás Valiente, *Los validos en la monarquía española del siglo XVII* (Madrid: Instituto de Estudios Políticos, 1963), p. 40.

[41] *Ibid.*

[42] Charles Howard Carter, *The Secret Diplomacy of the Habsburgs, 1598-1625* (New York and London: Columbia University Press, 1964), p. 70.

[43] *Ibid.,* p. 281.

[44] Jaime Vicens Vives, "Estructura administrativa estatal en los siglos XVI y XVII," p. 5.

[45] Gregorio Marañón, *Antonio Pérez, O.C.,* VI [Biografías], p. 61.

[46] Jaime Vicens Vives, *Historia crítica de la vida y reinado de Fernando II de Aragón,* p. 8.

[47] *Ibid.,* p. 7.

[48] *Ibid.,* p. 6.

[49] *Ibid.,* p. 7.

[50] *Ibid.* .

[51] Jaime Vicens Vives, *Fernando el Católico, Príncipe de Aragón, Rey de Sicilia* (Madrid: Consejo Superior de Investigaciones Científicas, 1952), p. 15.

[52] *Ibid.*

[53] *Ibid.*

[54] Jaime Vicens Vives, "Presentación y propósito," p. xii.

[55] *Ibid.*

[56] *Ibid.,* p. x.

[57] Jaime Vicens Vives, *Historia crítica de la vida y reinado de Fernando II de Aragón,* p. 6.

[58] *Ibid.,* p. 9.

[59] Gregorio Marañón, *El Conde-Duque de Olivares, O.C.,* V, p. 706.

[60] *Ibid.,* p. 708.

[61] *Ibid.,* p. 709.

[62] Gregorio Marañón, "Influencia de Francia en la política española a través de los emigrados," *O.C.,* III, p. 631.

[63] Gregorio Marañón, *Antonio Pérez, O.C.,* VI, p. 232.

[64] Pedro Laín Entralgo, "Vida, obra y persona de Gregorio Marañón," in Gregorio Marañón, *O.C.,* I, p. LXXIX.

[65] Gregorio Marañón, *Antonio Pérez, O.C.,* VI, pp. 12-13.

[66] *Ibid.,* p. 57.

[67] *Ibid.*

[68] *Ibid.,* p. 65.

[69] *Ibid.,* p. 69.

[70] *Ibid.,* p. 71.

[71] *Ibid.,* p. 70.

[72] *Ibid.*

[73]*Ibid.*, p. 59. Elsewhere in the book Marañón states that from his examination of Antonio Pérez's genealogy, one fact stands clear, the impossibility of Antonio Pérez to declare his ancestry with exactitude. This leads to the following statement, remarkable for its speculativeness: "I, impartially speaking, am inclined to believe that this fact is congruent with his need to hide his Jewish origin." (*Ibid.*, pp. 36-37.)

[74]*Ibid.*, p. 71.

[75]*Ibid.*, p. 67.

[76]*Ibid.*, p. 63.

[77]See Manuel Fernández Alvarez, *Política Mundial de Carlos V y Felipe II* (Madrid: Consejo Superior de Investigaciones Científicas, Escuela de Historia Moderna, 1966), for a very considered summary of Antonio Pérez's intrigues, which although explicitly based on Marañón's work, carefully avoids the latter's excesses. I should note that Marañón is occasionally cited by Spanish historians such as Fernández Alvarez, Tomás Valiente as well as Eulogio Zudaire Huarte, *El Conde-Duque y Cataluña* (Madrid: Consejo Superior de Investigaciones Científicas, Escuela de Historia Moderna, 1964), typically in terms of a perspicacious psychological insight. Other historians such as José Deleito y Piñuela, *El declinar de la monarquía española*, 2nd ed. (Madrid: Espasa-Calpe, 1947) and J.M. Gómez-Tabanera, *A Concise History of Spain* (Madrid: Cronos, 1966), follow Marañón wholeheartedly. Unfortunately (through no fault of Marañón) these latter two have written works of abominable quality.

[78]Gregorio Marañón, "Las mujeres y el Conde-Duque de Olivares," *O.C.*, II, p. 140.

[79]James Hoddie, Jr., "El concepto de la labor del historiador y biógrafo en las obras de Gregorio Marañón," p. 111.

[80]Pedro Laín Entralgo, "Vida, obra y persona de Gregorio Marañón," p. LXXIV.

[81]*Ibid.*

[82]*Ibid.*, citing Gregorio Marañón, "Prólogo," to Melchor de Almagro San Martín, *Crónica de Alfonso XIII y su linaje.*

[83]Gregorio Marañón, "Las mujeres y el Conde-Duque de Olivares," *O.C.*, II, p. 140.

[84]See Hippolyte A. Taine, *History of English Literature* (New York: Frederick Ungar Publ. Co., 1965), for an historiographical treatment which contains numerous close analogues to Marañón. Marañón probably acquired his Tainism through the intermediary of Cánovas del Castillo whom he admired deeply.

[85]Gregorio Marañón, "La endocrinología y la ciencia penal," *O.C.*, I, p. 572.

[86]James Hoddie, Jr., "El concepto de la labor del historiador y biógrafo en las obras de Gregorio Marañón," p. 107.

[87]Francisco López Estrada, "Marañón y las letras," *Anales de la Universidad Hispalense*, XX (1960), 4.

[88]Gregorio Marañón, "Un libro sobre Felipe II," *O.C.*, I, pp. 615-616.

[89]I have noted Marañón's lack of speculation concerning the possibility of deriving systematic laws for the explanation of history. Nevertheless, perhaps reflecting this tendency characteristic of the period, Marañón, on

several occasions went so far as to attempt to explain history in terms of biological laws. (See p. 208 for a discussion of Marañón's explanation of revolution in terms of biological motives.) In the historical biographies, the most notable attempt occurs in *Conde-Duque* where Marañón hypothesizes three phases through which, almost without exception, all absolute rulers pass: (1) The enthusiastic phase where the leader has not consolidated himself yet, but relies on his capacity for suggestion and his magnetic following with the people. (2) The stage of consolidated power where order is achieved and certain long standing national problems are resolved but during which public opinion begins to turn hostile due to the ruthlessness and violence of rule. (3) The stage of decline during which the *dictadura* becomes a *dictablanda*. The weakening dictator now craves the assent of all, yet the powers of opposition build up inexorably until the dictator falls resoundingly. Gregorio Marañón, *El Conde-Duque de Olivares, O.C.*, V, pp. 543-553.

Chapter IV.

[1]Gregorio Marañón, "Biología y feminismo," *O.C.*, III, pp. 9-34.

[2]Gregorio Marañón, "Nuevas notas médicas sobre la pintura del Greco," *Revista de las Españas*, II, 5-6 (1927), pp. 3-7.

[3]See: Manuel B. Cossío, *El Greco* (Madrid: 1908); José Martínez Ruiz, "Azorín," "El tricentenario del Greco," *Clásicos y modernos* (Madrid: Editorial Renacimiento, 1913), pp. 183-90; J. Salas, "La valoración del Greco por los románticos españoles y franceses," *Archivo Español de Arte y Arqueología*, 14 (1940-41), p. 387; J. Camón Aznar, *Dominico Greco* (Madrid, 1950); Ramón Gómez de la Serna, *El Greco* in *Biografías completas* (Madrid: Aguilar, 1959).

[4]Manuel B. Cossío, *op. cit.*, p. 239.

[5]*Ibid.*

[6]*Ibid.*, p. 535.

[7]*Ibid.*, p. 241.

[8]An excellent summary of these pathological studies is to be found in J. Camón Aznar, *op. cit.* See also Paul Guinard, *El Greco* (Lausanne: Imprimeries Réunies S.A., 1956) for additional bibliography on the pathological studies. Marañón comments on the widespread exposure that these medical studies had in society and the intense debate that they inspired among educated laymen and art critics alike: "The influence which is exercised by Medicine in modern times is curious; it is like the influence of myth on primordial tribes." (*El Greco y Toledo*, 5th ed. [Madrid: Espasa-Calpe, 1968], p. 227.) About forty years after this first wave of medical studies, and for the same reason, "due to its medical character," Marañón feels that his publication of photographs of inmates at the asylum in Toledo, together with reproductions of the heads of several of El Greco's saints, had the same inspiring effect.

[9]J. Camón Aznar, *op. cit.*, p. 1262, quoting David Katz.

[10]*Ibid.*, quoting Ricardo Jorge, *El Greco* (Universidad de Coimbra, 1913).

[11]*Ibid.*

[12]J. Camón Aznar separates from the other pathological studies and distinguishes with commendation only the work of Goyanes and Marañón: "It is fitting to underline the most effusive kind of admiration felt for doctors like Goyanes and Marañón, who have seen in El Greco's forms a mystical transcendence and spiritual profoundness which have nothing to do with facile diagnoses." (*Ibid.*, p. 1259.)

[13]Marañón's works on El Greco, in chronological order, are the following: "Nuevas notas médicas sobre la pintura del Greco," *Revista de las Españas*, II, 5-6 (1927), 3-7; "El hombre a quien el tiempo no impidió ver la eternidad" (1935), *O.C.*, I, pp. 579-83; "El secreto del Greco" (1939), *O.C.*, III, pp. 591-608; "El Greco otra vez" (1951), *O.C.*, IV, pp. 825-28; "Meditaciones sobre el Greco" (1953), *O.C.*, I, pp. 1917-1922; "Las academias toledanas en tiempo del Greco" (1956), *O.C.*, IV, pp. 951-58; "El Toledo del Greco" (1956), *O.C.*, II, pp. 209-32; *El Greco y Toledo* (1956), *O.C.*, VII, pp. 415-542.

In addition a version of the 1939 conference "El secreto del Greco" with slight revisions can be found in the first edition only of *Elogio y nostalgia de Toledo* (Madrid: Espasa-Calpe, 1941). Subsequently, this version was transferred to the 4th and succeeding editions of *Tiempo viejo y tiempo nuevo* (Madrid: Espasa-Calpe, 1947). For an explanation of the transfer see the *Advertencia* to *Tiempo viejo y tiempo nuevo* in *O.C.*, IX, p. 397.

[14]Gregorio Marañón, "Nuevas notas médicas...," p. 6.

[15]*Ibid.*, p. 3.

[16]*Ibid.*

[17]*Ibid.*, p. 5.

[18]*Ibid.*, p. 6.

[19]*Ibid.*, p. 3.

[20]*Ibid.*, p. 5.

[21]Gregorio Marañón, "El hombre a quien el tiempo no impidió ver la eternidad," *O.C.*, I, p. 581.

[22]*Ibid.*, pp. 580-81.

[23]*Ibid.*, p. 579.

[24]See footnote number 13.

[25]Gregorio Marañón, *Elogio y nostalgia de Toledo,* 3rd ed. (Madrid: Espasa-Calpe, 1958), p. 121.

[26]*Ibid.*

[27]*Ibid.*

[28]Gregorio Marañón, "El secreto del Greco," *O.C.*, III, p. 595.

[29]*Ibid.*

[30]*Ibid.*, p. 599.

[31]*Ibid.*, p. 595.

[32]*Ibid.*, p. 602.

[33]*Ibid.*, p. 603.

[34]Marañón quotes the well-known anecdote that once El Greco remarked in Rome that Michaelangelo was a poor fellow who didn't know how to

Gary D. Keller

paint. Marañón interprets the alleged remark by El Greco in the following way: ". . .for El Greco, painting was something quite different. It was not molding, which is "existing" (*estar*), but rather, aspiring: making the human figure into a hieroglyphic in order to come to an understanding with God." (*Ibid.*, p. 597).

[35] *Ibid.*

[36] *Ibid.*, p. 603.

[37] *Ibid.*, p. 604.

[38] *Ibid.*, p. 606.

[39] See Otto Rank, *Une étude sur le double* (Paris, 1932).

[40] Gregorio Marañón, *loc. cit.*

[41] *Ibid.*, p. 607.

[42] *Ibid.*, p. 606.

[43] See Harold E. Wethey, *El Greco and His School,* I (Princeton, New Jersey: Princeton University Press, 1962), pp. 95-96.

[44] Marañón cites Mayer in *El Greco y Toledo* and almost certainly knew Pijoán's work, inasmuch as this critic collaborated on the *Summa Artis* with Manuel B. Cossío, with whom Marañón was quite friendly.

[45] August L. Mayer, "El Greco, An Oriental Artist," *Art Bulletin,* XI (1929), 146.

[46] *Ibid.*, p. 148.

[47] See Manuel B. Cossío and José Pijoán y Soteras, *Summa artis, historia general del arte,* 1st ed., 18 vols. (Madrid: Espasa Calpe, 1931-1961).

[48] José Pijoán y Soteras, "El Greco, a Spaniard," *Art Bulletin,* XII (1930), p. 14.

[49] *Ibid.*

[50] Julián Ribera, *Disertaciones y opúsculos,* I, edición colectiva que en su jubilación del profesorado le ofrecen sus discípulos y amigos (Madrid: Imprenta de Estanislao Maestre, 1928), p. 151.

Although Ribera points to an Arabic influence in Spanish thought, he does so on the basis of similarity and comparability, in simple one to one correspondences. His orientation is quite opposed to the theories of Américo Castro, particularly as formulated in the constructs of *vividura* (functional context) and *morada vital* (dwelling place of life). Castro hypothesizes the formation of Spanishness from the fourteenth century on, as involving an official exclusion of Oriental elements together with a cultural assimilation of these elements through the medium of converts. Furthermore, Julián Ribera attempts to present the accomplishments of the Arabs in Iberia as Spanish, thereby paying homage to an understanding of Spanishness which stretches back to the original Iberians. Américo Castro, of course, spent much energy refuting this "historical fantasy." The following quotation of Ribera indicates clearly the gap between this pioneering Arabist and Castro: "I believe that for any impartial and unbiased person Abderrahmen III must be as Spanish as Trajan, with the difference that Abderrahmen was king of Spain in Spain and Trajan was emperor of Rome in Rome. Similarly, Averröes is as Spanish as Seneca, with the distinction that Averröes was born, studied, lived and wrote in Córdoba, whereas Seneca, who was also born there, flourished in Italy. . . .Therefore, those Moslems have as much right or more to be entered as Spaniards in our national history and literature as the Ibero-Romans who already figure in it from time immemorial; we treat the latter affectionately as countrymen and friends even if they were pagans." (*Ibid.,* p. 468).

⁵¹See Manuel Gómez-Moreno and José Pijoán y Soteras, *Materiales de arqueología española* (Madrid, 1912), as well as the following by Gómez-Moreno: *Iglesias mozárabes: arte español de los siglos IX a XI* (Madrid: Centro de estudios históricos, 1919); *Palacio del emperador Carlos V en la Alhambra* (Madrid: El Correo, 1885); *Las águilas del renacimiento español* (Madrid: Gráficas Urguina, 1941). In his 1943 book, Gómez-Moreno paid homage to El Greco's orientalism in terms quite similar to Marañón's 1939 statements: "He was to abandon his country, which was suffering under Venetian oppression, only to react [once in Venice] against the Venetian esthetic. He had to submit to a Titian, who had already outlived his own glory.... Let us recognize the Oriental aspect in El Greco, the lover of clouds and snow-covered mountains, the lover of the flowers which he affectionately painted and of that monumental Toledo which he so often brought to his canvases as an obsession, a dream-like reality." (*El Greco,* [Barcelona: Ediciones Selectas, 1943], p. 16).

⁵²Miguel Asín Palacios, *La escatología musulmana en la Divina Comedia seguida de la historia y crítica de una polémica.* 3rd ed. (Madrid: Instituto Hispano-Arabe de Cultura, 1961).

⁵³Miguel Asín Palacios: *El Islam Cristianizado: Estudio crítico del "Sufismo" a través de las obras de Abenarabi de Murcia.* 1st ed. (Madrid: Editorial Plutarco, 1931), p. 274.

⁵⁴*Ibid.*

⁵⁵*Ibid.* As with respect to his teacher, Julián Ribera (see footnote number 50), Miguel Asín's orientation is far different from that of Américo Castro. For a brief discussion and biography of early authors who pointed to the influence of Arabic and Jewish elements in the formation of Spanish culture, see Angel del Río and Mair José Bernadete, *El concepto contemporáneo de España; Antología de Ensayos 1895-1931* (New York: Las Américas Publishing Co., 1962), pp. 307-309. Curiously A. del Río and M.J. Bernadete do not mention the work of Ramiro de Maeztu. This author *does* strike close to Castro's thesis when he discusses Fernando de Roja's attitudes in *La Celestina* as the consequence of a rejection of Judaism together with a lack of sincere conversion to Christianity. Maeztu concludes: "*La Celestina* is, in short, one of the first books in which the Spanish people learned of the possibility of living without ideals." (*Don Quijote, Don Juan y La Celestina,* 6th ed. [Buenos Aires: Espasa-Calpe, 1948], p. 151).

⁵⁶See Emilia de Zulueta, *Historia de la crítica española contemporánea* (Madrid: Editorial Gredos, 1966) and Juan Marichal, *La voluntad de estilo (Teoría e historia del ensayismo hispánico)* (Barcelona: Editorial Seix Barral, 1957) for a survey of the evolving historiographical and literary concepts of Américo Castro. Both are in agreement that Castro entered his second period sometime during the Spanish Civil War. Emilia de Zulueta cites the 1939 essay "Lo hispánico y el erasmismo" as the first substantial result of Castro's new orientation. In this work Castro confesses that, fearful of falling into a "philo-Orientalism," he attempted to explain Spanishness within the frame-

Gary D. Keller

work of Western Europe without taking into account the eight centuries of "living-togetherness" (*convivencia*) between Christians, Arabs and Jews.

[57]Marañón is following here Maurice Legendre, who, based on a comment by Manuel de Falla, made this association in simple, picturesque terms. Cf., Maurice Legendre and A. Hartmann, *Domenikos Theotokopoulos called El Greco* (London: The Commodore Press, 1937), pp. 26-27.

[58]Gregorio Marañón, "El secreto del Greco," *O.C.*, III, p. 600.

[59]Américo Castro, *España en su historia. Cristianos, moros y judíos.* (Buenos Aires: Editorial Losada, 1948), p. 397.

[60]*Ibid.*, p. 407.

[61]Américo Castro, *Santa Teresa y otros ensayos* (Madrid: Historia Nueva, 1929), p. 10.

[62]*Ibid.*, p. 18.

[63]Américo Castro, *España en su historia*, p. 330.

[64]*Ibid.*, p. 639.

[65]*Ibid.*

[66]Ch. Zervos, *Les oeuvres du Greco en Espagne* (Paris, 1939); Marcel Bataillon, *Erasme en Espagne* (Paris, 1937); P. Sáinz Rodríguez, *Introducción a la historia de la literatura mística en España* (Madrid, 1927).

[67]Harold E. Wethey, *op. cit.*, p. 52.

[68]*Ibid.*

[69]Walter Friedlaender, *Mannerism and Anti-Mannerism in Italian Painting* (New York: Schocken Books, 1965), p. 42.

[70]Harold E. Wethey, *op. cit.*, p. 53.

[71]*Ibid.*

[72]*Ibid.*, p. 55.

[73]*Ibid.*, p. 56.

[74]*Ibid.*, p. 98.

[75]*Ibid.*

[76]Walter Friedlaender, *op.cit.*, p. 52.

[77]Harold E. Wethey, *op. cit.*, p. 57.

[78]*Ibid.*, p. 54.

[79]*Ibid.*, p. 55.

[80]I have not located any academician who talks of El Greco's use of shadow in the way that Marañón does. Wethey describes, presumably, the same phenomenon that Marañón had in mind in terms of ghostliness or disembodiment produced by the detachment from realistic background, the use of white light and bright and shocking color juxtapositions such as red-orange against green.

[81]Harold E. Wethey, *op. cit.*, p. 57.

[82]*Ibid.*, p. 60.

[83]*Ibid.*, pp. 60-61.

[84]*Ibid.*, p. 58.

[85]Paul Guinard, *El Greco* (Lausanne: Imprimeries Réunies S.A., 1956), p. 90.

[86]In an article entitled "El viaje de Cocteau por España," *O.C.*, IV, pp. 937-40, Marañón evokes Cocteau's attitudes toward El Greco and Góngora (Cocteau translated Góngora's sonnet dedicated to El Greco) as well as toward Hieronymous Bosch, Velázquez, Gaudí, Picasso, etc.

[87]Gregorio Marañón, "El Greco otra vez," *O.C.*, IV, p. 827.

[88]Gregorio Marañón, "Las academias toledanas en tiempo del Greco," *O.C.*, IV, p. 957.

[89]See Gregorio Marañón, "El Toledo del Greco," *O.C.*, II, pp. 209-232.

[90]Gregorio Marañón, *El Greco y Toledo, O.C.*, VII, p. 440.

[91]*Ibid.*, figure 26 (between pp. 440-445).

[92]*Ibid.*, p. 441.

[93]*Ibid.*

[94]*Ibid.*, pp. 441-442.

[95]*Ibid.*, p. 442.

[96]Eugenio d'Ors y Rovrera, *Poussin y El Greco, El Nuevo Glosario,* V (Madrid: Caro Raggio, 1922), pp. 14-16.

[97]José Ortega y Gasset, *Obras Completas,* II, 5th ed. (Madrid: Revista de Occidente, 1961), p. 153.

[98]Gregorio Marañón, *El Greco y Toledo,* p. 455.

[99]*Ibid.*, p. 460. As an object lesson on the hazardous inconsistency of this sort of projective criticism, let us note the almost antithetical appreciation of Manuel B. Cossío concerning the very same portrait: "The doctor is cadaverous...in his hands and face there is something of the angular harshness of the carving." (*El Greco* [Madrid, 1908], p. 401.)

[100]Gregorio Marañón, *El Greco y Toledo,* p. 443.

[101]*Ibid.*, p. 467.

[102]*Ibid.*, p. 485.

[103]See Helmut Hatzfeld, *Estudios literarios sobre mística española,* 2nd ed. (Madrid: Editorial Gredos, 1968), pp. 243-76.

[104]Gregorio Marañón, *El Greco y Toledo,* p. 487.

[105]*Ibid.*

[106]*Ibid.*

[107]*Ibid.*

[108]*Ibid.*, p. 488.

[109]*Ibid.*, p. 486.

[110]*Ibid.*, p. 488.

[111]*Ibid.*, p. 495.

[112]*Ibid.*, pp. 495-496.

[113]Marañón found it odd that his old student and friend, the Argentine psychoanalyst Angel Garma, could find but one minor psychoanalytic work referring to El Greco. On the other hand, a copious psychoanalytic literature exists on Hieronymous Bosch. (*Ibid.*, p. 511).

[114]*Ibid.*, p. 498.

[115]*Ibid.*

[116]*Ibid.*

[117]Américo Castro, *España en su historia,* p. 66.

[118]Gregorio Marañón, *El Greco y Toledo,* p. 520.

[119]Harold E. Wethey associates El Greco's landscapes with Mannerism and feels they have been influenced by Tintoretto. Wethey asserts: "Even his landscapes...belong in the same unreal Mannerist existence as his religious pictures." (*Op. cit.,* p. 58.)

[120]In this item Marañón is following the observation of J. Lhermitte, in his interesting monograph "Considérations psycho-phisiologiques nouvelles

Gary D. Keller

sur la peinture. L'image corporelle dans l'espace pictural," *Presse Médicale,* Vol. 63 (1955), where the author comments on the parallels between dreams and paintings with reference to iconography, and symbolic, physical and spatial relationships.

[121]Marañón cites the appropriateness of the following aphorism by Ramón Gómez de la Serna, referring precisely to this problem in the interpretation of El Greco: "Sane men who practice sanity as an obsession cannot understand insanity." (Ramón Gómez de la Serna, *op. cit.,* p. 8.)

[122]Gregorio Marañón, *El Greco y Toledo,* p. 503. Marañón was partisan to the widespread tendency to connect genius with mental imbalance: "...without a little bit of what is officially called insanity, humanity would come to a standstill in a few generations." (*Ibid.*)

[123]Cossío claims, on one hand, that El Greco and Góngora were, in their own day, attacked for "a lack of sincerity," for parting with the traditional molds. (*Op. cit.,* p. 576.) On the other hand, Cossío applauds that finally now (in 1908) "is when it has been possible not only to understand and pardon but also to admire and applaud the bizarre, scandalous and *daft* El Greco." (*Ibid.,* p. 537.)

[124]See Gregorio Marañón, *El Greco y Toledo,* pp. 505-507 for a discussion of M.B. Cossío's relationship to the experiment.

[125]*Ibid.,* p. 506.

[126]*Ibid.,* p. 508.

[127]Wethey claims: "...it is not necessary to believe, as did Dr. Gregorio Marañón, that the artist used as models the inmates of the local insane asylum." (*Op. cit.,* p. 60.) Similarly, with respect to Marañón's contention that many of the female figures were modeled on someone in an asthenic, hyperthyroid condition, Guinard asserts: "These are ingenious ideas certainly, but it may be questioned whether they are really needed to "explain" El Greco. (*Op. cit.,* p. 110.)

[128]Gregorio Marañón, *El Greco y Toledo,* p. 532.

[129]Gregorio Marañón, "Comentarios a una vida ejemplar," *O.C.,* III, pp. 57-74.

[130]Gregorio Marañón, *El "Empecinado" visto por un inglés,* in *O.C.,* V.

[131]Gregorio Marañón, *Ensayo biológico sobre Enrique IV de Castilla y su tiempo,* in *O.C.,* V.

[132]See Gregorio Marañón, "La moral de Amiel y otras cosas. (Crítica de críticos)," *O.C.,* IV, pp. 463-66; Gregorio Marañón, "Todavía Amiel," *O.C.,* I, pp. 653-58.

[133]James Hoddie, Jr., "Gregorio Marañón, Historian and Man of Letters," unpubl. Ph.D. thesis, Brown University, 1965, p. 100.

[134]In the book *Amiel,* Marañón emphasizes the identification of Amiel as a mystic during the first period of his popularity. On the other hand, in the *Revista de Occidente* article Marañón focuses on the "malady of the ideal" diagnosis which was concurrent with the "mystic" notion.

[135]Gregorio Marañón, "La moral de Amiel y otras cosas," p. 464.

[136]Gregorio Marañón, *Amiel. Un estudio sobre la timidez, O.C.,* V, p. 183.

[137]See G. Monteil, *La religion d'Amiel* (Paris, 1907); G.B. Marchesi, *Il Pensieroso* (Milan, 1908); A. Severino, *Il sentimento religioso di F. Amiel* (Rome, 1921); H. Delacroix, "Les états extatiques d'Amiel," in *Vers l'unité,*

Notes

October-November, 1921; Manuel Toussaint y Ritter, *El tesoro de Amiel (selección del Diario íntimo)* (México: Editorial Cultura, 1918). The following sample from Toussaint is fairly indicative: "Many times the contemplation of landscape gives rise to a mystical thought. Upon writing his first lines, the author seems uncertain of where his pen is leading him. And the idea begins to elevate and extend itself until it is in harmony with the rhythm of this world or the other world, shrouded in cosmogonic nebulae. . . .One could form a homogeneous all with those passages from the *Diary* that have a mystical character. The book is so profound and subtle that it is able to extend the mystical treasures of humanity." (*Ibid., p. 10*).

[138]Paul Bourget, *Essais de Psychologie Contemporaine*, Edition définitive augmentée d'appendices, tome second (Paris: Librairie Plon, 1937), p. 270.

[139]*Ibid.*

[140]Note Marañón's own variation on this theme: ". . .Amiel's problem, like that of so many men, was that of the strangulation of love by knowledge. . . ." (*Amiel. Un estudio sobre la timidez, O.C.,* V, pp. 180-81).

[141]Ernest Jones, *Hamlet and Oedipus* (Garden City, New York: Doubleday and Company, Inc. 1954). See chapter II, "The Problem of Hamlet and the Explanations Proffered," for an extensive discussion and bibliographical treatment of the topic.

[142]*Ibid.*, p. 35.

[143]Paul Bourget, *op. cit.*, p. 275.

[144]*Ibid.*, p. 278.

[145]*Ibid.*, p. 279.

[146]Charles Du Bos, "Pour le centenaire d'Amiel," *Revue de Paris,* Sept. 15, 1921.

[147]Alberto Insúa, *Don Quixote en los Alpes* (Madrid: Biblioteca Nueva de Escritores Españoles 1907).

[148]See Gregorio Marañón, *Amiel. Un estudio sobre la timidez, O.C.,* V, pp. 180-81 for a survey as well as the bibliographic details.

[149]A. Severino, "Un martyre dell'Ideale" in *L'Orma,* Naples, 1919.

[150]Van Wyck Brooks, *The Malady of the Ideal: Obermann, Maurice de Guerin and Amiel* (Philadelphia: University of Pennsylvania Press, 1947). While Van Wyck Brooks suscribes to the "malady of the ideal" notion, in contrast to the dominant point of view, he does not consider this malady at all noble.

[151]John Sheridan Zelie, "In Search of Amiel," *Atlantic Monthly,* January 1907, p. 136.

[152]Miguel de Unamuno contrasts the expurgated and unexpurgated editions in the following way: "Fanny Mercier. . .to judge by the passages that she elected to leave out, the ones that she omitted, and by her retouching and abridgement of other sections, was a sort of Calvinist prude or puritan. . .who was frightened by the naked truths that Amiel reveals in his intimate diary. Bouvier's new edition gives us a different Amiel, but it gives us a more complete Amiel, an Amiel of flesh and blood. There are passages, like the one where he speaks of his own virginity at the age of twenty-eight and those others where he relates the terrible agony of his last month of suffering with the illness that was destroying his body, which show us a less ethereal and

much more worldly, more human Amiel." (*Obras completas*, IX [Madrid: Afrodisio Aguado, S.A., 1958], pp. 95-96).

[153]Gregorio Marañón, *Amiel, O.C.,* V, p. 181.

[154]M. Bernard Bouvier, *Journal Intime,* 3 vols. (Paris, Geneve, 1923); M. Bernard Bouvier, *Philine,* introd. by Edmond Jaloux (Paris, 1927).

[155]José de la Luz León, *Amiel o la incapacidad de amar* (Madrid: 1927).

[156]Edmond Jaloux, "Introduction" in *Philine: From the Unpublished Journals of Henri-Frédéric Amiel,* trans. by Van Wyck Brooks (Boston and New York: Houghton Mifflin Company, 1930), p. xviii.

[157]*Ibid.,* p. xxiii.

[158]Gregorio Marañón, *Amiel, O.C.,* V, pp. 231-32.

[159]Gregorio Marañón, "La moral de Amiel y otras cosas," *O.C.,* IV, p. 465.

[160]Gregorio Marañón, *Amiel, O.C.,* V, p. 183.

[161]Jérôme-Louis-Georges Miniconi, *Amiel: Étude médico-psychologique,* Thèse pour le Doctorat en Médicine, Université de Bourdeaux, 1935-1936, No. 128; Henry Gilbert Medioni, *Essai sur le caractère d'Amiel à la faveur des Conceptions Psycho-pathologiques Contemporaines* (Paris: Faculté de Medicine de Paris, 1927).

[162]Joseph L. Haimovici, *Amiel ou L'Introspection Morbide en Littérature* (Paris: Faculté de Medecine de Paris, 1928), p. 15.

[163]Gregorio Marañón, *Amiel, O.C.,* V, p. 186.

[164]Gregorio Marañón, "Amiel. Un estudio sobre la timidez, (Article originally publ. in the *Revista de Occidente*), *O.C.,* IV, p. 206.

[165]Gregorio Marañón, *Amiel, O.C.,* V. p. 183.

[166]Gregorio Marañón, "La moral de Amiel y otras cosas," *O.C.,* IV, p. 465.

[167]Pedro Laín Entralgo has consistently noted an important element in Marañón's historical philosophy: the concept of biography as "redemption" from distortion and prejudicial interpretations. Concerning *Enrique IV,* Laín claims: "If the essays may be called 'redemptions,' according to an old and delightful Spanish term, in other words, if they are intellectual and literary endeavors to save the subjects or persons they deal with from oblivion, indifference, ignorance, or injurious interpretation; never has the old name been so well used as in the case of this essay dealing with Enrique IV and his times. It is an effort that is visibly directed towards removing, to the extent that it is possible, the stigma that a certain self-interested and merciless legend has attached to a man and a woman. There is a fundamental nobility of spirit at the outset of Marañón's first adventure in the field of historiography." Similarly, with respect to Amiel, Laín observes: ". . .Marañón's essay has had great success all over the world. But perhaps the hidden redemptive intent of its author when he wrote it has not been sufficiently seen." (Introduction in Gregorio Marañón, *O.C.,* I, [Madrid: Espasa-Calpe, S.A., 1968], p. LXXXIX.).

It is our intention to demonstrate that a partial aspect of this goal of redemption involves the reaffirmation of the "noble malady of the ideal" concept on biopsychological grounds.

[168]Anonymous, "Amiel o la timidez," *Indice Literario. Archivos de Literatura Contemporánea,* Madrid, Centro de Estudios Históricos, Año I, Núm. V (December 1932), p. 133.

[169]Gregorio Marañón, "Una carta sobre Amiel y mi Amiel," (Prólogo a la edición francesa) in *O.C.*, V, p. 168.

[170]*Ibid.*, pp. 188-89.

[171]*Ibid.*, p. 190.

[172]*Ibid.*

[173]*Ibid.*

[174]For information on Marañón's political role during this period see: Conde de Romanones, *Historia de cuatro días* in *O.C.*, III (Madrid: Editorial Plus Ultra, 1949); R. Salido Orcillo, "Marañón y la política," *Novedades*, Mexico, April 16, 1960; I. Prieto, "La ideología de Marañón," *Cuadernos Americanos* Año XIX-4, Mexico, 1960; E. Ramos Meza, *Marañón, gran médico y humanista* (Guadalajara, Mexico: Universidad Autónoma de Guadalajara, Folia Universitaria No. l, 1961).

[175]See Gregorio Marañón, "Los estados intersexuales en la especie humana," *O.C.*, III, pp. 155-86; and Gregorio Marañón, *La evolución de la sexualidad y los estados intersexuales, O.C.*, VII.

[176]Because of his discovery, Marañón is moved to defend Freud and other psychoanalysts with reference to infantile sexuality: "The child does not always lack an active sexuality, as Freud has demonstrated to the astonishment of those who live in the limbo of repression." *(Amiel, O.C.*, V, p. 195.)

[177]*Ibid.*, p. 197.

[178]*Ibid.*, p. 198.

[179]*Ibid.*

[180]Miguel de Unamuno, *Nada menos que todo un hombre* in *Tres novelas ejemplares y un prólogo*, 9th ed., (Madrid: Espasa-Calpe, 1958), p. 139.

[181]Gregorio Marañón, *Amiel, O.C.*, V, p. 195.

[182]*Ibid.*

[183]*Ibid.*, p. 199.

[184]*Ibid.*

[185]*Ibid.*, p. 200.

[186]*Ibid.*

[187]*Ibid.*

[188]*Ibid.*, p. 211.

[189]*Ibid.*

[190]*Ibid.*, p. 210.

[191]*Ibid.*, pp. 210-11.

[192]*Ibid.*, p. 212. Furthermore, Marañón cites evidence indicating that in many religions and mythologies a dissociation is maintained between the sexual act and the concept of procreation. Marañón cites B. Malinowski, *La sexualité et sa repression dans les sociétés primitives* (Paris: Payot, edic. franc., 1932); Ernest Jones, "Mother Right and the Sexual Ignorance of Savages," *International Journal of Psychoanalysis*, 1925, p. 109; Otto Rank, *Don Juan. Une étude sur le double*, Paris, 1932.

[193]Gregorio Marañón, *Amiel, O.C.*, V, p. 213 quoting H.F. Amiel, *Journal Intime*, I, ed. Bernard Bouvier, (Paris: Geneva, 1923), p. 255.

[194]*Ibid.*, p. 212.

[195]*Ibid.*, p. 216.

[196]*Ibid.*

[197]*Ibid.*

257

Gary D. Keller

[198]*Ibid.*

[199]Marañón values the incident so highly that he claims: "Our new knowledge, during these last few years, of the background and results of this adventure has completely changed our conception of the author of the *Journal*; in addition, these new facts constitute one of the most useful documents that we have at our disposal today for the explanation of the male instinct." (*Ibid.*, p. 228.)

[200]*Ibid.*, p. 230.

[201]*Ibid.*, p. 231.

[202]*Ibid.*, p. 230.

[203]*Ibid.*, p. 223.

[204]*Ibid.*, p. 231.

[205]*Ibid.*, p. 222.

[206]*Ibid.*

[207]*Ibid.*, p. 207.

[208]*Ibid.*, pp. 207-208.

[209]F. Oliver Brachfeld makes note of the autonomy between art and personality: "Nietzsche said that it would be better to publish works anonymously so that people would judge them more objectively. Marañón says, on the other hand, 'that all books should be published at least with a picture and a short biography of the author. . .because the work is the author to such an extent that without a knowledge of the latter the true meaning of the former remains incomplete.' Amiel, for his part, protested the custom of judging the artist on the basis of his life. . . .For many years the same error was committed by psychoanalysts: they believed that the genesis of a work or of an idea tells us everything. As if it mattered whether a brilliant idea was born in the brain of a schizophrenic or in that of a genius! As if the idea and the work were not valuable in themselves, independently of their genesis. As if the work of Henri-Frédéric Amiel were not interesting in itself without the need to know that its author went to bed with a woman only once in his entire life. . . ." (*Polémica contra Marañón* [Barcelona: Editorial Europa, 1933], p. 157.) Yet, despite this unheeded caveat, Oliver Brachfeld leaps into the fray with his own Adlerian thesis.

[210]*Ibid.*, p. 35. We recall, as I have noted in my chapter evaluating the theoretical foundations of Marañón's theories, that Brachfeld accuses Marañón of letting psychoanalysis "through the back door," that is, of utilizing the psychoanalytic constructs extrapolated into a more or less eclectic framework.

[211]*Ibid.*

[212]The book of Otto Rank to which Marañón invariably refers, *Don Juan. Une étude sur le double*, is a French translation of *Die Don Juan-Gestalt* (Vienna: Psychoanalytischer Verlag, 1924). During the period when this book was written, Rank was a committed adherent to Freudianism. For details on Rank's philosophic evolution, see Ira Progoff, *The Death and Rebirth of Psychology* (New York: The Julian Press, 1956).

[213]This work is better known in its second edition, 1930, with a changed title: *La evolución de la sexualidad y los estados intersexuales*. It is in *O.C.*, VIII.

[214]Gregorio Marañón, *Ensayo biológico sobre Enrique IV de Castilla y su tiempo*, *O.C.*, V, p. 143.

[215]*Ibid.*, p. 141.

[216]*Ibid.*, p. 109. With respect to the biological characteristics of Enrique IV, Marañón judges him to be abnormal but not pathological: "However, I want to call attention to the fact that I do not describe Don Enrique... using a classification...that is strictly pathological, but rather using a constitutional and hereditary state that approaches the eunuchoid one but is closer to normality." (*Ibid.*, p. 127.)

[217]Pedro Laín Entralgo, *Introducción* in Gregorio Marañón, *O.C.*, I, p. LXXIII.

[218]For bibliography on Marañón's role during this period, see footnote number 174.

[219]F. Oliver Brachfeld, *Polémica contra Marañón*, p. 158.

[220]See chapter VII of *Amiel*, "Femineidad y Afeminamiento," for Marañón's evaluation of the many fears that Amiel expressed about his manhood in his diary.

[221]Juan Pablo Muñoz Sanz, *Glosario de Amiel. Reflexiones sobre la timidez y réplica al doctor Marañón* (Quito, Ecuador: Imprenta Nacional, p. 217).

[222]F. Oliver Brachfeld, *Los sentimientos de inferioridad* (Buenos Aires: Editorial Siglo Veinte, 1942), p. 113. Oliver Brachfeld misconstrues Marañón's argument when he claims that the doctor measures timidity with some quantitative scale. As I have taken pains to point out, the difference between the inferior *tímido* and the superior *tímido* lies in the highly differentiated object that the latter's libido (Marañón's term) attaches itself to.

[223]Gregorio Marañón, *Amiel*, *O.C.*, V, p. 265.

[224]*Ibid.*, p. 266.

[225]*Ibid.*, p. 267.

[226]*Ibid.*

[227]Anonymous, "Amiel o la timidez," *Indice Literario. Archivos de Literatura Contemporánea*. Madrid, Centro de Estudios Históricos, Año I, No. V (December 1932), p. 137.

[228]Gregorio Marañón, *Amiel*, *O.C.*, V, p. 271.

[229]*Ibid.*, p. 269.

[230]*Ibid.*

[231]*Ibid.*, p. 270.

[232]F. Oliver Brachfeld, *Los sentimientos de inferioridad*, pp. 129-30.

[233]Juan Pablo Muñoz Sanz, *op. cit.*, p. 221.

[234]*Ibid.*, p. 290-10.

[235]*Ibid.*, p. 213.

[236]Clara Campoamor quoted by Oreste A. D'Aló, *Algunos hombres, algunas ideas: Amiel, Renan, Becher, Ingenieros*, p. 32.

[237]Oreste A. D'Aló, *Algunos hombres, algunas ideas*, p. 37. See also Bernard Halda, *Amiel et les femmes* (Lyon-Paris: Editions Vitte, 1963).

[238]Alain Girard, *Le journal intime* (Paris: Presses Universitaires de France, 1963), p. 450.

[239]Gregorio Marañón, "Ambivalencia," *O.C.*, IV, p. 637. Marañón mentions that he attempted to introduce "ambivalence" into the dictionary

Gary D. Keller

of the Real Academia de la Lengua, but that "the rest of the academicians rejected my definition energetically and unanimously." (*Ibid.*, p. 638.)

[240] *Ibid.*

[241] *Ibid.*, p. 637.

[242] *Ibid.*, p. 638.

[243] *Ibid.*

[244] Gregorio Marañón, "El destierro de Garcilaso de la Vega," *Españoles fuera de España*, O.C., IX, p. 308.

[245] Gregorio Marañón, "Garcilaso, natural de Toledo," *Elogio y nostalgia de Toledo*, O.C., IX, pp. 510-11.

[246] Gregorio Marañón, "El destierro de Garcilaso de la Vega," *Españoles fuera de España*, O.C., IX, p. 308.

[247] Marañón is referring to El Brocense's suggestion that *nemus* is an acronymn for *bosque*, and therefore Nemoroso represents Garcilaso's friend, Boscán. See Tomás Navarro Tomás, *Introducción* in Garcilaso de la Vega, *Obras* (Madrid: Espasa-Calpe, 1963), p. xxxv for an evaluation of this long-discarded idea. On the other hand, Hayward Keniston suggests that *nemus* does not only signify *bosque* but also *vega*. Thus Salicio may be an anagram for "Garcilaso" and Nemoroso may symbolize "de la Vega." (*Garcilaso de la Vega. A critical study of his life and works* [New York, 1922], p. 242.)

[248] Gregorio Marañón, "Garcilaso, natural de Toledo," *Elogio y nostalgia de Toledo*, O.C., IX, p. 508.

[249] *Ibid.*, p. 513.

[250] *Ibid.*, p. 514.

[251] *Ibid.* A similar association between ambivalence and liberalism is expressed by Marañón in his essay on ambivalence: "In public life the ambivalent man is the liberal. I have said many times that being liberal is not being affiliated to a particular political party, but rather possessing a certain spiritual outlook; and, as a result, it is an attitude that governs not only one's public life but also the most insignificant aspects of one's inner life." ("Ambivalencia," O.C., IV, p. 639.)

[252] Gregorio Marañón, "Garcilaso, natural de Toledo," *Elogio y nostalgia de Toledo*, O.C., IX, pp. 515-16.

[253] *Ibid.*, p. 516.

[254] Gregorio Marañón, "El destierro de Garcilaso de la Vega," *Españoles fuera de España*, O.C., IX. p. 316.

[255] For details on Garcilaso's stay in Italy see: B. Croce, *Intorno al saggiorno di Garcilaso de la Vega in Italia* in *Rass. Stor. Napol. di Lettere ed Arti*, Naples, Vol. I, fasc. No. 1 (1894); and E. Mele, "Las poesías latinas de Garcilaso de la Vega y su permanencia en Italia," *Bulletin Hispanique*, XXV (1923), 108-48, pp. 361-70, and Vol. XXVI (1924), pp. 35-51.

[256] Gregorio Marañón, *loc. cit.*

[257] Gregorio Marañón, "Garcilaso de la Vega (Estudio Preliminar)," O.C., I, p. 1000.

[258] *Ibid.*

[259] Gregorio Marañón has written the following on Quevedo: "Quevedo y el Conde-Duque," Chapt. XI of *El Conde-Duque de Olivares. La pasión de mandar*, O.C., V; "La España de Quevedo," O.C., IV, pp. 307-11; "Sobre Quevedo y su leyenda. (Gloria y miseria del intelctual)," O.C., IV, pp. 561-66.

[260]Gregorio Marañón, *El Conde-Duque de Olivares*, *O.C.*, V, p. 499.

[261]Dámaso Alonso, *Poesía española*. *Ensayo de métodos y límites estilísticos*, 5th ed. (Madrid: Editorial Gredos, 1966), p. 518.

[262]Gregorio Marañón, *El Conde-Duque de Olivares*, *O.C.*, V. p. 269.

[263]*Ibid.*, p. 623.

[264]*Ibid.*, p. 618.

[265]*Ibid.*, p. 628.

[266]Marañón has written the following on Galdós: "Galdós, íntimo," *O.C.*, IV, pp. 27-31; "Un profeta de España," *Raíz y decoro de España*, *O.C.*, IX, pp. 73-76; "Galdós en Toledo," *O.C.*, IV, pp. 349-54; "Galdós en Toledo," *Elogio y nostalgia de Toledo*, *O.C.*, IX, pp. 548-570; "Aparece en Inglaterra la traducción de una novela de Galdós," *Efemérides y comentarios*, *O.C.*, IX, pp. 598-601.

[267]Gregorio Marañón, "Un profeta de España," *Raíz y decoro de España*, *O.C.*, IX, p. 75.

[268]Gregorio Marañón, "Aparece en Inglaterra la traducción de una novela de Galdós," *Efemérides y comentarios*, *O.C.*, IX, p. 599.

[269]Gregorio Marañón, "Ensayo sobre la generación del 98," *O.C.*, I, p. 802.

[270]Gregorio Marañón, *Idearium de Marañón*, ed. by A. Juderías (Madrid: Editorial Cultura Clásica y Moderna, 1960), p. 220.

[271]Gregorio Marañón, "Ensayo sobre la generación del 98," *O.C.*, I, p. 804.

[272]Marañón has written the following on Unamuno: "Unamuno y los españoles magistrales," *O.C.*, IV, pp. 185-87; "El ejemplo de Unamuno," *O.C.*, IV, pp. 319-21; "Muerte y resurrección del profeta," *O.C.*, IV, pp. 321-24; "Miguel de Unamuno," *O.C.*, IV, p. 1081; "Unamuno en Francia," *O.C.*, IV, pp. 925-28.

[273]Gregorio Marañón, "Muerte y resurrección del profeta," *O.C.*, I, p. 324.

[274]Gregorio Marañón, "Miguel de Unamuno," *O.C.*, IV, p. 1081.

[275]Marañón has written the following on Pío Baroja: "Contestación al discurso de recepción, en la Real Academia Española, de don Pío Baroja," *O.C.*, II, pp. 319-30; "Baroja," *O.C.*, IV, pp. 367-72; "Pío Baroja vuelve a su casa de Vera," *Efemérides y comentarios*, *O.C.*, IX, pp. 682-685.

[276]Gregorio Marañón, "Contestación al discurso de recepción en la Real Academia Española, de don Pío Baroja," *O.C.*, II, p. 320.

[277]*Ibid.*, p. 321.

[278]*Ibid.*, pp. 321-22.

[279]*Ibid.*, p. 321.

[280]Gregorio Marañón, "Sobre la novela picaresca," *O.C.*, I, p. 1021.

[281]Gregorio Marañón, "Contestación al discurso de recepción, en la Real Academia Española, de don Pío Baroja," *O.C.*, II, p. 325.

[282]*Ibid.*

[283]*Ibid.*, p. 326.

[284]Gregorio Marañón, "Baroja," *O.C.*, p. II, p. 325.

[285]Gregorio Marañón, "Sobre Azorín," *O.C.*, III, p. 655.

[286]*Ibid.*, p. 656.

287 *Ibid.*, p. 655.

288 Gregorio Marañón, "Cumpleaños de Azorín," *Efemérides y comentarios, O.C.,* IX, p. 596.

289 *Ibid.*

290 Gregorio Marañón, "Contestación al discurso de entrada, en la Real Academia Española, de don Pedro Laín Entralgo," *O.C.,* II, pp. 507-16; "Contestación al discurso de ingreso en la Real Academia Española de don Camilo José Cela," *O.C.,* II, pp. 557-64.

291 Gregorio Marañón, "Rubén Dario y la España de su tiempo," *O.C.,* III, pp. 10ll-1022; Gregorio Marañón, "Maurice Legendre y España," *O.C.,* III, pp. 803-808.

292 See the following by Marañón: "Sobre Arniches y el género chico," *O.C.,* II, pp. 761-74; "Homenaje a Alejandro Casona," *O.C.,* II, pp. 277-78; "Un gran académico sin academia," *O.C.,* II, pp. 611-14; "Se celebra el medio siglo de la muerte de Castelar," *Efemérides y comentarios,* pp. 587-91; "Universidad y retórica en Ortega," *O.C.,* IV, pp. 929-30; "Ortega y Gasset, Europa, España," *O.C.,* IV, pp. 931-36; "Ortega y Gasset," *O.C.,* IV, pp. 941-46; "Juicio crítico a la obra, *Vida ejemplar y heróica de Miguel de Cervantes Saavedra,*" *O.C.,* IV, pp. 1005-1008.

293 Gregorio Marañón: "Con Descartes por Holanda," *O.C.,* IV, pp. 971-75; "Los amigos del país y Victor Hugo," *O.C.,* IV, pp. 711-16; "El viaje de Cocteau por España," *O.C.,* IV, pp. 931-36; "Valery desde Castilla," *O.C.,* IV, pp. 685-88.

294 See the following prologues by Marañón: "Diálogo antisocrático sobre Corydon," *O.C.,* I, pp. 465-72; "Gabriel Miró," *O.C.,* I, pp. 557-60; "La Fundadora," *O.C.,* I, pp. 837-40; "Los versos de Icaza," *O.C.,* I, pp. 433-36; "Aquella España," *O.C.,* I, pp. 625-32; "Mi antigua admiración por Clarín," *O.C.,* I, pp. 845-48; "Felix Lope de Vega," *O.C.,* I, pp. 595-600.

Chapter V.

1 See Pedro Laín Entralgo, *El problema de España en el siglo XIX* in *España como problema* (Madrid: Aguilar, 1957), for a more detailed and complicated grouping of the different factions in the nineteenth-century polemic over Spanish science. Laín distinguishes, on the *progresista* side, *krausistas, positivistas* and *doctrinarios.* On the *tradicionalista* side, we have *tradicionalismo intelectual a ultranza o "medievalista"* and *tradicionalismo "moderno."*

2 Pedro Laín Entralgo, *España como problema,* p. 647.

3 José Ortega y Gasset, "La ciencia romántica," *Obras completas,* I, 4th ed. (Madrid: Revista de Occidente, 1957), p. 41.

4 *Ibid.*, p. 42.

5 *Ibid.*

[6]José Ortega y Gasset, "Asamblea para el progreso de las ciencias," *Obras completas,* I, p. 103.

[7]*Ibid.,* p. 109.

[8]*Ibid.,* p. 104.

[9]Gregorio Marañón, *Quemoterapia moderna según Ehrlich. Tratamiento de la sífilis por el 606* (Madrid: Editorial Vidal, 1910).

[10]Pedro Laín Entralgo, *op. cit.,* p. 651.

[11]José Ortega y Gasset, "Vieja y nueva política," *Obras completas,* I, pp. 280-81.

[12]Gregorio Marañón, "Biología y feminismo," *O.C.,* III, pp. 9-34.

[13]See the following articles by Marañón in *O.C.,* IV: "Médicos extranjeros en España," "El asunto de los médicos extranjeros, I," and "El asunto de los médicos extranjeros, II."

[14]Gregorio Marañón, "Contestación al discurso de ingreso, en la Real Academia Española, de don Camilo José Cela," *O.C.,* II, p. 559.

[15]Gregorio Marañón, "Aquella España," *O.C.,* I, p. 625.

[16]*Ibid.,* p. 626.

[17]Julián Marías, "Gregorio Marañón," *Obras* (Madrid: Revista de Occidente, 1966), p. 163.

[18]See the following articles by Marañón in *O.C.,* I: "Literatura sexual," pp. 27-34; "Un libro de ciencia," pp. 75-78; "Notas a un libro de antropología sexual," pp. 111-20.

[19]Gregorio Marañón, "Notas a un libro de antropología sexual," *O.C.,* I, p. 112.

[20]Marañón was often subject to the severest criticism, usually for his political role. See, for example, José Bergamín, "Carta Abierta" in *Sur,* Buenos Aires, VII (1937), pp. 67-69. Here Bergamín calls Marañón a "criminal renegade to the Republic." On the other hand, the Catholic priest Antonio Sánchez Maurandi, in his *Reparos a los tres Vélez de Marañón* (Murcia, 1961), attacks the physician as a friend of Russia whose religious beliefs are suspect, and so forth.

[21]Gregorio Marañón, "Liberalismo y comunismo," *O.C.,* IV, pp. 373-87.

[22]Pedro Laín Entralgo, *op. cit.,* p. 756.

[23]Santiago Ramón y Cajal, "Nuestro atraso cultural y sus causas pretendidas," in Angel del Rio and Mair José Bernadete, *El concepto contemporáneo de España* (New York: Las Américas Publishing Co., 1962), p. 61.

[24]José Ortega y Gasset, *Obras completas,* Vol. I, p. 108, quoted by Gregorio Marañón, "Cajal," *O.C.,* II, p. 168.

[25]Gregorio Marañón, "Notas sobre Huarte," *O.C.,* III, pp. 265-82.

[26]*Ibid.,* p. 266.

[27]*Ibid.*

[28]*Ibid.,* p. 267.

[29]Arturo Farinelli, *Dos excéntricos: Cristóbal de Villalón—El Dr. Juan Huarte* (Madrid: Revista de Filología Española, Anejo XXIV, 1936), p. 74. Farinelli was acquainted with Marañón's study and judges it "an admirable profile of Huarte, with very humane intuitions." (*Ibid.,* p. 99.) See the notes in Farinelli for bibliographic details on other works written on Huarte during these years.

[30]*Ibid.,* p. 96.

Gary D. Keller

[31]*Ibid.*

[32]Gregorio Marañón, "Notas sobre Huarte," *O.C.*, III, pp. 276-78.

[33]Gregorio Marañón, "El deber de las edades," *O.C.*, III, p. 131.

[34]Arturo Farinelli, *op. cit.*, pp. 60-61.

[35]Gregorio Marañón, "Notas sobre Huarte," *O.C.*, III, p. 276.

[36]Arturo Farinelli, *op. cit.*, p. 60. Marañón is particularly enthused over Huarte's judgment that studiousness requires the sacrifice of Man's sensual inclinations and, therefore, the student should not be mothered nor should he be permitted to study at home, but rather, he should be forced to attend a distant university. The very same innocent dicta of Huarte, centuries remote from the historical phenomena of the 1930s, are associated by Farinelli with fascist policy. (*Ibid.*, p. 61.)

[37]*Ibid.*

[38]Gregorio Marañón, "Notas sobre Huarte," *O.C.*, III, p. 282.

[39]Gregorio Marañón, "Gota y humor del maestro. (El centenario de Vives)," *O.C.*, IV, pp. 629-36; "Teoría de la sobriedad," *O.C.*, IV, pp. 641-50; "El intelectual desterrado," *O.C.*, IV, pp. 651-58.

[40]Gregorio Marañón, *Luis Vives (Un español fuera de España)* (Madrid: Espasa-Calpe, 1942), reprinted in *O.C.*, VII.

[41]Eugenio D'Ors, Gregorio Marañón, et al., *Vives, Humaniste Espagnol* (Paris: Collection Occident, Etudes Hispaniques, Librairie Plon, 1941).

[42]Gregorio Marañón, *Españoles fuera de España* (Madrid: Espasa-Calpe, 1947), reprinted in *O.C.*, IX.

[43]Gregorio Marañón, *Luis Vives, O.C.*, VII, p. 264.

[44]José Ortega y Gasset, *Obras Inéditas: Vives-Goethe (Conferencias),* (Madrid: Revista de Occidente, 1961), pp. 64-65. See also José Ortega y Gasset, "Vives," *Obras Completas,* V, 4th ed. (Madrid: Revista de Occidente), pp. 493-507. Both Marañón and Ortega may have known the influential article by Foster Watson, "The Father of Modern Psychology," *The Psychological Review,* Vol. XXIII, No. 5 (September 1915), pp. 333-53. Watson's claim that Vives represents the father of modern psychology has been well accepted by psychologists and historians of psychology developing out of the introspectionist school.

[45]Gregorio Marañón, *Luis Vives,* pp. 290-291.

[46]*Ibid.*, p. 283.

[47]*Ibid.*, p. 282.

[48]*Ibid.*, p. 285.

[49]*Ibid.*

[50]*Ibid.*, p. 283.

[51]*Ibid.*, p. 274.

[52]For a detailed bibliography of studies on Vives as a psychologist (primarily dealing with the *De anima et vita*), see the article by Foster Watson, *op. cit.*, as well as Henryk Misiak, *The Philosophical Roots of Scientific Psychology* (New York: Fordham University Press, 1961); Henryk Misiak and Virginia Staudt Sexton, *History of Psychology* (New York and London: Grune and Stratton, 1966); R.S. Peters, ed., *Brett's History of Psychology* (New York: The Macmillan Company, 1953).

[53]Gregorio Marañón, *Luis Vives,* p. 265. It should be noted that Marañón treats this aspect of personal hygiene in Feijoo. See, for example, the

chapter "Ideas naturalistas de Feijoo sobre el régimen alimenticio," in *Las ideas biológicas del Padre Feijoo.*

[54]See Juan Luis Vives, *Obras completas,* 2 vols. (Madrid: Aguilar, 1947).

[55]J. Martínez Ruiz, "Azorín," *Lecturas españolas,* 4th ed. (1st ed., 1938; Madrid: Espasa-Calpe, 1943), p. 17.

[56]See Foster Watson, *op. cit.,* and others mentioned in footnote number 52.

[57]Gregorio Marañón, *Luis Vives,* p. 256.

[58]*Ibid.,* p. 276.

[59]Marañón compares Vives's *Institutio foeminae christianae* with Fray Luis de León's *La perfecta casada:* "Vives's feminine archetype, also profoundly Christian, has a certain puritanical inflexibility, a severity typical of Central European orthodoxy, which recalls the attitudes present in the books of the *reformistas.* It is less Spanish than Fray Luis de León's model." (*Ibid.,* pp. 276-77.) The conclusion here, based on the poles of puritanism versus Spanishness, we recall, is used also in the interpretation of El Greco's popularity.

[60]*Ibid.,* p. 277.

[61]See Gregorio Marañón, "Comentarios a una vida ejemplar," *O.C.,* III, pp. 57-74.

[62]Gregorio Marañón, "La literatura científica en los siglos XVI y XVII," in Guillermo Díaz-Plaja, ed., *Historia general de las literaturas hispánicas,* III (Barcelona, 1953); Gregorio Marañón, "Cisneros y la Universidad de Alcalá," *O.C.,* III, pp. 829-32; Gregorio Marañón, "Servet. Psicología de una heterodoxia," *O.C.,* III, pp. 855-68. The lecture on Servet is also published with the title "Se recuerda en Tudela el suplicio de Miguel Servet," *Efemérides y comentarios, O.C.,* IX, pp. 665-681. Obviously a misprint is the date (1958) ascribed to this lecture, since it had already been published in 1955.

[63]See J.M. López-Piñero, *La introducción de la ciencia moderna en España* (Barcelona: Ed. Ariel, 1969), for a detailed bibliography and treatment.

[64]Gregorio Marañón, "Servet. Psicología de una heterodoxia," *O.C.,* III, p. 866.

[65]*Ibid.,* p. 863.

[66]*Ibid.,* p. 861.

[67]*Ibid.,* p. 867.

[68]*Ibid.,* p. 856.

[69]Gregorio Marañón, "Prólogo de la segunda edición (1941)," *Las ideas biológicas del padre Feijoo, O.C.,* V, p. 292.

[70]Marcelino Menéndez Pelayo, quoted by Gregorio Marañón, *ibid.,* p. 308.

[71]*Ibid.,* p. 307.

[72]*Ibid.,* p. 310.

[73]Gregorio Marañón, "La literatura científica en los siglos XVI y XVII," in Guillermo Díaz-Plaja, ed., *Historia general de las literaturas,* III, p. 936.

[74]Fray Benito Jerónimo Feijoo, "Descubrimiento de la circulación de la sangre" in Angel del Río, *Antología general de la literatura española,* II (New York: Holt, Rinehart and Winston, 1960), p. 15.

[75]Gregorio Marañón, "La literatura científica en los siglos XVI...," p. 938.

Gary D. Keller

[76]*Ibid.*

[77]*Ibid.*

[78]See José Ortega y Gasset, "La ciencia romántica," *op. cit.,* pp. 38-43.

[79]Gregorio Marañón, *Las ideas biológicas del Padre Feijoo, O.C.,* V, p. 310.

[80]*Ibid.*

[81]*Ibid.,* p. 311. The above accusation of the Inquisition is written during the Republican years. By 1947 Marañón had completely changed his position: "The Inquisition never set up obstacles to excellence in the natural sciences. The difficulty was that there hardly existed any concern for science . . .it is absurd to say that it persecuted our few investigators in their role as men of science. If on any occasion it placed any of them under interdict, it was not because of his science but rather because of possible heterodoxy." ("Cajal," *O.C.,* II, p. 175). This defense of the Inquisition is also restated in "La literatura científica en los siglos XVI y XVII."

[82]*Ibid.,* p. 312.

[83]*Ibid.,* p. 311.

[84]*Ibid.*

[85]*Ibid.*

[86]*Ibid.,* p. 309.

[87]Marcelino Menéndez y Pelayo quoted in *ibid.*

[88]*Ibid.*

[89]Marañón cites, among others, works by Menéndez Pelayo, Pí y Margall, Morayta, Azorín, R. Pérez de Ayala, A. Castro, L. Araujo Costa, etc. For an excellent bibliography of Feijoo, past and present, both primary and secondary sources, see José Antonio Pérez-Rioja, *Proyección y actualidad de Feijoo* (Madrid: Instituto de Estudios Políticos, 1965).

[90]Gregorio Marañón, *Las ideas biológicas del Padre Feijoo, O.C.,* V, p. 305.

[91]*Ibid.*

[92]Gregorio Marañón, "Los amigos del Padre Feijoo," *Vida e Historia, O.C.,* IX, p. 151.

[93]Carlos Clavería, "Apostillas al lenguaje de Belarmino," *Cinco estudios de literatura española moderna* (Salamanca: Colegio trilingüe de la Universidad, 1945).

[94]Max Müller quoted in Ernst Cassirer, *Language and Myth,* trans. by Susanne K. Langer (New York: Dover Publications, 1946), p. 5.

[95]*Ibid.*

[96]*Ibid.*

[97]See Ernst Cassirer, *ibid.,* for a criticism of this association of myth and untruth. Cassirer traces linguistic conceptualization and mythical conceptualization back to a common, inseparable root. Although Marañón may have thought myths are the subject of scientific disentanglement, he was just as adept at myth-making as any other human being, as J.P. Muñoz Sanz well pointed out in his criticism of *Amiel.* (See p. 121 and 137).

[98]Gregorio Marañón, *Las ideas biológicas del Padre Feijoo, O.C.,* V, p. 451.

[99]*Ibid.,* p. 483.

[100]*Ibid.*

[101]*Ibid.*

[102]*Ibid.*, p. 328.

[103]*Ibid.*

[104]*Ibid.*, p. 329.

[105]*Ibid.*

[106]*Ibid.*, p. 317.

[107]*Ibid.*

[108]*Ibid.*

[109]*Ibid.*

[110]Marañón states: "Menéndez Pelayo does not hesitate to include these Societies among the heterodox manifestations, confusing them, to the deep distress of the impartial reader, with *Enciclopedismo;* he incurs, therefore, in the error of equating the sectarian French movement with all the universal, renewing spirit of the century." (*Ibid.*, p. 464.)

[111]*Ibid.*, p. 317.

[112]*Ibid.*

[113]*Ibid.*

[114]Gregorio Marañón quoted in Jean Sarrailh, *La España ilustrada de la segunda mitad del siglo XVIII* (Mexico-Buenos Aires: Fondo de Cultura Económica, 1957), p. 290.

[115]See Gaspar Delpy, *Bibliographie de sources françaises de B. Feijoo* (Paris: Librairie Hachette, 1936) as well as the following articles by Charles N. Staubach: "Feijoo on Cartesianism," *Papers of the Michigan Academy of Science, Arts and Letters,* Vol. XXIV, Part IV (1938), pp. 79-87; "The Influence of Bayle on Feijoo," *Hispania,* Stanford, California, XXII (1939), pp. 79-92; "Fontenelle in the Writings of Feijoo," *Hispanic Review,* Philadelphia, VIII (1940), pp. 46-56; "Feijoo and Malebranche," *Hispanic Review,* Philadelphia, Vol. IX, No. 2 (1941), pp. 287-97.

[116]Gregorio Marañón, *Las ideas biológicas del Padre Feijoo, O.C.,* V, p. 318.

[117]*Ibid.*

[118]*Ibid.*, pp. 318-19.

[119]Jean Sarrailh terms Feijoo, "This experimentalist 'by predestination,' as Marañón has defined him. . ." (*Op. cit.*, p. 414.)

[120]José Antonio Pérez-Rioja, *op. cit.*, p. 101.

[121]Gregorio Marañón, *Las ideas biológicas del Padre Feijoo, O.C.,* V, p. 344.

[122]*Ibid.*

[123]James Hoddie, Jr., "Gregorio Marañón, Historian and Man of Letters," Unpubl. Ph.D. dissertation, Brown University, 1965, p. 180.

[124]Gregorio Marañón, "Roberto Novoa Santos," *O.C.,* I, pp. 142-43.

[125]James Hoddie, Jr., *op. cit.*, p. 181.

[126]Gregorio Marañón, "Cajal," *O.C.,* II, pp. 186-87.

[127]Gregorio Marañón, *Vocación y ética y otros ensayos, O.C.,* IX, p. 382.

[128]Padre Fray Benito Jerónimo Feijoo y Montenegro, *Obras Escogidas,* Biblioteca de Autores Españoles, Vol. 56 (Madrid: Rivadeneyra, 1863), p. 45.

[129]Fernando Lázaro Carreter, *Las ideas lingüísticas en España durante el siglo XVIII* (Madrid: Consejo Superior de Investigaciones Científicas, 1949), p. 285.

Gary D. Keller

[130]*Ibid.*, pp. 286-87.

[131]Gregorio Marañón, *Las ideas biológicas del Padre Feijoo*, *O.C.*, V, p. 339.

[132]*Ibid.*, pp. 340-41.

[133]*Ibid.*, p. 342.

[134]*Ibid.*

[135]Angel del Río, "Sobre Gregorio Marañón: Las ideas biológicas del Padre Feijoo," *Revista Hispánica Moderna*, Columbia Univ., N.Y., I (1934), 201-202. (J.A. Pérez-Rioja has misinterpreted the initials A.R. which follow the book review, erroneously attributing it to Rafael Altamira.)

[136]Fernando Lázaro Carreter, *op. cit.*, pp. 209-210. On the other hand, Lázaro Carreter judges that, "harassed by the attacks of his critics, Feijoo launches forth into the frankly dangerous attitude. . .of affirming that 'in order to justify the introduction of a new word, the absolute lack of another which means the same is not necessary. It is enough that the new one be either more appropriate, or more beautiful, or more dynamic,' " (*Ibid.*, p. 261.)

[137]See Joaquín de Entrambasaguas, *Prólogo* a la edición antológica de Feijoo, 3 vols. (Madrid: Ediciones FE, 1942); Juan Marichal, *La voluntad de estilo (Teoría e historia del ensayismo hispánico)* (Barcelona: Editorial Seix Barral, 1957).

[138]Gregorio Marañón, *Las ideas biológicas del Padre Feijoo*, *O.C.*, V, p. 331.

[139]*Ibid.*, p. 332.

[140]Pí y Margall, "Prólogo" al *Teatro Crítico del Padre Feijoo* (Oporto, 1887), quoted in *ibid.*

[141]J. Montero Díaz, "Las ideas estéticas del Padre Feijoo," *Boletín de la Universidad de Santiago de Compostela*, IV (1932), quoted in *ibid.*

[142]Miguel Morayta, *El Padre Feijoo y sus obras*, quoted in *ibid.*

[143]*Ibid.* Marañón does concede that Feijoo, on rare occasions, did bow to ecclesiastical pressure, as in the case of the church bell of Velilla, which allegedly sounded by itself. ". . .in all of this discourse, what is certain is that his arguments strive to destroy the famous legend of this bell, which so impressed Spaniards for many years. The final affirmation. . .seems to be a timid concession to the high authorities of the Church, who conceded the miracle." (*Ibid.*, p. 315.)

[144]I.L. McClelland, *Benito Jerónimo Feijoo* (New York: Twayne Publishers, 1969), p. 13.

[145]*Ibid.*

[146]Gregorio Marañón, *Las ideas biológicas del Padre Feijoo*, *O.C.*, V, p. 333.

[147]*Ibid.*, p. 482.

[148]Jean Sarrailh, *op cit.*, p. 613.

[149]Raquel Sajón de Cuello, "Feijoo y el enciclopedismo," *Fray Benito Jerónimo Feijoo y Montenegro: Estudios reunidos en conmemoración del II centenario de su muerte* (La Plata, Argentina: Universidad Nacional de la Plata, 1965), p. 166. See, in addition, Arturo Ardao, *La filosofía polémica de Feijoo* (Buenos Aires: Editorial Losada, 1962).

[150]Gregorio Marañón, *Las ideas biológicas del Padre Feijoo*, *O.C.*, V, p. 295.

268

Notes

[151] Ibid.
[152] Ibid.
[153] Ibid.
[154] Ibid.
[155] Ibid., p. 379.
[156] Ibid.
[157] Ibid.
[158] Ibid., p. 378.
[159] Ibid., p. 420.
[160] Ibid., p. 350.
[161] Ibid., p. 349.
[162] Ibid., p. 449.
[163] Gregorio Marañón, "Fecundación artificial," *O.C.*, III, p. 229.
[164] Ibid.
[165] Ibid.
[166] Ibid.
[167] Ibid.
[168] Gregorio Marañón, *Las ideas biológicas del Padre Feijoo*, *O.C.*, V, p. 378.
[169] Ibid., p. 408.
[170] Ibid., p. 378.
[171] Ibid., p. 392-93.
[172] Ibid., p. 394.
[173] See the section entitled "Feijoo en el pleito del agua. Un Rinconete de la medicina: Don Vicente Pérez," *Ibid.*, pp. 399-404.
[174] Ibid., p. 412.
[175] Ibid., p. 413.
[176] Ibid., p. 417.
[177] Ibid.
[178] Ibid., p. 418.
[179] Ibid., p. 394.
[180] Ibid., p. 391.
[181] Ibid.
[182] Ibid., p. 406.
[183] Marañón provides only errors pertaining to the natural sciences, but cites bibliography where different categories of misassumptions have been evaluated. See *ibid.*, pp. 315-16.
[184] Ibid., p. 315. Marañón explains the last item in the following way: "This belief, very wide-spread in all countries, has a basis, which is that in old hens the plumage is transformed in such a way as to become similar to that of the cock. Therefore this is the false cock that lays eggs." (*Ibid.*)
[185] Julio Caro Baroja alleges that "Marañón in a sense has wanted to excuse Feijoo's bizarre defense of the reality of the Fish-man of Liérganes by means of various medical speculations. . . .I do not see here anything but the amplification of several folkloric motifs that had been on the scene during those times." Julio Caro Baroja, *Algunos mitos españoles y otros ensayos* (Madrid: Editorial Nacional, 1944), p. 133. Caro Baroja is not quite accurate. While Marañón does take the position that Feijoo actually *saw* something (a case of icthyiosis) he is in complete agreement with Caro Baroja's

Gary D. Keller

observation that "most likely it is in his treatment of sea nymphs and other similar fantastic creatures that the habitual judgment of Feijoo suffers a major breakdown." *Ibid.*

[186]*Ibid.*, p. 447.

[187]*Ibid.*

[188]*Ibid.*, p. 439.

[189]*Ibid.* Marañón reproduces the following two comments by Feijoo in order to support his speculation that the monk was terrified and awed by the sea: "I have never swum, nor learned how to swim." (*Teatro*, VI, VIII, 24.) "How much we might learn from it [the sea] about things appertaining to the wandering nation of fish; things which are not known by naturalists up to now." (*Teatro*, VI, VIII, 17.)

[190]*Ibid.*

[191]*Ibid.*, p. 459.

[192]*Ibid.*, p. 461.

[193]*Ibid.*, p. 462.

[194]*Ibid.*, p. 366.

[195]*Ibid.*, p. 365.

[196]*Ibid.*, p. 364.

[197]*Ibid.*, p. 365.

[198]*Ibid.*, p. 368.

[199]*Ibid.*, p. 465.

[200]*Ibid.*, p. 469.

[201]See Pedro Laín Entralgo, *Gaspar Casal y la medicina de su tiempo* (Oviedo, 1959); R. Sancho de San Román, *Vida y obra de Gaspar Casal* (Salamanca, 1959).

[202]Gregorio Marañón, *Las ideas biológicas del Padre Feijoo*, O.C., V, p. 373.

[203]*Ibid.*

[204]See Marañón's bibliography for a listing of unedited manuscripts in his personal collection.

[205]*Ibid.*, p. 375.

[206]Gregorio Marañón, "El siglo XVIII y los Padres Feijoo y Sarmiento," O.C., III, pp. 671-72.

[207]*Ibid.*, p. 671.

[208]Marino Gómez-Santos, *Gregorio Marañón cuenta su vida* (Madrid: Aguilar, 1961), pp. 68-69.

[209]Angel del Río, "Sobre Gregorio Marañón: *Las ideas biológicas del Padre Feijoo.*" *Revista Hispánica Moderna*, Columbia Univ., N.Y., I (1934), 201.

[210]G. Cirot, "Sobre Gregorio Marañón, *Las ideas biológicas del Padre Feijoo*," *Bulletin Hispanique*, XXXVIII, I (1935), 114.

[211]Santiago Montero Díaz, "A propósito de un libro de Marañón," *Boletín de la Universidad de Santiago*, No. 23 (January-March 1935).

[212]Gaspar Delpy, *Feijoo et l'esprit européen* (Paris: Librairie Hachette, 1936), p. IX.

[213]*Ibid.*

[214]José Antonio Pérez-Rioja, *op. cit.*, pp. 22-23.

[215]*Ibid.*, p. 101.

270

216Gregorio Marañón, *Las ideas biológicas del Padre Feijoo*, *O.C.*, V, p. 348.

217Eugenio d'Ors quoted in Jean Sarrailh, *op. cit.*, p. 708.

218Gregorio Marañón quoted in *ibid.*

219Paul Hazard, *European Thought in the Eighteenth Century from Montesquieu to Lessing* (London: Hollis and Carter, 1954), p. 89.

220*Ibid.*

221Cf. V. Peset Llorca, "Acerca de la difusión del sistema copernicano en España," *Actas del II Congreso Español de la Historia de Medicina*, I (Salamanca, 1965), 309-324; V. Peset Llorca, "La doctrina intelectualista del delirio de Pedro Miguel de Heredia," *Archivo Iberoamericano de Historia de la Medicina y Antropología Médica*, 14 (1962), 133-206; L. García Ballester, "El galenismo de transición en la España del siglo XVII: Luis Rodríguez de Pedrosa," *Actas del II Congreso Español de la Historia de Medicina*, I (1965), 385-392; R. Marco Cuéllar, "El *Compendio Mathemático* del Padre Tosca y la introducción de la ciencia moderna en España. I. Las matemáticas. II. La astronomía. III. La física," *Actas del II Congreso Español de la Historia de Medicina*, I (1965), 325-358; Luis S. Granjel, *La doctrina antropológico-médico de Miguel Sabuco* (Salamanca: Publicaciones del Seminario de Historia de Medicina de la Universidad de Salamanca, 1956); Luis S. Granjel, *El ejercicio de la medicina en la sociedad española del siglo XVII* (Salamanca: Universidad de Salamanca, 1971); Luis S. Granjel, "Vida y obra de Pedro Miguel de Heredia," *Boletín de la Sociedad Española de Historia de la Medicina*, II, 1 (1961); Luis S. Granjel, *La obra de Gaspar Bravo de Sobremonte* (Salamanca: Universidad de Salamanca, 1960); Luis S. Granjel, *Aspectos médicos de la literatura antisupersticiosa española de los siglos XVI y XVII* (Salamanca: Universidad de Salamanca, 1963); J.M. Morales Meseguer, "La introducción en España de la psicología médica moderna: *Las cartas* (1691) de Juan Bautista Juanini," *Actas del II Congreso Español de la Historia de Medicina*, I (1965), 423-30; E. Portela Marco, "La obra química de Juan de Bercebal (1707)," *Actas del II Congreso Español de la Historia de Medicina*, I (1965), 431-438; Olga Victoria Quiroz-Martínez, *La introducción de la filosofía moderna en España: El ecletismo español de los siglos XVII y XVIII* (México: El Colegio de México, 1949); J.R. Zaragoza, "La defensa de la quina de Tomás Fernández," *Actas del II Congreso Español de la Historia de Medicina*, I (1965), 393-402; J. Reglá, "La crisis del siglo XVII (1621-1713)," *Introducción a la historia de España* (Barcelona, 1963), pp. 289-344; J. Nadal, "La contribution des historiens catalans à l'histoire de la démographie générale," *Population*, 16 (1961), 91-104; P. Vilar, "1660-1705: Segon redreçament català. Renovació de l'esperit d'iniciativa," *Catalunya dins l'Espanya moderna*, Vol. II (Barcelona, 1964), pp. 373-411; Antonio Domínguez Ortiz, *La sociedad española en el siglo XVII* (Madrid: Instituto Balmes de Sociología, 1963); Antonio Domínguez Ortiz, *La sociedad española en el siglo XVIII* (Madrid: Instituto Balmes de Sociología, 1955); Antonio Domínguez Ortiz, *Política y hacienda de Felipe IV* (Madrid: Editorial de Derecho Financiero, 1960); S. García Martínez, *Els fonaments del País Valencià modern* (Valencia, 1963); R. Ceñal, "Cartesianismo en España," *Revista de la Universidad de Oviedo* (1945), 3-95; M.L. Terrada Ferrandis, "La anatomía normal y patológica en la

Gary D. Keller

España de Carlos II," *Actas del II Congreso Español de la Historia de Medicina*, I (1965), 359-368.
The above bibliography is merely a partial listing. For additional bibliography see: J.M. López Piñero, *La introducción de la ciencia moderna en España* (Barcelona: Ed. Ariel, 1969); J.M. López Piñero, "La medicina del Barroco español," *Revista de la Universidad de Madrid*, 11 (1962), 479-515; J.M. López Piñero, "Galileo en la España del siglo XVII," *Revista de Occidente*, 40 (1966), 99-108; J.M. López Piñero, "Los comienzos de la medicina y la ciencia modernas en España en el último tercio del siglo XVII," *Actas del II Congreso Español de la Historia de Medicina*, I (1965), 271-292; J.M. López Piñero, "La doctrina de Harvey acerca de la circulación de la sangre en la España del siglo XVII," *Actas del II Congreso Español de la Historia de Medicina*, I (1965), 369-384; J.M. López Piñero, M. Peset Reig, L. García Ballester, J.R. Zaragoza and M.L. Terrada, *Bibliografía histórica sobre la ciencia y la técnica en España*, 2 vols. (Granada: Secretariado de Publicaciones de la Universidad, 1973); J.M. López Piñero y J.M. Morales Meseguer, *Neurosis y psicoterapía: Un estudio histórico* (Madrid: Espasa-Calpe, 1970); P. Laín Entralgo and J.M. López Piñero, *Panorama histórico de la ciencia moderna* (Madrid, 1963); Luis S. Granjel, *Bibliografía histórica de la medicina española* (Salamanca: Universidad de Salamanca, no date); and R. Muñoz Garrido, *Ejercicio legal de la medicina en España (Siglos XV al XVIII)*, (Salamanca, 1967).

[222]J.M. López Piñero, *La introducción de la ciencia moderna en España*, p. 8. See also, "La introducción de la ciencia moderna en España," *Revista de Occidente*, 35 (1966), 133-156.

[223]Gregorio Marañón, "Vocación, preparación y ambiente biológico y médico del Padre Feijoo," *O.C.*, II, p. 93.

[224]Gregorio Marañón, "Nuestro siglo XVIII y las Academias," *O.C.*, III, p. 309.

[225]*Ibid.*, p. 310.

[226]*Ibid.*, p. 311.

[227]*Ibid.*, p. 315.

[228]The title of this ridiculous monograph by Torres de Villarroel is the following: *Desengaños razonables para sacudir el polvo del espanto y del aturdimiento producido en los espíritus acoquinados por el cadáver de don Roberto Le Febre Demoulinel, cadete de los reales guardias de Corps, por haberle visto flexible y sudando después de algunos días, expuesto en su salón del Hospital General de Madrid. Lo escribe para que se limpien sus admiraciones y sustos los genios atolondrados y los físicos de cortos alcances.*

[229]Gregorio Marañón, "El siglo XVIII y los Padres Feijoo y Sarmiento," *O.C.*, III, p. 662.

[230]*Ibid.*, p. 663.

[231]*Ibid.*

[232]Paul Hazard, *op. cit.*, see the table of contents, pp. v-xv.

[233]Gregorio Marañón, "El siglo XVIII y los Padres Feijoo y Sarmiento," *O.C.*, III, p. 666.

[234]Gregorio Marañón, "Feijoo en Francia," *O.C.*, IV, p. 412.

[235]Gregorio Marañón, "Evolución de la gloria de Feijoo," *Cuadernos de la Cátedra Feijoo,* Universidad de Oviedo, No. 1 (1955).

[236]Gregorio Marañón, "Enciclopedismo y humanismo," *O.C.*, I, p. 225.

[237]*Ibid.*, p. 226.

[238]Gregorio Marañón, "Milagros y milagrerías," *La medicina y nuestro tiempo*, 3rd ed. (Madrid: Espasa-Calpe, 1963), pp. 57-66. In addition, see the section "Crítica de la medicina dogmática" (pp. 15-56) in the same, which contains numerous references to Feijoo.

[239]Gregorio Marañón, "Vida y andanzas de Don Pablo de Olavide," *O.C.*, III, pp. 928-29.

[240]*Ibid.*, p. 928.

[241]*Ibid.*, p. 931.

[242]*Ibid.*, p. 932.

[243]Jean Sarrailh, *op. cit.*, pp. 621-22.

[244]Richard Herr, *The Eighteenth-Century Revolution in Spain* (Princeton, New Jersey: Princeton University Press, 1958), p. 369.

[245]*Ibid.*

[246]Gregorio Marañón, "Vida y andanzas de Don Pablo de Olavide," *O.C.*, III, p. 932.

[247]Marañón pursues his attack on the University that we have seen in his writings on Vives and Cajal: "The university had already begun to be the torpid and graceless mastodon that it is now the world over. And Jovellanos would not have been able to accomplish any transcendent work if he had to occupy a musty, pedantic professorship." ("Jovellanos," *O.C.*, III, p. 876.)

[248]*Ibid.*, p. 870.

[249]*Ibid.*, pp. 870-71.

[250]*Ibid.*, p. 880.

[251]*Ibid.*

[252]Gregorio Marañón, "Vida y andanzas de Don Pablo de Olavide," *O.C.*, III, p. 929.

[253]Gregorio Marañón, "La historia moderna de España," *O.C.*, I, pp. 951-56; Gregorio Marañón, "El afrancesamiento de los españoles," *O.C.*, I, pp. 907-14. For a related topic, on the emigrations of Spaniards to France, see Gregorio Marañón, "Influencia de Francia en la política española a través de los emigrados," *O.C.*, III, pp. 627-50.

[254]Gregorio Marañón, "La historia moderna de España," *O.C.*, I, p. 955.

[255]*Ibid.*

[256]*Ibid.*

[257]Jean Sarrailh, *op. cit.*, p. 573.

[258]*Ibid.*

[259]Gregorio Marañón, "El afrancesamiento de los españoles," *O.C.*, I, p. 908.

[260]*Ibid.*

[261]*Ibid.*

[262]*Ibid.*

[263]*Ibid.*, p. 909.

[264]*Ibid.*

[265]*Ibid.*

[266]*Ibid.*

[267]Gregorio Marañón, "Recuerdos de Menéndez y Pelayo," *O.C.*, III, pp. 529-44; Gregorio Marañón, "Se celebra el centenario del nacimiento

Gary D. Keller

de Menéndez Pelayo," *Efemérides y comentarios, O.C.,* IX, pp. 661-664; Gregorio Marañón, "Aquella España," *O.C.,* I, pp. 625-32; Gregorio Marañón, "Menéndez Pelayo visto desde su precocidad," in Enrique Sánchez Reyes, ed., *Trabajos escolares de Menéndez Pelayo,* edición patrocinada por el Ministerio de Educación Nacional y costeada por el Banco de Santander (Santander: Hermanos Bedía, 1959), pp. 185-211.

[268]Pedro Laín Entralgo, *Menéndez Pelayo: Historia de sus problemas intelectuales,* in *España como problema* (Madrid: Aguilar, 1957).

[269]Gregorio Marañón, "Recuerdos de Menéndez y Pelayo," *O.C.,* III, p. 538.

[270]*Ibid.*

[271]*Ibid.*

[272]Gregorio Marañón, "Menéndez Pelayo visto desde su precocidad," *Trabajos escolares de Menéndez Pelayo,* pp. 192-93.

[273]Gregorio Marañón, "Recuerdos de Menéndez y Pelayo," *O.C.,* III, p. 539.

[274]*Ibid.*

[275]*Ibid.*

[276]*Ibid.,* p. 540.

[277]*Ibid.,* p. 535.

[278]*Ibid.*

[279]Gregorio Marañón, "Se celebra el centenario del nacimiento de Menéndez Pelayo," *Efémerides y comentarios, O.C.,* IX, p. 661.

[280]Pedro Laín Entralgo, *op. cit.,* p. 76.

[281]*Ibid.,* p. 78.

[282]Gregorio Marañón, "Menéndez Pelayo visto desde su precocidad," in *Trabajos escolares de Menéndez Pelayo,* p. 203.

[283]I should note that in 1934 Ramón y Cajal protested a festival in honor of Toledo, Ohio, taking place in Toledo, Spain: "...to entertain the Yankees because they happened to remember our Toledo upon baptizing one urb among the innumerable cities of North America, is the height of naiveté." (*Obras literarias completas* [Madrid: Aguilar, 1954], p. 368.) Cajal ironically notes the presence of "genteel and obsequious Marañón." (*Ibid.*)

[284]Gregorio Marañón has written the following on Ramón y Cajal: "Cajal," *O.C.,* II, pp. 165-208; *Cajal, su tiempo y el nuestro* (Madrid: Espasa-Calpe, 1947); "Conmemoración del centenario del nacimiento de Cajal," *Efemérides y comentarios, O.C.,* IX, pp. 592-594; "Investigadores clásicos y rómanticos," *O.C.,* I, pp. 165-68; "Hombres de ciencia," *O.C.,* I, pp. 194-204; "El esfuerzo intelectual en España," *O.C.,* I, pp. 377-78.

For a bibliography on Ramón y Cajal oriented toward his literary works, see Helene Tzitsikas, *Santiago Ramón y Cajal, obra literaria* (México: Ediciones de Andrea, Colección Studium—53, 1965).

[285]Gregorio Marañón, "Nicolas Achúcarro," *O.C.,* IV, pp. 9-10; "José Francisco Tello," *O.C.,* IV, p. 1106; Gregorio Marañón, "Severo Ochoa," *O.C.,* III, pp. 607-10.

[286]Gregorio Marañón, "Recuerdo a Cajal," *O.C.,* III, p. 317.

[287]*Ibid.*

[288]Gregorio Marañón, "Cajal," *O.C.,* II, p. 165.

274

[289]*Ibid.*, p. 167.

[290]*Ibid.*, p. 168.

[291]Luis S. Granjel, *Baroja y otras figuras del 98* (Madrid: Ediciones Guadarrama, 1960), pp. 33-35.

[292]For a discussion of Lafora's and Marañón's attitudes toward Letamendi, see Gregorio Marañón, "Arte y medicina," *O.C.*, I, pp. 423-236.

[293]Gregorio Marañón, "Psiquiatras de España," *Raíz y decoro de España, O.C.*, IX, p. 82.

[294]*Ibid.*, p. 84.

[295]*Ibid.*, p. 86.

[296]See Santiago Ramón y Cajal, *Charlas de café* in *Obras literarias completas* (Madrid: Aguilar, 1954), pp. 1051-73. Perhaps the most famous of these aphorisms is the following which was paraphrased both by Ortega y Gasset and Marañón: "Just as the great mountain peaks emerge strictly from mountain ridges, scientific or artistic geniuses rise only from the high cultural plateaus of a society." (*Ibid.*, p. 1053).

[297]Gonzalo Lafora, "La influencia de la personalidad y el carácter de Cajal sobre su obra," *Tierra Firme*, I (1935), 32.

[298]*Ibid.*, p. 35.

[299]Pedro Laín Entralgo, *Cajal y el problema del saber* (Madrid: Ateneo, Colección "O crece o muere," 1952), p. 10.

[300]*Ibid.*

[301]*Ibid.*

[302]Pedro Laín Entralgo, *Estudios y apuntes sobre Ramón y Cajal, España como problema* (Madrid: Aguilar, 1957), p. 287.

[303]Gregorio Marañón, "Cajal," *O.C.*, II, p. 179.

[304]*Ibid.*

[305]*Ibid.*

[306]Pedro Laín Entralgo, *España como problema*, p. 340.

[307]Luis S. Granjel, *op. cit.*, p. 229.

[308]Gregorio Marañón, "Cajal," *O.C.*, II, p. 174.

[309]*Ibid.*, p. 176.

[310]See, for example, Gregorio Marañón, "Crítica de la medicina dogmática," *La medicina y nuestro tiempo*, 3rd ed. (Madrid: Espasa-Calpe, 1963), pp. 15-56; Gregorio Marañón, "Un español regresa del Brasil," *Efemérides y comentarios, O.C.*, IX, pp. 606-17.

[311]Gregorio Marañón, "Cajal," *O.C.*, II, p. 177.

[312]*Ibid.*, p. 203.

[313]Pedro Laín Entralgo, *España como problema*, p. 296

[314]Gregorio Marañón, "Cajal," *O.C.*, II, p. 188.

[315]*Ibid.*, p.189.

[316]*Ibid.*, p. 191.

[317]*Ibid.*, p. 192.

[318]Francisco Javier Almodóvar and Enrique Warleta, *Marañón o una vida fecunda* (Madrid: Espasa-Calpe, 1952), p. 174, quoting Gregorio Marañón.

[319]Gregorio Marañón, "Cajal," *O.C.*, II, p. 184.

[320]*Ibid.*

[321]Gregorio Marañón, "Médicos escritores," *O.C.*, I, p. 566.

Gary D. Keller

[322]Francisco López Estrada, "Marañón y las letras," *Anales de la Universidad Hispalense*, XX (1960), 5.
[323]Gregorio Marañón, *Ensayos liberales, O.C.,* IX, p. 252.
[324]Gregorio Marañón, "Fecundación artificial," *O.C.*, III, p. 230.
[325]Gregorio Marañón, "Gloria y miseria del conde de Villamediana," *O.C.*, III, p. 551.

Conclusion

[1]Gregorio Marañón, *Liberalismo y comunismo* in *Revue de Paris,* December 15, 1937; subsequently published as a separate pamphlet. It is reprinted in *O.C.*, IV.

BIBLIOGRAPHY

Works by Marañón

This bibliography of the works of Gregorio Marañón does not pretend to be complete. The publication of such a bibliography would require a separate volume in itself. See Almodóvar and Warleta's work for a bibliography that includes both humanistic and scientific titles through the year 1950.

This bibliography *does* include, however, all titles in the areas of literary criticism, biography and history that I have been able to locate during the nine years of this research project (1967-1976), and therefore it does presume to relative completeness in the aforementioned areas. However it is subject to certain limitations.

(1) The so-called *Obras completas* are not complete in actuality. (Hoddie, "En torno a cuatro prólogos 'desaparecidos' de G.M." makes a compelling case for the suppression of certain titles because they were politically offensive to post-Civil War Spain. Many others undoubtedly are missing because of the carelessness of the editor, facilitated by the enormous body of Marañón's writings and the fact that he published material all over the world.) If a title written by Marañón appears in the bibliography that follows, it is because it has been omitted totally or in part from the *Obras completas*.

(2) While I have referred to works published in the *Obras completas* wherever possible, because the first four volumes contain scores, and in the case of the prologues, hundreds of titles, the actual contents of those books are masked; they are not itemized here. The interested reader should consult the text and notes for a broad view of the contents in volumes I-IV of the *Obras completas*, at least in the humanistic areas.

(3) This bibliography does not list the various editions of Marañón's works; titles are only listed once. If the work is not listed in the *Obras completas*, then usually the last or definitive edition is cited, since Marañón regularly revised and expanded his work. There are one or two exceptions where I was unable to secure a later edition and was forced to use an earlier one. However, in the areas of interest to this study (Don Juan, El Greco, Amiel, etc.) a complete listing (to the best of my knowledge) *does* appear of the various works as they were issued in editions earlier than or separate from the *Obras completas*. This listing is located in the chapter notes and can be readily supplemented by reference both to Almodóvar and Warleta and to the *Obras completas* themselves, which also list earlier editions.

Gary D. Keller

(4) See pp. 7-8 in the introduction to this book for additional guidelines on how to best use the bibliographic data in this study.

"*El conocimiento de las naciones* y el *Norte de príncipes*, ¿son obras de Antonio Pérez o de don Baltasar Alamos de Barrientos?" *Estudios dedicados a Ramón Menéndez Pidal.* Madrid, 1950. Vol. I, 317-47.

Crónica y gesto de la libertad. Buenos Aires: Hachette, 1938.

Cuatro comentarios a la revolución española. Madrid: España Nueva, 1931.

La doctrina de las secreciones internas. Su significación biológica y sus aplicaciones a la clínica. Madrid: Corona, 1915.

La edad crítica. Madrid: Siglo Médico, 1919.

España fuera de España. Buenos Aires: Publicaciones de la cátedra de historia de la medicina, Universidad de Buenos Aires, 1946.

"Evolución de la gloria de Feijoo." *Cuadernos de la cátedra Feijoo*, Universidad de Oviedo, No. 1 (1955).

Gómez Moreno, Manuel y Gregorio Marañón. "Los restos de Enrique IV de Castilla." *Boletín de la Real Academia de la Historia*, CXXI (1947), 41-50.

"La homosexualidad como estado intersexual." *Revista médica de Chile*, 57 (1929), 413-20.

Idearium de Marañón, Ed. Alfredo Juderías. Madrid: Editorial Cultura Clásica y Moderna, 1960.

Juventud, modernidad, eternidad. Madrid: Editorial Historia Nueva, 1930.

"La leyenda de Don Juan." *Cuadernos de Adán*, No. 1 (1944), 25-51.

El libro y el librero. Madrid: Espasa-Calpe, 1953.

"La literatura científica en los siglos XVI y XVII." *Historia general de las literaturas hispánicas.* Ed. Guillermo Díaz-Plaja. Barcelona: Editorial Barna, 1953. III, 933-66.

La medicina y los médicos. Ed. Alfredo Juderías. Madrid: Espasa-Calpe, 1962.

La medicina y nuestro tiempo. 3rd ed. Buenos Aires: Espasa-Calpe, 1963.

"Menéndez Pelayo visto desde su precocidad." *Trabajos escolares de Menéndez Pelayo.* Ed. Enrique Sánchez Reyes. Santander: Hermanos Bedia, 1959, pp. 185-211. [Edición patrocinada por el Ministerio de Educación Nacional y costeada por el Banco de Santander.]

"Nuevas notas médicas sobre la pintura del Greco." *Revista de las Españas*, Año II, Nos. 5-6 (1927), 3-7.

Obras Completas, Vol. I [Prólogos]. Ed. Alfredo Juderías, introd. by Pedro Laín Entralgo. 2nd ed. Madrid: Espasa-Calpe, 1968.

Obras completas, Vol. II [Discursos]. Ed. Alfredo Juderías. Madrid: Espasa-Calpe, 1966.

Obras completas, Vol. III [Conferencias]. Ed. Alfredo Juderías. Madrid: Espasa-Calpe, 1967.

Bibliography

Obras completas. Vol. IV [Artículos]. Ed. Alfredo Juderías. Madrid: Espasa-Calpe, 1968.

Obras completas, Vol. V [Biografías: *El "empecinado" visto por un inglés; Ensayo biológico sobre Enrique IV de Castilla y su tiempo; Amiel; Las ideas biológicas del Padre Feijoo; El Conde-Duque de Olivares*]. Ed. Alfredo Juderías. Madrid: Espasa-Calpe, 1970.

Obras completas, Vol. VI [Biografías]: *Antonio Pérez; Los procesos de Castilla contra Antonio Pérez*]. Ed. Alfredo Juderías. Madrid: Espasa-Calpe, 1970.

Obras completas, Vol. VII [Biografías: *Tiberio; Don Juan; Luis Vives; Cajal; San Martín, el bueno y San Martín, el malo; El Greco y Toledo; Los tres Vélez; Notas sobre la vida y la muerte de San Ignacio de Loyola*]. Ed. Alfredo Juderías. Madrid: Espasa-Calpe, 1971.

Obras completas, Vol. VIII [Ensayos: *Climaterio de la mujer y del hombre; Ensayos sobre la vida sexual; Gordos y flacos; Amor y eugenesia; La evolución de la sexualidad y los estados intersexuales*]. Ed. Alfredo Juderías. Madrid: Espasa-Calpe, 1972.

Obras completas, Vol. IX [Ensayos: *Raíz y decoro de España; Vida e historia; Ensayos liberales; Españoles fuera de España; Vocación y ética y otros ensayos; Tiempo viejo y tiempo nuevo; Elogio y nostalgia de Toledo; Efemérides y comentarios*]. Ed. Alfredo Juderías. Madrid: Espasa-Calpe, 1973.

"Les origines de la légende de Don Juan." *Revue Hebdomadaire.* Paris, January, 1939.

"Los orígenes de la leyenda de Don Juan." *Revista de la Universidad de San Francisco Javier,* 4 (1939), 197-212.

"Prólogo" to Luz León, José de la. *Benjamin Constant o El donjuanismo intelectual.* Havana, 1937.

"Prólogo" to Benzo, Eduardo. *Al servicio del ejército.* Madrid, 1931.

"Prólogo" to Ruiz, Nicolás. *Obras selectas.* Madrid, 1947.

"Prólogo" to Valera, Fernando. *Tópicos revolucionarios.* Madrid, no date. Marañón's prologue is dated, August, 1932.

Quemoterapia moderna según Ehrlich. Tratamiento de la sífilis por el 606. Madrid: Editorial Vidal, 1910.

"Quevedo, Calderón de la Barca y el Conde-Duque de Olivares." *Academia Dominicana de la Lengua* (May, 1944), 25-37.

Una "relación" inédita de Antonio Pérez. Madrid: Editorial Maestre, 1949.

"Sex and Religion in Spain." *Birth Control Review.* 6 (1929), 150-57.

"Socialismo, inteligencia, civilidad." [Prologue] in Domingo, Marcelino. *¿Adónde va España?* Madrid, 1929.

Veinte y cinco años de labor. Historia y biografía de la obra del Prof. G. Marañón y sus discípulos. Madrid: Espasa-Calpe, 1935.

Gary D. Keller

Translations of Marañón's Works into Other Languages

Amiel. Paris: Nouvelle Revue Française, 1938.
Amiel o della timidezza. Turin: Ginardi, 1938.
Antonio Perez, Spanish Traitor. Trans. C.D. Ley. New York, 1954.
Don Giovanni. Tre saggi sull' origine della leggenda. Milan: Gentile, 1945.
Don João. Ensaios sobre a origen da sua lenda. Porto: Tavares Martins, 1947.
"Don Juan." Trans. Lloyd D. Teale. *The Theatre of Don Juan.* Ed. Oscar Mandel. Lincoln, Nebraska: University of Nebraska Press, 1963, pp. 637-40.
Don Juan et le donjuanisme. Trans. Marie Berthe Lacomb. Paris: Stock, 1958.
Olivares. Trans. and prol. by Ludwig Pfandl. Munich, 1940.
Tiberius, the Resentful Caesar. Trans. Warren Bradley Wells, foreword by Ronald Syme. New York, 1956.
Vives, Humaniste Espagnol. with Eugenio d'Ors and others. Paris: Collection Occident, Etudes Hispaniques, Librairie Plon, 1941. [Marañón's article is "Le Docteur melliflu."]

Books, Articles, and Pamphlets about Marañón

Albár, Manuel. "Las angustias del doctor Marañón: El liberalismo, los liberales y sus verdugos." *España Nueva.* México, October 18, 1947.
Aleixandre, Vicente. "En la academia." *Indice de Artes y Letras.* Madrid, Vol. XII, Nos. 137/138 (1960).
Allúe y Morer, Fernando. "Marañón y la poesía." *Poesía Española.* Madrid, No. 89 (1960).
Almodóvar, Francisco Javier and Warleta, Enrique. *Marañón o una vida fecunda.* Madrid: Espasa-Calpe, 1952.
Alvarez Sierra, J. *El Hipócrates de la medicina española. Biografía del Doctor Marañón.* Madrid, 1960.
Aranguren, José Luis. "El humanismo moral de Marañón." *Papeles de Son Armadans,* Año VI, Vol. XX, No. 60 (March 1961), 302-307.
Baquero, G. "El sentido americano de Gregorio Marañón." *Indice de Artes y Letras.* Madrid, Vol. XII, Nos. 137/138 (1960).
Barco Teruel, Enrique. *Elogio y nostalgia de Marañón.* Barcelona, 1961.
Bergamín, José. "Carta abierta a Victoria Ocampo." *Sur,* Vol. VII, No. 32 (1937), 67-69.
-----. "José Bergamín desmiente al Dr. Marañón." *Repertorio Americano.* San José, Costa Rica, April 17, 1937, pp. 230-31.
-----. "Traidor." *Nuevo Continente.* México, No. 3 (1937), 12.

Bibliography

Botellá Llusía, José. "Marañón y la academia de medicina." *Papeles de Son Armadans*, Año VI, Vol. XX, No. 60 (March 1961), 267-74.

Caba, P. "Filósofo del hombre." *Indice de Artes y Letras*. Madrid, Vol. XII, Nos. 137/138 (1960).

Candau, A. "Marañón y el humanismo." *Arbor*, Vol. XLVIII (1961), 346-52.

Casariego, J.E. "Marañón de cerca." *Abside*. México, Vol. XXIV, No. 3 (1960), 255-71.

Castillo de Lucas, A. *Glosa refraneada de la vida y obra de Marañón*. Tenerife: Instituto de Fisiología y Patología Regional, 1962.

Cela, Camilo José. "Marañón, el hombre." *Cuatro figuras del '98*. Barcelona: Aedos, 1961, pp. 101-18.

Colberg, Juan Enrique. "Culto de Marañón a Toledo." *Orfeo*. Ponce, Puerto Rico, Vol. III, No. 6 (1956), 3-6.

-----. *Del orbe ideológico de Marañón*. Barcelona: Ediciones Rumbos, 1962.

Collazo, J.A. "Gregorio Marañón, espíritu selecto y eximio maestro de juventudes." *El Debate*. Montevideo, March 13, 1937.

Cortés, Guillermo A. "Un apunte elemental sobre Gregorio Marañón." *Cultura Hispánica*. El Salvador, 2 (1967), 23-45.

Cuatrecasas, Juan. "El sentido hipocrático de Marañón." *Cuadernos Americanos*, Año XIX, No. 4 (July-August 1960), 80-91.

Cueva Tamariz, Agustín. *Elogio de Gregorio Marañón*. Cuenca, Ecuador: Universidad de Cuenca, 1955.

Díaz Plaja, Guillermo. "Marañón y la literatura española." *La Nación*. Buenos Aires, July 10, 1966.

-----. "Marañón y la literatura española." *La Nación*. Buenos Aires: May 29, 1966.

-----. "Marañón y la literatura española. (El derecho del Amor.)" *La Nación*. Buenos Aires, April 30, 1966.

-----. "Marañón y Cataluña." *Insula*, Vol. XV, Nos. 164/165 (1960), 10.

Díaz-Sal, Braulio. "Un itinerario íntimo de Gregorio Marañón." *La Nación*. Buenos Aires, January 28, 1962, p. 4.

Doménech, R. "Ideas de Marañón sobre los jóvenes." *Insula*, Vol. XV, Nos. 164/165 (1960), 11.

Doreste, Ventura. "Humanismo y estilo en Gregorio Marañón." *Insula*, Vol. VI, No. 61 (1951), 1-2.

Eisenberg, Daniel. "Enrique IV and Gregorio Marañón." *Renaissance Quarterly*, XXIX (1976), 21-29.

Fredinnick-Afasto, Felipe. "El psiquiatra cabal." *Américas*. Unión Panamericana, Washington, D.C., Vol. XIII, No. 1 (1961), 34-35.

García de Castro, Rafael G. "Los intelectuales y la iglesia." *Revista de Estudios Hispánicos*. Madrid, No. 10 (1935), 459-60.

García Díaz, Sebastián. "Humanismo y magisterio de Marañón." *Atlántida*, V (1967), 383-89.

García Sabell, Domingo. "Españoles mal entendidos." *Insula*, Año XV, Nos. 164/165 (July-August 1960), 8.

Garciasol, Ramón de. "Teoría del prólogo en Marañón." *La Torre*, Vol. XIV, No. 54 (1966), 157-73.

García Vicente, Saturnino. *Baroja, Marañón, Toledo y otras narraciones*. Madrid: Espasa-Calpe, 1958.

281

Gary D. Keller

Gassió Contell, E. "Valoración literaria y humana del Dr. Marañón." *Libros selectos*. México, No. 19 (1966).

Girón de Segura, Socorro. *Gregorio Marañón, escritor*. Palma de Mallorca: Imp. Mossén Alcóver, 1962.

Gómez de la Serna, Ramón. "En el hospital con el doctor Marañón." *El Norte*. Trujillo, Peru, July 11, 1926.

Gómez-Moreno, Manuel. "Marañón en la Real Academia de Bellas Artes." *Papeles de Son Armadans*, Año IV, Vol. XX, No. 60 (March 1961), 261-66.

Gómez-Santos, Marino. *Gregorio Marañón cuenta su vida*. Madrid: Aguilar, 1961.

-----. *Vida de Gregorio Marañón*. Madrid: Taurus, 1971.

González, Nasario. "Marañón, periodista." *Razón y Fe*. 179 (1969), 403-10.

González-Ruana, César, "Gregorio Marañón." *Siluetas de escritores contemporáneos*. Madrid: 1949, pp. 143-46.

Granjel, Luis S. *Gregorio Marañón: Su vida y su obra*. Madrid: Ed. Guadarrama, 1960.

Hernández Díaz, José. "Marañón y las bellas artes." *Anales de la Universidad Hispalense*. Sevilla, Vol. XXI, No. 1 (1960), 87-91.

Hoddie, Jr., James. "El concepto de la labor del historiador y biógrafo en las obras de Gregorio Marañón." *Bulletin Hispanique*, Vol. LXIX, Nos. 1-2 (1967), 106-21.

-----. "En torno a cuatro prólogos 'desaparecidos' de Gregorio Marañón." *Bulletin Hispanique*, 74 (1972), 43-60.

-----. "Gregorio Marañón, Historian and Man of Letters." Unpubl. Ph.D. dissertation. Brown University, 1965.

-----. "El liberalismo de Gregorio Marañón." *La Torre*, Vol. XVI, No. 61 (1968), 182-201.

Izquierdo, M. de. *Gregorio Marañón, médico, escritor e historiador*. Madrid: Ed. Cid, 1965.

Izquierdo Hernández, M. "Marañón, trabajador." *Gaceta Médica Española*, 1962, pp. 3-29.

Junco, Alfonso. "Feijoo y Marañón." *Abside*. México, Vol. XXIV, No 2 (1960), 233-43.

Junior, Peregrino. "Lección y ejemplo de una vida grande." *Cuadernos Hispanoamericanos*, Vol. XLVI, No. 136 (1961), 41-49.

Laín Entralgo, Pedro. *Gregorio Marañón. Vida, obra y persona*. Madrid: Espasa-Calpe, 1969. [Reprint of Laín Entralgo's Introduction to Gregorio Marañón's *Obras completas*, Vol. I.]

-----. *Marañón y el enfermo*. Madrid: Revista de Occidente, 1962.

-----. "La persona de Marañón." *Revista de Occidente*, Vol. III (1965), 133-53.

Lastres, Dr. Juan B. "El profesor Gregorio Marañón." *Mercurio Peruano*. Lima, Vol. XXVIII (1947), 483-87 and 518-46.

León Pagano, José. "Una visita a Toledo con Marañón." *La Nación*. Buenos Aires, September 23, 1956.

López de Toro, José. "Marañón en la Real Academia de la Historia." *Papeles de Son Armadans*, Año VI, Vol. XX, No. 60 (March 1961), 234-260.

Bibliography

López Estrada, Francisco. "Marañón y las letras." *Anales de la Universidad Hispalense*, Vol. XX (1960), 5-18.

Loudet, Osvaldo. "Azorín y Marañón." *La Nación*. Buenos Aires, April 16, 1967, p. 1.

-----. "Gregorio Marañón: un poeta ignorado." *La Nación*. Buenos Aires, September 24, 1967, pp. 1 and 3.

-----. "Gregorio Marañón, médico humanista." *La Nación*. Buenos Aires, July 17, 1960.

Magaña Esquivel, Antonio. "¿Don Juan, canonizado?" *El Nacional*. México, November 10, 1960.

Mañach, Jorge. "Marañón." *Visitas españolas. Lugares, personas*. Madrid: Revista de Occidente, 1960, pp. 190-207.

-----. "Visita a Marañón." *Insula*, Vol. XV, Nos. 164/165 (1960), 6.

-----. "Marañón contra los comuneros de Castilla." *España Republicana*, Buenos Aires. March 26, 1949.

Marías, Julián. "Gregorio Marañón." *Obras*. Madrid: Revista de Occidente, 1966, pp. 152-68.

Marías, Julián and Cano, José Luis. "Evocación de un liberal: Gregorio Marañón." *Cuadernos del Congreso por la Libertad de la Cultura*. Paris, No. 43 (1960), 93-95.

Menéndez Pidal, Ramón. "Recuerdo de Marañón en la Academia Española." *Papeles de Son Armadans*, Año VI, Vol. XX, No. 60 (March 1961), 231-33.

Micó Buchon, J.L. "Ideas religiosas del doctor Marañón." *Cuadernos Hispanoamericanos*. Madrid, Vol. XLVI (1961), 351-69.

Morente, Manuel G. "Consulta al Dr. Marañón." *Cervantes*. La Habana, Vol. XI, Nos. 8-9 (1936), 19-20.

Muñoz, Andrés. "Mi visita a Gregorio Marañón." *La Nación*. Buenos Aires, November 2, 1950.

Muñoz Pérez, J. "Marañón, historiador." *Revista del Instituto de Avila*, No. 1 (1961), 11-18.

Muñoz Sanz, Juan Pablo. *Glosario de Amiel. Reflexiones sobre la timidez y réplica al Doctor Marañón*. Quito, Ecuador: Imprenta Nacional, 1936.

Mussió Fournier, Juan César. "Marañón, abogado de la mujer." *Revista Nacional*. Montevideo, Vol. V, No. 205 (1960), 375-84.

Ocampo, Victoria. "Carta abierta a José Bergamín." *Sur*, Vol. VII, No. 32 (1937), 69-74.

Olaya Restrepo, Max. "Valor universal de Gregorio Marañón." *Universidad Pontificia Bolivariana*. Medellín, Colombia, Vol. XXIV, No. 86 (1960), 226-35.

-----. *Gregorio Marañón*. Bucaramanga: Editorial Salesiana, 1962.

Oliver Brachfeld, F. *Polémica contra Marañón*. Barcelona: Editorial Europa, 1933.

Olsen, Manuel. "La última vez que vi a D. Gregorio Marañón (Hablaba de Rubén Darío y Gómez Carrillo)." *Cultura*. El Salvador, No. 34 (1964), 135-38.

Ors, Eugenio d'. "En España. —Marañón y la Endocrinología." *Nuevo Glosario*. Madrid, Vol. I (1947), 604-608.

-----. "Juliano y San Pablo." *Nuevo Glosario*. Madrid, Vol. II (1947), 258.

Gary D. Keller

Ors, Eugenio d'. "Marañón, una mente lúcida." *El Norte.* Trujillo, Peru, July 11, 1926.

-----. "Paréntesis cerrado." *Nuevo Glosario.* Madrid, Vol. I (1947), 866.

Palencia, Ceferino. "El doctor don Gregorio Marañón en su obra literaria." *Cuadernos Americanos,* Vol. XIX, No.4 (1960), 92-109.

Pereda, V. de. "Feijoo y Marañón." *Costumbres y Tradiciones.* Zaragoza, Vol. L (1934), 7-75.

Pérez de Ayala, Ramón. "El doctor Marañón." *Amistades y recuerdos.* Barcelona, 1961, pp. 227-36.

-----. "Ensayo liminar." In Gregorio Marañón, *Tres ensayos sobre la vida sexual.* Madrid: Espasa-Calpe, 1934.

Perrín Tomás G. "Dos Jornadas, La de Plata y la de Oro—en la Vida de Gregorio Marañón." *Cuadernos Americanos,* Vol. XIX, No. 4 (1960), 73-91.

Prévost, Jean. "Où Marañón, sociologue espagnol, rejoint la morale anglosaxonne." *Les Nouvelles Littéraires.* Paris, March 27, 1937.

Prieto Indalecio. "La ideología de Marañón." *Cuadernos Americanos,* Año XIX, No. 4 (1960), 110-31.

Ramos Meza, Enrique. *Gregorio Marañón, gran médico y humanista.* Guadalajara: Universidad Autónoma de Guadalajara, Folia Universitaria, No. 1 (1961).

Reforzo Membrives, J. "Gregorio Marañón." *Universidad.* Universidad Nacional del Litoral, Santa Fe, Argentina, No. 45 (1960), 51-72.

-----. "La personalidad polifacética de Marañón." *Cuadernos Americanos,* Vol. XIX, No. 4 (1960), 132-49.

Ridruejo, Dionisio. "La autoridad de Marañón." *Indice de Artes y Letras.* Madrid:, Vol. XII, Nos. 137/138 (1960).

-----. "Un liberal." *En algunas ocasiones (Crónicas y comentarios).* Madrid: Editorial Aguilar, 1960, pp. 417-22.

Ruiz Chacón, Enriqueta. *Ideas literarias de Marañón.* Unpubl. Thesis. Seville, Universidad de Sevilla, 1962.

Salazar Chapela, E. "Carta de Londres." *La Nación.* Buenos Aires, July 17, 1960.

Salido Orcilla, R. "Marañón y la política." *Novedades.* México, April 16, 1960.

Sampelayo, Juan. "Marañón y sus academias." *Arbor,* Vol. LXXV (1970), 103-106.

Sánchez, José. "El doctor Gregorio Marañón: Médico, literato, humanista." *Hispania,* Madrid, Vol. XLV, No. 3 (1962), 451-57.

Sánchez Agesta, L. "Gregorio Marañón, historiador político." *Indice de Artes y Letras.* Madrid, Vol. XII, Nos. 137/138 (1960).

Sánchez Maurandi, Antonio. *Reparos a los tres Vélez de Marañón.* Murcia, 1961.

Sendrail, M. "Gregorio Marañón et la pensée médicale hispanique." *La Table Ronde.* Paris, Nos. 169, 21-30.

Urmeneta, F. de. "Sobre la estética marañoniana." *Revista de Ideas Estéticas.* Madrid, Vol. XXI (1963), 247-49.

Bibliography

Vasconcelos, Taborda de. "Gregorio Marañón e a inteligência ibérica." *Gazeta Literaria*. Porto, Nos. 10/11 (1960). [Republished in *Cronos*, Lisbon, 2 (1966), 33-39.]

"El viaje al Brasil de don Gregorio Marañón ha sido triunfal." *Correo Literario*. Madrid, Vol. IV, No. 80 (1953).

Vicens Vives, Jaime. "Marañón y los comuneros." *Destino*. 2a época. XII, December 11, 1948, p. 13.

Viñole, Omar. "Gregorio Marañón es un exógeno de tipo poliformista hereditario." *Claridad*. Buenos Aires, Vol. XV, No. 312 (1937).

Book Reviews

Adams, Phoebe. "Marañón Gregorio, *Tiberius*." *Atlantic Monthly*, August, 1957.

"Amiel o la timidez." *Indice Literario. Archivos de Literatura Contemporánea*. Madrid, Centro de Estudios Históricos, Año I, No. 5 (December 1932), 131-34.

Arambaru, Julio. "Un libro de Marañón." *Conducta*. Buenos Aires, No. 9 (1939), no pagination. [Review of *Las ideas biológicas del Padre Feijoo*.]

Bataillon, Marcel. "*El 'Empecinado' visto por un inglés*, traducción y prólogo de Gregorio Marañón." *Papeles de Son Armadans*, Año VI, Vol. XX, No. 60 (March 1961), 291-98.

Bonilla, E. "Gordos y flacos." *La Gaceta Literaria*. Madrid, March 1, 1927.

Cano, José Luis. "El Greco y Toledo. Sobre un nuevo libro de Gregorio Marañón." *El Nacional*. Caracas, March 14, 1957.

-----. "Marañón y sus *Obras completas*." *Insula*, Vol. XXI, No. 233 (1966). [Review of Vol. I, *Prólogos*, of the projected *Obras completas*.]

-----. "Gregorio Marañón: Toledo y el Greco." *Insula*, Vol. XII, No. 123 (1957), 6.

-----. "Gregorio Marañón. *Los tres Vélez. Una historia de todos los tiempos*." *Insula*, XVI (1960), 9-10.

Castaneda, C.E. "Marañón, Gregorio, *Antonio Pérez*." *New York Times*, January 1, 1956.

Cereceda, Feliciano. "Sobre: *Antonio Pérez*." *Razón y Fe*, CXXXVI (1947), 389-409.

Cirot, G. "*Enrique IV de Castilla*." *Bulletin Hispanique*, XXXIII (1931), 352-353.

-----. "*Ensayo biológico sobre Enrique IV de Castilla y su tiempo*." *Bulletin Hispanique*, Vol. XXXIII (1931), 352-53.

-----. "Sobre Gregorio Marañón, *Las ideas biológicas del P. Feijoo*." *Bulletin Hispanique*, Vol. XXXVII (1935), 114.

Deleito y Piñuela, J. "*Enrique IV de Castilla*." *Revista de la Biblioteca, Archivo y Museo del Ayuntamiento de Madrid*, VII (1930), 410-12.

Gary D. Keller

Delgado, H. "Sobre: Gregorio Marañón, *Don Juan. Ensayos sobre el origen de su leyenda*." *Revista de la Universidad Católica del Perú*. Lima, Vol. VIII (1940), 353-55.

Díaz Fernández, J. "*Tres ensayos sobre la vida sexual*." *El Sol*. Madrid, December 18, 1927.

Domenchina, J.J. "El Amiel de Marañón." *Crónicas de "Gerardo Rivera*." Madrid, 1935, pp. 64-68.

Erasmo Buceta, V. "*Enrique IV de Castilla*." *Revista de Filología Española*, XVIII (1931), 404-6.

Espina, Antonio, "*Las ideas biológicas del Padre Feijoo*." *Revista de Occidente*, Vol. XLIV (1934), 329-35.

Feliz García, P. "*Raíz y decoro de España*." *Religión y Cultura*. Madrid, Vol. XXIV, 464-67.

-----. "Reivindicación de Feijoo." *Cruz y Raya*. Madrid, No. 15 (1934), 131-41.

García Gallo, Alfonso. "Sobre *El Conde-Duque de Olivares*." *Anuario de Historia del Derecho Español*, XIV (1942-1943), 655-57.

Garciasol, Ramón de. "Marañón: *Los tres Vélez (Una historia de todos los tiempos.)*"*Cuadernos Hispanoamericanos*, Vol. XLIV, No. 131 (1960), 285-93.

Gil Novales, Alberto. "Gregorio Marañón, *Obras completas*, tomo V." *Revista de Occidente*, XXXII (1971), 249-51.

Gómez Galán, A. "Obras completas de Marañón." *Arbor*, Vol. LXIV, Nos. 247/248 (1966), 115-17. [Book review of Vol. I, *Prólogos*.]

González, Nazario. "Gregorio Marañón." *Razón y Fe*. Madrid, Vol. CLXXIII, No. 818 (1966), 317-23. [Book review of M. de Izquierdo, *Gregorio Marañón, médico escritor e historiador*.]

-----. "Marañón, periodista." *Razón y Fe*. Madrid, Vol. CLXXIX, No. 855 (1969), 403-10. [Book review of Vol. IV, *Artículos* of the *Obras completas*.]

Julián Martínez, Eduardo. "Sobre: Gregorio Marañón, *Luis Vives (Un español fuera de España.)*" *Revista de Filología Española*. Madrid, Vol. XXVI (1942), 116-17.

Hadas, Moses, "Marañón, Gregorio, *Tiberius*." *New York Herald Tribune*, August 4, 1957.

Lafuente Ferrari, Enrique. "Toledo y el Greco: Sobre el libro del doctor Marañón." *Insula*, Año XI, No. 125 (1957), pp. 1 and 8.

Lapeyre, H. "*Antonio Pérez*." *Revue Historique*, CCI (1949), 124-26.

Keller, William. "*Antonio Pérez, Spanish Traitor*." *The Catholic Historical Review*, XLI (1955), 208-209.

Koenigsberger, H.G. "*Antonio Pérez, Spanish Traitor*." *Bulletin of Hispanic Studies*, XXXII (1955), 58-59.

Konetzke, R. "*Olivares*." *Historische Zeitschrift*, CLXVI (1942), 411-15.

"Marañón, Gregorio, *Antonio Pérez*." *San Francisco Chronicle*. January 8, 1956.

Maura, duque de. "*Antonio Pérez*." *Boletín de la Real Academia de Historia*, CXXII (1948), 23-49.

Montero Díaz, S. "A propósito de un libro de Marañón." *Boletín de la Universidad de Santiago,* No. 23 (January-March 1935). [Book review of *Las ideas biológicas del padre Feijoo.*]

Moreyra, P.S.M. "Sobre: Gregorio Marañón, *Tiempo viejo y tiempo nuevo.*" *Revista de la Universidad Católica del Perú.* Lima, Vol. VIII (1940), 442-44.

Mostaza, Bartolomé. "Sobre: Gregorio Marañón, *Ensayos liberales.*" *Revista de Estudios Políticos.* Madrid, Vol. XIX, Nos. 35-36 (1947), 340-93.

Negrete, P.E. "Sobre Gregorio Marañón, *Vocación y ética.*" *Religión y Cultura.* Madrid, Vol. XXXIII (1936), 173-90.

Panichas, G.A. "Marañón, Gregorio, *Tiberius.*" *Springfield Republican,* September 8, 1957.

Pazos, P. Manuel R. "Marañón, Gregorio: *Antonio Pérez.*" *Archivo Ibero-Americano,* XIII (1953), 511-12.

Peers, E. Allison. "*El Conde-Duque de Olivares.*" *Bulletin of Hispanic Studies,* XXVI (1949), 187-88.

Pérez Villanueva, V. Joaquín. "Sobre: *Antonio Pérez.*" *Arbor,* IX (1948), 616-29.

Ricard, R. "Sobre Gregorio Marañón, El conde-duque de Olivares." *Bulletin Hispanique,* Vol. XLIX (1947), 101-106.

Río, Angel del. "Sobre Gregorio Marañón: *Las ideas biológicas del Padre Feijoo.*" *Revista Hispánica Moderna,* Vol. I (1934), 201-202.

Sánchez-Camargo, Manuel. "El último libro de Marañón." *Cuadernos Hispanoamericanos,* No. 88 (April 1957), 110-12.

Santacruz, V. Pascual. "*El empecinado.*" *Nuestro Tiempo,* Madrid. XXVI (1926), 279-282.

Schoeffler, V.H. "*Olivares.*" *Romanische Forschungen,* LIV (1940) 99-101.

Torrendell, V.J. "*El Conde-Duque de Olivares.*" *Nosotros,* 5 (1936), 554-57.

Werner, E. "*Olivares.*" *Deutsche Literaturzeilung.* Berlin-Leipzig, LXI (1940), 280-1.

Homenajes and Necrologies

Alonso, Dámaso, "Don Gregorio Marañón." *Boletín de la Real Academia Española,* 51 (1971), 43-45.

Aleixandre, Vicente. "Ojos humanos." *Insula,* Año XV, Nos. 164-165 (July-August 1960), 5.

Bastid, Paul, "Hommage d'un liberal a un liberal." *Papeles de Son Armadans,* Año VI, Vol. XX, Núm. 60 (March 1961), 291-98.

Bataillon, Marcel. "Necrologie: Gregorio Marañón (1887-1960)." *Bulletin Hispanique,* Vol. LXII, No. 3 (1960), 357-59.

Batllori, Miguel. "El Doctor Marañón." *Razón y Fe.* Madrid, Vol. CLXI (1960), 528-37.

Boeta, J.R. "Luto por Marañón." *Arbor,* Vol. 45 (1960), 110-13.

Gary D. Keller

Cano José Luis. "Un recuerdo personal." *Insula*, Año XV, Nos. 164-165 (July-August 1960), 5.

Cela, Camilo José. "Gregorio Marañón." *Boletín de la Real Academia Española*, 51 (1971), 29-30.

Ciriquián Gaiztarro, M. "Don Gregorio Marañón." *Boletín de la Real Sociedad Vascongada de Amigos del País*. San Sebastián, Vol. XVI (1960), 221-22.

Chacón y Calvo, J.M. "Don Gregorio Marañón." *Boletín da Academia das Ciencias de Lisboa*. Coimbra, Vol. IX (1960), 146-50.

Cortejoso, Leopoldo. "Elogio y nostalgia de Marañón." *Clínica y Laboratorio*, Vol. LXIX (May 1960), 398-400.

Cossío, José M. de. "Recuerdo de Gregorio Marañón." *Boletín de la Real Academia Española*, 51 (1971), 35-38.

Díaz Plaja, Guillermo. "Gregorio Marañón: Esquema del intelectual puro." *Boletín de la Real Academia Española*, 51 (1971), 15-20.

Endara, Julio. "Gregorio Marañón, Guión de cultura." *Letras de Ecuador*, Vol. XV, No. 118 (1960).

Esteva Fabregal, Claudio. "Marañón: sentido de una vida." *Horizontes, Revista Bibliográfica*. México, Vol. III, No. 13 (1960), 5-6.

García, P. Felix. "Elegía a Marañón." *A.B.C.* Madrid, March 30, 1960.

García de Diego, Vicente. "Gregorio Marañón." *Boletín de la Real Academia Española*, 51 (1971), 41-42.

Garciasol, Ramón de. "Correo para la muerte." *Insula*, Año XV, Nos. 164-165 (July-August 1960), 8.

"Glosa y loa de la vida y obra del insigne Gregorio Marañón." *Gaceta Médica Española*, Año XXXIV, No. 5 (1960), 161-217; and Sec. Paramédica 112P-29P.

Hernando, Teófilo. "Marañón, maestro." *Insula*, Vol. XV, Nos. 164/165 (1960), 4.

Hommage à Gregorio Marañón. Textes receuillés, traduits et publiés par Marie-Berthe Lacombe. La Colombe, Paris, 1963.

"Homenaje a Gregorio Marañón." *Indice de Artes y Letras*. Madrid. Vol. XII, Nos. 137/138 (1960).

Homenaje a Gregorio Marañón. Madrid: Prensa Española, 1960.

Homenaje a Gregorio Marañón. Córdoba: Reunión Hispano-Lusa de Endocrinología, 1962.

Laín Entralgo, Pedro. "Gregorio Marañón (1887-1960)." *Boletín de la Real Academia Española*, Vol. XL, No. 159 (January-April 1960), 7-19.

-----. "Gregorio Marañón." *Insula*, Vol. XV, Nos. 164/165 (1960).

-----. "Gregorio Marañón, médico." *Archivo Iberamericano de Historia de la Medicina y de Antropología Médica*. Madrid, Vol. XII (1960), 3-22.

-----. "Por la integridad del recuerdo de Marañón." *Cuadernos Hispanoamericanos*, 246 (1970), 511-18.

López Ibor, J.J. "Marañón, médico humanista." *Cuadernos Hispanoamericanos*, 246 (1970), 519-25.

Marías, Julián. "Gregorio Marañón, lo que se ha perdido y lo que ha quedado." *Insula*, Vol. XV, Nos. 164/165 (1960), 7.

-----. "Llamar a Marañón." *Boletín de la Real Academia Española*, 51 (1971), 21-22.

Marín, Juan. "Tránsito de Gregorio Marañón." *La Nueva Democracia*, Vol. XV, No. 3 (1960), 54-55.

Molina, Antonio. "Marañón y su proyección filipina." *Boletín de la Real Academia Española*, 51 (1971), 9-13.

Pereira Rodríguez, José. "Gregorio Marañón." *Revista Nacional*. Montevideo, Vol. IV, No. 203 (1960), 142-46.

Pérez, T. "La gloria de Don Gregorio." *Indice de Artes y Letras*. Madrid, Vol. XII, Nos. 137/138 (1960).

Rof Carballo, Juan. "Marañón como médico." *Blanco y Negro*. Madrid, No. 2500 (April 2, 1960).

-----. "Marañón, médico." *Papeles de Son Armadans*, Año VI, Vol. XX, No. 60 (March 1961), 308-41.

-----. "Marañón y España." *Cuadernos Hispanoamericanos*. 246 (1970), 526-539.

-----. "La superficie de la fructura." *Insula*, Año XV, Nos. 164/165 (July-August 1960), 3.

Roquér, P. Ramón. "In Memoriam." *Revista Gran Vía*, Año IX, No. 416 (April 5, 1960).

Sagarra, J.M. de. "Homenaje a Marañón." *Insula*, Vol. XV, Nos. 164/165 (1960), 10.

Sánchez Cantón, F.J. "Necrología del Excmo. Sr. D. Gregorio Marañón y Posadillo." *Boletín de la Real Academia*, Vol. CXLVI, No. 2 (1960), 209-15.

Sander, Carlos. "Gregorio Marañón y Toledo." *Cuadernos Hispanoamericanos*. Madrid, Vol. XLIV, No. 131 (1960), 293-301.

"Sesión necrológica en memoria del Excmo. Sr. D. Gregorio Marañón y Posadillo." *Anales de la Real Academia Nacional de Medicina*, Vol. LXXVII, No. 3 (1960).

Sopeña, P. Federico. "La fe de don Gregorio." *A.B.C.* Madrid, April 5, 1960.

Valdecasas, Alfonso. "Gregorio Marañón, el Español." *Boletín de la Real Academia Española*, 51 (1971), 23-25.

General Bibliography

Agustín, Francisco. *Don Juan en el teatro, en la novela y en la vida*. Madrid: Editorial Paez, 1928.

Alonso, Dámaso. *Poesía española. Ensayo de métodos y límites estilísticos*. 5th ed. Madrid: Editorial Gredos, 1966.

Altamira y Crevea, Rafael. *Proceso histórico de la historiografía humana*. México: El Colegio de México, 1948.

Amezúa y Mayo, Agustín G. de. *Isabel de Valois*. 2 vols. Madrid: Gráficas Ultra, 1949.

Amiel, Henri Frédéric. *Journal Intime*. Ed. M. Bernard Bouvier, 3 vols. Paris: Genève, 1923.

Gary D. Keller

Amiel, Henri Frédéric. *Philine*. Ed. M Bernard Bouvier, Introd. Edmond Jaloux. Paris, 1927.

-----. *Philine: From the Unpublished Journals of Henri-Frederic Amiel.* Trans. Van Wyck Brooks, introd. Edmond Jaloux. Boston and New York: Houghton Mifflin Company, 1930.

Araya, Guillermo. *Evolución del pensamiento histórico de Américo Castro.* Madrid: Taurus, 1969.

Arco, Ricardo del. *Fernando el Católico, artífice de la España imperial.* Zaragoza: Edit. Heraldo de Aragón, 1939.

Ardao, Arturo. *La filosofía polémica de Feijoo.* Buenos Aires: Editorial Losada, 1962.

Asín Palacios, Miguel. *La escatología musulmana en la Divina Comedia seguida de la historia y crítica de una polémica.* 3rd ed. Madrid: Instituto Hispano-Arabe de Cultura, 1961.

-----. *El Islam Cristianizado: Estudio crítico del "Sufismo" a través de las obras de Abenarabi de Murcia.* 1st ed. Madrid: Editorial Plutarco, 1931.

Barga, Corpus. "Don Juan y los doctores." *El Sol.* Madrid, December 18, 1926.

-----. "Don Juan y los placeres renanos." *Revista de Occidente*, IX (1925), 374-81.

Basarde, Jorge. "En torno a la teoría de la historia." *Historia y Cultura.* Lima, I (1965), 1-11.

Bataillon, Marcel. *Erasme en Espagne.* Paris, 1937.

Binet-Sanglé, Charles. *L'epilepsie chez Gustave Flaubert.* Paris: Chronique Médicale, 1900.

-----. *La Folie de Jésus*, 4 vols. Paris: Maloine, 1908-15.

-----. *La maladie de Blaise Pascal.* Paris: Annales Médico-psychologiques, 1899.

Bolles, Robert C. *Theory of Motivation.* New York: Harper and Row, 1967.

Bourget, Paul. *Essais de Psychologie Contemporaine.* Edition définitive augmentée d'appendices, tome second. Paris: Librairie Plon, 1937.

Brooks, Van Wyck. *The Malady of the Ideal: Obermann, Maurice de Guerin and Amiel.* Philadelphia: University of Pennsylvania Press, 1947.

Bryson, Frederick Robertson. *The Point of Honor in the Sixteenth Century: An Aspect of the Life of the Gentleman.* New York: Columbia University Press, 1935.

Cadoux, Cecil John. *Philip of Spain and the Netherlands: An Essay on Moral Judgments in History.* London, 1947.

Camón Aznar, José. *Dominico Greco.* Madrid, 1950.

Camus, Albert. *The Myth of Sisyphus and Other Essays.* Trans. Justin O'Brien. New York: Random House, 1955.

Cannon, W.B. *Bodily Changes in Pain, Hunger, Fear and Rage.* New York: Appleton-Century, 1929.

Capouya, Emile. "Apropos of Don Juan." *The Nation*, August 29, 1959.

Caro Baroja, Julio. *Algunos mitos españoles y otros ensayos.* Madrid: Editorial Nacional, 1944.

-----. "Honor and Shame: A Historical Account of Several Conflicts." *Honor and Shame: The Values of Mediterranean Society.* Ed. J.G. Peristiany. London: Weidenfeld and Nicolson, 1965.

Bibliography

Carter, Charles Howard. *The Secret Diplomacy of the Hapsburgs, 1598-1625.* New York and London: Columbia University Press, 1964.

Casalduero, Joaquín. *Contribución al estudio del tema de Don Juan en el teatro español.* Northampton, Mass.: Smith College Studies in Modern Languages, Vol. XIX, Nos. 3-4 (1938).

Cassirer, Ernst. *Language and Myth.* Trans. Susanne K. Langer. New York: Dover Publications, 1946.

Castro, Américo. *De la edad conflictiva.* Madrid: Ediciones Taurus, 1961.

-----. "Don Juan en la literatura española." In *Cinco ensayos sobre Don Juan.* Santiago de Chile: Editorial Cultura. [Gregorio Marañón, Ramiro de Maeztu, José Ingenieros, "Azorín," Pérez de Ayala.]

-----. *Dos ensayos.* México: Porrúa, 1956.

-----. *España en su historia. Cristianos, moros y judíos.* Buenos Aires: Editorial Losada, 1948.

-----. *La realidad histórica de España.* México: Porrúa, 1954.

-----. *Santa Teresa y otros ensayos.* Madrid: Historia Nueva, 1929.

Ceñal, R. "Cartesianismo en España." *Revista de la Universidad de Oviedo,* (1945), 3-95.

Cereceda, Feliciano. *Semblanza espiritual de Isabel la Católica.* Madrid: Ediciones Cultura Hispánica, 1946.

Clavería, Carlos. "Apostillas al lenguaje de Belarmino," *Cinco estudios de literatura española moderna.* Salamanca: Colegio Trilingüe de la Universidad, 1945.

Cortés, Narciso A. *La muerte de Villamediana.* Valladolid, 1928.

Cossío, Manuel Bartolomé. *El Greco.* 2 vols. Madrid: Suárez, 1908.

-----, and Pijoán y Soteras, José. *Summa artis, historia general del arte.* 1st ed. Madrid: Espasa-Calpe, 1931-1961.

Cotarelo y Mori, Emilio. *El conde de Villamediana.* Madrid: Sucesores de Rivadeneyra, 1886. [Estudio biográfico-crítico con varias poesías inéditas del mismo.]

Croce, Benedetto. "In torno al saggiorno di Garcilaso de la Vega in Italia." *Rassegna Storica Napolitana di Lettere ed Arti.* Naples, Vol. I, fasc. No. 1 (1894).

D'Aló, Oreste. *Algunos hombres, algunas ideas: Amiel, Renan, Becher, Ingenieros.* Santa Fe, Argentina: Librería y Editorial Castellri, 1955.

Delacroix, H. "Les états extatiques d'Amiel." *Vers L'unité,* October-November 1921.

Deleito y Piñuela, José. *El declinar de la monarquía española.* 2nd ed. Madrid: Espasa-Calpe, 1947.

Delpy, Gaspar. *Bibliographie de sources françaises de B. Feijoo.* Paris: Librairie Hachette, 1936.

-----. *Feijoo et l'esprit européen.* Paris: Librairie Hachette, 1936.

Domínguez Ortiz, Antonio. *Política y hacienda de Felipe IV.* Madrid: Editorial de Derecho Financiero, 1960.

-----. "The revolt of Catalonia against Philip IV." *Past and Present,* 29 (1964), 105-11.

-----. *La sociedad española en el siglo XVII.* Madrid: Instituto Balmes de Sociología, 1963.

Gary D. Keller

Du Bos, Charles. "Pour le centenaire d'Amiel." *Revue de Paris*, September 15, 1921.

Ellis, Havelock. *Views and Reviews*. London, 1932.

Entrambasaguas, Joaquín de. *Prólogo* a la edición antológica de Feijoo. 3 vols. Madrid: Ediciones FE, 1942.

Fagg, John E. "Rafael Altamira," in *Some Historians of Modern Europe: Essays in Historiography*, ed. Bernadotte E. Schmitt. Port Washington, N.Y.: Kennikut Press, 1942.

Farinelli, Arturo. "Cuatro palabras sobre Don Juan y la literatura donjuanesca del porvenir." *Homenaje a Menéndez y Pelayo*. Madrid, 1899, I, 205-22.

-----. *Divagaciones hispánicas*. 2 vols. Barcelona, 1936.

-----. *Dos excéntricos: Cristóbal de Villalón—El Dr. Juan Huarte*. Madrid: Revista de Filología Española, Anejo XXIV, 1936.

-----. *Ensayos y discursos de crítica literaria hispano-europea*. 2 vols. Rome, 1925.

Feijoo, Benito Jerónimo. "Descubrimiento de la circulación de la sangre," in Del Río, Angel. *Antología general de la literatura española*. vol II, New York: Holt, Rinehart and Winston, 1960, p. 15.

-----. *Obras escogidas*. Biblioteca de Autores Españoles, vol. 56. Madrid: Rivadeneyra, 1863.

Fenichel, Otto. *The Psychoanalytic Theory of Neurosis*. New York: W.W. Norton, 1945.

Fernández Alvarez, Manuel. *Política Mundial de Carlos V y Felipe II*. Madrid: Consejo Superior de Investigaciones Científicas, 1966.

Fitzmaurice-Kelly, Julia. *Antonio Pérez*. Oxford: Oxford University Press, 1922.

Friedlander, Walter. *Mannerism and Anti-Mannerism in Italian Painting*. New York: Schocken Books, 1965.

Freud, Sigmund. *Leonardo da Vinci: A Psychosexual Study of an Infantile Reminiscence*. Trans. A.A. Brill. New York, 1910.

-----. *Moses and Monotheism*. Trans. K. Jones. New York: Knopf, 1939.

-----. *New Introductory Lectures on Psychoanalysis*. Trans. James Strachey. New York: W.W. Norton and Co., 1964.

-----. *Totem and Taboo*. Trans. A.A. Brill. New York, 1927.

-----. *Wit and Its Relation to the Unconscious*. Trans. A.A. Brill. New York, 1916.

García Ballester, L. "El galenismo de transición en la España del siglo XVII: Luis Rodríguez de Pedrosa." *Actas del II Congreso Español de la Historia de la Medicina*. Vol. I. Salamanca: 1965, 385-392.

García Martínez, S. *Els fonaments del País Valencià modern*. Valencia, 1963.

García Morente, Manuel. *Ideas para una filosofía de la historia de España*. Madrid: Univ. de Madrid, 1943.

Garraty, John A. "The Interrelations of Psychology and Biography." *Psychological Bulletin*, LI (1954), 569-82.

-----. *The Nature of Biography*. New York: Alfred A. Knopf, 1957.

Gendarme de Bévotte, Georges. *La légende de Don Juan, son évolution dans la littérature des origines au romantisme*. 2 vols. Paris: Librairie Hachette, 1911.

Bibliography

Gener, Pompeyo. *Literatura malsana; estudios de patología literaria contemporánea.* Barcelona: J. Llordachs, 1900.

Girard, Alain. *Le Journal intime.* Paris: Presses Universitaires de France, 1963.

Gombrich, E.H. *Art and Illusion: A Study in the Psychology of Pictorial Representation.* The A.W. Mellon Lectures in the Fine Arts, 1956. National Gallery of Art, Washington: Bollingen Series, XXXV (1956).

Gómez de la Serna, Ramón. *El Greco in Biografías completas.* Madrid: Aguilar, 1959.

Gómez-Moreno, Manuel. *Las águilas del renacimiento español.* Madrid: Gráficas Uguina, 1941.

-----. *El Greco.* Barcelona: Ediciones Selectas, 1943.

-----. *Iglesias mozárabes: arte español de los siglos IX a XI.* Madrid: Centro de Estudios Históricos, 1919.

-----. *Palacio del emperador Carlos V en la Alhambra.* Madrid: El Correo, 1941.

-----. and Pijoán y Soteras, José. *Materiales de arqueología española.* Madrid, 1912.

Gómez-Tabanera, J.M. *A Concise History of Spain.* Madrid: Cronos, 1966.

Goyanes Capdevila, José. *Tipología del Quijote.* Madrid: Aguirre, 1932.

Granjel, Luis S. *Aspectos médicos de la literatura antisuperticiosa española de los siglos XVI y XVII.* Salamanca: Universidad de Salamanca, 1963.

-----. *Baroja y otras figuras del 98.* Madrid: Ediciones Guadarrama, 1960.

-----. *Bibliografía histórica de la medicina española.* Salamanca: Universidad de Salamanca, no date.

-----. *La doctrina antropológico-médica de Miguel Sabuco.* Salamanca: Publicaciones del Seminario de Historia de Medicina de la Universidad de Salamanca, 1956.

-----. *El ejercicio de la medicina en la sociedad española del siglo XVII.* Salamanca: Universidad de Salamanca, 1971.

-----. *La obra de Gaspar Bravo de Sobremonte.* Salamanca: Universidad de Salamanca, 1960.

-----. "Vida y obra de Pedro Miguel de Heredia." *Boletín de la Sociedad Española de Historia de la Medicina,* II, 1 (1961).

Grau, Jacinto. *Don Juan en el tiempo y el espacio: Análisis histórico-psicológico.* Buenos Aires: Editorial Raigal, 1953.

Guinard, Paul. *El Greco.* Lausanne: Imprimeries Réunies S.A., 1956.

Haimovici, Joseph. *Amiel ou l'introspection morbide en littérature.* Paris: Faculté de Médecine de Paris, 1928.

Halda, Bernard. *Amiel et les femmes.* Lyon-Paris: Editions Vitte, 1963.

Halkin, Léon E. *Initiation à la critique historique.* Paris: Librairie Armand Colin, 1953.

Hatzfeld, Helmut. *Estudios literarios sobre mística española.* 2nd ed. Madrid: Editorial Gredos, 1968.

Hazard, Paul. *European Thought in the Eighteenth Century from Montesquieu to Lessing.* London: Hollis and Carter, 1954.

Herr, Richard. *The Eighteenth-Century Revolution in Spain.* Princeton, New Jersey: Princeton University Press, 1958.

Gary D. Keller

Hoffman, Frederick J. *Freudianism and the Literary Mind.* 2nd ed. Baton Rouge, Louisiana: Louisiana State University Press, 1957.

Holland, Norman N. *The Dynamics of Literary Response.* New York: Oxford University Press, 1968.

-----. *Psychoanalysis and Shakespeare.* New York: McGraw Hill, 1964.

Icaza, Francisco A. de. *Introducción* in Juan de la Cueva, *El Infamador.* Madrid: Espasa-Calpe (Clásicos Castellanos), 1941.

Ingenieros, José. *La psicopatología en el arte.* Buenos Aires: Editorial Losada, 1961.

Insúa, Alberto. *Don Quijote en los Alpos.* Madrid: Biblioteca Nueva de Escritores Españoles, 1907.

-----. "Perspectivas. Naturalismo y freudismo." *La Voz.* XIII, October 7, 1932, p. 1.

Jarnés, Benjamín. *Sor Patrocinio.* Madrid: Espasa-Calpe, 1929.

Jones, Ernest. *Hamlet and Oedipus.* New York: Doubleday (Anchor), 1949.

-----. "Mother Right and Sexual Ignorance of Savages." *International Journal of Psychoanalysis,* 1925.

Jones, George Fenwich. *Honor in German Literature.* Chapel Hill: University of North Carolina Press, 1959.

Jorge, Ricardo. *El Greco.* Coimbra: Universidad de Coimbra, 1913.

Jung, Carl G. *Memories, Dreams, Reflections.* Recorded and edited by Aniela Jaffe. New York: Vintage Books, 1961.

Keniston, Hayward. *Francisco de los Cobos, Secretary of Emperor Charles V.* Pittsburgh, 1960.

-----. *Garcilaso de la Vega. A Critical Study of His Life and Works.* New York, 1922.

Knights, L.C. "How Many Children Had Lady Macbeth?" [1933]. In *Explorations.* London: Chatto and Windus, 1951.

Kris, Ernst. *Psychoanalytic Explorations in Art.* New York: International Universities Press, 1952.

Lafora, Gonzalo. *Don Juan, Los milagros, y otros ensayos.* Madrid: Biblioteca Nueva, 1927.

-----. "La influencia de la personalidad y el carácter de Cajal sobre su obra." *Tierra Firme,* I (1935), 31-54.

-----. "Las psiconeurosis de situación." *El Sol.* Madrid, December 17 and 24, 1926.

-----. "Sobre el problema de Don Juan." *El Sol.* Madrid, December 21, 1926.

Laín Entralgo, Pedro. *Cajal y el problema del saber.* Madrid: Ateneo (Colección "O crece o muere"), 1952.

-----. *España como problema.* Madrid: Aguilar, 1957.

-----. *Gaspar Casal y la Medicina de su tiempo.* Oviedo, 1959.

-----. *Ocio y trabajo.* Madrid: Revista de Occidente, 1960.

-----. "Otra vez, Don Juan." *Obras.* Madrid: Plenitud, 1965, p. 1154.

-----, y López-Piñero, J.M.. *Panorama histórico de la ciencia moderna.* Madrid: Ed. Guadarrama, 1963.

Lapeyre, H. "Autour de Phillipe II." *Bulletin Hispanique.* LIX (1957), 152-75.

Lázaro Carreter, Fernando. *Las ideas lingüísticas en España durante el siglo XVIII.* Madrid: Consejo Superior de Investigaciones Científicas, 1949.

Legendre, Maurice and Hartmann, A. *Domenikos Theotokopoulos Called El Greco.* London: The Commodore Press, 1937.

Leman, Auguste. *Richelieu et Olivarès: Leurs negociations secrètes de 1636 à 1642 pour le rétablissement de la paix.* Lille: Fasc. XLIX des Facultés cathol. de Lille, 1938.

Lesser, Simon O. *Fiction and the Unconscious.* Boston: Beacon Press, 1957.

Lewis, C.S. "Hamlet, the Prince or the Poem?" Annual Shakespeare Lecture of the British Academy. *Proceedings of the British Academy,* XXXVIII (1942), 7-9.

Lhermitte, J. "Considérations psycho-physiologiques nouvelles sur la peinture. L'image corporelle dans l'espace pictural." *Press Médicale,* XLIII (1955).

-----. *Mystiques et faux mystiques.* Paris, 1952.

Lida, Raimundo. "Cartas de Quevedo." *Cuadernos Americanos.* XII (1953), 193-210.

Lizcano, Manuel. "La sociología de las religiones en España." *Revista de Estudios Políticos.* Madrid. LVII (1956), 115-131.

López Piñero, J.M. "Los comienzos de la medicina y la ciencia modernas en España en el último tercio del siglo XVII." *Actas del II Congreso Español de la Historia de Medicina.* Vol. I. Salamanca, 1965, 271-292.

-----. "La doctrina de Harvey acerca de la circulación de la sangre en la España del siglo XVII." *Actas del II Congreso Español de la Historia de Medicina.* Vol. I. Salamanca, 1965, 369-384.

-----. "Galileo en la España del siglo XVI." *Revista de Occidente.* 40 (1966), 99-108.

-----. *La introducción de la ciencia moderna en España.* Barcelona: Ed. Ariel, 1969.

-----. "La introducción de la ciencia moderna en España." *Revista de Occidente.* 35 (1966), 133-156.

-----. "La medicina del Barroco español." *Revista de la Universidad de Madrid.* 11 (1962), 479-515.

-----, y Morales Meseguer, M.J., *Neurosis y psicoterapía: Un estudio histórico.* Madrid: Espasa-Calpe, 1970.

-----, Peset Reig, M., García Ballester, L., Zaragoza, J.R., and Terrada, M.L. *Bibliografía histórica sobre la ciencia y la técnica en España.* 2 vols. Granada: Secretariado de Publicaciones de la Universidad, 1973.

Ludwig, Emil. *Genius and Character.* New York, 1927.

Luz León, José de la. *Amiel o la incapacidad de amar.* Madrid, 1927.

McClelland, I.L. *Benito Jerónimo Feijoo.* New York: Twayne Publishers, Inc., 1969.

Madariaga, Salvador de. *De Galdós a Lorca.* Buenos Aires: Editorial Sudamericana, 1960.

-----. "Don Juan and Don Juanism." Trans. Lloyd D. Teale in Oscar Mandel, *The Theatre of Don Juan.* Lincoln, Nebraska: The University of Nebraska Press, 1963, pp. 646-58.

-----. *El Hamlet de Shakespeare, ensayo de interpretación.* Buenos Aires: Editorial Sudamericana, 1949.

-----. *Semblanzas literarias contemporáneas.* Madrid: Biblioteca Cervantes, 1923.

Gary D. Keller

Maeztu, Ramiro de. *Don Quijote, Don Juan y la Celestina.* 6th ed. Buenos Aires: Espasa-Calpe, 1948.

Mandel, Oscar, ed. *The Theatre of Don Juan.* Lincoln, Nebraska: The University of Nebraska Press, 1963.

Malinowski, Bronislaw. *La sexualité et sa répression dans les societés primitives.* Paris: Payot, 1932.

Maravall, José Antonio. *Antiguos y modernos: la idea de progreso en el desarrollo inicial de una sociedad.* Madrid: Sociedad de Estudios y Publicaciones, 1966.

-----. *Carlos V y el pensamiento político del renacimiento.* Madrid: Instituto de Estudios Políticos, 1960.

-----. *Las comunidades de Castilla; una primera revolución moderna.* Madrid: Revista de Occidente, 1963.

-----. *La teoría del estado en el siglo XVII.* Madrid: Instituto de Estudios Políticos, 1944.

-----. *Teoría del saber histórico.* Madrid: Revista de Occidente, 1958.

Marchesi, G.M. *Il Pensieroso.* Milan, 1908.

Marco Cuéllar, R. "El *Compendio Mathemático* del Padre Tosca y la introducción de la ciencia moderna en España. I. Las matemáticas. II. La astronomía. III. La física." *Actas del II Congreso Español de la Historia de Medicina,* Vol. I. Salamanca: 1965, 325-358.

Marichal, Juan. *La voluntad de estilo (Teoría e historia del ensayismo hispánico.)* Barcelona: Editorial Seix Barral, 1957.

Marichalar, Antonio. *Riesgo y ventura del Duque de Osuna.* Madrid: Espasa-Calpe, 1930.

Martínez Fernando, Jesús Ernesto. *Jaime II de Aragón. Su vida familiar.* Barcelona: Consejo Superior de Investigaciones Científicas, 1948.

Martínez Ruiz, José, "Azorín." "El tricentenario del Greco." *Clásicos y modernos.* Madrid: Editorial Renacimiento, 1913, pp. 183-90.

-----. *Lecturas españolas.* 4th ed. Madrid: Espasa-Calpe, 1943.

Matisse, Henri. "Notes d'un peintre sur son dessin." *Le point,* IV, XXI (1939).

Maurois, André. *Aspects of Biography.* New York: Frederick Ungar, 1966.

Mayer, August L. "El Greco, An Oriental Artist." *Art Bulletin,* XI (1929), 146-52.

Medioni, Henry Gilbert. *Essai sur le caractère d'Amiel à la faveur des conceptions psycho-pathologiques contemporaines.* Paris: Faculté de Médicine de Paris, 1927.

Mele, E. "Las poesías latinas de Garcilaso de la Vega y su permanencia en Italia." *Bulletin Hispanique,* XXV (1923), 108-48, 361-70 and Vol. XXVI (1924), 35-51.

Menéndez Pelayo, Marcelino. *La ciencia española (Polémicas, proyectos y bibliografía.)* Cuarta edición refundida y aumentada. 3 vols. Madrid: Colección Escritores Castellanos, 1918.

Menéndez Pidal, Ramón. *Estudios literarios.* 6th ed. México-Buenos Aires: Espasa-Calpe, 1946.

Miniconi, Jérôme-Louis-Georges. *Amiel: Étude médico-psychologique.* Thèse pour le Doctorat en Médicine. Université de Bordeaux, 1935-1936, No. 128.

Bibliography

Misiak, Henryk. *The Philosophical Roots of Scientific Psychology.* New York: Fordham University Press, 1961.

-----, and Sexton, Virginia Staudt. *History of Psychology.* New York and London: Grune and Stratton, 1966.

Monteil, G. *La religion d'Amiel.* Paris, 1907.

Montero Díaz. "Las ideas estéticas del Padre Feijoo." *Boletín de la Universidad de Santiago de Compostela,* IV (1932).

Morales Meseguer, J.M. "La introducción en España de la psicología médica moderna: *Las cartas* (1691) de Juan Bautista Juanini." *Actas del II Congreso Español de la Historia de Medicina.* Vol. I. Salamanca: 1965, 423-430.

Muñoz Garrrido, R. *Ejercicio legal de la medicina en España (Siglos XV al XVIII).* Salamanca, 1967.

Nadal, J. "La contribution des historiens catalans à l'histoire de la démographie générale." *Population.* 16 (1961), 91-104.

Navarro Tomás, Tomás. *Introducción* in Garcilaso de la Vega, *Obras.* Madrid: Espasa-Calpe, 1963.

Nordau, Max Simon. *Degeneration.* Introduction, George L. Mosse. New York: H. Fertig, 1968.

Novoa Santos, Roberto. *El advenimiento del hombre y otras conferencias.* Madrid, 1933.

-----. *La indigencia espiritual del sexo femenino.* Madrid, 1908.

-----. *Patografía de Santa Teresa de Jesús.* Madrid, 1932.

Oliver Brachfeld, F. *Los sentimientos de inferioridad.* Buenos Aires: Editorial Siglo Veinte, 1942.

O'Gorman, Edmundo. *Crisis y porvenir de la ciencia histórica.* Mexico: Imprenta Universitaria, 1947.

Ortega y Gasset, José. "Amor en Stendhal." *El Sol.* August 24, 1926.

-----. "Asamblea para el progreso de las ciencias." *Obras completas.* 4th ed. Madrid: Revista de Occidente, 1957. I, 99-110.

-----. "La ciencia romántica." *Obras completas.* 4th ed. Madrid: Revista de Occidente, 1957. I, 38-43.

-----. "La estrangulación de 'Don Juan.' " *Obras completas.* 4th ed. Madrid: Revista de Occidente, 1957. V, 242-51.

-----. *Estudios sobre el amor.* Madrid: Espasa-Calpe, 1964.

-----. *Goethe desde adentro* in *Obras completas.* Vol. IV. 4th ed. Madrid: Revista de Occidente, 1957.

-----. *Historia como sistema. Obras completas.* VI. 5th ed. Madrid: Revista de Occidente, 1961.

-----. "Ni vitalismo ni racionalismo." *Obras completas.* 4th ed. Madrid: Revista de Occidente, 1957. III, 270-82.

-----. *Obras inéditas: Vives-Goethe (Conferencias).* Madrid: Revista de Occidente, 1961.

-----. *El tema de nuestro tiempo* in *Obras completas.* Vol. III. 4th ed. Madrid: Revista de Occidente, 1957.

-----. "La vida en torno: Muerte y resurrección." *Obras completas.* 4th ed. Madrid: Revista de Occidente, 1957. II, 149-57.

-----. "Vieja y nueva política." *Obras completas.* 4th ed. Madrid: Revista de Occidente, 1957. I, 276-84.

Gary D. Keller

Ortega y Gasset, José. "Vives." *Obras completas.* V. 4th ed. Madrid: Revista de Occidente, 493-507.

Oosthendorp, H.Th. *El conflicto entre el honor y el amor en la literatura española hasta el siglo XVII.* La Haya: G.V. Van Goor Zonen's U.M.N.V., 1962.

Ors y Rovira, Eugenio d'. *Poussin y el Greco* in *El nuevo glosario.* Vol. V. Madrid: Caro Raggio, 1922.

Palacio Atard, Vicente. *Derrota, agotamiento, decadencia en la España del siglo XVIII.* Madrid: Rialp, 1958.

Pérez Ballestar, Jorge. "Ideas para una ordenación metódica de la historiografía." *Estudio de Historia Moderna,* III (1953), 1-24.

Pérez Bustamante, Ciriaco. *Felipe III: Semblanza de un monarca y perfiles de una privanza.* Madrid, 1950.

Pérez de Ayala, Ramón. *Las máscaras* in *Obras Selectas.* Barcelona: Editorial AHR, 1957.

Pérez Gómez, Antonio. *Antonio Pérez: Escritor y Hombre de Estado. Ensayo de Bibliografía razonada.* Ceiza: Talleres de Tipografía Moderna, 1959.

Pérez-Rioja, José Antonio. *Proyección y actualidad de Feijoo.* Madrid: Instituto de Estudios Políticos, 1965.

Peset Llorca, V. "Acerca de la difusión del sistema copernicano en España." *Actas del II Congreso Español de la Historia de Medicina.* Vol. I. Salamanca, 1965, 309-324.

-----. "La doctrina intelectualista del delirio de Pedro Miguel de Heredia." *Archivo Iberoamericano de Historia de la Medicina y Antropología Médica,* 14 (1962), 133-206.

Peters, R.S., ed. *Brett's History of Psychology.* New York: The Macmillan Company, 1953.

Phillips, William, ed. *Art and Psychoanalysis.* New York: The World Publishing Company, 1963.

Pí y Margall, Francisco. *Opúsculos.* Madrid, 1884.

-----. "Prólogo" al *Teatro Crítico del Padre Feijoo.* Oporto, 1887.

Pijoán y Soteras, José. "El Greco, a Spaniard." *Art Bulletin,* SII (1930), 13-18.

Pitt-Rivers, Julian. "Honour and Social Status." In *Honour and Shame: The Values of Mediterranean Society.* Ed. J.G. Peristiany. London: Weidenfeld and Nicolson, 1965.

Portela Marco, E. "La obra química de Juan de Bercebal (1707)." *Actas del II Congreso Español de la Historia de Medicina.* Vol. I. Salamanca, 1965, 431-438.

Progoff, Ira. *The Death and Rebirth of Psychology.* New York: The Julian Press, 1965.

Quiroz-Martínez, Olga Victoria. *La introducción de la filosofía moderna en España: El ecletismo español de los siglos XVII y XVIII.* México: El Colegio de México, 1949.

Ramón y Cajal, Santiago. "Nuestro atraso cultural y sus causas pretendidas" in del Río, Angel and Benardete, Mair José. *El concepto contemporáneo de España.* New York: Las Américas, 1962.

-----. *Obras literarias completas.* Madrid: Aguilar, 1954.

Rank, Otto. *Art and Artist.* Trans. C.T. Atkinson. New York, 1932.
-----. *Die Don Juan-Gestalt.* Vienna: Psychoanalytischer Verlag, 1924.
-----. "The Don Juan Figure." trans. Walter Bodlander in *The Theatre of Don Juan.* Ed. Oscar Mandel. Lincoln, Nebraska: University of Nebraska Press, 1963, 625-33.
-----. *Un étude sur le double.* Paris, 1932.
Reglá, J. "La crisis del siglo XVII (1621-1713)." *Introducción a la historia de España.* Barcelona, 1963, 289-344.
Rennert, Hugo Albert. *The Spanish Stage in the Time of Lope de Vega.* New York: Dover Publications, 1963.
Ribera, Julián. *Disertaciones y opúsculos.* Edición colectiva que en su jubilación del profesorado le ofrecen sus discípulos y amigos. 2 vols. Madrid: Imprenta de Estanislao Maestre, 1928.
Río, Angel del. *Antología general de la literatura española.* 2 vols. New York: Holt, Rinehart and Winston, 1960.
-----, and Bernadete, Mair J. *El concepto contemporáneo de España; Antología de ensayos 1895-1931.* New York: Las Américas Publishing Co., 1962.
Rof Carballo, Juan. *Entre el silencio y la palabra.* Madrid: Aguilar, 1960.
-----. *Medicina y actividad creadora.* Madrid: Revista de Occidente, 1964.
-----. *Mito e realidade da terra nai.* Vigo: Editorial Galaxia, 1957.
Romanones, Conde de. *Historia de cuatro días* in *Obras completas,* Vol. III. Madrid: Editorial Plus Ultra, 1949.
Romero, José Luis. *La historia y la vida.* Buenos Aires: Edit. Yerba Buena, 1945.
-----. *Sobre la biografía y la historia.* Buenos Aires: Edit. Sudamericana, 1945.
Rosales, Luis. *Pasión y muerte del Conde de Villamediana.* Madrid: Editorial Gredos, 1969.
Sacristán, José M. *Genialidad y psicopatología.* Madrid: Biblioteca Nueva (no date).
Said Armesto, Víctor. *La leyenda de Don Juan.* México-Buenos Aires: Espasa-Calpe, 1946.
Sáinz Rodríguez, P. *Introducción a la historia de la literatura mística en España.* Madrid, 1927.
Sajón de Cuello, Raquel. "Feijoo y el enciclopedismo." *Fray Benito Jerónimo Feijoo y Montenegro: Estudios reunidos en conmemoración del II centenario de su muerte.* La Plata, Argentina: Universidad Nacional de la Plata, 1965, 150-66.
Salas, J. "La valoración del Greco por los románticos españoles y franceses." *Archivo Español de Arte y Arqueología,* Vol. XIV (1940-1941), 387-99.
Saldaña, Quintiliano. *Siete ensayos sobre sociología sexual.* Madrid, 1929.
Sánchez-Albornoz, Claudio. *España, un enigma histórico.* 2 vols. Buenos Aires: Edit. Sudamericana, 1956.
-----. *Españoles ante la historia.* Buenos Aires: Edit. Losada, 1958.
Sánchez Alonso, Benito. "Epílogo," in *Historia de la historiografía española.* Vol. III. Madrid: Consejo de Investigaciones Científicas, 1950.
-----. *Historia de la historiografía española.* 3 vols. Madrid, 1947-1950.
Sancho de San Román, R. *Vida y obra de Gaspar Casal.* Salamanca, 1959.

Gary D. Keller

Sarrailh, Jean. *La España ilustrada de la segunda mitad del siglo XVIII.* México-Buenos Aires: Fondo de Cultura Económica, 1957.

Severino, A. *Il sentimiento religioso di F. Amiel.* Rome, 1921.

-----. "Un martyre dell'Ideale." *L'Orma.* Naples, 1919.

Silió Cortés, César. *Isabel la Católica, fundadora de España.* Valladolid: Santarén, 1938.

Singer, Armand E. "A Bibliography of the Don Juan Theme." *West Virginia University Bulletin,* 1954. Supplements: 1956, 1958, 1959 in *West Virginia University Philological Papers.*

Sobejano, Gonzalo. *Nietzsche en España.* Madrid: Editorial Gredos, 1967.

Staubach, Charles N. "Feijoo and Malebranche." *Hispanic Review.* Philadelphia, Vol. IX, No. 2 (1941), 287-97.

-----. "Feijoo on Cartesianism." *Papers of the Michigan Academy of Science, Arts and Letters,* Vol. XXIV, Part IV (1938), 79-87.

-----. "Fontanelle in the writings of Feijoo." *Hispanic Review.* Philadelphia, Vol. VIII (1940), 46-56.

-----. "The Influence of Bayle on Feijoo." *Hispania.* Stanford, California, Vol. XXII (1939), 79-92.

Taine, Hippolyte A. *History of English Literature.* New York: Frederick Ungar, 1965.

Tellechea, Idígoras José Ignacio. "Antonio Pérez a través de la documentación de la Nunciatura de Madrid." *Anthologica Annuí.* Rome, V (1957), 654.

Terrada Ferrandis, M.L. "La anatomía normal y patológica en la España de Carlos II." *Actas del II Congreso Español de la Historia de Medicina.* Vol. I. Salamanca, 1965, 359-368.

Torrente Ballester, Gonzalo. *Panorama de la literatura española contemporánea.* 3rd. ed. Madrid: Ed. Guadarrama, 1965.

Toussaint y Ritter, Manuel. *El tesoro de Amiel (Selección del Diario Intimo).* México: Editorial Cultura, 1918.

Trilling, Lionel. "Art and Neurosis," in *Art and Psychoanalysis.* ed. William Phillips. New York: The World Publ. Co., 1963.

Tzitsikas, Helene. *Santiago Ramón y Cajal, obra literaria.* México: Ediciones de Andrea (Colección Studium—53), 1965.

Unamuno, Miguel de. *Nada menos que todo un hombre* in *Tres novelas ejemplares y un prólogo.* 8th ed. Madrid: Espasa-Calpe, 1958.

-----. "Una vida sin historia: Amiel." *Obras completas.* Madrid: Afrodisio Aguado, S.A., 1958. IX, 95-100.

-----. *Teatro completo.* Madrid: Aguilar, 1959.

Unguer, Gustav. "Bibliographical Notes on the Works of Antonio Pérez." *"Jerónimo Zurita" Cuadernos de Historia.* Zaragoza. XVI-XVIII (1963-1965), 247-260.

Valbuena, Angel. "En torno al psicoanálisis de Don Juan." *Revista de Psicología i Pedagogía.* Barcelona, V (1937).

Valiente, Francisco Tomás. *Los validos en la monarquía española del siglo XVII.* Madrid: Instituto de Estudios Políticos, 1963.

Vela, Fernando. "Freud y los surrealistas." *El Sol.* July 31, 1936.

Vicens Vives, Jaime. "Al cabo de tres años." *Estudios de Historia Moderna,* III (1953), v-viii.

Vicens-Vives, Jaime. *Aproximación a la historia de España*. 3rd. ed. Barcelona: Edit. Vicens-Vives, 1962.

-----. "Estructura administrativa estatal en los siglos XVI y XVII." *Eleventh International Congress of Historical Sciences, Rapports*. IV. Stockholm: Almqvist and Wiksell, 1960.

-----. *Fernando el Católico, Principe de Aragón, Rey de Sicilia*. Madrid: Consejo Superior de Investigaciones Científicas, 1952.

-----. *Historia crítica de la vida y reinado de Fernando II de Aragón*. Madrid: Consejo de Investigaciones Científicas, 1952.

-----. *Juan II de Aragón. Monarquía y revolución en la España del siglo XV*. Barcelona: Edit. Teide, 1953.

-----. *Política del Rey Católico en Cataluña*. Barcelona: Destino, 1940.

-----. "Presentación y propósito." *Estudios de Historia Moderna*, I (1951), i-xii.

-----. "Progresos en el empeño." *Estudios de Historia Moderna*, II (1952), v-vii.

Vilar, P. "1660-1705: Segon redreçament català. Renovació de l'esperit d'iniciativa." *Calunya dins l'Espanya moderna*. Vol. II. Barcelona, 1964, 373-411.

Vives, Juan Luis. *Obras completas*. 2 vols. Madrid: Aguilar, 1947.

Watson, Curtis Brown. *Shakespeare and the Renaissance Concept of Honor*. Princeton, New Jersey: Princeton University Press, 1960.

Watson, Foster. "The Father of Modern Psychology." *The Psychological Review*. Vol. XXII, No. 5 (September 1915), 333-53.

Wethey, Harold E. *El Greco and His School*. 2 vols. Princeton, New Jersey: Princeton University Press, 1962.

Zaragoza, J.R. "La defensa de la quina de Tomás Fernández." *Actas del II Congreso Español de la Historia de Medicina*. Vol. I. Salamanca, 1965, 393-402.

Zelie, John Sheridan. "In Search of Amiel." *Atlantic Monthly*. Boston, January 1907, 122-36.

Zembrano, María. "El freudismo, testimonio del hombre actual." *Hacia un saber sobre el alma*. Buenos Aires, 1950.

Zervos, Charles. *Les oeuvres du Greco en Espagne*. Paris, 1939.

Zudaire Huarte, Eulogio. *El Conde-Duque y Cataluña*. Madrid: Consejo Superior de Investigaciones Científicas, 1964.

-----. "Ideario político de D. Gaspar Guzmán, privado de Felipe IV." *Hispania*. Madrid, XXV (1965), 413-425.

Zulueta, Emilia de. *Historia de la crítica española contemporánea*. Madrid: Editorial Gredos, 1966.

Zweig, Stefan. *The World of Yesterday*. New York, 1943.

INDEX

Index

Index

Index

Index

Index

Index